A CELEBRATION OF POETS

GREAT LAKES
GRADES 4-12
FALL 2011

creativeCOMMUNICATION
A CELEBRATION OF TODAY'S WRITERS

A Celebration of Poets
Great Lakes
Grades 4-12
Fall 2011

An anthology compiled by Creative Communication, Inc.

Published by:

creativeCOMMUNICATION
A CELEBRATION OF TODAY'S WRITERS

PO BOX 303 · SMITHFIELD, UTAH 84335
TEL. 435-713-4411 · WWW.POETICPOWER.COM

Authors are responsible for the originality of the writing submitted.

ISBN: 978-1-60050-480-8

FOREWORD

In January of this year, I was watching the Miss America Pageant. I thought of all the accomplishments that culminate in this one ending competition. These outstanding women had decided what they wanted, paid the price and now were reaping the rewards of their hard work. While watching the pageant, the finalists were on stage and a few of their accomplishments were written across the screen. For Miss Arizona, Jennifer Sedler (who ended as 3rd runner-up), one of her accomplishments was having a poem published in 5th grade. In checking our records, it was our company, Creative Communication, that published her poem "Hawaiian Seas" in the Fall of 2002.

Jennifer wrote to us about the experience of being published:

> "I had a poem published by Creative Communication in 5th grade, and I will never forget how special and inspired it made me feel. I have since gone on to win numerous essay contests, many which earned me scholarship money for college, and I may have never believed in myself if it wasn't for Creative Communication. And as Miss Arizona, I write pages and pages of creatively-written updates for all of my followers. Now of course I still take time on my own to read, study, and write poetry. When you choose to be an active learner and writer, I think you will find, just as I did, that truly anything is possible."

When a poet enters our writing contest, they are students like everyone else. As they move on in life, talents are developed. A 5th grade student becomes Miss Arizona. Another student, novelist Angela Bishop, also wrote to me the following:

> "My name is Angela Bishop, and almost ten years ago you selected one of my poems to be published in the Southern edition of your book. I was 15 and it was the highlight of my young life. Although it has been nearly a decade, I just wanted to finally express the thanks I have felt all these years. I cannot thank you enough for accepting my work and publishing it. I have been writing since I was a child and have continued to write. I am currently working on my second novel. So, thank you, thank you, for the confidence you unknowingly gave me in 1999. I plan to keep writing for as long as I possibly can. Your poetry contest is a wonderful thing, and you open a window for tomorrow's great writers to find their way through and gain the confidence in their work. Keep it going, you are making dreams into realities."

To both Jennifer and Angela and the students in this anthology, I am glad that we are here for you. We helped you in creating an accomplishment that you can be proud of and add to your resume. When students wonder if they should enter a contest, I give a strong affirmative. You may not be accepted to be published, but if you don't enter, there isn't a chance of being published or being a Top Ten winner. Sometimes you have to take a risk and enter a contest. It may change your life. Just ask Jennifer and Angela.

I hope you enjoy the poems that are included in this anthology. We are pleased to help provide the spark that makes lifelong writers. Each of these students took a risk in entering and has the potential to achieve great things in their lives. Good luck.

Tom Worthen, Ph.D.
Editor

WRITING CONTESTS!

Enter our next POETRY contest!
Enter our next ESSAY contest!

Why should I enter?
Win prizes and get published! Each year thousands of dollars in prizes are awarded throughout North America. The top writers in each division receive a monetary award and a free book that includes their published poem or essay. Entries of merit are also selected to be published in our anthology.

Who may enter?
There are four divisions in the poetry contest. The poetry divisions are grades K-3, 4-6, 7-9, and 10-12. There are three divisions in the essay contest. The essay divisions are grades 3-6, 7-9, and 10-12.

What is needed to enter the contest?
To enter the poetry contest send in one original poem, 21 lines or less. To enter the essay contest send in one original non-fiction essay, 250 words or less, on any topic. Please submit each poem and essay with a title, and the following information clearly printed: the writer's name, current grade, home address (optional), school name, school address, teacher's name and teacher's email address (optional). Contact information will only be used to provide information about the contest. For complete contest information go to www.poeticpower.com.

How do I enter?
Enter a poem online at:
www.poeticpower.com
or
Mail your poem to:
    Poetry Contest
    PO Box 303
    Smithfield UT 84335

Enter an essay online at:
www.poeticpower.com
or
Mail your essay to:
    Essay Contest
    PO Box 303
    Smithfield UT 84335

When is the deadline?
Poetry contest deadlines are August 16th, December 6th and April 9th. Essay contest deadlines are July 19th, October 18th and February 19th. Students can enter one poem and one essay for each spring, summer, and fall contest deadline.

Are there benefits for my school?
Yes. We award $12,500 each year in grants to help with Language Arts programs. Schools qualify to apply for a grant by having 15 or more accepted entries.

Are there benefits for my teacher?
Yes. Teachers with five or more students published receive a free anthology that includes their students' writing.

For more information please go to our website at **www.poeticpower.com**, email us at editor@poeticpower.com or call 435-713-4411.

TABLE OF CONTENTS

STATES INCLUDED IN THIS EDITION:

MICHIGAN
MINNESOTA
WISCONSIN

Fall 2011
Poetic Achievement
Honor Schools

*Teachers who had fifteen or more poets accepted to be published

The following schools are recognized as receiving a "Poetic Achievement Award." This award is given to schools who have a large number of entries of which over fifty percent are accepted for publication. With hundreds of schools entering our contest, only a small percent of these schools are honored with this award. The purpose of this award is to recognize schools with excellent Language Arts programs. This award qualifies these schools to receive a complimentary copy of this anthology. In addition, these schools are eligible to apply for a Creative Communication Language Arts Grant. Grants of two hundred and fifty dollars each are awarded to further develop writing in our schools.

Abbott Middle School
West Bloomfield, MI
Julia Music*
Erin Wynn*

Allegan High School
Allegan, MI
Nancy Hascall*
Jane Kiel

Blue Heron Elementary School
Lino Lakes, MN
Curt Gutbrod*

Boulan Park Middle School
Troy, MI
Cheryl Megahan
Audrey Wright

Campbellsport Elementary School
Campbellsport, WI
Michelle Dahlinger*
Shelly Gassner*

Clarkston High School
Clarkston, MI
Nancy Brown
Kathy Kuehn*

Detroit Country Day Middle School
Beverly Hills, MI
Carla Chennault
Victoria Chiakmakis
Charles Duggan
Cheryl Duggan
Michael Mencotti
Carol M. Tabaka
Stephanie Trautman

Detroit Lakes Middle School
Detroit Lakes, MN
Nicky Courneya*

Dibble Elementary School
Jackson, MI
Pat Elsey*

Dr Dyer Intermediate School
Burlington, WI
Sue Fleshman
Angela Mangold

East Rockford Middle School
Rockford, MI
Denise Visger*

Falcon Heights Elementary School
Falcon Heights, MN
Gwaynel Donatell*
Meggan Lovick*

Floyd Ebeling Elementary School
Macomb, MI
Jacquelyn Barker*
Tracy Bettys*
Lisa Bruce*
Rachel D'Angelo*
Robin Pizzo
Mrs. Taubitz*
Mrs. VanGilder*
Mrs. Vittiglio

Galesburg-Augusta Middle School
Augusta, MI
Laura Britain*
Katie Fotis
Mr. Musialczyk

Gesu Catholic School
Detroit, MI
Judy P. Kuzniar*

Gillett High School
Gillett, WI
Rebecca Rousseau*

Gilmore Middle School
Racine, WI
Linda Broesch*
Sherry Coburn*

Grand Rapids Christian School -
Evergreen Campus
Grand Rapids, MI
Matt Christians*

Hewitt Texas Elementary School
Wausau, WI
Linda Davis*

Kalkaska Middle School
Kalkaska, MI
Pam Ciganick
Collette Sabins

Lenawee Christian School
Adrian, MI
Angela Smelser*

Lincoln Jr/Sr High School
Alma Center, WI
Diane Kujak*

Manistique Middle & High School
Manistique, MI
Brenda Fleck*

Maple Lake Elementary School
Maple Lake, MN
Jennifer DesMarais-Holland*

Martin County West Trimont Elementary
School
Trimont, MN
Jackie Royer*

Menominee Jr High School
Menominee, MI
Sharon Brey*

Michigan Lutheran Seminary School
Saginaw, MI
Melissa LaBair*

Montgomery-Lonsdale High School
Montgomery, MN
Jen Davidson*
Sarah Mejia
Jessica Weller

Nellie B Chisholm Middle School
Montague, MI
Jennifer Szegda*

Osceola High School
Osceola, WI
Amanda Meyer*

Our Lady Star of the Sea School
Grosse Pointe Woods, MI
Alice Dandy*

Perry Middle School
Perry, MI
Kim Hewitt*
Sharon Johnson*

Pleasant View School
Lansing, MI
Annette Shauver*

Riley Upper Elementary School
Livonia, MI
Dona Gossett*

River Heights Elementary School
Menomonie, WI
Lynn Ruhland
Kayla Williams

Riverdale Elementary & Middle School
Muscoda, WI
Jill Nankee*

Round Lake High School
Round Lake, MN
Shari Nelson*

Ruth Murdoch Elementary School
Berrien Springs, MI
Philip E. Giddings*

Sault Area Middle School
Sault Sainte Marie, MI
Mrs. McClenny
Janice Theriault*

St Clare of Montefalco School
Grosse Pointe Park, MI
Angela LoVasco*

St Gerard School
Lansing, MI
Marie Hickey
Kitty Zelenka*

St Jerome Elementary School
Maplewood, MN
Sharon Grundtner*

St John Neumann School
Oshkosh, WI
Ginny Hathaway
Mary Uecker*

St Paul Evangelical Lutheran School
Lake Mills, WI
Susan Thorman*

Star International Academy
Dearborn Heights, MI
Leif Batell
Amy Gullekson
Lisa Stranyak

Stocker Elementary School
Kenosha, WI
Diane Aiello
Jill Francis*
Denise Gifford*
Nancy Granger*
Steve Hartfield
Mrs. Mardon*
Marilyn Siedjak*
Margaret Unger*
Ruth Walls*

T J Walker Middle School
Sturgeon Bay, WI
Kasee Jandrin*

The Potter's House Christian School
Grand Rapids, MI
Sherry Leyendecker
Mark Van Zanten

Tracy Area Jr/Sr High School
    Tracy, MN
        Paul Skoglund*

Wagner Elementary School
    Litchfield, MN
        Nikki Knochenmus*

Language Arts Grant Recipients 2011-2012

After receiving a "Poetic Achievement Award" schools are encouraged to apply for a Creative Communication Language Arts Grant. The following is a list of schools who received a two hundred and fifty dollar grant for the 2011-2012 school year.

Annapolis Royal Regional Academy, Annapolis Royal, NS
Bear Creek Elementary School, Monument, CO
Bellarmine Preparatory School, Tacoma, WA
Birchwood School, Cleveland, OH
Bluffton Middle School, Bluffton, SC
Brookville Intermediate School, Brookville, OH
Butler High School, Augusta, GA
Carmi-White County High School, Carmi, IL
Classical Studies Academy, Bridgeport, CT
Coffee County Central High School, Manchester, TN
Country Hills Elementary School, Coral Springs, FL
Coyote Valley Elementary School, Middletown, CA
Emmanuel-St Michael Lutheran School, Fort Wayne, IN
Excelsior Academy, Tooele, UT
Great Meadows Middle School, Great Meadows, NJ
Holy Cross High School, Delran, NJ
Kootenay Christian Academy, Cranbrook, BC
LaBrae Middle School, Leavittsburg, OH
Ladoga Elementary School, Ladoga, IN
Mater Dei High School, Evansville, IN
Palmer Catholic Academy, Ponte Vedra Beach, FL
Pine View School, Osprey, FL
Plato High School, Plato, MO
Rivelon Elementary School, Orangeburg, SC
Round Lake High School, Round Lake, MN
Sacred Heart School, Oxford, PA
Shadowlawn Elementary School, Green Cove Springs, FL
Starmount High School, Boonville, NC
Stevensville Middle School, Stevensville, MD
Tadmore Elementary School, Gainesville, GA
Trask River High School, Tillamook, OR
Vacaville Christian Schools, Vacaville, CA
Wattsburg Area Middle School, Erie, PA
William Dunbar Public School, Pickering, ON
Woods Cross High School, Woods Cross, UT

Grades 10-11-12 Top Ten Winners

List of Top Ten Winners for Grades 10-12; listed alphabetically

Maria Capitano, Grade 11
Pittston Area High School, PA

Anna Daavettila, Grade 10
Houghton High School, MI

Anna Groeling, Grade 11
Arapahoe High School, CO

Arniecia Hinds, Grade 10
Germantown High School, TN

Sabrina Maus, Grade 10
Haynes Academy for Advanced Studies, LA

Erin McCune, Grade 10
Bellarmine Preparatory School, WA

Declan Routledge, Grade 12
Webber Academy, AB

Jacob Schriner-Briggs, Grade 12
Liberty High School, OH

Lianna Scott, Grade 11
Xavier College Preparatory School, AZ

Alexander Wimmer, Grade 10
Home School, GA

All Top Ten Poems can be read at www.poeticpower.com

Note: The Top Ten poems were finalized through an online voting system. Creative Communication's judges first picked out the top poems. These poems were then posted online. The final step involved thousands of students and teachers who registered as the online judges and voted for the Top Ten poems. We hope you enjoy these selections.

Addicted

Running through your body
and coursing through your veins,
it makes you act insane and also melts your brains.
Shoot it up, snort it, smoke it, or drink it.
There's no way around it, face it,
you're addicted.
Doping as coping is no way to live.
It's a mistake that's made that you'll never forgive.
You party.
You blaze,
And life becomes a haze.
You waste away your days
as life continues to play.
One days a party,
the next is a chore.
It doesn't matter what way you enter,
it's always a trap door.
So quit while you're ahead,
before you're in a hospital bed,
or even before you're dead.

Rikki Doers, Grade 11
Lincoln Jr/Sr High School, WI

Senior Year, This Is It…

This is it…we made it;
last year of football games,
homecoming dances,
and pep rallies.

This is it…almost completed
one chapter of our lives: high school

This is it…last chance to see all of our friends
who we have grown up with in the halls, lunches, and classrooms.

This is it…let's live it up,
have no regrets,
and always remember what it meant to be an Eagle.

Lucine Markarian, Grade 12
Dwight D Eisenhower High School, MI

Quit Being Lazy

I want success but habits push me away
For the sake of my dreams I don't want to go through another day
To reach my goals I can no longer just get by
I might have a rough time but that is the price I'm willing to pay
I need to stay away from bad habits that take my life astray
Hard work is needed to walk down the right path
Being lazy feels so easy, easier than you think
But over time it will put your life on the brink
Striving for success does not mean pushing away from failure
I know now that breaking the habit should be easy
All I have to do is realize what it is doing to my life
Quit being lazy

Mohamed Moubadder, Grade 12
Star International Academy, MI

Travis Pastrana

He isn't afraid to die.
He jumps way up in the sky.
He rides motocross like a boss.
He can rap like Rick Ross.
He did a double back flip.
His heartbeat didn't even skip
His number is 199.
I love it though it is mine.
He has a great TV show.
Only because he is a pro.
He can pull a back flip with a Monster Truck.
It didn't work but it didn't suck.
He can hydroplane.
It is so insane.
He can jump a trike.
No one can dislike.
He snow boards and skis.
And never hits trees.
He jumps out of planes with no chute.
But the guys after are in hot pursuit.

Walton Christopherson, Grade 11
Lincoln Jr/Sr High School, WI

The Sorrows of Living

The sorrow of old men
Hidden in the faces of children
Lacking that which is
Only gained by living;
Mocking life as carcasses
Become all that remain.
Approaching, slowly as a planed attack,
The Ferryman, cloaked in blue,
Comes bearing a fortune subdued.
Shuddering are all of those souls
Who stir
The cold and angry stew
Fighting eternally for a glimmer
Hope of a savior swells when payment is due.

Cloē Edna Becher, Grade 12
Stevens Point Area High School, WI

Afraid of the Dark

I am afraid, afraid of the dark,
but for some reason tonight my night light won't spark,
The darkness surrounds me getting close to my face,
maybe I shouldn't have spent hours playing *Dead Space*.
Then out of the black I hear a slight gurgle,
and the darkness gets darker, squeezing me like a girdle.
The gurgling grows into a soft grumble,
I'm too scared to get up, afraid I might stumble.
I finally stand to find the source of the noise,
but when I turn on the light, all I see is toys.
There are no monsters or zombies before me,
I hear the grumble again…I guess I was hungry.

Noah Hoeft, Grade 12
Dilworth Glyndon Felton Sr High School, MN

Scary Movies

You sit in the basement and turn out the lights
Turn on the TV — you are in for a fright
Grab your blanket — a buddy, your man
Squeeze him tight, as tight as you can
How much of the movie do you actually see?
You scream and jump, you're scared but is he?
The room goes silent, the movie's intense
He jumps and screams, it's in a boy's sense
To wait for his girl to calm down for a scare
He hides behind the couch when you run up the stairs
The movie's on pause, and you wait till you sit
If you push play too soon, your heart throws a fit
Snuggled back up, you're ready for more
You tuck up your feet so they're not on the floor
The movie ends, but you don't want to get up
You hear noises upstairs, but it's just your pup
If you can relate to the story I told
Let's hope you had a hand to hold
If you get bored on a Friday night
Watch a scary movie and you're in for a fright

Megan Kutney, Grade 12
Osceola High School, WI

Christmas at Home

Home, where I always want to be
with family all around me.
Smelling the scent of a home-cooked meal
the fire is warm; how good it feels!
Sitting around the table, before we eat,
saying our prayers while in our seats.
Outside there are snowflakes falling to the ground;
I am glad we're all here, safe and sound.
Later, we go and pick out a Christmas tree,
set it in the front window for all to see.
String it with lights, hang the ornaments, put on the star,
having so much fun so far.
Having fun with others too,
all I can say is, "I love you."

Lauren Stanton, Grade 11
Round Lake High School, MN

Your Face Makes Me Wonder: The View Through Asperger's

Emotions scare me more then actions
I do not know for sure what you are going to do
But I can try to listen and find out
I cannot know what you are thinking
More than that I have no control over your thoughts
And that scares me
I see your face and I do not know
I am confused so I ask questions
But you do not get what I am trying to ask
So I look at your face again and try to see
But your face makes me wonder
What am I doing wrong?

Molly Sell, Grade 11
Kalamazoo Christian High School, MI

The Unknown Mind in the Maze

It's the middle of the night
I wake up with a desperate need
To find someone that's lost
But I know exactly where to be
I follow my soul that's making
Me lost but in a familiar place
But unknowingly I'm entering
The secrets of my maze
I see the water in the reflecting lake
It's inches but miles away
I scream as I see my haunted face
Could this be the cause of unknown pain
Is this the cause of being alone
How can emotional scars be physically shown
I'm so detached I don't understand
How could the body that's mine be who I am
This view makes me desperate
For a painful longing to see
If I'm near but far away
Why can't I find me?

Rachel Bownik, Grade 10
Home School, MN

A Little Thought Makes a World of Difference: Do You Care?

From the narwhal to the great polar bear
They're still at the pole, however rare
From the snow leopard to the mountain goat
They remain high in mountains, still remote
From the huge elephant to the black rhino
They're being poached for their ivory cargo
Orangutans, pandas, and manatees too
What does it matter to me and you?
Stocks, markets, and high profit
What's it worth if you lose part of the planet?
They're living, breathing, with hearts full of blood
Weren't they here too after the flood?
So tell yourself this, next time you don't care
Take care of our planet, please do your share

Mason VanEssen, Grade 11
Tracy Area Jr/Sr High School, MN

Class of 2012

It's the year we have all been waiting for,
When we start saying goodbye and some leave for war.
It is the end of a chapter about this last great year
It's losing touch that's our biggest fear.
We will go our separate ways and maybe make a new friend,
But don't you worry this is not the end.
In years to come we will meet again,
To catch up with the life of at least one friend.
We will start our own families and have stories to tell,
But to keep things short I wish you all well.
Congrats to you all, we have made it this far.
Our wish has come true from that one shooting star.

Lauren Fellows, Grade 12
Montgomery-Lonsdale High School, MN

Moving On

You left me here all alone
We were the best of friends
Did everything together
You decided to move on
Go somewhere else with your life
It wasn't much of your decision
More of your parents'
I was stuck here in this little town
And you moved on to much bigger dreams
Yea you had to make new friends too
But for most of the time you were here,
I ignored the rest of the class
We kept in touch
Over the years we moved on
Made other friends
Got involved in school
We don't talk much anymore
But that's okay
We have our own lives now

Joelle Holzl, Grade 12
Rib Lake High School, WI

Reprise

The glass slipped idly from my fingers,
Shattered on the floor,
Twinkled just like a prism in the sun.

I wrote you a letter,
In seven different inks.
I wanted you to know,
I was thinking of you.

The glass slipped idly from my fingers,
Shattered on the floor,
Twinkled,
just like a prism…
Remnants of my former self.

Alexandra Grosskurth, Grade 10
Portage Central High School, MI

Entranced

The lapping of the sea is
Hypnotizing,
Ever swaying,
Whispering,
Chanting,
Pleading for me
To wade
In its calm waters;
To splash
In the white crests
Of its rolling waves,
Amid the sea's heavy
Trance.

Kathleen Roark, Grade 12
Allegan High School, MI

Sailing Away

Summer time, perfect time to travel,
Leaving home to explore.
Bringing with you new stories.
Exploring new places.

Family telling to travel safe and return.
Sailing on the blue ocean, hoping that storms don't come.
Clouds becoming less so that the sun comes out.

Men calling "Land," you hoping to find riches.
Coming on the shore, hoping and wondering if people are watching you.
Having guns nearby in case there is a battle.
Searching and looking out during the day.
Wondering what will come with this experience.

Coming home, months later.
Telling stories and hugging your family and friends.
Wondering when the next time it will be to find new things.

Damaris Stahlmann, Grade 12
Clarkston High School, MI

Winter Draws Near

As the cold starts to come, and the winter draws near,
the only thing they are able to hear is the soft stillness in the forest this year.
Many of the animals are hibernating in their dens,
while other animals are out and about like the wren.
The leaves have fallen and are long gone,
as the snow takes the place of the green lawn.
The chimney gives off a frosty smoke
as a cozy cabin can be seen by the travelers who tuck in their cloaks.
The smell of a warm meal is in the air,
but whether or not they will be welcome is how they are unaware.
Yet a man opens the door with a smile,
and invites them in to come in and stay awhile.
The long day's journey is over
as they visit while sitting and drinking tea of the alpine clover.

Karli Tholen, Grade 12
Tracy Area Jr/Sr High School, MN

I Wouldn't Ask for Another

He was handsome, he had charm.
And close, he could hold me up, with just one arm.
He showed me no fear, but kept me afraid.
And even if it seems odd, I never made his mistakes, ones that could never be repaid.
He kept me close, within hearts reach.
And though he tried to shy his wrong, his actions were the best to teach.
He kept me warm, he helped me achieve.
And so for him, I never deceived.
Even when he left me lonely, I never gave my love away.
And as he taught me, I always said what I wished to say.
So today, I have to say that I am thankful — so proud.
And that I wouldn't be who I am, if he hadn't been around.
He taught me the most, better than any other.
And although he has a disease called addiction, I wouldn't ask for another brother.

Monica Paar, Grade 10
Osceola High School, WI

First Pep Band

It's the beginning of football season
The players are practicing hard
And the band is too.

We play our songs
That we haven't played since last year
Our excitement grows
As the first home game draws near.

The day has come
And we can hardly wait to start
Win or lose
We are here to pump up the crowd.

We play loudly
We have a blast
Maybe get a little crazy
But hey —
That's why we're the pep band.

Chelsea Picha, Grade 12
Montgomery-Lonsdale High School, MN

We Don't Belong

We don't belong,
In a world so cold,
Too much enmity,
For a purified soul,

So much cold,
It's picking at my skin,
I'm starting to freeze up,
From the outside in,

I should move on,
But it's hard to do,
Because in this world,
There are people like you,

We're one of a kind,
I wish you could see,
There aren't many people,
People like you, or people like me,

We don't belong,
In a world so cold,
Too much enmity,
For a purified soul.

Devin Droster, Grade 10
Visions Jr/Sr High School, WI

I Am a Child

What say do I have?
For I am a child.

I color outside the lines,
And always smile.

I cry when I am sad,
I turn red when I am mad.

I am foolish and silly,
And know nothing about life.

For I am a child.

I think you are wrong.
Yes, I do those things.

But guess what?
I am strong.

You don't listen to me,
Because you think I am wrong.

I am a child.
I am strong.

Sarah Wilde, Grade 10
Minnehaha Academy, MN

Never Alone

I don't know how it ends here
and I don't know where to go
but what I know
is that you are not all alone

no matter
where you are
near or far
I shall always be
in your heart
and we will never be apart

you may not think about
where I am all the time
but you are always on my mind
take the road you are led
by your heart
and I will always be
happy as long as you think of me

that is how it ends here
only you know where to go
that I surely know
just remember you are never alone.

Tyler Escue, Grade 12
Southgate Anderson High School, MI

For Grandma

When we were young
We looked to our parents
They were always strong
They never got nervous

The older we get
The more we realize
The elderly forget
They lose sight in their eyes

Grandparents grow weak
They suffer a stroke
They have only a week
Death's no longer a joke

Now we start to notice
Feelings begin to churn
Our parents grow older
Soon it will be their turn

And finally, when our time comes
And swiftly ends our last of days
We leave our friends and homes behind
And join our family in eternal praise.

Caleb Krueger, Grade 10
Michigan Lutheran Seminary School, MI

Squeezed

Have you ever held sand
In the palm of your hand
And then as you squeeze
It slips out the cracks
'tween your fingers?
Joining the sand
That is on the ground
And you will never get it back
Because it goes invisible
It gets blown to the wind
Or taken into the sea
If you are not one of them
There are some who have done this
Some who have squeezed
Until the sand
Falls
Out of
Their
Hand

Amy Prescott, Grade 11
iQ Academy, WI

What Do You Think of Me?
What is it like to be free?
All these people are looking at me, waiting for me to break.

So I go away, because in my mind, I'm finally free.
What do you think of me?

If only there was a way to get back what I've paid.
Because I've paid too much, I didn't ask for this price.
This price is too high.

So I go away, because in my mind, I'm finally free.
So I ask you again, what do you think of me?

I don't care; think what you want.
I'm not going to stand here and be judged for what I'm not.
You don't have anything on me.

So I'll give up now, because you're not worth it.
Because really, what are you but worthless?

So goodbye sweet world, I guess it doesn't matter…
What you think of me now.

Kaitlyn Miller, Grade 12
Bay Arenac Community High School, MI

Life Goes On
Remembering you so healthy and strong,
Seeing you tremble, I begin to break.
Whenever I visit, I try to get along,
But seeing you like this my heart begins to ache.

Seeing you so sick kills me inside;
Watching you drift away is just so much to bare.
I could see all your thoughts beginning to collide,
Of life, death, and the bitterness of not being here.

To my horror I've found
Life without you is hard.
You went away without one little sound,
And my heart is now permanently scarred.

I sit and wonder why God took you away;
Now I pray that I will see you again someday.

Allison Linneman, Grade 11
Belmont High School, WI

Memories
Sitting here as I hear you speak,
It's been more than a few weeks,
Since you've been this close to me.
We've fallen apart but you still have a hold on me.
As my lungs cave in, and I can't breathe.
I've lost the words that meant anything to me.
You've come and gone again like the ship's raging on the sea.

Rachel Goodell, Grade 11
Huron High School, MI

A Flight and a Promise
Shadows disappear in the light
As a new generation begins its flight.

Those things most familiar fade
Quickly as the sun chases the shade.

The future glitters like gold.
Make your life count. Have hope. Be bold.

You're ready to be on your own,
But never forget the life where you've grown.

You'll be looking one day to find
That life, those people that cross your mind.

But never be afraid to fly.
Smile and learn and laugh and cry.

You think you've reached your end?
I'm always here when you need a friend.

So hold up your head and don't pout;
The future is waiting for you to go out.

And so begins a new flight,
The whole world waits to be consumed in light.

Alyssa Maxson, Grade 12
Montgomery-Lonsdale High School, MN

Memory Lane
Driving by that old, familiar road,
I stop to watch the sun go down.
I think about the times spent,
At this quaint little hideaway.

I step out of the car,
And walk down to the water.
I can't help but giggle at that old rope swing,
Still hanging from the willow tree.

I slip my shoes off,
Dig my feet in the sand.
No trouble comes to mind,
When I think of what I felt then.

I take a step forward,
And shiver at the water's touch.
Before I know it, I'm waist deep,
Listening to the cricket's song.

Here I watch the sun vanish before me,
Time gone by too fast.
I take a breath and one more step,
And consume myself in the past.

Meg McGuire, Grade 12
Montgomery-Lonsdale High School, MN

The Saints

When I first became a fan
They were known as the New Orleans Aints
That first season they went three and thirteen
I thought I could faint
Then a hero came to town
And raised them from the dead
And it made me raise my head
Drew Brees was his name
Lead by coach Sean Payton
They rose quickly to fame
And more games they won
They kept winning games and took some bashes
But like a newborn Phoenix they rose from the ashes
The winning streak continued
A new superpower team was found
And just like that they were Super Bowl bound
They beat the Colts and won Super Bowl forty-four
From nothing to something they evened the score
They beat the odds and heard no complaints
No more are they the Aints they are the New Orleans Saints!

Shane Ballard, Grade 11
Osceola High School, WI

The Redwood Tree

Standing tall and proud it's the king of the forest
Casting its shadow over all before it
It's stood for a thousand years it will a thousand more
Never will it crash to the forest floor

Tough and strong it will not be broken
No ill word would ever be spoken
Its beautiful color is something to love
Looking down on all people from above

Its vast canopy covers the sky
Giving shelter to all sorts of creatures on high
Providing shade for all who adore it
It is the mighty redwood the king of the forest

Seth Bauer, Grade 10
Michigan Lutheran Seminary School, MI

Determination

You have to be willing to try, try again
You're mindset should be, "Yes, yes I can!"
Do not let fear strike in your heart,
Worrying and fear will tear you apart.
Don't let the little things get you down,
Don't be willing to stay on the ground.
You have to stop moaning, sighing and crying
But instead start smiling and keep on trying.
Failure is just a step to success,
Just remember to always do your best.
Determination and willpower is the key,
You decide the person you want to be.

Kaitlyn Cole, Grade 10
Michigan Lutheran Seminary School, MI

Withering

And so it seems as all before
The presence of winter once every year,
The pine trees shiver, to add one age
The pigeons perch, to mourn existence

Must we old our lives away?

The teardrop that won many wars and battles
The good speech that brought together many friends
To one day perish — like summer —

Famous literature will eventually rip
The tallest buildings will eventually fall
Will eventually rot, and lose their beauty
The knowledge of a million men
The secrets of a million books —

My lovely swan — the trumpeter kind —
The one who sat within my pond
Did not return to rendezvous
Did not return to love me more
Did not return to show her beauty

Som Thao, Grade 12
East High School, WI

Ode to My Grandmother – A Sonnet

My grandmother is always full of fun
And she makes the most of the little things
She never takes for granted anyone
And freely gives all her love without strings

My grandma has a ready ear for those
Who need someone with whom to talk or cry
She's a hopeful sun breaking through clouds closed
Her optimism driving woe aside

I feel I should appreciate her more
Her ready smile and loving, tender hugs
And steady hands which open wide the door
With a heartfelt welcome home in her eyes

She is like a steady rock on the shore
Who faces the storms though they beat her sore

Elisabeth Kyro, Grade 10
Wayzata High School, MN

Life Is Like a Machine

Life is like a machine
Working men and women are the parts
But sometimes they malfunction
And maybe even rust
And need to be replaced
But if everything works, it's a perfect harmony
Life is like a machine

Mack Wilda, Grade 12
Osceola High School, WI

Down by the Ocean

She dug her feet into the scorching sand.
Running down to the water,
She flopped her feet into the icy bath.
Children splashed around,
Like swans searching for fish.
The waves were crashing,
Reminding her of planes roaring overhead.
The aroma of the ocean tasted like a saltine cracker
She was concentrating on the children,
When her eyes darted back in the distance,
As a dolphin fin cut through the glassy water.
As her dress ruffled in the wind,
Her mother shouted her name over and over,
"Kayla! Kayla!"
Finally her mother came over and grasped her shoulder.
She suddenly snapped out of hypnosis.
"It's time for lunch," she told her.
And she looked back and it was gone.
A feeling of sadness accelerated through her.
She turned around abruptly.
"Okay mom," she sighed and they wandered away from paradise.

Kayla Holmes, Grade 12
Clarkston High School, MI

Remember Me

Your heart is my vintage,
Yet everything is so touch-and-go nowadays.

For everything that is clear,
It has been too far obscure these past few years.

Won't somebody set me free?

My essence still lingers,
Though my soul is so far detached.

When I'm too fragile to persevere,
Promise me one thing —

Please keep me in your heart.

Macy Veith, Grade 10
Appleton North High School, WI

American Soldiers

They fight for the red, the white, and the blue
For honor and glory and liberty too
They fight through the danger, no matter the cost
Some live through the battles and some, they are lost
Some get enlisted and some volunteer
And though they have courage, most do have fear
Siblings, relatives, friends and spouses
We hope they all can come back to their houses
And even when they're gone, in our hearts they'll be
The ones who fought so we could be free

Justine Hanan, Grade 10
Michigan Lutheran Seminary School, MI

Who Would Understand?

Open up wide swallow down deep,
No spoonful of sugar can make it sweet.
Day and Night it keeps haunting me.
Who can undo what I have done?

If they knew who knows what they would do to me?
Never before has someone tried to help me to live.
Something sincere, surely they might understand.
Abused, misused and confused am I,
They would always think the truth is a lie.

My life is lived like a nightmare home after home no one ever cares.
Daily and nightly I always pray for a family.
One who will care for me
not just toss me around like an object.

I've tried that before. Nothing ever worked,
They always shipped me off to another,
Then they would pretend to be like my mother.
It's all my fault.

It's like a cancer inside. I know it's there,
And I know of no one who will ever care.
But who would dare to love me,
after what I have already done.

AnaMarie Jackson, Grade 11
Prairie Du Chien High School, WI

Again, with Feeling!

Crazy, they say,
As if they've never even
Tasted the hunger, the chaos,
On their tongue; crazy, they
Say, as clinical, intellectual, dead.

Clearly, they've never felt the
Guttural roar of clarity, never
Felt the pulse of insanity, truth
Shoot through arteries and words and
Spread through the air, seedling.

Clearly, in their clean white coats,
They can examine and judge, gavels
Swinging down, shunning stray thought.
"Stay on path," grunts the jailor,
"Keep your thinking to your head, give up."

No, dear sir, no way, I won't,
I can't, these seedlings have taken root
In my head, be free, I'll save you,
I'll let you grow. This flower is all
I have to own. In here, I'm dead.

Oh, dear God, I'm dead.

Genevieve O'Fallon, Grade 12
Centennial High School – Red Building, MN

William Russel Peterson

W illing time ends and life shortens
I llness covers the sky as lives burn to ash
L ove for his wife till inside his mind as he feels fire around his soul
L ong hard breathes as smoke fills his lungs and the feeling of falling all around him
I 'll live he said as he runs to find his way out
A good man and a loving husband taken away from his wife
M aking his job his resting place

R olling smoke over his office makes seeing hard
U nlikely to see the future he never made it out alive
S mall children missing their father after coming home from school
S mells covers the room as people are burning
E very breath is cherished as it may be the last
L iving is the only thing the people see not money not cars but their own lives

P ain is the feeling that over comes the body
E very body wants to run but don't know what way as they can't see their ways through the fire and black smoke
T ension of love makes the man feel unsafe and forgotten
E very step is cherished as he walks among fire
R unning is not an option after he sees the fire around his body
S ad and never forgotten he will be remembered after every day passes
O n this day no one stands among you without pity for the fallen
N o lives are better than another and life is a dream that's unspoken for this man

Zakary Peterson, Grade 12
Gillett High School, WI

Dandelion Bouquets

She lies in her crib.
Sheets gently ripple as she breathes.
Her small pink lips crinkle into a smile, as she sleeps.
And while I slowly stroke her hair,
the splendor of the moon whispers wisdom to me…"remember this"
She skips through the yard chasing her youth,
while summer lullabies hum through the trees.
Her hair sticks to her face. Her clothes, smeared with dirt.
And as she hands me a dandelion bouquet,
the scent of summer whispers wisdom to me…"remember this"

I sit here silently, surrounded by the frigid stillness of a new place
And I begin to remember
the songs my baby brother would sing repeatedly
the brush of my mother's kiss, her hair shielding my innocence
the symphony of crickets serenading me to sleep
the dusty feeling of chalk covering my fingers, like pixie dust
dancing in the kitchen, around my father's knees, while sunlight slowly poured in from the window

…we slowly drowned in the bliss.

And I remember,
wilting dandelion bouquets on the front porch step.

Lauren Sander, Grade 10
Fruitport High School, MI

Death Row

For the anonymous executioners of death row
Some people might just not know
Pulling the lever is our 'high'
The look we get in our eye
Followed by a lifetime of doubt
Only few know what that is about:
They take an innocent life
With a pistol or a sharp knife —
I wasn't there to witness it.
Was it a false accusation, or legit?
I have to appear somewhat normal.
Death is never casual; it is always formal.
I can't always remember their names
At times, it may seem inhumane.
"Please forgive me."
That is how they plea
I'd show some mercy if I were kind
But that is not what is on my mind.
My fingers itch
I look to the electrician and order him to pull the switch.

Shawn Forsting, Grade 11
Lincoln Jr/Sr High School, WI

I Don't Understand

I don't understand
Why people don't know when to stop talking
Why some care so much about what others think of them
Why it gets so cold outside

But most of all
Why people are dishonest
Why there is so much pain in the world
Why people insult others to make themselves feel better

What I understand most is
Why I love animals
Why I like warm weather
Why I try to help

Jacqy Hall, Grade 12
Osceola High School, WI

Hiding

I have to stay in my shell,
cramped in this increasingly dark place.
The solitude is beginning to destroy
my once lovable emotions,
I am forced to stay in cover
in fear of being stripped
of all remaining safety,
wanting simply to come out of this dark place
and stretch my cramped body,
without being ridiculed for what I am
by the voices surrounding me
that were born "normal"

Daniel Lehto, Grade 10
MI

The Movement

A single spotlight lights the floor
A single dancer and nothing more
She moves with poise, with charm, with grace
And every last inch of her, dressed with lace

Yet she feels alone, unloved and scared
If only she'd see it, she'd be prepared
She'd know I am here with her, though quiet, enshrouded
If she'd close her eyes, she shan't be so clouded

But it's not just her eyes that aren't seeing me too
It's also her heart, but I wish it wasn't true
If she knew I was here, it would be okay
We could dance together, lose the time, and fly away

But someday she'll discover
What I am and I'll say
"I am the movement
And have always lit your way"

Ethan Liss, Grade 10
Pacelli High School, WI

The Mistake That Took Everything

The sound of the rain hitting the dark brown coffin
Sends chills down my spine
My breath catches, and I want to cry
But my eyes have nothing left in them
I feel like my soul's been ripped out
And I know I'll never be the same again
I wish that I'd told him to stop
To let me drive, instead of him
But I didn't, and now the crunch of glass breaking
Metal upon metal, will forever haunt my dreams
They lift the coffin down into the bleak earth
That seems to be rising up to take him away forever
As they cover it with dirt, I know what was left of my soul
Is buried forever with my love

Emilee Rhode, Grade 10
Brown City High School, MI

The Beach

Remembering the sounds of the ocean,
The feeling of the sand against my skin
The sound of the squawking seagulls
Resting my head on the sand
Staring at the clear blue iridescent sky
My head overflowing with thoughtful memories,
Picturing the moments of my life
Feeling the warmth of the sun
Triggering every part of my body, relaxing every muscle inside me
Hearing the sounds of the ocean as I close my eyes,
It's one of those days where I put everything aside,
Laying on the beach with nothing on my mind,
Just enjoying every second as I feel alive!

Rabab Alkaabi, Grade 12
Star International Academy, MI

Unconditional

God's love is unconditional.
He loves you when the sun comes up, he loves you when the sun goes down.
God's love is unconditional.
He loves you when you have made a mistake, even when it is so great you cannot forgive yourself.
But God forgives you,
Because no matter what, he loves you.
God's love is unconditional.
It is not influenced by color of skin, or by sexual orientation.
Not by our past, no matter how rough.
None of this matters to God.
God's love is unconditional.
He will never leave you or give up on you,
Even when you have given up on yourself.
When you turn your back on God,
He waits patiently for you to face him again.
God's love is unconditional.
He loved you enough to die for you,
And even if you were to hate him for doing so,
He would do it again in a heartbeat.
Because he loves you.
God's love is unconditional.

Cheyenne Vargo, Grade 10
West Bend West High School, WI

Dear Papa

I have spent a while, trying to figure out what to say. Papa, I never got to tell you who you are in my eyes.
From when you held me for the first time, to when you would tuck me in at night.
You have always been more than just my grandpa. In all honesty you were the hero that I was so blessed to meet.
Hey Papa, remember when you saved that one guy's life when he fell off the dock at Big Bass Lake?
He said he owed his life to you.
Remember when you would pick me up from school every day in 1st grade?
Hey Papa, remember when you, me and grammy would sit on the couch every night and watch *Wheel of Fortune?*
In that exact order, you, me, gram.
Remember when you and I stayed up until two in the morning the night before Christmas Eve
and we would eat all the caramel turtles? Papa, you're so silly. Did you know that?
I remember when you would come to all my cheer competitions to watch me.
In fact you and grandma are the reason I was in cheer to begin with.
If I could tell my babies one thing, that you have taught me, is that you start and end with family. No matter what.
I was so blessed to be in ours. Our big family.
You never let anyone feel out of place.
Any one of us could tell any person that you accepted everyone for who they were and always had a joke to share.
Papa, during the Cancer Walk my candle never went out. I'd like to think that it's a sign.
Papa, your light will always be lit inside of me, because you always kept mine lit.
I'll keep yours lit. I pinky promise.
I love you Papa. The angels are very lucky to have you. Just like I was.
Sleep peacefully, say hi to Jesus for me. I'll see you again one day, and we will dance in purple rain.

Katelynn Phillips, Grade 12
Wayland High School, MI

Never Ending Battle

My life is like a never ending battle. The people I see, the things I do, they're like a never ending path to pain and hurtfulness. My family's all I have but that's not enough for me. My emotions are a never battle, like a road to nowhere that continues to appear before me as I walk this lonely path. My life is like a novel each chapter tells a new part but there's a difference this book never ends. So I'll say it again I am in a never ending battle and it continues on.

Chyenne Stewart, Grade 10
Northwestern High School, MI

Beautiful Blue Eyes

People may love me,
People may hate me,
And some people may even adore me,
But they do not know…
What's hiding behind these beautiful blue eyes,
Nothing in my life is perfect, as matter of fact it is far from perfect.
So if you wish you were me try to look deep into my beautiful blue eyes.
Look behind my fake smile I put on every day to fool everyone.
I put a fake smile on to hide all the tears I have shed, to hide all the pain, hurt, and suffering.
But even though I had it rough, I am built strong.
But if you wish you were me, look deep into my beautiful blue eyes.
And tell me what you see.

Khali Kellogg, Grade 12
Gillett High School, WI

Courage

Courage means standing up for what you believe in, and not turning the other cheek. It means doing what is right, but does not mean doing what is popular. It is doing what is best, not what is the easiest. Most importantly, courage is saddling up for your principles and not hiding from the truth.

Jeffrey Rachu, Grade 12
Greenwood High School, WI

Good Friend

you said it was my voice
i never even knew
           YOU
we were in sixth grade
we never talked or hung out

you want to judge me
sure, why not
that makes you look bad not
           ME
you have to like everyone for
their good qualities
the bad qualities and everything in between
doesn't matter who they are or if you like them
remember the golden rule?
treat others how you want to be treated

so you know what? that's ok
i will still talk to you
act like we are friends
even though i know what you say
behind my back

i like me for me
so if you don't like me i will push through that

because i am and always will be the one and only
           ME

Caitlin Fairbanks, Grade 11
Deer River High School, MN

Ours to Conquer

One army marched, another wept.
The sea swallowed the rest.
We fought for men lost and freedom kept.
Death took the best.

The world was ours to conquer.

We faced the enemies' wrath.
The battle cry echoed through history,
As we forged our path.
This is our requiem, this is our glory.

The world was ours to conquer.

The drums were wild to match the victory,
Of fury and death and freedom to come.
We spun and pounded for the blood that ran free.
We sang and screamed for the memory burdensome.

The world was ours to conquer.

We clashed, but it was our own choice.
We stood for the destiny we conceived.
We spoke for ourselves as one voice.
And all who died did it for what they believed.

The world is ours to conquer.

Margaret K. Collins, Grade 10
Bay City Central High School, MI

A Silent Scream for Help

it happens every day
        some people only imagine it
        others live it
it breaks some people's hearts when they know they can't prevent it
or when they know they could have prevented it and didn't

        for children living it
it's a living nightmare every day
a child screams, a child cries
        no one listens

        years later the pain that haunted them
        is inflicted on their children
it's a cycle that seldom breaks
the child inside screams, the child inside cries
        still   no one listens

        it happens every day
some people only imagine it
others live it
        ignoring it won't stop it
        a new home every year won't stop it
Kerrie Humble, Grade 10
Deer River High School, MN

American Soldiers

Blood, sweat, and countless tears,
Struggling, surviving, facing all their fears.
Fighting for their life,
Easing others strife
Night and day
While civilians play.
They keep our country safe from harm,
Protecting us from dread alarm.
The land of the free and the home of the brave.

Their life they give
That we might live.
Unselfish, proud, and loyal too,
They love our country through and through.
Their bravery and commitment we adore,
In debt we shall be ever more.
Jessica Friebe, Grade 10
Michigan Lutheran Seminary, MI

The Finish Line

Driving fast is a blast from the past,
When I race down the track
Ahead of the pack.
The pedal's to the floor,
With a top speed of 244
I pushed the button I thought was cursed…
Then realized, I'd flown by the leader
And came in first!
Zach Poole, Grade 12
Neil E Reid High School, MI

Braun, Fielder

The Home of the Brewers! Miller Park!
Prince Fielder and Ryan Braun!
They are both just 27 years old.
Training and timing is what matters
Two-run double to the right field
Two-run home run to right field in the fifth inning
Turns into a 6-5 leading for the Brewers
Shut down the Cardinals in final three innings.
Bouncing a single
Followed with a double
Then comes BRAUN!
Double to right field
One pitch and a two-run homer for Fielder.
The one-two hammer
Comparing them to Hank Aaron and Eddie Mathews.
The two had their fingerprints all over the games.
Career-high hitting streak.
This could be the last of the one two hammer,
But it also could be the last of Prince Fielder,
In Miller Park, for the Brewers!
Stephanie Kalina, Grade 11
Lincoln Jr/Sr High School, WI

Lost in Reality

I've got no plans, I ain't going nowhere
and neither are you.
I'll stay stranded here until the day
I see your face,
moved by hope and the future.

But we have no future.
There are no plans to go anywhere,
we'll just sit here, and wish away all our dreams
on each other.
I don't want that.
I want to see these dreams become reality.

No longer lost in a dream
but rather lost in reality.
Lindsay Borkin, Grade 12
Trillium Academy, MI

Who Are We?

We live in a world of media frenzy
where the grass is supposedly greener on the other side,
fast is never fast enough,
skinnier equals prettier,
self should always come first,
more possessions and money equals a happier life,
trends are followed for fear of standing out,
and where getting ahead is always more important than giving help.
We don't live for ourselves anymore…
So who are we
really?
Rachael Miner, Grade 12
Waterford Kettering High School, MI

Messy Room

Oh, what a mess, I can barely dress
The floor is like a jungle.
I would slip on some shoes, but I have some bad news
I think I may have misplaced them.

The bed's a disaster, and now I must muster
The strength to reform its beauty.
The covers are a mess, it's tougher than chess
To position them back into order.

Where is my shirt? Ew! It's covered in last night's desert,
I'll just have to find another.
The dressers are bare, I realize in terror
I haven't done the laundry in ages.

My clock rings aloud, and it feels like a black cloud
Is hovering over my head.
I've just about had it, with my messy old habit
It's time to make a change.

Then and there I promise, to always be honest
To my mom about cleaning my room.
Was I truthful you say? On no there's no way
And one simple phrase is what caused it…

…I'll do it later.

Wyatt Towne, Grade 10
Michigan Lutheran Seminary School, MI

Fritz

The days after you died
I will never forget
I had never been so sad
I had never been so upset

You lay there so still
With a smile on your face
As I stood there and cried
You stood watching from a better place

We each walked by
Crying more with every step
Saying our last goodbyes
Reliving every memory kept

The gunshots were fired
The horn began its call
They gave the flag to Grandma
And my tears began to fall

I miss you so much
And I know you are finally free
But sometimes I wish God's gates were closed
So you'd come back home to me

Mitch Vosejpka, Grade 11
Montgomery-Lonsdale High School, MN

Losing You — A Process

The day I lost you hurt like ice,
when it feels so hot but you're cold.
The way it burned,
how I stung with pain,
and still do though I've grown old.
You may say that I look young,
like any other little girl,
but on the inside I've grown up,
my heart's an empty shell.
My heart has turned to cold cold ice,
my innocence it seems snatched up by mice,
who made me cry day and night,
day and night.
But now my eyes cry no more.

I wish I could talk to you.
I miss you dearly.
Who is it that took you?
How I wish I knew.
Why don't you talk to me anymore?
Why is it I hear silence?

Micala Burns, Grade 10
Jefferson High School, MN

Stay Within Serenity

Scorning at you in dimness
Pain is the aggressive darkness
Undermining your hope
Fail is the threatening calamitousness
But don't be afraid
Light shines on you
Just stay within serenity

Bringing chaos
Discordance within opinions is the source of separateness
Putting you in trouble
Misery is the incurable sadness
But have hope in your mind
Eternal peace resides within you
Just stay within serenity

Jae-Young Park, Grade 11
Michigan Lutheran Seminary School, MI

Impenetrable Storm Waters

The scream of the sea
is disruptive,

thundering,
roaring,
raging,

rejecting
intruders to inhibit the black waters of solitude,
damning them to unknown territory.

Elizabeth Kunz, Grade 12
Allegan High School, MI

My Angel

there she lay so cold
...so still
purple washed over her skin
foam trickling from her mouth
she was gone...

the bottles of pills lay beside her
empty...

why did God have to take my mommy
I will never understand
was it a night of fun gone wrong
or...meant to end this way

after a year of missing you...
I get this feeling of numbness
it's still not real
the shock and disbelief still lingers

now up above in heaven...
my guardian angel
watching me grow from above
Shelby Geving, Grade 10
Deer River High School, MN

My Angel

Angel, can you hear me,
As I'm praying on my knees?
Angel, can you see me,
As I whisper quiet pleas?
Angel, can you feel me,
As I long for only he?
There's nobody but him.
No one else for me.
Baby, can I tell you,
Exactly how I feel?
Baby, can I show you,
That what I say is real?
Baby, can you listen,
And take heart to what I say?
That baby, you're MY angel,
For forever and a day.
Amanda Sleen, Grade 12
South Sr High School, MN

Through All the Damned

The lonely nights and sullen days
Beaten and broken a thousand ways
The blackened heart and shrouded soul
Oh how this love takes its toll

But here I am, through all the damned
Facing dread with a heavy sigh
It's not yet my day to die
Will Stuttz, Grade 11
Onsted High School, MI

Dreams

It's hard to wake up when you've only just started;
You've only just begun the dream with which you're prematurely parted.
You ignore the time and grab with an outstretched hand.
You grab at the safety left behind in blissful dreamland.

It is the place where impossible is possible, and good times never end.
The place where ideas are sparked, and where rules are quite easy to bend.
The place where silly childhood fairy tales take flight.
The place your mind goes to wander during the night.

It is in dreamland where answers are found.
It is in dreamland where you're no longer stuck on the ground.
But wander too long and you'll lose your grip on reality,
Because life isn't always what you dream it will be.

Although you must be careful not to get lost,
Not dreaming at all also comes with a cost.
If you refuse to dream, you lose insight not found when you're awake.
Insight into the things you truly want, which might be at stake.

So when you dream, you must take great care.
For if you get lost in fiction, you'll forget what's truly there.
Sarah Harvin, Grade 12
University High School Academy, MI

Synethesia

A warm July night with street lamps and celestial perforations
providing enough light to see without touching the magic of an impeccable summer's eve.
Intoxicated off summer's energy,
the synth beats flowing from the speakers, remixing with the hum of the cicadas.
I could feel the noise
as if it came from within.
We performed a series of rhythmic bodily movements to the music
through the mosquitoes, numb to their bite,
off the porch,
through the dusty breezeway,
and out to the backyard with the intention of clambering into the pool
for the refreshing cool escape from the heat.
We bounced with the bass lines and sung to the lyrics in discord.
Creating a whirlpool dizzying, and blurred.
I did everything I was not supposed to,
and everything
that felt right.
Maranda McCain, Grade 12
Clarkston High School, MI

Why We Fight

War means death, war means pain, but war can also be triumph and gain.
We fight all night so people back home don't have to fright.
War can be good, war can be bad. It can make us glad or sad.
Millions have died which gave the U.S. its pride.
War isn't glorious, war isn't fun, we try to kill each other with a gun.
Freedom isn't free, it's paid in blood and tears of moms who gave their sons to die
For our freedom. "War is pain, war is cruel, so pray for our troops, don't be a fool."
J.C. Newcomer, Grade 10
Michigan Lutheran Seminary School, MI

Love Song, Love Song

I want to remember how it feels,
to feel new.
To touch every atom,
to breathe from your breath.
But your words are shattering,
yet your voice silencing.
Every second and I'm ice
You freeze and then melt me;
melt and then freeze me,
And I'm dripping with ardor.
Dear puppeteer,
Untangle my strings,
the ones in your hands and in my heart.
Or just pull tighter,
but want to this time.
Untangle the knots in my stomach,
ease the pain,
Because the pace is quickening,
and the Earth is spinning,
and with living like this,
I'll soon detonate.

Eileen Martin, Grade 11
Stevenson High School, MI

You Didn't Have to Be

Six was when we first met,
And I couldn't help but feel scared.
I wasn't ready to open up just yet
To love you — I wouldn't dare.

You didn't push me to like you,
I took it slow
And you did too.
Which allowed our relationship to grow.

We began to do everything together
Like play games, hunt, and fish.
I realized you were here forever,
And there's nothing more I could wish.

You are everything to me.
You are the father you didn't have to be.

Cassandra McCarthy, Grade 11
Belmont High School, WI

As My Soul Softly Weeps

Into the deep
I fall
Without a single breath
Only small ripples remain
No memories or thoughts
No survivors
The dark blue engulfs my heart
As my soul softly weeps

Anastasia Welnetz, Grade 11
Random Lake High School, WI

Man's Best Friend

I sit and try to write the words I want your heart to hear.
Hoping to find some comfort in the fact that you're not here.
I look out into the places that you once occupied,
Knowing now that your favorite spots are empty, because, my love, you've died.
I do believe with all my heart that your soul has gone to be,
With all the other angel dogs that you were meant to see.
We will have to stay behind, until God calls us too,
So do not be afraid that he has only called for you.
The water is still where you have played,
And you bed is so empty, where you once laid.
The four people who loved you now only dream,
That one day our eyes will shut one last time,
And you will come greet us, angel of mine.
Until then, I'll keep trying to see through the tears,
With memories you left us, to reflect through the years.
And I dread the day that your scent disappears
For it's proof to me, Moose, that you were once here.
But one day will come, when we'll start to see through,
The pain of the moment and just remember you.
Now you go on and play, and look down when you can,
Remembering we love you, and just like I told you, this isn't the end.

Jessica Schirmeister, Grade 12
Osceola High School, WI

The Pieces to My Heart

My heart is made of many pieces, they come together as one
Because they are so special they bright up like the sun
They glow and sparkle to light up my world
They make me happy, they make me enjoy

Each one is its own piece making it so special
Their care and support always makes me feel better
Their character and beauty makes them who they are
In my heart they come together shining like a star
Without them my heart will not remain together
They are the pieces to my heart
Each piece needs the other, each piece cannot be alone

I cannot imagine living without them
Each one is a puzzle piece of my heart
They will always remain a part of me, I will never let go

Their beauty will always shine like the sun, they will always sparkle
Their character will never fade away, they will always remain special
In my heart they are the pieces that will always remain together
They are not only my world and my happiness, they are my sisters that I love

Fatima Ghanem, Grade 12
Star International Academy, MI

My Everything

baseball is my
   everything
I love the
   pressure
the intense feeling
I get when
   on the mound
knowing that
every
   pitch
      counts
the team
      relies on the pitcher
   to read EVERY batter
what pitch to throw
   fastball
      curve
         change
Eythan Stangland, Grade 12
Deer River High School, MN

For Every

For every war that is one,
Many die.

For every job that's taken,
Many go homeless.

For every teacher,
Many students succeed.

For every broken heart,
Only one person can repair it.
Kaylee Kiggins, Grade 12
North High School, WI

Aunt!

Surgery and pain. Visits and tears.
Is it a cyst or is it cancer?
Saying good luck and saying you'll be okay.
In seven days, surgery will happen.
At the hospital, waiting for surgery to end.
Four to eight hours later there she is!
Happy, hurting, hugging, smiling.
Asking how she is or how she feels.
Finally, surgery ended. Asking the doctors,
Was is a cyst or was it cancer?
Until then, we will never know…
Amanda Dvorak, Grade 12
Eagan High School, MN

No Longer Trustworthy

Trust is a must as we
travel through this dusty road.
When the trust is broken
anger can develop like a blistering cut.
Life without trust is like toast
without butter, breathing without air,
a pool with no water.
I trusted you with my personal thoughts
and came to you for advice.
The day you broke our trust
was the day my life changed.
No more carefree days,
always being analyzed.
Closed off, keeping to myself
I can no longer find comfort
in the ones I surround myself with.
I try not to hold this against you,
you were only trying to help.
But didn't you know that wasn't
your stuff to tell?
Nicole Frank, Grade 11
Clarkston High School, MI

Advice for Country Living

Do get lost in a corn field,
Don't do it at night.
Do shoot a big buck,
Don't fall asleep in the stand.
Do shine deer,
Don't let the boys drive.
Do go in haunted houses,
Don't chicken out before you leave.
Do ride around on "all terrain vehicles,"
Don't get caught by the police.
Do go on road trips,
Don't follow the map.
Do go fishing,
Don't fall in the water.
Do live it up in the country,
Don't forget this advice.
Rachel Davis, Grade 11
Lincoln Jr/Sr High School, WI

You Are

Beauty is from within.
You may not look pretty to others because
People see you differently.
You see what you don't want to see.
Everyone has flaws.
You see more than others that
You may feel like hiding.
Your thoughts are wrong.
Well,
You are not pretty.
Logan Klatt, Grade 11
Random Lake High School, WI

I Love You

I feel upendi,
I feel my heart,
I feel amore,
I have from the start.

I feel liebe,
Hey, "je t'aime,"
If only I could tell you,
And I could make you see.

I feel ai,
And everything in between,
I can't even describe,
What it is you mean.

Every Beatles song,
Says what I will in time,
So let me find the lyrics to ask,
"Will you be my Valentine?"
Nichole Vann, Grade 10
Hartford High School, MI

Tour of Europe

Pasta in Roma,
Croissant in Paris,
Cappuccino in Wien,
Chocolate in Bern.

Big Ben in London,
Cathedral Sta Maria del Mar in Barcelona,
Buchenwald in Weimar,
Coastlines in Belfast.

Full of culture,
Full of people,
A mixture of language,
An American in Europa.
Alli Kremers, Grade 11
St John's Preparatory School, MN

A Great Man

He took me to the farthest lands
He told me the ancient stories
He was a great man

He was a Lion
But was as sweet as sugar
He helped the needy
Even if they needed to see

To some, he was Chuck
To others, Mr. Weir
But to me, he was just
Grandpa
Kaelene Gulick, Grade 10
Michigan Lutheran Seminary School, MI

A Cold Winter Day

That day was cold
Your warm glove grabbing my hand
When we touched you melted my heart
My fingers had fit perfectly between yours
That day was the day I fell
I didn't just fall, I fell for you, specifically you
We were inseparable
Well, until that horrid day
You turned your back, said we're through
You chose your friends over me
I've loved you since that cold winter day
When you picked me up and said
Everything will be okay
But stupid me, I was so blinded
Your charm cast a spell
Just like your stupid smile
Ever since that horrid day
You say everything will be okay
But silly you, charms don't last forever
My love faded long ago
Just like that ice cold winter day

Kenzie Taylor, Grade 10
Owen Gage High School, MI

Bedtime at Age Three

Your little eyes twinkle like the stars.
Your little hands are holding your favorite stuffed animal.
With your blanket wrapped in your arms,
You create a bed for your little friend.
As I read you a bedtime story,
I see a smile with two twinkling eyes staring back at me.
I'm your hero.
I make fairy tales and action adventures come to life.
I sing you lullabies so you can go to sleep in peace.
All cozy in your warm, little bed;
I see a child whose eyes are closed, but still smiling while sleeping.
A heart full of joy;
A head full of imagination;
A peaceful night sleep;
As it should be at age three.

Latisha Thomas, Grade 12
Martin Luther High School, MN

Whoville

Up in the mountain sits the Grinch.
His heart beats slowly barely a flinch
Never to come down from his cave
The town is scared no one that's brave
Christmas around the corner
But the Grinch has never gave.
Still time to believe in old Saint Nick
Best to hurry for time will go quick
He comes down for a night
The Grinch can believe and makes things right.

Mariah Schrock, Grade 12
Osceola High School, WI

Irreplaceable

I've met people that make jokes
But nobody makes me laugh as they do
I've met people that solve world's problems
But nobody solves my problems as they do
I've met weird people
But nobody is weirder than them
There are people that support me at my game
But nobody cheers like they do
I don't even remember how I met them
But now we talk every day
We talk about important things and even random things
I could spend all day hanging out with them
Our fight lasts less than a day
We could read each other's mind though our eyes
Every time I have problems, I run to find them
I cry and they listen
I smile and they laugh
I'm bored and we have fun
They are irreplaceable

Lidyanila Gusman, Grade 12
Osceola High School, WI

The Battle Within

There she shall lie,
through her bloodshot eyes,
her body trembling like thunder,
and the truth coming out from under
another cold haunting night
she will take flight
in the dead of her addiction
injecting her own prescription
the solution crawls through her bloodstream
feeling relief and disgust, she screams
staring hopelessly into the mirror
she watches her soul disappear
this would be the last time
that she would see the light
as her small heart melts down…
she crashes…to the ground

Josie Antrim, Grade 12
Deer River High School, MN

Passionate Love

Great big long hugs around your body,
Deep long kisses upon your lips,
Passionate gazing in your eyes,
To whisper I love you at first sight,
To wake and find you in my sight,
To never let you go through this world alone,
To hold you close when you are cold,

I'll love you just as much when you lose control,
I love you baby with all my heart,
So how about we grow old together and never fall apart.

Cody Vlaminck, Grade 11
Lincoln HI High School, MN

The Hunt

The time is here
the cool fall air the nights getting shorter
the time is here
all the time I spent getting ready finally
the time is here
I set my alarm
the time is here

the alarm goes off I shoot out of bed
and grab my gear
lace up my boots
and head out the door

I grab my bow and start the walk
the first glossy frost sitting on the now-dying grass
I hit the trail to my stand
to start my sit I smile
                    the time is here!
                    Max Villeneuve, Grade 10
                    Deer River High School, MN

That Really Big Fish

On the muddy brown water we sit,
    my Grandpa and I trying to fish.
We're catching some big Bluegills,
    and catching the slimy seaweed,
    but no luck catching that really big fish.
We crack open our Coca-Cola's
    on that hot, steamy day,
    with hopes of catching that fish in some way.
Then all of a sudden the bobber started bobbing,
    and soon, my clear line goes running and running.
So I start reeling and my grandpa starts cheering,
in hopes that my hook pulls up and I can start screaming.
When the fish comes up to the small boats mast,
    my Grandpa starts shouting that's a really big bass.
So he grabs the fishing net to pull the bass in,
    And now and forever the great memory of then.
                    Aaron Crocker, Grade 11
                    Gillett High School, WI

My Truck

I picked up my truck yesterday at the repair shop
I got the top chopped.
I got really fancy tires
I hope it don't catch on fire.
The truck might have a little rust
But I'll leave you in the dust.
Whenever I want it to start, she cranks
But only if there is enough fuel in the tank.
Hit the trail
And the truck will never fail.
My truck is a Chevy
And I'll drive it to a levy.
                    Ryan Bruder, Grade 12
                    Tracy Area Jr/Sr High School, MN

Beauty

Beauty can be as simple as a thunderstorm,
    Or a frost-bitten field of glinting snow.
Beauty is the sunshine that keeps her warm,
    Or this feeling deep inside I may never know.

Beauty is the clouds sailing across the sky,
    Or the crunchy fall leaves littering the ground.
Beauty is that look she holds in each eye,
    Or her voice equal to an angelic sound.

Beauty can be the sun set upon the sand,
    Or the way she carries her sweet smile.
Beauty is the way she holds my hand,
    Or the way she walks in a charming style.

Beauty is defined in the rhythm of my words,
    Or can be seen in the clear blue sea.
In the end the only thing that should be heard,
    Is that beauty is as simple as you and me.
                    Stephen Lyon, Grade 10
                    Dewitt High School, MI

Crescendo

Shall I compare thee to a winter's night?
    Drawn over me and I can't run away
    It covers with a strength I cannot fight,
    And somehow makes it into every day
These vivid memories aren't good for me
Next pain increases with each single word,
    And darkness streaming far as I can see
    To feel as if my voice is still unheard
Let tears build up, crescendo anger now
Evoke the thoughts I'd hate to cloud my head
    Forget it all allegrissimo how?
Come follow me and see the tears I've shed,
    But its piano builds to forte fast,
And I'm amazed at how much time has passed.
                    Delphanie Wu, Grade 10
                    Saline High School, MI

Is It Me?

Piercing green eyes stare back at me
Every time I look in the mirror
I don't know what I should see.
And life doesn't seem to make it any clearer
I keep asking myself, is it me?
That reflection I see is not,
A girl so stupid and blunt.
She thought for once she could be happy
But the world stood against her angry and snappy.
That girl inside is so dead,
So gone, and so unread
So I go back and ask is this really me?
Maybe it is but it's not who I want to be…
                    Nourhan Mahmoud, Grade 12
                    Star International Academy, MI

The Timeless Dream
The azure mass perpetually floating above.
In times long past man has dreamt of soaring through its depth.
Of embracing the ivory wisps that glide lazily by.
This wonder, this, diving splendor…
A mere shadow of what once was.
It clings desperately to its last vestiges of immortality, a vain attempt at preserving that which remains.
Freedom. A promise that this horizon once boasted now remains a fleeting dream.
We, the dreams who have labored to embrace such perfection, now corrupt our beloved with taint unthinkable.
In humanity's youth we gazed upon the night sky in amazement. A color symbolizing the coldest of hearts,
made warm, and alluring.
With our rise, the night gradually declined.
Now our eyes are met with a bleak outline of what once was.
Only in the remote corners, man's taint has not yet spread. It is here that our gazes can still be met
with the glittering stars of old.
The final frontier in which the gods themselves were once said to call home.

Mircea Sucigan, Grade 10
Dwight D Eisenhower High School, MI

10 Years…
My imagination is no longer my inspiration, it is my next expectation.
But it seems like anytime I find my way, something happens to ruin the day.
I dream of the life we could have and wonder if I'm on the right path.
I've made a pact to get to where you are at.
But it seems like finding my way to you, is like painting the sky blue.
You're a lot bigger than me and even stronger too, I wonder if I'll ever get a clue.
The happy little lives of three that you lead, is something that is hard for me to see.
Life's tests and trials make me doubt, I'll get to where you are.
But I think about their faces and it gives me the power.
Money and cars are the foundation of who you are, why is it you always seem to leave me in the dark?
Your power and strength are something, I'm afraid I won't be able to match to.
Just when I feel I'm at your level, something always knocks me back down to size.
When everything here is so gray and doesn't seem right, I thinks about you and your Chicago life and it helps me see the light.
As much as I might despise how you see blue skies, I remember to give it time and I'll soon find myself in you.

Georgina Gjonaj, Grade 12
Dwight D Eisenhower High School, MI

In Detroit
You see hooligans, tagging buildings, I see artists.
You see a smart-mouthed little girl, who always has to have the last word, I see a defense attorney.
You see the disrespectful boy in the back of the class who loves banging beats on the desk while you speak,
I see a music composer.
You see a hard-headed girl who never complies with the dress code, I see a fashion designer.
You see a city, a "ghetto war zone."
I see a community trying, I see a place, a place I call home.

Rolanda Carty, Grade 11
Martin Luther King High School, MI

My Guardian Angel
I'm so in love it's crazy, when you touch me I feel clam, safe, and warm instantly but when you let go I feel scared, lost, and cold. I want to hold you for the rest of my life. What amazes me the most is when you found me my heart was broken along with me but when you found my heart you started to put it back together like a puzzle. Also when I look into those eyes it's like a black hole, one look and I'm hooked. And when I see you it's hard to look away because you are like an angel on water, when you walk it's so graceful. And every time I see you I want to pick you up and run away with you, you are my guardian angel so take me away with you. And I plead don't ever leave me alone.

Trever A. Oaks, Grade 11
Visions Jr/Sr High School, WI

Done
I'm sorry to say
But I have to go
Because I can't
Deal with the pain.

I'm sorry to say
But I'm sick of dealing
With everything you have done.
I'm sorry to say but I'm going away.

I know you don't like it
But it has to be done
I need to get out
To get rid of the pain
To get rid of the past
And move to the future.

No more dealing with the past
No more dealing with the pain
Now I am free and that's all I need.
I'm sorry today had to come
But it had to be done.
Tayler Wilson, Grade 12
Gillett High School, WI

Think
Anger
Pain
Confusion
All are running
Taking over my mind
What he did
Horrible to think
Think —
He did it to me
I loved him so
All I have
Somehow gone
Case of a broken heart
No cure
I'll live in fear
Fear of meeting someone like him
Brittany Paa, Grade 12
Hamilton High School, WI

Waltzing Waves
The waves are playful,
Forever pushing and pulling.
They prance and dance,
Tip and dip —
It's a joyful tempo
That sloshes and washes from the mind
All things serious;
All things dull.
Elizabeth Straub, Grade 12
Allegan High School, MI

I Am the Greatest
Full of energy, strength, and quickness, Muhammad Ali delivers punch after punch.
Not a person watching is using the seat they paid for.
Thousands on their feet yelling or watching in amazement.
All in anticipation of a finishing strike, a knockout.

The occasional grunt or moan from the competitors is muted
by the screams and cheers of fans.
Ali's opponent is wounded and afraid.
Blood from his nose trickles into his mouth.

Muhammad Ali can smell the fear in every breath his opponent takes.
The intensity builds inside everyone as Ali delivers blow after blow.
Finally his opponent collapses.
The People's Champion is victorious by knockout once again.

He elevates one fist towards the crowd,
"I am the greatest."
Shawn Achenbach, Grade 11
Viroqua High School, WI

Forever in My Life
Without you life would be unthinkable
With you sometimes it's unbearable
Sometimes you're the only thing that makes me laugh
Sometimes you're the only thing that makes me cry
Losing you is something I never want to think about
The days we spent together are the days I'll always want to remember
The days we spent apart are the days I'm pushing to forget
With her around we'll never be the same
The way we talked is something I'll never forget and always miss
I wish we could go back
Back to the way things were
When I had you, for you
The things I say aren't always meant
Cause with you things are hard to forget
But in the end with or without you
I'll move on
Kaitlyn Garczynski, Grade 11
Gillett High School, WI

Grandpa
Grandpa you have left me now.
From this cold, forsaken place you go.
Into the clouds, above the ground, with Jesus I see you now.
Sitting there talking and laughing, asking all the questions you had.
Grandpa, I see you face down here, but where have you gone?
I think, and I think, and I say I know, you are in a better place.
I see you working on your farm, sowing, plowing and reaping.
I know you loved it but you had your time down here.
It was time for you to go with Jesus up above.
I know you are woodworking with God by your side, making dogs and flowers and hearts,
But, oh, how I wish it was me by your side.
I know you had to leave but I miss you so.
I just want you to know I love you and will never let you go.
Taylor Eastin, Grade 10
Michigan Lutheran Seminary School, MI

Thank You

You've taught me so much without even trying
you're not the type of guy who scores his points by lying
You started off as a shoulder to lean on and a truly good friend
but turned out to be so much more in the end
I'll never forget the silly conversations over strawberry shakes
and your gentle hands to soothe my seemingly endless belly aches
You never taunt or tease
being with you is such a breeze
Through touching slimy fishes and
ten minute long goodbye-chapstick kisses
Through many a giggling fit
and being so nervous I could barely sit
I can confide in you about anything with such ease
You'll even bust a move with me if I play the puppy dog eyes
and give a "pretty please"
For late nights
belly button tickle fights
Fried peanut butter and bananas
And for all our future extravaganzas
For everything you do…
Thank you.

MyKayla Hilgart, Grade 12
Chequamegon High School, WI

A Place for Me

Water washes past,
full of life
more vibrant than my own.
Sun strikes the surface
lighting the world on fire.
Skimming rows of multicolored planets,
as sand caresses my body.
The cold engulfing at ocean's depths
clears my mind and slows my breath.
How I wanted to stay under the waves,
never to come up for air.
How I wanted to be held in the current's grasp,
to be swept away.
How I wanted to watch the sun turn the water to gold,
each and every night.
How I wanted to stay forever,
much longer than oxygen's need would allow.

Corrie Irving, Grade 12
St Joseph High School, MI

Lost Love

I stand here above your lonely grave.
To you, my heart will forever be a slave.
You will always be in my head, in my thoughts,
You are my inspiration when I'm alone — distraught.
You taught me to never give up, to fight,
You are the strength in my soul, the bright light.
Flowers will forever be on your grave in remembrance,
Of the gift you gave me, a second chance.

Thomas Dixon, Grade 12
Charlotte Sr High School, MI

Dear Moe

Dear Moe,

You sit and wait all day.
Until I come home for you to play.
Some days you'll jump up in the truck.
Headed out to field after pheasants or ducks.
Blazing through to grass.
Huntin' up every bird that you pass.
When the sun going down to the final light.
We watch the last of the teal on their final flight.
By this time you're ready for bed.
On the truck ride home you sit out my lap and rest your head.
I lay to rest back in your house,
And I sneak away quiet as a mouse
Thank you, friend, for the time together and time yet to come.

Your owner,
Don

Donald Houser, Grade 11
Lincoln Jr/Sr High School, WI

Memory Gazing

As I lay on the grass, at ease,
I ponder under the blazing sun
How similar the last few years seem to be
To the sky full of drifting clouds. Some
Are feathery and wisp lazily along,
While others are brisk, caught by the wind.
I close my eyes and listen to the song
Of twittering birds and silence   .
A cloud covers the sun. It's like a time
Of doubt; reasons and the future unsure.
But on the winds of prayer, patience, time,
God blows away my troubles and the Devil's lures.

I see them come and go steadily across the sky.
Soon they're long gone and in the past,
Only a memory, an image in my mind,
And the most memorable, good or bad, are what last.

Mikayla McDonald, Grade 11
Immanuel Lutheran High School, WI

Regret Nothing

From trouble's last breath
We regret what we have done.
Things seem different yet profound
A new perspective, unimaginable.
Aged like your favorite cheese,
I too have found rest, at last,
Regret nothing.
For it was I who once bared the burden of lie,
The burden of regret,
The burden of jealousy.
Be still, Regret Nothing.

Patrick Mork, Grade 12
North Branch Sr High School, MN

Moon

The sun's underminer
they intercept each other
the sun glaring rays of hate
at the moon
whose pale face smirks back apathetically
as he rises
the moon's nocturnal light looms
out of dark clouds
flooding empty darkness
with haunting lambency
preparing us
for the radiant light
of its daytime oppressor
the creatures of
the underworld
crawl out
from under depths of the earth
and roam
in the dark evil elements
until the sun rises.

Jared Teune, Grade 12
Holland Christian High School, MI

This Ground Is Hard and Cold

This ground is hard and cold
The Ziegler is still running bold
The headlights are a glare
For bypassers to drive by and stare

Every time I hear a clatter
I'm waiting for a disk to shatter
The shanks are tripping out
But I know there is no doubt

This field will be done
By the break of dawn
Yawn after yawn
I can see the crack of dawn

Brad Peterson, Grade 12
Tracy Area Jr/Sr High School, MN

The Most Important Days

As I'm sitting here
I find myself looking at a deer.
He's standing in the field across from me
Eating all the leftover sugar beets
Next I see the chirping birds
Flying all over from one tree to the next
As I see them flying around
To where destinations have no bounds,
I hear a whinny coming from beside me
I turn to face my horse
These are the days I live for of course!

Holly Nunnari, Grade 10
Michigan Lutheran Seminary School, MI

United

People and wars
And traveling far
Searching for equality
Getting ready to do reality
Stop thinking
And start doing
Whatever happens between one country and another will happen to others
With respect I should call them my sister or brother
Nobody's perfect
Trust me it's not worth it
People fought for healthiness and happiness
They've struggled now isn't that enough?
Men and women have to be strong and tough
No life to feed a child
Now tell me for all these years where have you people been?
After all these years it has been complicated
I promise you in the future you won't be devastated
For everything that you've done that you hated
If you come to the future you'll see the things that you've never seen before
All the years just for freedom
Don't wait you just get them

Nadia Husaini, Grade 12
Star International Academy, MI

Scott

I run through the woods hopping over small streams and fallen trees.
I hear shots fired, I keep running.

I meet the end of the woods; the scent of freshly cut grass fills the air.
Rows and rows of homes. I turn back around towards the wet and cold woods.

I'm trapped. Nowhere to go.
I lay low to the ground, I'm tickled by the tall grass going up my nose.
I slowly crawl into a bush and unexpectedly feel thorns prick my skin.

I see two of my friends walk up. I'm unseen. They look around then turn back.
As my two friends walk away I jump from the bush.
I aim my empty squirt gun at them and imitate the loud crashing sound of a real gun.

The battle is over.
I have won.

George Haight, Grade 10
Clarkston High School, MI

The Me in Me

A tree with many branches
The very complex Rubic's cube
Living life as a turtle in a shell: slowly comes out, one bump, he's back in
I wish you could stop looking at this tree with rose-colored glasses on
When are you going to let the light in this dark and cold room?
Weak as the smile on a bitter man's face
Being plowed to the side as snow
Being like a horse with no legs wanting to take that walk
Good god shut up, I don't want to hear another soul speak.

Jesse Halimon, Grade 11
Cody-Academy Critical Thinkers, MI

Light Show

Fire's stronger, lasts much longer,
but lightning takes the show
Fire will take your heart,
but wily lightning steals the soul

Lightning's airy, temporary,
and followed by the storm
Fire dances when it's fed
and hides the light of dawn

Lightning can't make up its mind,
dancing through the strands of time
Fires, you will stay quite true,
as long as something's feeding you

So which is truly better?
Fire, fierce bloodletter?
Or lightning, captivating minds
with murky storms, disastrous finds?

Who can ever really know?
We only sit and watch the show.
Brooke Kadrlik, Grade 10
Montgomery-Lonsdale High School, MN

Heaven and Hell

I've been to Heaven and Hell
Heaven was quite nice
Hell, I wish had ice
They both have a lot of room
Heaven has gates
Hell has lakes
I met a lot of people when I was there
Some were cool
Some were fools
I saw a lot of things when I was there
I saw our maker
I saw our taker
If I could go back I would
The maker was wise
The taker despised
I've been to Heaven and Hell
Cody Wilgus, Grade 11
New Buffalo Sr High School, MI

Seafood Buffet

Snapped crustacean limbs
like shrapnel
lodge
in trimmed steaks.
ragged survivors hustle
to pick up checks
from behind cover
before the crab bin is reloaded.
Steven McKeever, Grade 12
Allegan High School, MI

Decide

One day can change a lifetime.
That's one cold, true fact.
It's not your fault,
You're not to blame.
One thing leads to the next.
Life can be gained,
Love can be lost.
But those are just two things.
There's millions more, and open doors.
Just take a look around.
There's loss and pain, there's love and gain.
Your path has not yet been chosen. So take a look, and choose a door.
To see where life goes next. Some doors are good, but some are bad.
There's one thing you must know,
The door's not locked, you can get out. But memories can change you.
That's not bad, they shape us all. And we all make mistakes.
So when you fail, or when you lose,
Get up, and try again.
Sumiyah McCarty, Grade 12
Osceola High School, WI

Sitting, Watching, Waiting

Sitting, watching, waiting,
The whistle blows, the orange inflated basketball is so craving,
It's the start of basketball season, but I'm not on the floor,
Instead I'm at the table, counting the score,
Still sitting, watching, waiting.
Still going through all the practice and training,
But when it comes to game time, still watching and waiting.
My teammates, enjoying the winning,
While I'm stuck envying,
And I'm still stuck sitting, watching, and waiting.
But the clock is ticking, and the season's just getting entertaining,
My body does not feel normal without the game, it's hard to be taking,
But as soon as I get on the court it's just the beginning,
The only thing on my mind is winning,
And no more of this sitting, watching, and waiting.
Julian L. Reeves, Grade 10
Andover High School, MI

Your Touch

It's so cold, it's all around me and I can feel it in my heart, in my veins,
It cuts at my wrists, my throat, my heart, and it maims,
But then you came and I am not the same
For it you tame
In your touch I find warmth and love
And I have faith in a God above
And when you go
My heart sinks so low
Again the cold seeps into me
And it is so dark I cannot see
But again you come back to me
And the light is so bright and brilliant, I can see
So please, never leave.
Jessica Miehlke, Grade 10
Manton Consolidated High School, MI

A Day of Hunting and Fishing

I throw my gun in the back of my truck
With it I hope to kill a 12-point buck
While in the woods, BANG! I see the deer fall
I take him home, freeze the meat, and mount his horns on my wall

I grab my pole and tackle box and head to the lake
At this time in the morning, I feel barely awake
There is no school today, I'm glad there is no class
A mighty tug on my line, I hook a large mouth bass

There is nothing like hunting; waiting for the kill
Cutting and cleaning the meat my freezer I'll soon fill
Deer stakes and deer jerky have such a great taste
And with his head on my wall nothing goes to waste

I like fishing, fishing is fun
Fishing underneath the rising sun
I like catching the fish and putting them in a net
Fish is a great dish when the table is set

Timothy Sullivan, Grade 10
Michigan Lutheran Seminary School, MI

Inspiration

Inspiration, like morning dew
Here one second, then gone for a few,
Deep as the ocean, shallow as a clue;
Inspiration, like morning dew.

Creativity, fragile and framed
One man's trash is another man's gain,
A woman's style, a child's way;
Creativity, fragile and framed.

Influence, considered wrong
Whether you're above the temptation or under the throng,
You can be too good or you are just not strong;
Influence, considered wrong.

Revolution, strong and powerful
Subtle as a whisper, hectic as a crowd,
You can take part, or you can stand astounded;
Revolution, strong and powerful.

Cait Colby, Grade 10
Michigan Lutheran Seminary School, MI

Tears

Tears were streaming down on my cheeks
It's been like this for weeks.
I closed the bathroom door,
I started to cry and bawl more.

The fact that I cannot see her again,
A lot of memories that she made for me will stay in.
It is just too early to me
She promised to come to my wedding someday for me.

Always got choked up and brought tear,
But it is time to leave here.
My heart will keep her forever,
Always love, miss, and sorry for my grandmother.

Maria Ha, Grade 10
Michigan Lutheran Seminary School, MI

Judy

It has been a year to this day,
that we found out you could not stay.
We know you're in a better place,
but one more day to see your face…
We all miss you very much,
just one more day to feel your touch.
No one knew you were so sick.
Why'd you have to be His pick?
You had pushed on very strong,
It's sad that you couldn't stay that long.
The 50 great years you stayed,
all the people's days you've made.
You would always finish what you started,
but now you're gone and we are broken-hearted.

Anna Dvorak, Grade 10
Eagan High School, MN

Pride

I use to think
    that having pride meant knowing who you are
    and being totally okay with it.
Now I feel that
    having pride is being okay with who you are and
    not letting anyone change you.
I used to feel that
    having pride meant loving labels that are given to you.
Now I feel that pride is giving yourself labels and loving them
    I used to feel that
    pride was something that you could have too much of.
Now I feel that
    you can never have too much pride.

Allison Pamperin, Grade 12
Bay Port High School, WI

Nerves

I await on the end line to serve my heart-racing
the screams from the enormous crowd gives me butterflies
a million messages running through my mind
"you can't miss this serve"
"just get it over"
"don't serve it into the net"

the shriek of the whistle echoes throughout the gymnasium
I throw the ball up and serve it over the net
it catches the net, plopping over the other side
I hear my teammates yelling…
A.C.E! What's that spell Ace…Ace…Ace!!
with excitement I run up and high five my teammates

Alexandra Vickerman, Grade 11
Deer River High School, MN

Grandpa: My Hero

You've been there since day one.
You've done so much for me.
You've treated me like your son.
You've really made me see.

I stood on that bench and looked out that window.
You picked me up for the day.
You would drive rather slow.
It was a great day I'd have to say.

I've learned so much from you.
You've always loved me and made sure I knew it.
You even lost your leg for me in World War II.
So now, here we sit…

I can't imagine my life without you.
I want you to know…
Grandpa, you are my hero.

Nick Casales, Grade 11
Belmont High School, WI

White Beauty

December starts,
The winter is coming,
It's getting freezing cold outside.
The first snow is falling slowly and quietly.
There it lays down,
On trees, streets, and roofs of houses.
Everything turns white and beautiful.
It makes the world look like one of those typical winter paintings,
And seems so quiet
That people can forget the Christmas stress.
The beauty of snow keeps you thinking
About so many things.
How will other people celebrate their Christmas?
The poor might celebrate a different Christmas,
But the snow is a gift for everybody,
And its beauty,
Is showing peace.

Sandra Keck, Grade 10
Amery High School, WI

Just Me

Day in and day out it's always the same
What I do is never good enough for you
What I say is never right
How I dress is never appropriate
I'm sorry I am never good enough
But you know what
I'm done
I'm done trying to make you happy
I'm done trying to live up to your standards
I'm happy just the way I am
And you can and never will change me.

Bobbi Atkinson, Grade 11
Montgomery-Lonsdale High School, MN

Awaken Life

Awaken life

Fill the empty depressions
Give me more than impressions

Don't tickle my desires
Thrust the sword into my hand

Let me breathe the stable air
Of foreign, far-off lands

Make the questions chill my blood
And my answers dangerous ones

Make all things eternal blaze
Make insight mine, not the naive

Make mercy spill in silver drops
Tears that cover all disgrace

Make me see behind the glass
Explore the soul beyond the face

Catch distortions in the song
Give to love its wanting grace

Mold my soul to spring and soar
Inspire my voice to take on wings

Reflect the stars across my path
Instruct me to live.

Kayla Austin, Grade 11
Home School, MI

Nature

What I like best
Is the outdoors and forest
I like the green grass
And fishing for bass

There is so much to see
And it makes me feel free
It smells like a dirt floor
And it never seem to bore

The birds chirp
And the frogs burp
The waters run cold
And the animals walk bold

The trees grow tall
And make me feel small
With all the things that grow
They still seem to flow

Crystal Demuth, Grade 12
Tracy Area Jr/Sr High School, MN

Whenever I See You

Whenever I see your face,
I feel my heart race.
Whenever I see your smile,
My body goes wild.

Whenever I feel you near,
I never have fear.
Whenever I hear your voice,
I feel I've never had a choice.

Whenever I think about you,
My mind feels like a zoo.
Whenever we converse,
I never need to rehearse.

Whenever you talk to me,
I can barely breathe.
Whenever I see you,
All I want to do is be with you.

Lindsay Liljenberg, Grade 12
Osceola High School, WI

Love Is the Truth

Her smile brings out mine
I will love her until
The end of time
Make-up or not she always shines
I laid eyes on her and it just clicked
I knew I had found the one
She stuck out from everyone
Like she was the sun
When our lips lock I
Get chills like a cold breeze
I hope she will never leave
When she hugs me I
Wanna spin and twirl
Truth is…this girl is my world

D.J. Micik, Grade 12
Gillett High School, WI

Grief

The year 2004 brought lots of grief
The world can be cruel and life can be brief
Tragedies happen when least expected
Why can't death be ahead of time detected?

Both my grandfathers left this world
Leaving me filled with fear
And covered in tears
Why tragedies happen no one will know
The world can be tough
We all live with it
Why it happened to me
I never will know

Dylan Klimpke, Grade 12
Rib Lake High School, WI

I'm Gonna Come Back a Brand New Me, After This Tragedy

There's this demon within me, it craves life and got it;
everything is crumbling down faster than burning buildings, it's like I'm going psychotic.
I always say I'm fine, but we all know I lied;
it seems like it's taking over, the demon called love, that is inside.

The aches, and throbbing is going to be the death of me;
some say if I believe in God, He will help me but that's what they believe.
They say if I don't believe in him, this is what happens before I go to hell;
nothing could possibly get worse than this and you can already tell.

I feel like all that's happening is me losing control of myself;
coming to an understanding, I can't always pretend I'm okay, I need help.
Too weak, too weak, to do anything worthwhile;
my days consist of dwelling over things I can't fix, in continuous denial.

Somehow someway, I have a feeling that I'ma be able to pull through;
maybe I need to be locked away, if I promise to come back bulletproof.
Or just maybe, I'll do what I do, and just tough it out.
Like mama always said to me, this is what life is all about.

Brianna Silva, Grade 11
Forest Park School, MI

Waiting

When I'm lying on my deathbed, I must pray,
"God, oh Lord take me away, for I want to spend eternity with you someday."
But I guess right now is not the time.
For I am lost, not even found.
There is lawlessness because there is nothing left to do.
I sit around and sigh, waiting for my dreams to come true.
"Oh God, hear my prayers. It seems like the end is coming quite soon."
The people worry because they never had a chance to make a change.
I don't get why they wouldn't' want to leave,
For this miserable town is giving me the creeps.
And here it comes, the finale; 1, 2, 3.
Goodbye for now, I must leave.
God is calling me by name to the throne,
To judge me if I am accepted into my new home.
If not, I'll be dragged by demons themselves to be burned over and over again.
By the Satan to hell!

Alyssa Palazzolo, Grade 12
Dwight D Eisenhower High School, MI

Gratitude

I share my debt of gratitude with all my spiritual friends.
My gratitude begins with "I've learned that we are one."
I'm grateful and thankful for the right to dream, hope, wish, and know.
I'm also grateful for being a blessed child of God.
I'm thankful for the joy.
And
I am grateful for the fear.
My gratitude goes deeper for my breath, for my sight, and my life.
I'm grateful for all nature, the birds, the grass, and the trees.
And
I'm grateful for all the wisdom gained as I journey through this life.

Keauna Cornelius, Grade 10
Medicine & Community Health @ Cody High School, MI

Keep My Mind in My Pocket

Keep my mind in my pocket
My people tell me I'm a prophet
Unknown people tell me stop it
I'm using my senses no luck
Emotions I've had enough
I'm rock solid built like a truck
Hard scars like elephant tusk
Not making enough bucks
See so many John Does, do you know?
Have you heard? From a little bird
My vision is blurred
Trouble is stirred
But this trouble deterred
Nothing now I'm something that's absurd
I feel the hit but I pretend I never heard
I see a lot of change
Got money but it's all in change
My situation I'm trying to change
As I board the plane, I remain low
Consistent flow, my boat I just row
Where I'm going to end up I don't know
Marco Rivera, Grade 11
Osceola High School, WI

My Everything

You're on my mind every single day
You're the one I think about
The one I know I love
You took my heart away
We belong together
I'd give anything to be your anything
You're my everything
The guy I cry for
The guy who holds me tight
The guy who says he loves me
The one who makes me laugh
The only one I want
The love of my life
Whenever you need me
I'll be right there next to you
You're my everything
Amanda Young, Grade 11
Breckenridge Sr High School, MN

Hockey

Hockey players skate down the ice
With the hockey puck
And try to make a goal,
but the goalie tries
To stop the puck
And make sure
This team will win.
Austin Boots, Grade 10
Round Lake High School, MN

Summer's Story

I do not remember exactly when I first met Summer.
I only remember her green eyes, the greenest I've ever seen.
She took my hand, and I was surprised by its warmth.
She wrapped me in her arms as we headed down the road.

I cannot say how many days I spent with Summer.
I can only say that they were long and lazy days,
Days that made you want to sleep forever and that made you never want to close your eyes.
I saw flecks of brown in her once green eyes, but I thought nothing of it.
I thought of nothing except Summer.
Her warmth, her smile, her whispers that hinted of something Greater.

We walked a dusty road, sun-baked and empty.
I asked her why her eyes became more brown each day.
She kissed me and said; "Do not think of it. We have a while yet. We have time."
So we continued down the road.

After many days, Summer fell.
I caught her in my arms, and watched the last green in her eyes give in to brown, then gold.
She whispered one last "I love you" and closed her eyes.
A winter rain fell on her face as Summer faded away in my arms.
Anna Daavettila, Grade 10
Houghton High School, MI

Home

The sun is shining in, making the room bright
Everything is put perfectly and orderly

In the corner there are teacups set up, for a little girl
The pictures on the wall are perfectly hung,
The wall looks as if it were on a slant

From looking at the style of the room, as well as the darker more quiet colors
It seems a long time ago, that she lived there

No shadows emerge, just a different brightness on every side of the room
The room is fresh, smelling like fresh linen
The colors are all soft and all go together,
The red blanket stands out

Both chairs are placed separately
One in the corner and one in the middle of the wall by the
Half-opened blue closet

She cannot picture herself here.
Jordan Lawson, Grade 11
Clarkston High School, MI

Him

He is always there…
Ever since you've been born
He knows all about you
He was there…
For everything, for all of your birthdays
For all of your games
All of your practices, all of your scrimmages
For every single fall…
Every single mistake and embarrassment
For every failed test quiz and assignment…
When you learned how to walk
Riding your bike for the first time
When you read your first book without pictures
Even the first time you tied your shoes
He knows every move you make
He knows your every weakness
Every breath you take
He stalks you everywhere you go
Except for at night…
Because without light,
Your Shadow is just a memory.

Aaron Squanda, Grade 10
Michigan Lutheran Seminary School, MI

I Love You

Your face brightens up my day
You just being here makes everything okay
Your love is like an unending river that does flow
Your warm brown eyes melt my heart like sun does snow
When I can't feel your soft touch
I miss you so much
There's not a second that goes by that I don't think about you
And you're the one right now I wish I was next to
I just love the smell of you
You're the one that my heart goes out to
To me you're the best
So much better than the rest
We may fight about a thing or two
But there's nothing we can't get through
Because I don't want to lose you
You mean everything to me
And that I can guarantee
In my world you're my only guy
You have something money can't buy
You have the key to my heart and no one can change the lock
Because I love you a lot

Sarah Fournier, Grade 10
Michigan Lutheran Seminary School, MI

Lloyd's Ned

Skin black as night,
Rough and weathered,
Yet touch as soft as a feather.
When the blanket of darkness covers the world,
And nature is still,
I feel a sense of hope.
I'm risking it all,
Everything I've worked for,
But I can't stay away.
What I wouldn't give,
For things to be a little different,
But I don't have a say.
When we're together,
Everything changes,
The pain and fear, it all disappears.
You make me,
Forget the troubles, forget the suffering.
You make me believe, believe in a dream.
A dream of freedom.
You give me hope.
Lloyd's Ned.

Jazmyn Patterson, Grade 10
Waverly Sr High School, MI

Prince Fielder

Fellow first baseman and free agent-to-be
Eighth inning final at-bat in the final game we
Give the fans a few more goodbye reasons
A rival facing a similarly uncertain off-season.
Prince left a mark
At Miller Park.
Fielder may exercise his right as a player with six years
With the fans many tears
With a few more ranks
Milwaukee fans had a chance to say thanks.
Prince's great creation
He's done well for this organization.
With no more slugs
They lined up and gave Fielder hugs.
The beautiful weather
Braun told Fielder he was proud of what they had together.
Fielder's little boy crying
He told him he was trying
He will be remembered for his wonderful plays
On the end of his day.
Thanks, Fielder!

Chelsie Soppa, Grade 11
Lincoln Jr/Sr High School, WI

The Boy Who Never Could Cry

As he lies on the floor feeling wanted no more
joyous people chatter outside.
As he beats on his chest, he can get no rest
for the pain won't ever subside.
When he gets to his feet, all tangled in sheet
he falls with no strength to stand.
Then he curls in a ball to forget it all
and grips his face in his hand.

But the boy never cries, never tears in his eyes
'cause he feels too much to shed.
From morning till night he'll feel no delight
as he lies writhing in sorrow in bed.
See the boy never cares because nobody dares
to ask him what's wrong or what's right.
The boy never weeps, only moans when he sleeps
for a curse upon him, full of might.
This poor boy will never cry, have a tear in his eye
He will never make a peep.
A sad little boy, who's never known joy
and has never been able to weep.

Hayli Cox, Grade 12
Morenci Area High School, MI

Empty Space

The thoughts in my head,
Are more than crowded.
I pace back and forth,
While I'm waiting on my porch.
My mother is gone, and I'm alone like a little fawn.
Waiting for someone to come along,
To put me out of my misery and keep me company.
When I'm alone, I get this feeling that someone is watching me.
I want to put this feeling back, but it won't let me be.
All I want is a friend.
'Cause when I'm alone, it feels like the world is coming to an end.
I feel darkness, but I want to feel the light.
It's hard to do when you're full of fright.
I cry when I'm alone for too long,
But I think of my mother and her happy song.
This helps me cope with the emptiness that I am feeling,
Thinking of this makes me feel like I'm dreaming.
Being single is like being alone,
I want someone there when I come home.
I want someone there both night and day,
And "I love you" is what I want them to say.

Kelly Guy, Grade 11
Lincoln Jr/Sr High School, WI

The Dark

Walking outside in the dark,
Feeling like anything could be watching me.
I never know what could be
Just waiting around the next corner.
Even the slightest noise could make me jump,
It may be little as a mouse or as big as a bear.
As I walk I try to tell myself
That nothing is behind me.
It's only me out there, and nothing can get me.
I park the tractor in the shed and turn off the lights,
Jump out and tell myself nothing can
Get me. I'm by lights, and I'll okay.
I hear something creak.
Then my heart starts pounding fast,
I just take off running to the house.
Just trying to not fall flat on my face,
My work boots weighing my feet down, all
I can think is run for the house!
I finally reach the house and I can finally relax
A little bit. I'm out of breath but
I now know I'm safe from the dark.

Paige Janke, Grade 11
Lincoln Jr/Sr High School, WI

Wicked Twilight My Delight

Snap, CRACKLE! Boom and Twirl
My soul lashes out as we begin to whirl
A fire burns you as you run away
Afraid of the beast inside
Someone too strong for me to hide
A Fragile eternity begins again
With the wicked lovely thoughts flooding my brain
It tears my twin souls in twain
No, I'm not afraid of your pain
But I am afraid of being alone
My fragile, Agile soul is hurt by the pure black sky
Sometimes I wish I could. just. hide
I fear the light, I love the night
And for once my heart again takes flight
I don't want to hurt you
I'd like to keep you safe
But your life is not mine to keep or take
Radiant shadows flood in my wake
But I'm not sleeping for fear of dreaming
In the night I wake up screaming
Seeing your face again

Kasey Haight, Grade 12
Apollo High School, MN

Kardashian Family

For all the attention you receive
You would think that you were all queens.
Kris, Kourtney, Kim, Khloe, Kendall, and Kylie
So many K's, you'd have to agree.
Although you do have too much money,
You girls are just too funny.
From the places you visit and the things you do,
All of the things you've been through.
Becoming famous and the TV show,
All the vacations, and the money you blow.
Seeing baby Mason for the first time,
And watching Scott be quite the slime.
The first wedding with only nine days to prepare,
Khloe and Lamar had quite the affair.
The surgeries plus the photo shoots,
And the boyfriends they all go through.
The lawyer father and the Olympian step dad,
Six seasons going with three run off shows, and boy am I glad.
Kim's fairy tale wedding, only 72 days,
Its all right Kim, you were just in a daze.

Katie Sproul, Grade 11
Lincoln Jr/Sr High School, WI

Snow Road

Snow is falling, and falling
From a hole in Heaven that God made.

I came out with my darling, with my darling.
Her eyes are just like snow.
So pure and adorable

Trees are dancing, and dancing.
All lined up together,
Dancing with snow and breeze.

Now I am walking, and walking
With my darling
On a special, magical snow road,
Where snow and trees are with us.

James Lee, Grade 10
Michigan Lutheran Seminary School, MI

Bed of Roses

Surrounded by my murderous blush and bloom
Of a thousand red blossoms;
My flesh torn by thorns, as if I had been rolled in a bed of roses

I laugh at the moon and the clouds, the wind in my ears, speaking;
Whispering clearly that this is where my future lies
And where I now reside

Sin is where it starts, sin is where it stops
Many who live deserve death,
Many who die deserve life

Heather Springer, Grade 11
Centreville High School, MI

Christmas with Family

This Christmas I am not alone
I have something to hold
a memory in my heart

Christmas Carols through the night
people smiling at the sight
Of children playing joyously
Cookies and everlasting glee
Spending close time with your family

This year I promise, To do what I do best
Spend time with people I love
And remind them they're constantly blessed
Singing warm songs
Giving loving hugs
By sharing warm embraces and hot chocolate filled mugs
Christmas is the holiday, where we all reunite
Let us bypass the hate, the pain and the constant fights
Let us cuddle with our warm love and stop the blusterous nights

Saleria J-Cunningham, Grade 10
Martin Luther King High School, MI

The Beginning and the End

It all started with a new school
Then we ended up in a pool
A pool made of happiness
Love, care and kindness
Then the pool started to dry
And the "see you soon" turned into a goodbye
The pool turned into a desert
A desert that left me alone and alert
I kept on looking around
And you were all I found
Everywhere I look I see you in front of me
Smiling at me lovingly
Then you disappear
And I realize that we were never meant to be
You were only a once upon a time
That will always be stuck in my head like a rhyme

Nahla Naser, Grade 12
Star International Academy, MI

This Crush

This child like crush, an innocent thing by thee.
Is just the start you see, this romance grows as do we.
Until we are as tall as a tree…
The branches are the loose ends you see,
And the trunk well that's the support we need.
As we grow others see just how meant to be are we,
The day we put upon our rings, we join as one
While the choir sings.
And as we say the words I do
I'll know right then we'll make it through.
Our tree may change as we do just know I love you

Jade Overton, Grade 10
Lakeville South High School, MN

Dream Scape

Can anyone hear me?
I scream my pain, I cry my sorrow.
In the darkness I lie
Shuddering, hurt
Bruised, broken.

In the darkness I lie
thinking, seeing
things that are
truly not there.

Can anyone hear me?
agony flows into me
as I realize no one
hears me. No one is there.

But suddenly, I awake
no longer do I lie in darkness
but in the comfort of my bed.
And it's just another dream.
another dream of pain and sorrow.

Alexis DePaoli, Grade 12
Marion High School, WI

Reliving My Past

I need a cloudy day,
something to mask the sun.
I'm tired of hiding the pain
and putting on a smile for everyone.
So bring on the rain,
let the thunder roll.
You better take shelter,
because this storm is out of control.
I can only fake it for so long
before the walls come tumbling down.
Thought I had it all together;
guess I should've known
that what I had
would never last.
It would only leave me sitting here
reliving my past.

Kari Louwagie, Grade 12
Lakeview High School, MN

Soaring

Flying is freedom,
looking down on the birds.
Using the clouds as an endless road,
uninterrupted by traffic.
Clouds rushing past the plane,
as darkness falls.
The plane turns on its lights,
it looks like a dislodged star.
Moving about the night sky.

Cody Decker, Grade 12
Random Lake High School, WI

A Man for Our Country

My old grandpa used to be a soldier
He fought for our country
He stood strong for what he believed in
What is he now?
A lifeless body
An abounding box of bones
Tears at the funeral become a plentiful amount
Tears on his finished, polished wood casket
A widow now alone sits crying in the front seat of the funeral home
Family weeping over his maple wood glossy box
His skin was cold like a freezer
White and pale he lay in cotton and silk as if he were someone special
The truth is he was he was special to us
To us he was someone great, a hunter of deer
A man of wisdom.
He will always be admired by his family
My old grandpa will dearly be missed.

Christian Lobo, Grade 12
Clarkston High School, MI

Unfaltering

I walk into the crisp, breathtaking dawn, there is so much ambiguity,
My family and future — all plans unknown,
I've perceived too much and cannot grasp the certainty,
As I almost recall my dreams — the thoughts of the past, all slip away un-grown.
I wish and pray for guidance from the mightiest power of all,
From the ground, to the river bed, great oak and edge — I find the right,
How life should feel — the unfaltering love — the colors of the wind in fall.
Day by day in the assumed reality, I lose the feel, 'til I reach the reassuring sunlight.
On the path to the future unknown, I'm sure to be guided.
Now instead of looking out the void window into the cold,
I see the world in a new light, thoroughly enjoying every moment, the love decided.
With a great stimulation of emotions, a new certainty will hold.
Into the twilight I spread my wings and learn to fly
Onward into the graceful stars, 'til I touch the sky.

Kalyn Kamps, Grade 11
Belmont High School, WI

Love

Lightning without darkness,
Thunder with no rain living without you will never be the same
Life with no breath
Speech with no sound I remember when your love stayed around
Speechless days
Horrible nights love with you is lost it's no longer in sight
Dry mouth heart beating
I wonder if you can hear the sound of my blood heating
Soul with no body
Eyes with no tears no one knows about my silent scares
I loved so hard
I loved so long
And in a blink of an eye our love was gone

Aarionna Richardson, Grade 11
Jackson High School, MI

That Did Not Just Happen!

One fine day
I visited a friend
Beautiful day
Horrible end
I start my vehicle
I check all mirrors
I start backing out
I'm struck with horror
The van comes to a sudden stop
And my stomach sinks to my feet
I made quite a big flop
Our vans decided to greet
Good size dent in Tom's
Softball dent in mine
He was very calm
I thought I'd be fined
I bought a new door
He accepted it with joy
I went from rich to poor
I could've bought a new toy

Eric Minett, Grade 11
Tracy Area Jr/Sr High School, MN

What Happened to You

What happened to you!
Where's the real you;
The one who was fun;
Who always cared;
What happened to you!
You used to listen;
Why are you down;
Hiding the real you;
You loved life;
And loved everything about
It;
I think that is why;
I miss you most;
What happened to you!

Brooke L. Jaeger, Grade 10
Visions Jr/Sr High School, WI

My Thanksgiving

Thanksgiving day
Is here another year.
Families gather together for a feast.
Where we all relax and eat like beasts.
We talk about how thankful we are
For all the bounty of food we have.
The sight of chocolate pudding pie.
Glistens in my eye.
After we eat like beasts.
We are tired and have to rest our feet.
Another Thanksgiving day
Is past, I almost didn't think I could last.

Devyn Roe, Grade 12
Osceola High School, WI

Little Princess

I am the youngest of five,
And unlike them, I am so full of life.
My brothers are so strict and overprotective,
And when it comes to friends, they are very selective.
It's like they try to deprive my life of fun,
And without them, I can't even go out into the sun.
And when they are out doing their royal duties,
I'm stuck in my ivory tower, wondering about cooties.
I have never met a single person that my brothers hate,
But I guess that changed, when I met my best friend Blake.
He came one night in my little tower,
And to my surprise, he gave me a blue flower.
This is something I only saw when my brothers escorted me outside,
I couldn't pick or touch them, no matter how hard I cried.
His eyes, so blue, unlike my dark brown,
Both in jeans, and black shirts, though I suppose I should wear a gown.
His skin is as white as the moon, but mine is dark as wood,
But he don't seem to care, despite my brothers, he comes and visits as much as he could.
And from that magical night, I had an enchanting vision,
Me outside my tower with Blake, and my brothers starring with no tension.
Even if there's no crown on my head, I'm treated like a little princess.

Lakota Butterfield, Grade 11
Lincoln Jr/Sr High School, WI

Family

Family is something you always need
Family is forever, side by side
With family you can do anything
When people leave you, they will be waiting
They have the patience of a saint
They will wait up for you until you get home from and important date
Wondering how everything went
Mothers are there for a shoulder to cry on
Fathers are there waiting on the porch with a shot gun waiting for your return
Aunts are there to make you laugh
Uncles are there to give advice
Cousins are the best friends that you can tell anything to
Grandmas are there to spoil you
Grandpas are there to pick on you
Friends are family God never gave you
Sisters are pains but you love them anyway
Brothers are people who will look out for you and only want the best for you.

Amanda Mallin, Grade 12
Osceola High School, WI

Strength

Strength is something not everyone has.
It is something that has to be discovered and lured out of the innermost crevices.
It is what is found in athletes at the end of a race
— pushing themselves even harder than ever thought possible.
It is what it takes to be truthful to a close friend,
What your heart needs to survive and be true
And yet it is so much more than just these things.
Strength is something not everyone has.

Mariama Dryak, Grade 11
Blair-Taylor High School, WI

The Clock Chimes Again

The loss and grief are far too great,
Not even nightmare's thirst shall they merely sate.
Death to ye who feel this pain,
For only liars survive this black rain.
Misery loves company, but suppose your company's cold?
Lying interred in your soul, heart beating there alone?

The clock chimes.
Time falls fast away; it slips through our fingers,
Water, that we could hold it only a moment longer.
Would that it would fall faster for the grieving.

The clock chimes again, but it has been hours since the first.
If only life, that bane of the broken, would tick away faster.
I beg my life to drain away, so as only pain would die.
I can escape nevermore those eyes burned in mine,
Nor the deafening ticking of the clock this night.

The clock chimes again and I beg for reprieve.
Madness and grief grow ever within me,
Black plague consuming and suffocating me.
I gasp for air, but tears drown me,
Kill me if only to stop the agony.

The clock chimes once more, once alone.
Rachel Martens, Grade 12
Hortonville High School, WI

The Little Peach Tree

Back in the garden where the grass grows free
A little girl planted her own peach tree
She loved it, and watered it, and watched it grow
But would it have peaches? No one knows

Back in the garden where the leaves blow free
The autumn wind rustles the little peach tree
The little girl laughed as it danced to and fro
But would it have peaches? No one knows

Back in the garden where the snow falls free
Deep in the sleep stood the little peach tree
The little girl watched window glass to her nose
But would it have peaches? No one knows

Back in the garden where the sun glows free
Pink blossoms popped on the little peach tree
The little girl clapped and her mouth made an "O"
But would it have peaches? No one knows

Back in the garden, summer's bounty we see
Fuzzy round fruits on the little peach tree
The little girl's chin with sticky juice flows
Did it have peaches? Now she knows
Miriam Willitz, Grade 10
Michigan Lutheran Seminary School, MI

Him

His eyes glimmer like fireflies, in the night sky
His breath on my skin drives me to win.
I know that I would do anything for him.

The way that he looks at me,
Makes my heart pound a million, billion beats per second.
When I'm not talking to him,
I'm thinking about him.

He always finds a way into my mind,
Whether or not I want him to.
And he's definitely sweet, funny and kind.

When I'm in his arms
I can't help but feel safe and cared about.
I'm sad when he has to leave
But happy that I know I'll see him again soon.

We may be apart now
But that won't last forever
Because I know in my heart that
We'll always have each other.
Hannah Bubolz, Grade 12
Gillett High School, WI

Beach Side Oasis

I remember going to Mexico
The smell of Señor Frog's coming down the block
Mad drivers buzzing by
Foreigners yelling to buy their stuff
Spanish being spoken everywhere

Water so blue
You can see your reflection right through
Like a glass window
The salty ocean
Splashing up on shore
Spanish being spoken everywhere

Drinks by the shoreline
All day service
Life couldn't be any more relaxing
Than sitting and soaking up the sun
Jessica Lowry, Grade 11
Clarkston High School, MI

Snow

I look around and what do I see?
No snow to show for December. I smile with relief.
I don't know why I live in Minnesota. I don't like the snow.
I cry when it comes.
I cheer when it is time for it to go.
I do not like the snow.
Shawna Wilkett, Grade 10
Round Lake High School, MN

Our Last Moments

The Earth sweats at a hundred and fifty
As silent as the moon
Not even the birds chirp outside
Still as a sleeping bear
In hibernation
Breathing in and out
Our nostrils flare close and then open
For the last few breaths
The world has left
The wind suffocating as the walls close in
On everything we once believed in
Trees dehydrate at the thought of no return
Squeezing the life of the already dead grass
And this time
We don't get a second chance
The decisions made
And the last breath has been taken
As a whole
For the home we called Earth
Is dead

Alexis Matthews, Grade 11
Clarkston High School, MI

So Long Cinderella

Paint chips
from my fingernails
like a house that's aging
leaving rough patches of scales
as my hair turns crusty
hardening around my face
the mirror displays the debris
this condition wasn't always the case
but now sweat smothers my skin
entrapped by the layers of my dress
free from the bobby pin
my hair frames my face in a tangled mess
aching from limb to limb
my body submits to weakness
no longer swaying with him
I face reality's bleakness
staring at my reflection
I say farewell to Cinderella
and hello again to imperfection.

Jessica Heintz, Grade 11
St Croix Lutheran High School, MN

Here Today, Gone Tomorrow

I walk through the door of the church,
look at the scattered ash on the floor
The flames touched heaven,
but the souls were already there

What once was white now is charcoal,
just like the spirits inside it
I watch the crow, as though,
it knew what once was there

A place for God.
A place for people,
young and old,
black and white

I walk to the cemetery,
put a flower at every grave
But when I come to a familiar one,
I sit and pray as the raven roses lay

I feel the cold wind on my face.
I feel the cold tears on my face
When I'm done I go back.
Walk down the aisle
and smile.

Kori Schuessler, Grade 11
Random Lake High School, WI

Futility

The voice of the sea is vicious —
never abating
gnawing gnashing churning
forcing
　　　　the
　　　　　　ship
　　　　　　　　towards
disaster
in the fury of waves
never relenting
thrashing throwing jarring
goading
the vessel into
abandoning all hope
　　　　　　in
　　　　the
　　　　　　darkness
　　　　　　　　of
　　　　　　endless
　　　　　　depths

Sarah McDaniel, Grade 12
Allegan High School, MI

Love

Think about love
How it is kind
How it is honest
How it is pure
How it is unmoving and unchanging

Something should come to mind
Whether a person or thing
Whether an animal or item
Whether personal or distant
Whether earthly or heavenly

Whatever comes to mind
Either something physical or imagined
It's yours

You accept them as who they are
Not who you want them to be
To you they are perfect
In every way shape and form

Don't give away what one could earn
If you earn love it lasts longer
We live to love
But we don't need to love to live

Grace Johnson, Grade 10
Michigan Lutheran Seminary School, MI

The Final Goodbye

This is it.
This is the end.
Finding some closure
is my goal for your descent.
I will miss you forever
and love you even more.
You are gone.
I must move on.
I feel guilt and anger,
hurt and sadness.
Most of all I feel emptiness.
Without you, I'm lost.
You are now with the Lord
peaceful and happy,
no more suffering.
I will see you again one day,
but for now
I must say goodbye.

Anamarie Loeb, Grade 12
Mishicot High School, WI

My Fearless Bull Rider

He tunes out the crowd, and focuses
The gates open, and the adrenaline smacks him
The bull whips him around like trees in a Kat 5 hurricane
His thoughts are focused, and locked on his target

One slip up, one wrong move and everything could end
Too late, he's in the air, and then the dirt breaks his fall
He has quick reflexes, like a shark catching his prey
In a few seconds he's over the gate, and in the safe zone

His mom says it was too close, and he just shakes his head
He'll love the sport 'til the day his heart stops beating
Lucky for him he's got a crazy redneck girlfriend
That supports, and loves everything he does
She keeps his head clear, and focused
When she's in his thoughts, the crowd disappears

"My Fearless Bull Rider" she whispers to him, every day
Keana Brummond, Grade 11
Breckenridge Sr High School, MN

Better Things Will Come

Every day when I woke up I saw your beautiful face.
I'd lie there and smile and stare into your eyes,
As you stared into mine.
You'd run your finger across my cheek
And you'd make me smile even more.
Every day I think about it.
I wish it'd still be real.
I always wondered why this happened to me,
But in the end I realized
That everything happens for a reason,
And if I set my mind to it,
I can someday find someone like you,
But better.

Hailey Mayer, Grade 11
Round Lake High School, MN

The Beavers and Their Dams

Castor Canadensis is its name,
If you are a scientist born to name,
The beaver is a rodent,
If you see a dam you should wait a moment,
The beaver's dams are very buoyant,
They are large and made of mud and twigs,
In their dams they have lots of tunnels,
The beavers have no troubles,
Below their dam lies all of the mussels,
Which the beaver's friends the muskrats eat,
They are packing a lot of meat,
The beaver's dam is as hard as concrete,
The beaver's dam is like a suite.

Jordan Lanoue, Grade 11
Tracy Area Jr/Sr High School, MN

Cry of Fighting

Fire! Fire! Fire!
Run! Run! Run!
Enemies are coming, with cannons and guns!
Cross the oceans and forests, then invade our hometowns!
Their horses' hoofs struck the ground
Lilies of peace are watching them, with resent and sorrow
But blood still incarnadines the earth and grass
Homes are gone
These evils destroyed our heart
Whirlwind of soul is calling us to come!
Come! Come! Come!
Darkness is always before dawn!
Our success is around!
In our blood
Never give up —
Hold our hands
To seek the light of sun!

Sarah Li, Grade 11
Pansophia Academy, MI

As I Climb the Mountain

As I climb the mountain
I see you watching over me

As I climb the thorny mountain
I feel you covering my feet

As I climb the mountain covered with snow
I feel the warmth that you provide me

As I climb the mountain with all my burdens on my shoulder
You make me free of those burdens

As I climb this mountain called world…

John Kim, Grade 11
Michigan Lutheran Seminary School, MI

Snow

Starting in November snow starts to fall
All the kids are waiting to throw snowballs
The first snow is always the best
Covering the streets, roofs, and all the rest
Christmas time would not be the same
If we didn't have the snow for all the games
The flakes glisten in the air on a cold winter day
And before people go out and about
They must shovel out their way
After a long day playing in the snow
The kids never complain or pout
Snow is cold and snow is wet, but you can never forget
That snow in the wintertime is never a threat

Becky Przybilla, Grade 11
Tracy Area Jr/Sr High School, MN

My Cherry Tree

I have a little cherry tree
Growing deep inside of me.
But I've closed it off from the world
So that nobody can see.

Cold nights and summer storms
May cause it to frown.
One word and its smile reforms,
Whereas another can uproot it,
And knock it down.

For every cherry tree
Blooms occasionally.
But no love can uphold
No matter how strong or how old.
For every tree
Loses its flowers and leaves
To the cold.

Abigail Fassbender, Grade 11
Random Lake High School, WI

Truth Within the Heart

I love you dear and true,
but when it seems so blurry,
everything begins to come unglued,
life is a mess of tangled lies,
is love just one of those,
or is it all we dream,
for a pretty dress, a solid sound,
in all life's two words are found,
what is truth,
what is lie,
for thus only time shall show,
thus all that must be found,
is hidden within our hearts inside.

Jessica Thimmesch, Grade 10
Glenville Emmons Sr High School, MN

My Mother

A mother you have always been,
Through thick and thin.
Still my mom until the end,
No matter what you do, I do love you.
I hope you know that's true.
I miss you—I wish to see you.
You have no clue, but I do need you.
There's not another mother like you.
That's true, it's why I love you.
I only have one mother, no other.
No one can love me as much as you.

Angel Frith, Grade 10
Visions Jr/Sr High School, WI

One Sad August Day

Why did you have to leave?
Was it because of me?
I remember one sad August day, it was such a horrible, rainy day.
I remember my mother holding me close, in a weary way
Telling me that everything was going to be okay.
I didn't know what she meant about that, I didn't know what to do or even say!
The, she told me that God has chosen to take you away
And how you died that very day.
I didn't know what to do or say; but my heart had a pain each and very day, in some way.
Why did you have to leave?
Was it because of me?
I miss your hugs; the way that you smiled, that too
I remember your deep brown eyes; and what we used to do.
Constant reminder that I didn't know what to say or do; I can't help but think about you!
I remember the sad song they played at the funeral that day
One I'll never forget that hurts in every way
One day Mike I will see you again,
One day Mike, we will live, laugh, and love again.
We just have to wait, until it's my turn for God to show me the way.
I understand the saying now; you never know what you have until it's gone!
I had a great friend, and now he is gone!

Bridget Tyranski, Grade 12
Dwight D Eisenhower High School, MI

The Flag

Passion is the flag the righteous man will hold.
I've decided it is time for me to play the villain.
Instead of living with this pain until I grow old,
I've used my heart to search within.
Love is everlasting, or so we've been told,
But at this age, our lives have yet to begin.

When your heart is broken, there is no way out,
Then your ambition collapses, and you feel you are done.
You remember the love, how could you live without?
You begin to give up, to feel that the depression has won.
But your mind wakes you up in the morning, and to your heart it gives a shout,
"Wake up! Your life is not yet done!"

Realizing that your emotions blow like a flag in the wind,
You know the wind has to change direction again.

Zane Potter, Grade 10
Brown City High School, MI

Key to Your Heart

Love is an endless road.
Your hair swaying in the wind as you clutch onto his hand on a walk through the park.
Butterflies in your stomach as he looks you in the eyes and says
I
Love
You
The smell of red roses as I walk through the door and see his smile.
The sound of my heart beating on a never-ending romantic night.
The taste of his soft lips on mine at the end of the night. Love is a key to your heart.

Hannah Samlow, Grade 10
Fruitport High School, MI

Mudding

Once a year I go mudding with the jeep
She has 40's for tires
When I pull in my dad gives his truck a beep, beep
At night we have a couple fires
Everyone has a chance
To be top dog
All the drivers give each other a little glance
At this mud bog
But once I start throwin' the mud
The drivers start to fear
Then their trucks start to flood
They turn and sneer
The jeep still has a loud roar
The mud is just flyin'
The pedal hasn't even touched the floor
The drivers start sighin'
Everyone tries to beat us
To tell you the truth, there is no chance
They better not fuss
'Cause there is no stoppin' a Bantz.

Jonathan Bantz, Grade 12
Osceola High School, WI

Boundless

The
wind
rushed
through
my hair as
I picked up speed
    fasterFasterFASTER
I felt like Magellan as he
explored the world before him.
Excitement and awe tingled
up my spine. As I trailed my hand
through the water, the coolness bit
at my skin. My eyes searched the
h
or
iz
on
for any monsters that might be lurking, but
all that was before me was endless water. It
was alive with possibilities, and I yearned to discover them.

Zoe Norr, Grade 12
Allegan High School, MI

Life and Death*

Happy birthday, Grandma
We will surely miss you
even though it's been a year
you will never be forgotten
we love you in life
and we love you in death
we know you are in heaven watching every day
showing hope even if we can't see
lifting us up to feel the joy you felt
and when we die
you will be there waiting
you will greet us and smile
"Welcome my children, you will enjoy this place"
and when it is time to return to life
we will follow you, go into a new world
and live as much as we did now
so happy birthday, Grandma
we will live as you did
and we will die gracefully as you did

Carley Peterson, Grade 10
Butternut School, WI
In loving memory of Rosalie Bailey (11/14/1938-12/09/10)

Death

Death
What will it behold?
   Darkness,
     Blackness,
       Nothingness.
Death
I'm so afraid. But what am I afraid of?
     The unknowingness of *Death*
     The uncertainty of *Death*
Where will I be when I die? Is there an afterlife?
   Or is there just Darkness,
     Blackness,
       Nothingness?
Will I see my passed family? My ancestors?
   The ones from Germany, Canada, Ireland, Scotland?
   All the history, from everywhere. Will I see them too?
Or is there just Darkness,
     Blackness,
       Nothingness
Of *Death*

Cassie Arellano, Grade 11
Deer River High School, MN

Behind the Curtain

Behind the curtain lies wonders
I stand, hat in hand
Ready to go, although I know
Behind the curtain lies wonders
Mysteries and blunders

Welding is no sport
It's more of an art
Some can do it
Many cannot

There's arc, there's wire
There's tig, all may cause a fire
There's mig, there's brazing
The metal is blazing

But behind the curtain is a wonder
Left for one's mind to ponder.
Jeremy Hall, Grade 12
Tracy Area Jr/Sr High School, MN

Dancing

It is dark, silent.
The lights come on,
And the music starts.
Movement begins around me.
I lift my head, then my arm.
We move in intricate designs;
Slowly at first, then faster.
Cloth swirls around me,
Drifting down in soft patterns.
They move apart as I move forward.
It's just me alone in the world.
I am nothing without the music.
I'm dancing.
Kirsten Kaat, Grade 11
Random Lake High School, WI

Procrastination

Procrastination.
It seems to creep up
on you at the worst times

Telling you: Do it later
put it off until tomorrow
it doesn't need to be done now.

But this needs to end.
I should give a speech.
Help people change their ways.

I will tomorrow.
Maggie Colwell, Grade 11
Montgomery-Lonsdale High School, MN

The Call

…The phone rang
Grandma Caroline
She asked to talk to my dad?
I thought WEIRD! She didn't want to talk to me?
He says hello
…
And a few moments later,
He dropped the phone. He has a shocked and scared look on his face.
    I heard nothing…

"I'll be back; don't worry. Everything is going to be fine."
I wondered where he went
I called my mom and thought maybe she had known what was going on…But she didn't

My cell phone rang
    …it's him
    …My father
I was told to get my mom and go to the hospital
It's my Grandma Mel, my favorite, my Grandma

The doctor said she wasn't going to make it
    …She had a stroke
ALL of my dad's brothers and sisters came. ALL 14 and their families
She's gone now.
The best cookie maker, the BEST GRANDMA EVER!
Lydia Daigle, Grade 12
Deer River High School, MN

Flower

Color so bright, so sunny and cheering; sweet smell that livens the place
Silk soft touch on my fingertips
Looking at the beauty you add to my home

The season passes; your bright color begins to fade
That smell so sweet becomes faint
Your silkiness turns brittle in the harsh weather
Still your beauty of summer lingers

So into my house I bring you, to try to escape fall's chill
In a small pot of soil I blanket you; stay a while longer, little flower

Where are you
            Going, little petals
        That float on
                Waves of air
        To the ground

It's saddening to say good-bye, when you're still wanted here
To chase away the cold frost from my window,
That turns the whole world white

Sparkles of snow begin to fall
Good-bye, sweet flower,
Until the summer, when you awaken again
Tessa Snyder, Grade 10
Michigan Lutheran Seminary School, MI

Comfort

Talking together, you take my hands
in that brief moment my world expands

Turquoise beads rolling, white whisking clouds
emerald clovers gleaming through crowds

Gentle blue raindrops, aquamarine
dim rays of sunlight but in olive green

Light lavender sunsets, round pearly rocks,
wrapped in indigo waves and the ticking of clocks

Sapphire satin, hollow sage trees
deep cobalt skies and an ivory breeze

Viridian grass blades, mauve in sight
rotating circles of teal in the night

The reds and the blacks all disappear
when you take my hands and hold me so near.

Sydney Lammers, Grade 12
Milan High School, MI

Rubber Boots

I've been writing a lot Lately.
My arms feel like warm, heavy Rubber
Like yellow rubber boots left outside in Summer
Floods rising after heavy rain, they fill quickly with Water
The water is not Clear
Not Muddy
Nor Red
Green
Or Blue
It's a Mirror
A mirror that Reflects
Circling ripples of mesmerizing distortion and Dissipation
At times beyond that with which we are Familiar
However, sometimes when all is Calm
Truth and reality is Reflected.

Spencer Berglund, Grade 11
Mayo High School, MN

Porcelain Ashes

Seams sewn shut with fragile lace.
Wrapped around a tiny waist.
Make-up covered, smothered skin.
Lies to make up perfection.
Counting stars that barely shine.
Wishing on anything she can find.
Distant eyes, silent prayers.
Hiding from accusing stares.
Weight loss liar, calorie cowards.
Coughing up blood as her body weight crashes.
Her body falls to porcelain ashes.

Kyshya Baker, Grade 11
Lincoln Jr/Sr High School, WI

Growing Up

New born baby
All gentle and meek
Looking up to his parents

Now 16, a teenager
Ready for what comes next
Looking up and wanting to be older

30 years old
Setting up their new life
Looking forward to that new promotion

At the age of 50
Almost done with work
Looking back on your life

Now they are 70
Old and frail
Looking at everything in life

They reach deaths icy grip
All is done
Life is over when it felt like it had just begun

Joel Prange, Grade 10
Michigan Lutheran Seminary School, MI

I Love You, Grandpa

Grandpa, Grandpa, how I love you.
In my heart you hold a special place.
I look up to you in all you do;
I find comfort every time I see your face.

I don't know how to thank you
For all you've done, you see.
You're the example I look up to
When looking for the other half of me.

So many memories that we share;
From when I was two I helped you rebuild,
To the last softball game, it's you who was there
To pick up my spirits when they were killed.

One thing I know will always be true
Is that Grandpa, forever, I will always love you.

Daisy Cunzenheim, Grade 11
Belmont High School, WI

Birth

Birth
Painful, crazy
Life-changing, anxious, beautiful
Happiness, tiresome, expensive, lovely
Depressing, scary, joyful, long-term, sentimental.
Birth

Samantha Beardslee, Grade 12
Neil E Reid High School, MI

What I Can Do!

I can be sweet as honey
Sorrowful as death
Smooth like satin
Flowing as a river
Short and sweet
Long and sad,

I can be put to music
Or told to small children,

I can go anywhere
See anything,

I can take you across the safari
Down the Mississippi
The smallest places
The biggest places
The detailed or the brief places of
Across the world,

I am a poem.
Alina Eisenbach, Grade 12
Dwight D Eisenhower High School, MI

The Awe of Welding

Two pieces of metal are made into one.
Doing this job can be fun.
Spending the day outside in the sun.
Able to look down and see everyone.
It's a wonder it can even be done.

Electricity, flying in the air.
The heat, is difficult to bear.
Do it, if you dare.
But, take great care.
With, what you wear.

Sparks…fly like a meteor shower.
Beauty…like the perfect weld
Welding…for hours and hours.
Hypnotized…by the raw power.
Awestruck…how high the building's tower.
Brady Townsend, Grade 12
Tracy Area Jr/Sr High School, MN

The Final Trial

I am dragged down into the depths of woe
I see demons dance and play all around me
I smell the smells of sulfur
I look out and see those who have gone before me
I look at a sign which reads "Wait here for jailer"
I wait patiently as the jailer draws near
I am taken to a court room and placed before God
I see the devil to my left and Jesus to my right
I see the devil sitting proudly thinking he has my soul
I hear the devil say, "He has sinned, his soul belongs to me"
I see the judge turn his head to me
I hear in a loud booming voice, "Is this true?"
I fall to my knees and begin to weep
I through my tear stained eyes say, "I have sinned"
I feel Jesus run to me and pick me up
I feel Jesus wiping my tears away
I hear Him say in a soft gentle voice, "He believes and I have died for him"
I hear the Judge say, "He is yours"
I feel Jesus taking me away to eternal life
Justin Petoskey, Grade 10
Michigan Lutheran Seminary School, MI

My Everything

To me you are my love,
You are my light, my life,
You are my everything.

You are the air I breathe,
And the shoulder I lean on.
You know what to say when things don't go my way
You make me stay and would never leave.
You are my everything.

You mean the world to me,
I would die for you and I would even kill for you.
I know in my heart you would do the same.
You are my everything.

I appreciate everything you do whether it is
Making me supper and taking care of me when I'm sick,
Or something serious like standing up for me when I can't fight my own fight.
You are my everything and I love you!!!
Briana Rudie, Grade 12
Gillett High School, WI

Winter Season

it's the most beautiful time of the year.
The temperature drops,
The snow falls,
Christmas music is played,
Presents are wrapped,
Love and joy fill the air.
Everyone loves a happy holiday season.
Megan Schmitz, Grade 10
Round Lake High School, MN

The Sonorous Sea

The sighing of the sea is listless,
    slow,
      sorrowful,
        slighted,
    inviting others to its shallows,
      into the softened sounds
    of the slipping tides.
Jessica Perez, Grade 12
Allegan High School, MI

Healing Currents

The lull of the sea is medicinal,
    alleviating,
      consoling,
        inspiring,
          absolving;
  soothing the soul of ails and miseries;
    silencing the voices of chaos.
Ashley Doolittle, Grade 12
Allegan High School, MI

Stressed?

Let your fears
Slide away,
They aren't important.
Not here,
Not today
Let your thoughts unravel.
Let your mind unwind.
Just let it go
And take some time.
Let all your worries
Slip away.
Don't try and save them for
Another day.
Let them go
And then you'll see
Just how beautiful
Life can be.
So take it slow,
Ease your mind
Don't clutch your troubles,
When they slide right by.

Aimee Hickman, Grade 10
Stoughton High School, WI

Break Free

I walk these streets,
Feeling like a freak.

Up and down, feel so strange.
Stranger in my own skin,
As every day goes by,
I forget my pain — it fades away.

No more,
I will not shy away,
No more,
I break free today.

I walk these streets,
Ah, so happy will I be.
Loving life,
Never taking her for granted.

Cory Tavares, Grade 10
Neil E Reid High School, MI

Walking with You

Walking in the snow
Leaving foot prints below,
Walking to the house
Almost as silent as a mouse,
Walking closer to you
So I can get a view,
Walking with my mittens
As soft as my kittens.

Halie Spessard, Grade 11
Round Lake High School, MN

King

The rock and the foundation
You are my hero
My security at all times, keeper of my well being

You are no stranger to my heart
My creator from the beginning of time
The only one I live for, king of kings, Lord of lords

You being light to the darkness, you heal the ones in need
You tell us who you are
Your words shake the Earth, you bring all to their knees
You deserve endless praise, you rule with a mighty fist

You have blessed me in countless ways
Every breath I take is given only by You
Serving you is the purpose in life

Living to glorify You is the challenge
A witness to Your indescribable power is all I am
Nothing but a sinner I am, anything and everything You are

To walk in Your kingdom is a day I dream of
Casting my eyes upon Your face living only with You for all of eternity
For You have saved me, you are my King

Andrew Gatz, Grade 12
Random Lake High School, WI

You're Always on My Mind

Not one day has gone by where you're not on my mind.
You were the best I've ever had,
You were one of a kind.

I keep telling myself it will work out in the end,
but there's just too much destruction,
too much to mend.

I wanted to live with no regrets,
but this one I cannot ignore.
Every day it hurts me more and more.

They say you don't know what you have until it's gone
and it hurts me to say that seeing you leave was what it took,
to make me realize I fell in love with you at first look.

All I want is to hold your hand, to hear your laugh, and to see your smile.
Because no one else could make me feel the way you did,
and every second spent with you is time that's worth my while.

Every day, you're on my mind,
and I swear I'm seeing all the signs.

They all point to you.

Abby Mikita, Grade 10
Kenowa Hills High School, MI

Golden Heart

A brightened heart began to fade,
As a child looked around her.
The blue sky walked the narrow path,
That seemed dim, as if a cloud was covering the sun.
Taking the slow steps, as a baby begins to learn,
The wind gently pushed the cloud to reveal the one at rest.
A fragile lady whose life had been full.
And now she lays as the morning glory sweeps her body.
The seeds of venom are missed and the weeds conquer its prey.
As the child looks at an empty face and frail body.
A quivering lip, as the eyes swell with rain.
Yet the food is suffering and tired.
The unwelcome plant is not satisfied,
As the child softly and mildly wraps her in love.
Through tearful eyes she watched her leave.
But that she was loved dearly.
Her golden heart stopped beating,
As the child got up and was on her way.
Yet it is now placed and kept safe,
In his hands that have the cure.

Angela Wick, Grade 10
Jordan Sr High School, MN

Dance Floor

Life is like a dance floor
There's hard times and good times.
You can feel the beat inside you
Trying to break free…
Until that one moment
When your heart stops beating.
Feeling like a whole new person
Leaving everything on the dance floor,
Until you can't give anymore.
At the end you feel like a winner
Getting the prize you've been waiting for.
Feeling special for the best prize you could ever get.
Knowing it was the best battle you ever fought for
Just leaving your life, on the dance floor.

Tosha Kay Arthur, Grade 10
Michigan Lutheran Seminary School, MI

Dr. Seuss

His name is Theodor Seuss Geisel, but he goes by Dr. Seuss,
He's a rhyming machine; he's even better than Mother Goose,
He wrote about an elephant named Horton who hears a Who,
He wrote about guy named Mr. Brown and how he can "Moo,"
He wrote about a Christmas hating, mean, green, man,
He wrote about eating odd things like green eggs and ham,
He wrote about Bartholomew Cubbins and his five hundred hats,
He wrote about two children and their adventures with a funny cat,
He wrote about crazy dogs having fun in a tree,
He wrote a book that's all about me,
All of his books have been so sweet and so clever
His books will inspire people everywhere, now and forever.

Anna Traynor, Grade 11
Osceola High School, WI

I'm Thankful for My Mom

Dear Mom,
Thank you for giving me birth,
Even before you knew my worth.
Thanks for teaching me wrong from right,
And how to stand up for myself and fight.
Thanks for teaching me how to obey,
Even though sometimes I choose my own way.
Thanks for dressing me warm in the cold,
And to throw away anything covered in mold.
Thanks for putting clothes on my back,
Even when being grateful is something I lack.
Thanks for teaching me the perfection of setting a volleyball,
And that it's disrespectful when I don't call.
Thanks for always just being there,
Even after I show no care.
Thanks for teaching me proper diet,
And that it's not polite to start a riot.
Thanks for reminding me why I'm really here,
And that, with God I must not fear.
Thank you for pushing me to be the real me,
And that loving others is the most important key.

Lauren Nelson, Grade 12
Osceola High School, WI

Valentine

You tell me you love me, I know it's true
You've shown me passion, that I never knew
You've taken all the darkness that once filled my life,
You changed it into something new, a white brilliant light.
Our love is like a river, so clear and strong.
Obstacles in its way, it always goes around
Living on through winter's wrath, and summer's blistering sun.
Suddenly it all makes sense.
The stories and songs, the tales of everlasting love,
That never seemed to once,
To my only true love.
I will forever stand by you, in sickness or in health.
One day soon a life will be made, for the both of us,
That brings with it the joys of life that none can live without.
You tell me you love me in so much more than words.
The way you touch, the way you kiss,
The language of life unheard.
You truly mean the world to me,
I hope you know it's true.
So please believe me when I say
"Baby, I love you."

Lazarus Ramlow, Grade 12
West High School, WI

Fact from Fiction

When contemplating fact from fiction
We learn to realize the true beauty of life
We realize what may or may not be true to oneself
Beyond this place of a human cal society

Emily Clutter, Grade 11
Random Lake High School, WI

Beautiful Day

It's the beginning of spring break
People everywhere and boats on the water
Lots of shopping, swimming and tanning
Day 1 and the sunshine is coming to a close

The sun is setting, fast and beautifully
Lighting up the ocean and the sky
With pinks, oranges, and yellows.
Palm trees slowly swaying left and right
The wind blowing the green and brown leaves
As some drop to the sandy beaches below
The sand cooling from the beating sun
People walking the waterline,
Splashing their feet and holding hands
Umbrellas are taken down and sunglasses too
Stopping, standing, and watching

Children tired, cranky, and in need of a nap
And young adults wide awake ready to set off
Grills are finishing up their meals and
Being shut off, beaches closing down
Lifeguards off duty and lighthouses on
It's a beautiful night for a spring vacation.

Paige Lucas, Grade 11
Clarkston High School, MI

Love Heals

When you think you have it all
Until you hit a brick wall
Everything is put on hold
Nothing will ever bet he same
Things are falling apart every step I take

When people leave your life they are gone for good
If you let yourself believe in feelings
They break easier

Love is like a ticking time bomb
When it goes off the world explodes
But for love your heart just shatters

Once you have a broken heart,
You can't trust anyone
You hide in a shell like a turtle does
But most of all love heals…

L ost
O utside
V igorous
E ngaging

Michelle Noffke, Grade 12
Gillett High School, WI

The Unborn

Lost in thought, she was never taught.
Confused and humiliated,
she was being hated.
First month gone by,
all she could do was lie.
Trying to hide the pain,
everyone thought she was insane.
Crying and hurt inside.
She doesn't know what to think,
a day gone by after every blink.
She couldn't tell anyone,
always afraid of what people would think.
The day came when she finally told,
the only thing they could do was stay bold.
As the thought came across her mind,
she knew she couldn't leave this poor little thing behind.
Crying and dying inside,
she stopped and thought,
what her life would be like in nine months.
Son or daughter,
This girl had nothing to do but ponder.

Misty Conner, Grade 11
Lincoln Jr/Sr High School, WI

I'm Only Seventeen

I can sometimes still hear the loud voices screaming in my head
The scream that made me cry, that woke me up in my bed.
I felt the vibration of the chair hitting the floor
I listen to the footsteps that leave and the slam of the door.

Why do they have to fight, it only makes it worse.
Nothing is getting better; I think our family has a long lasting curse.

Can they see it in my eyes, the tears that show the pain?
I watch them yell, how will I ever be the same.

Why did you choose to lean on me to take away your stress?
Does it make you feel better dragging me into your mess?

Because honestly it kills me to see you both cry
I hate coming home; it seems the days never pass by.

He slams his fist into the dry wall, she walks away
I will become stronger, better, and it starts with today
I will learn from this, discover what it means
But for now, stop, I saw so much, I'm only seventeen.

Kristen Jindra, Grade 11
Montgomery-Lonsdale High School, MN

The Victors

Football
Tough, brutal.
Strong focus, painful plays.
"Hail to the Victors."

Brandon Smith, Grade 11
Neil E Reid High School, MI

Bleed Out

He leaves
I bleed out tears
Reflection from the mirrors
Mascara smeared
Deletion, 'cause I stayed but you're not here
I cared like "married"
I carried love like every case of AIDS
Can't donate,
'Cause it sticks to where it stains
Necrotizing Fasciitis
Love kills slowly but we might as
Well, stand still closely
For the remaining time we have left
No theft will be here
So they'll grieve in fear
Not knowing it's a relief
But I don't care
And he doesn't either
So even though he leaves
I still bleed out tears

Armani Gregory, Grade 10
Northview High School, MI

Death Can Be Bliss

It comes at unexpected times.
It can shock and frighten you.
You grieve and cry and wail.
To know that they are gone is sad.
But you have a strong relief.
You can turn to Him and grieve.
You can pray to Him and he'll hear.
You can talk to Him and he listens.
To know that God is with you.
To know that they believed in Him.
To know that they went with Him.
It brings joy to my heart.
To know they are in heaven.
With God in eternal bliss.

Brandon Webster, Grade 10
Michigan Lutheran Seminary School, MI

What If…

What if tears were never shed…
and feelings were a secret?
What if friends didn't exist…
and all thoughts had to be kept boxed in?
What if trust just didn't exist…
And lives were kept hidden?
What if peace couldn't be found…
and the world went insane?
What if life ceased to exist…
and we are all unknowingly dead?
What if this was the after life…
and we are destroying again?

Kaitlin Gadzinski, Grade 10
Peck Jr/Sr High School, MI

I Did, Will You?

Every day how would you like to

Be called stupid,
Be told you were ugly,
Be threatened,
Have everything of yours damaged.

How would you like to be yelled at

Just because you are gay,
Or because you don't know an answer to a question,
Or even because you know the answer?

Even the little things make the difference
Like being left out of a game,
And not getting to hear a secret everyone keeps spreading,
Only to hear it was about you.

Every single day people are dealing with these things.
I admit that I was once the bullied and the bully,
But I have caught myself and fixed it.
It's time to stand up and admit that you have bullied someone before.

I did, now it's your turn.
Will you join me and
Admit you have been the bully?
Before someone else becomes another sad tragedy?

Hannah Reed, Grade 10
Detour Middle High School, MI

The Perfect Morning

The alarm clock rings out
Seems like I just went to bed
Ducks are quacking in the distance
Can't wait to get out to the duck blind

All dressed up in camouflage
Face covered in paint
Gun in hand, I sprint out the door
Drive out to the secret spot

Throw everything in the canoe and start paddling
The stars glitter in the night
Glide to the spot and set up
Time passes and I watch the decoys shine in the red and orange sunrise

Then something's coming in…

BANG
BANG
BANG

The ducks hit the water
It's the best way to start the day

Jack Carter, Grade 12
Deer River High School, MN

Friendship

Friends come and go,
they are there for you when you are feeling low.
You laugh, giggle, and go crazy with friends,
normally they are just around the bend.
They are supposed to be honest and kind,
in order to give you your piece of mind.
There will always be disagreements and times of sadness,
but at least you'll never have to guess.
You can count on them to be there when needed,
you'll never feel cheated.
Sometimes they're lost on the way,
and you have to pay the cost.
Friendship should be cherished,
no matter how embarrassed.
The more you have, the better off you'll be,
just wait and see.
Each friend is worth the fight,
because they will tell you what's wrong and what's right.
Sometimes there are too many to count,
but you never want to have a total amount!

Savanna Germain, Grade 12
Osceola High School, WI

Mirrors

Can you actually look in the mirror,
and see yourself for who you really are?
Or what you want to be?
Is it the right answer to be someone you're not?
Or is it just an escape from your reality?
Now you look away,
the mirror shatters
The pieces cuts the skin,
the blood rolls down,
dripping,
falling
Off of the body of who you think you are
There is no pain,
there is no guilt
Just the sadness of the realization,
of what you're not

Eileen Collins, Grade 10
Osceola High School, WI

My Soul

Waking up to the sunshine
Feeling the bright yellow rays
The feeling of life
The feeling of a real soul moving in my body
The feeling of my blood streaming through my veins
Hearing the thump-thump of my heart
Feeling my soul moving and yearning for release
Letting it go free into the sky
Letting my soul journey through the clouds

Amal Ismail, Grade 12
Star International Academy, MI

Through All the Darkness

Through all the struggles that I face
I am somehow able to hide the pain
On the outside I look just fine
But on the inside I want to die.

There's no way to understand
Unless you come and take my hand
I will try to show you my life
Even if it cuts my heart like a knife
Through all the darkness there is a light
And it's the girl I'm with tonight.

There is no other place I'd rather be
Than having you right next to me
When everything else is falling apart
I know that you will give me a fresh start
Through all the darkness there is a light
And it's the girl I'm with tonight.

Cole Sogge, Grade 11
Dilworth Glyndon Felton Sr High School, MN

Teachers

All teachers want to do
    is teach their students.
They can't do that,
    if we don't let them.
Teachers just want to teach us
    what we need to know about our future.
Someday later in life you will,
    want to thank your teachers for,
pushing you to the limits instead of
    just sitting back and passing you.
Your parents and your teachers are
    about half the reason why you are
where you are today.
    The other half is you.

Chelcie Busch, Grade 10
Mabel Canton Secondary School, MN

Michigan November

Withered leaves grace the skeletons of barren trees,
Not long ago, bursting with life.
They drift from their perches like tired birds;
Hollow shells tumbled by November wind, a cutting knife.

My mother sees this as a sign to rake;
She sweeps the featherweights in strong, bold blows.
They amiably tumble into piles, too sleepy to protest,
And nestle down together in the woods to doze.

Then one morning we awaken,
To the sounds of pure, untainted stillness,
Atop the soundly sleeping leaves, cozy in their piles,
A fresh, white world we witness!

Abby Tongue, Grade 11
Home School, MI

Deer Hunt

Motionless deer stands,
Cool air touches my hands.
The 7 point stares off into the woods.

I watch it, holding the gun,
Praying, "Please God, don't let it run!"
As I prepare my weapon for battle.

I wait for it to turn broadside,
Then it will be just right!
My buck fever starts to set in.

I open the window and stick the gun out,
I'm going to get him there's no doubt!
The deer has met its end.

With a bang, bang of the gun,
The deer doesn't even run.
It's been the best November 15th ever.
Bradley Bender, Grade 10
Michigan Lutheran Seminary School, MI

Leave It

Leave it at the door
Never look back for more
Even if the battle wasn't won
It's over and done
Kick in the determination
Or find some inspiration
Go with what you have
Just be glad
You're on the team
No matter what their scheme
Figure out what to do
It will someday come to you
If you leave it at the door
Never looking back for more
Katelynn Naujock, Grade 10
Michigan Lutheran Seminary School, MI

Broken

I stand alone,
staring in the mirror.
And what do I see?
A plain old face looking back at me.
Those baby blue eyes
tell a different story,
and that make-believe smile
isn't fooling anyone.
Underneath that beautiful girl,
lies a broken heart.
But as another tear falls,
I look down,
trying desperately to forget it all.
Kaycee Reed, Grade 11
Gillett High School, WI

Toy Soldier

It's been a year daddy
And I really really miss you
Mommy says you're in heaven now
I told her not to cry because you would be coming home soon
Every night I go to bed daddy, thinking all about you
I wish you could be here to see me and play with me daddy
Me and mommy went to see grandma and grandpa yesterday
They gave me a toy soldier that looked just like you daddy
I'm gonna keep it forever
I started first grade yesterday daddy
Mommy gave me a locket with your picture in it to carry all the time
When are you coming home daddy?
I really really miss you
I haven't talked to you in a while dad
I'm graduating high school this year
You would be proud of me dad; I know I'm proud of you
I now understand why you never came home, because you were home
I pray every day to one day see you again
Always, your little girl
Jena Owsiany, Grade 12
Dwight D Eisenhower High School, MI

Never Forget*

This is the end of the road
I refuse to believe anyone who says
that this life is for the better
We all believe and know
that our dreams always crumble
It is never real or true
the love we share among another
And nothing is greater than
the doubt we hold inside
We have to let go of all
the fantasies we dream about
for real life contains all of
those fears that hold us back
We realize we have to free
our dreams and desires
Because in this life, we never forget
Ola Hendler, Grade 12
Grand Ledge High School, MI
Read this poem once through, then read the poem backwards—line by line.

Everlasting Love

The inviting warmth of body heat combining.
Beginning the process of two souls intertwining.
Sustained breathing of two bodies, overflowing of emotion and love.
Everlasting love the incentive for the two souls from up above.
Anticipating the long journey of the lovely life of marriage.
Wanting nothing but the love of each other and a new soul awaiting in the carriage.
The precious scent of one another invading their noses.
The God-kissed lips touching once more to keep their focus.
Alas the time as come,
For two souls to become one.
Sinloria Macrae, Grade 11
Hastings High School, MN

Those Who

Those who work hard,
Blister, burst, burn, and hurt to succeed
Those who care
Treat others with compassion
Those who are devoted
Give up friends, family, food, and money
Those who believe
Have faith
Those who are motivated
Will fight for what they know is right
Those who are strong
Persevere through all
Those who love
Share it with the world
Those who dream
Accomplish greatness
Those who survive
Triumph.
I will succeed.

Haley Vogt, Grade 12
Dwight D Eisenhower High School, MI

Him

It's him
The man who taught me
Taught me how to be a man
Taught me how to shake a hand

It's him
The man who shaped me
Shaped me into who I am
Told me what I can and can't

It's him
The one that helped me with my strife
The one that helped me through my life
It's him, my grandpa

Ethan Doble, Grade 10
Michigan Lutheran Seminary School, MI

Reign

Reign pours
The once blue sky
Darkened by fire
The tainted clouds sing
A sorrow filled choir
Land turned to ash
Seas painted red
The sun begins to dim
Rays of light, now dead
There seems no hope
In this midnight hour
But in the distance I see
A lonesome white flower

Brandon Kennedy, Grade 12
Redford Union High School, MI

I Am From*

I am from yellow and brown yards,
the parched grass without sprinklers.
I am from the old rusted swing set,
the gathering place of neighboring children;
the one that has been passed down from older generations.
The propane grill that takes hours to ignite,
from the green grass stains tattooed on my knees.
I am from the diligent working class,
from the very dirt beneath my nails.
From arguments fought by child and parent,
as if cycles don't end.
I am from the alarm clock that rings at 6 a.m.,
from Folger's coffee in the morning, like a smooth, black river.
I'm from that long line of smokers and drinkers,
from bad cholesterol and diabetes.
I am from a kind heart and good morals,
but from sarcasm, stubbornness, and impatience.
I am from the salty water that runs down my face during a hard day's work,
and the cold, hard well water that washes it off at the end of the day.

Stefani Hoffman, Grade 12
St Joseph High School, MI
*Inspired by George Ella Lyon's, "I Am From"

The Power of Death

Black as night,
Tommy talks to the tumultuous tigers,
As night lurks upon him.
He speaks to himself, and walks down the steps that creak.
The door flies open and in the blink of an eye,
Death comes and its every breath covers Tommy like a sheath of a knife.

The wrench of his stomach is like the quench of his fight to stay alive.
Tommy flies away and cries and cries as death rises.
He needs his tigers and he leads his mind to think they are still out there.
With every last breath, he tries to defeat the power of death.
Out of the woods come all the tigers, and
The right moves of the Tigers and Tommy makes the fight end.
And in the light of the night,
The power of death vanishes
The tumultuous tigers take another victory!

Tanner Clausen, Grade 11
Prairie Du Chien High School, WI

A Family Christmas

Santa, snow, and sledding, it's that time of year.
When families come together to share in holiday cheer.
Presents, peppermint, and pine remind us it's the season.
To celebrate our blessings are the main reason.
Family, fudge, and flakes, so many things to enjoy.
Top item on our list, is that special toy.
Laughter, love, and lights are all around the tree.
Our favorite time of year for my family and me.
Caroling, cookies, and Christmas, it doesn't get much better than this.
Wishing you and your family a Christmas filled with bliss.

Kayla Lapworth, Grade 12
Dwight D Eisenhower High School, MI

Sunflowers

Tall sunflowers swing their golden heads in the breeze.
I am young.
And the world is a mystery.
Most memories have begun to retire,
But the sunflowers, those I remember.
We planted them,
Tiny seed by tiny seed
My dad and brothers and I, they grew up with us.
Every day I would run out to check, my face shining with discovery.
The sunflowers spread their petals to the sky,
Standing up to the world, braving the elements,
Petals becoming a deeper yellow, stunning in the summer heat.
I looked up to them.
The leaves began to sag and trees grew weak,
Leaves fell blanketing the ground in brown.
Their heads drooped.
I stopped visiting.
My dad and I still planted them for a while;
They grew shorter and shorter.
Summer woke up one day and they were gone,
And then so was I.

Whitney Kelley, Grade 12
Clarkston High School, MI

A Suffering-Storm

Thunder crashes in the distance.
A warning to all who hear.
Rich and poor,
Old and new,
Boy and girl.
And all who hear know:
A suffering-storm is near.
It rages and whips
Leaving destruction in its wake.
No one can see the end
But every storm ends with a rainbow and a sun,
Which only darkness can make us appreciate.
It lets us pick up the pieces new and old
Which only the heart knows what it makes.
Each storm leaves experience,
Making us stronger, wiser, happier.
Riding the storm is easier if you train the mind,
Train it to see the good in the bad,
The light in the dark,
In the mist of
A suffering-storm.

Ashley Pike, Grade 10
Waunakee High School, WI

Milwaukee

The best place to live in is Milltown.
No one there has a frown.
A true city that never sleeps.
Where the Brewers are always going for the sweep.
Sit-in right next to Lake Michigan.
Where people want to go fish again.
The city with bright lights.
And buildings that have got height.
Home of Summerfest.
Where the Bucks are the best.
University of Marquette battling in the Big East.
Vander Blue playing like a real beast.
There's the famous 3rd Ward.
Don't worry you'll never be bored.
Just off of the I-94.
There are always places to explore.
The city where they brew with barley.
And the home of Harleys.
The great Milwaukee Museum of Art.
You'll never want to part.
Milwaukee, the best city in the U.S.A.

Kelsey Olson, Grade 11
Lincoln Jr/Sr High School, WI

Wiggle Room

wonder, if you will
humor me
is this what happens
when two people connect on a plane
two universes…colliding
splitting at the seams and becoming something new
something different…completely different
yet exactly the same
identical
to what the first loves, the second enjoys
what they both despise
all of it sitting before them
like a gift…wrapped with ribbon
smiling, they both
watch their gift unwrap into roads
watching in reverence
at the dream
do they wake up?
or continue drooling ecstasy
think ridiculous
humor me.

Saranya Sundaram, Grade 11
Forest Hills Northern High School, MI

Me and You Dad

Sittin' here by the barbecue
just hangin' out, me and you.

It's a Monday night
and there's not a single cloud in sight.

We're lightin' up the briquets
and listenin' to the crickets.

Watchin' the waterfall
and listenin' to the coyotes call.

Lookin' at the filbert tree
we're best friends, you and me.

I'm sittin' in a lounge chair
he's sittin' in a white chair.

He's just a growlin' like a bear
Oops! I see a gray hair!

He's my dad
although I make him mad.

He loves me so
I'm his lil' Zoe.

We are in each other's hearts
and we will NEVER be apart!
Zoe Estep, Grade 10
Home School, MI

Fallen Warrior

Stands alone, Covered in sand
Looks at the picture
He holds in his hand
Bombs are around him
His buddies are down
Feels the wind
And the helicopters sound
But he's home
And has been for weeks
The memories won't leave him
From his eyes tears leak
His wife is now gone
She couldn't handle the pain
He was a hero when away
But now he's insane
He stood tall in bullets
And saved those he could
But now that he's home
He can't do what he should
He needs her back, And stares at his phone
The warrior is down, And completely alone
Madeline Zumbach, Grade 10
Apple Valley High School, MN

Monetary Judges

Blinded by the light
I step forward for judgment
the whole room is white

Nervously I sit
waiting for accusation
Unseen doors open

But they were not doors
they were bars to big cages
I saw my judges

I was horrified
the judges were snarling beasts
monsters that oozed slime

Their teeth long and sharp
the distinct shade of their fur
was monetary

On their armored chests
they had tattooed a man's face
as is their interest

They took their cursed seats
and began their corrupt trial
but I knew my doom
Ben Schroff, Grade 11
Lutheran High School Northwest, MI

Volleyball

Bump, set, SPIKE!
the crowd is wild
as a point is scored.

The winning team stays
not only physically fit,
but mentally tough.

Game point is served,
outside hitter!!
bump, set, spike!

And it's hit back up,
ready team ready!
the ball comes over,
and kill!!

The team crying with
joy and the coach explaining
that a game is never over
unless you have given up.
Kaylyn Nygaard, Grade 11
Cannon Falls Sr High School, MN

My Sister's Daughter

My sister walks toward me
With a bundle in her arms
I peek into the blankets eagerly
And suddenly, my heart warms

As I gaze at this tiny person
My heart is so filled with love
Her tiny face so precious
As innocent as a dove

She opens up her small blue eyes
Her dark, wispy hair on her head
She gives me a sweet, tired smile
As I place her in her bed

It seems like I waited an eternity
To finally hold her tonight
I turn around once more
And then turn out the light
Lana Schmitzer, Grade 10
Michigan Lutheran Seminary School, MI

Genderwar

Her smile's plunge:
Explosive,
The ruin of entire nations

And wailing as it plummets,
My heart strikes the hardwood

Why must I
Why must I
Allow these rounds
To fly?

I didn't aim
To split a gash
I only called her

Pretty
Kai Niezgoda, Grade 12
Royal Oak High School, MI

Soldier

Ready for battle
He readies his gear
He readies his arms
He goes in the fight
With all his might
He vanquishes his foes
And all of his woes
His glory shows
And this he knows
He returns home a hero
Matthew J. Smith, Grade 10
Michigan Lutheran Seminary School, MI

Deceiving Appearances

See those girls? Those tall, skinny, gorgeous girls?
Perfectly coifed honey blonde hair; wide, piercing ice blue eyes,
A smile always playing on those rosy red lips.
They're the prettiest, richest, and most popular girls at school,
Completed, of course, by their equally breathtakingly handsome boyfriends.
They're perfect.
Everybody wants to be them.
But look beneath the surface, and you'll see the fragmented souls hidden by the pretty candy coating.
One has an alcoholic father, and her parents constantly fight.
Another has a best friend who committed suicide two weeks ago.
Still another has a boyfriend who only likes her for her body.
Depression. Abuse. Cutting. Anorexia. Bulimia.
These girls are drowning, desperate, but all anyone sees is their "perfect" facade.
No one thinks they could possibly have the slightest problem.
No one is there to save them.
Everyone has their own cross to bear, and sometimes the seemingly flawless people are dealing with the toughest obstacles.
The most broken people can hide under the brightest smiles.

Rebecca Chen, Grade 11
Novi High School, MI

The Room

It all starts in one room, the room where champions are made.
The room where all humanity breaks at one point.
The room where everything is hot, and everything is hard, where everything has a meaning.
This one room, this one room where you can sweat and bleed and cry all at one time.
The room, where one person can achieve excellence in the greatest sport known to any real man.
In this room you don't dribble a ball up and down the gym.
In this room you don't throw around balls to other BOYS.
In this room you don't kick balls into a net.
But in this room, in this glorious but also hell of a room.
In this room, champions are made.
The room that's always the hottest in any building.
The room where boys are made into MEN.
The room in which these men spend countless hours trying to get better at the sport that they love.
The room where their Daddies Grandaddies and Great-Grandaddies once took mass.
This glorious but also hell of a room. That some dread, but others dread but know they have to keep coming back.
In this room.

David Lundgren, Grade 10
Amery High School, WI

Beneath Me

Blowing wind blows upon my face, snuggling close. Only in dreams could I have seen where this may have led. Having such power, such dignity, such gracefulness and I declare your love is not beneath me. Beautiful words, all put into songs, loving every inspirational tune you speak. Beats fill my head and I am zoned. Loving the tempo your heartbeat plays, loving this song, our kiss plays in our moment of love. Art of noise makes this even more lovable. May I remind you, your love is not beneath me. Loving every moment, cherishing the need to be loved. Tear drops melting my face, no makeup, bare faced. Love melts our burning candles, aroma of love, look of love, touch of love. Must I remind you, your love is not beneath me. Reminding looks of why we were here to begin with. Our love builds together, hearts tied, condescending stares and graceful approaches. Yet I remind you, your love is not beneath me. Understanding more than you ever could wonders me about the Complexity of everything, makes me think. Believing you only because I allow myself to. Loving you simply because my heart did not stop me. Engrossed in my thoughts I wonder, is your love beneath me? Beneath me, holding me high, making me so inclined to soar, making me rethink positions that I have already seen. Loving our memories, the ones we created together, made up from you and me. Love has always been spent away and spent in a way and we are always learning why. Depending on you makes it easy to survive. And yet you remind me, that still after praise and memories, your love is yet and still not beneath me.

MiShay Jefferson, Grade 12
Advanced Technology Academy, MI

Without

A book without chapters
A camera without captures
A sea without a shore
Kids without chores
America without poverty
A heart without an artery
A ring without a jeweler
A drug without a user
A life without cars
A jail without the bars
Money without a bank
Fish without a tank
An artist without a painting
Sports without spring training
People without racism
A car without a brake system
Soap without water
A wheel without a potter
A sky without the moon
A flower that doesn't bloom

Hannah Schreck, Grade 10
Osceola High School, WI

Spotlight

Center stage
The fluorescent yellow spotlight
Warm on my face
My leotard fits snugly against my pale skin
I see the crowd
Vigilant
Focused
Watching as though if they looked away,
They would miss some sort of trick
But I'm not here for tricks
No
In these slippers I am here for one thing
Each long brunette curl is tied up
Pinned into a bun
So I can focus on this single moment
A solo performance
My spotlight dance

Aubrey Meyer, Grade 10
Fruitport High School, MI

Echo No More Doubts

There is a heavy silence
I think I am losing my dream
My feet begin to wander
I think I am losing my dream
Time burns holes in my defense
I think I am losing my dream
Precious life I will squander

Madeline Ince, Grade 10
Eastview High School, MN

Night

When the stars appear
You can hear the Angels singing
Then the music begins

When the moon appears
So does the music
The music of Demons

When Night comes
So does Selene
When the Goddess appears
So does the wolf

When the moon is illuminated
The wolves come to see their lover
Then the music comes

The calls of the wolf
The draw to the wild
And the calls to a lost lover

'Come to us Selene'
The wolves howl
And she does

Stephanie Vickers, Grade 11
Novi Sr High School, MI

Take Chances

With every mistake you make,
Comes another chance for you to take.
To see if things just might,
Finally turn out right.
Don't regret the things you've done,
They were all part of the fun.
Remember what you've experienced so far,
Those events make you who you are.
When things don't seem to be going right,
Stay strong and put up the fight.
And when everything seems good and fair,
Just remember to beware.
The world changes every day,
Sometimes you don't have a say.
Be thankful for each moment until the end,
You weren't given this life to just pretend.
Sometimes words are hard to find,
But speak whatever comes to mind.
This may be your last day,
Take chances as they come your way.

Brandi Shramek, Grade 10
Lincoln Jr/Sr High School, WI

1929

I am weary, but I will endure
I wonder what tomorrow will bring
I hear the echoes of despair
I see faces full of sorrow
I want to believe in hope
I am weary, but I will endure

I pretend to be strong when I am not
I feel the shame of worthlessness
I touch my worn and empty pockets
I worry about our nation's future
I cry for those like me
I am weary, but I will endure

I understand that life is not easy
I say there is always another day
I dream of a better life for all
I try to find my inner strength
I hope for these times to end
I am weary, but I will endure

Kallie Zieman, Grade 10
Jefferson Sr High School, MN

A Woman

Once upon a time
There will have lived a woman
A woman of worth

She will search and search
For whom she is what what for
For what she wants, needs

She will have found love
Lost love, given love, taken it
Then loved the right one

She will have taken
Great chances and daring risks
Regretting nothing

She will be a wife,
A writer, a teacher, and
A mother and friend

Once upon a time
A woman will have lived and
She will be happy

Emily Eresh, Grade 11
Random Lake High School, WI

Hunting Time

In the arctic autumn air
In the middle of nowhere

Not a breeze
Not a movement
Not a sound
Not a…

And then

In the arctic autumn air
In the middle of nowhere

A breeze
A movement
A sound
A…

Big *Bold* Buck

A p p e a r s

In the arctic autumn air
In the middle of nowhere

BANG!
Allen Huju, Grade 11
Deer River High School, MN

Lighthouse

A place to go,
Like a lighthouse in a raging storm.
Safe haven,
Refuge from danger.

Protection and safety,
Home and family.
My stronghold to catch me,
Knight to rescue me.

I need you,
With you I am safe from harm.
Danger doesn't exist,
Only love and family.

You are my support,
To stand by your side forever.
Fear has vanished now,
Replaced by hope alone.

Even after everything,
We will be together.
I will stand by you,
No matter what.
Tina Foote, Grade 12
Sandusky High School, MI

Nine Eleven

We've all heard of the sad sorrowful day,
We saw something,
I'd only describe as betray

Our country stood,
as the smoke cleared
And there was,
our biggest fears

We saw the planes, that day on the news
We watched all,
those cleanup crews

I know its possible, terrorist attacks,
But its hard to imagine,
such violent acts

We saw it all,
on that now famous day
Americans families,
ripped away

We live in a country,
that had reached great heights
That shook in fear,
because of a few terrible flights.
Michaela Bemis, Grade 11
Lincoln Jr/Sr High School, WI

Procrastination

As I sit here in this seat
My mind keeps drawing blanks
I still have nothing but an empty sheet
And I have myself to thank

For I waited down 'til the very last second
To start this writing assignment
And now I sit here rather stunned
For no words are coming into alignment

Things like this don't happen to me
I've never had this problem
When the words in my head seem to be
A bunch of riddles and I can't solve them

I still can't think of what to say
Or how to make it rhyme
But when I do I'll type away
So I can hand this in on time

Now here's a message for all of you
You people across the nation
Don't do this thing I always do
This thing called procrastination
Travis Williams, Grade 10
Michigan Lutheran Seminary, MI

Bittersweet

You tell me
that leaving
is
bittersweet

I can feel the weight of
those words as they
Hit
my chest

Then you ask me, do I
understand?

I do

I understand;
if, indeed, after
all is said and done

Bittersweet
is simply another word for
horridly,
utterly,
heart —
wrenchingly…

Painful.
Katherine McAuly, Grade 12
IQ Academies, WI

Narwhal

Yearning for
Crisp, arctic air
The Narwhal surfaces
Overwhelmed
In a
Thick
Caustic
Oil slick
Assaulting its lungs and
Suppressing its Cetacean screams.

Thrashing about
In vain;
He
Realizes
How Alien
The water has become.

The sea wheezes
As its
Children's Last Breaths
Are Silenced
By a black death.
Maureen Massie, Grade 12
Allegan High School, MI

Uncontrolled

Uncontrolled, left to fate.
My heart and soul, disintegrate.

Until I believe, in the fairy tale of real…
My heart is hopeful! a tormented seal.

My fears hidden. My tears untold.
My heart betrothed, to the hopeless and cold.

The "friends" defend, the moral enemy.
Crumbling my supports, I fall to my aching knee.

Uncontrolled, my story speaks.
To anyone, my secrets leak.

The answers that'll help, linger in Past.
A Nightmare's dream! begins to elapse.

Faking the smile, and "living" the day.
Uncontrolled by Life.
Who cares anyway?

Addison Mumm, Grade 11
River Ridge High School, WI

Life Is Good

Life is good
Summer is the best time
Staying up well past one-thirty
Waking to the morning birds chirping
Smelling the fresh-cut grass at a Tigers game
Learning absolutely nothing
Life is good
Friends are great
Friends help you get through the bad times
Friends help pick you up when you are down
They make you laugh when you want to cry
Friends know what to say and when to say it
Friends make happiness
Life is good
Simple things in life
Skipping school and sleeping in
The taste of fresh-baked brownies, cupcakes, and cookies
Thanksgiving break, Midwinter break, Spring break
Christmas morning
THE WEEKEND
Life is good

Robby Milbrand, Grade 12
Dwight D Eisenhower High School, MI

Phoenix Rise and Fall

Rise from your ashes, oh fiery one,
you'll burst into flames, with plumes of the sun;
fly above them all, inferno spread among.
They tremble from your call,
your Phoenix screech, your song.
You're at your strongest point,
adult you've become.
Your brethren here to anoint,
your time is only some.
Fall of your time,
fire eagle you once were.
Nothing left but rhyme,
ashes you were secure.
Age had taken you,
back to the blackened.
Your long life, your flock just few,
you're falling back, you've come to slacken.
Rise and Fall of the mighty bird,
your life you held so great.
You call your only and last word,
a new Phoenix chick awaits.

Madeline Hunt, Grade 11
West High School, WI

A Stranded Leader

Things are racing
People are pacing
They believe an answer is you,
What am I suppose to do?

I take a breath
I look what's left
I say, "You, you, and you
Go find some food."

I get some wood
Build a fire as fast as I could
This is insane
How are we going to get to civilization again?

Over our head flies a plane
Get more wood, feed the flame.
Luckily they were looking for us
A sigh of relief comes out of all the fuss.

Let's go home.

Joey Felt, Grade 10
Tracy Area Jr/Sr High School, MN

Innocent Mirror

Look into your mirror,
And tell me what you see.
Is it really you?
Or someone you cannot be?

Don't look into someone else's mirror,
And tell them what they should see.
Looking into their mirror,
Will not change what your mirror sees.

When you look into your mirror,
Are you sure you see yourself?
As you gaze into your eyes,
Are you sure your eyes aren't reflecting someone else?

It is not the mirror's fault.
That it reflects someone else.
How do you expect a mirror to reflect you,
If you don't even know how you are yourself?

Cheryl Bailey, Grade 11
Athens Area High School, MI

The Truth

We all bleed and scar
Nobody here is different
Some people take things to heart
And some people make it so transparent

It's hard to really see someone for who they are
To get past the walls they have built
But once you get past those obstacles
You can really see that person and your similarities

Everyone has feelings
Some just hide them down where no one can see
But all I have to say
Is just show your feelings and be who you wanna be

Ed Patzer, Grade 11
Gillett High School, WI

Birthday

As I sit in my car seat
I hear squealing beneath my feet
Then all I see is black
At this time I can tell death is beside me
I feel pain in my side
I can hear faint sirens; I can hear talking and crying
When I open my eyes
I see my mom cut on forehead and crying beside me
Hoping I'm ok
As I look at my side; I see red
I get picked up in a strain and black out
I wake and see my family all around me
Happy to see me smile

William Vorpahl, Grade 11
Gillett High School, WI

Forever in the Darkened Room

sitting in a darkened room
in the corner of my mind
so many things pass me by
so many thoughts fill me in

sitting in the darkened room
the thoughts that push me down
make me overwhelmed
make my life not worth living

sitting in my darkened room
my thoughts pour out
not in front of you
but behind the light

always in this darkened room
because the thoughts that pour are too much
that's why I will forever hide
behind the light that you see

Emalie Leonard, Grade 11
Irondale Sr High School, MN

Bixby Canyon Bridge

I dream to walk along the Bixby Canyon Bridge
silent euphoria as the wind grazes the ridge
a gentle mist rises from the horizon grasping the sun
as the clouds above grasp the breeze and begin to run
the breeze brings a stinging cool across Bixby Canyon Bridge

The sun's light pierces the arches of the bridge
as I walk along the frigid ridge
chasing love's emotion is overdone
I dream to walk along the Bixby Canyon Bridge

The feelings sweep me a deep calm and warmth of passage
keeping me along the edge of the ridge
holding the heat of emotion that begins to run
from the grasp of my soul as I leave the ridge
I dream to walk along the Bixby Canyon Bridge

Niles Cox, Grade 12
Sauk Prairie High School, WI

Father

You raise me up, when I am in trouble
You raise me up from every difficulty
You raise me up, even though I did wrong
For you are with me, I can stand

You act as legs which support my body so that I cannot fall off
Even if I fall off, you raise me up again and again
You act as a guide when I walk a wrong way
You act as light in the darkness so that I would not be lost
You are the reason that I am breathing
You are my father

David Park, Grade 10
Michigan Lutheran Seminary School, MI

Raro Pez

They come big
Or they come small
Others are spotted
And others are striped
Some are pink
And some are orange
They may come with two gills
Or may have three
Some love eating minnows
And some love eating worms
Some can fly
And others can swim
Some dance merrily
And some sing beautifully
Some may laugh 'til they cry
And some may just cry
Some love other fish
And some may bully other fish
They can be silly
But mostly fish are happy as can be

Shauna Rein, Grade 12
Osceola High School, WI

Pinky Promises

It started the summer before third grade…
From the stupid fights that made us bawl
To the memories that will never fade,
It feels like we've been through it all.

People keep trying to tear us apart,
But it only brings us nearer.
You've left footprints in my heart,
And it couldn't be any clearer.

All those pinky promises we made together.
Even though you moved away,
You changed my life forever.
I know you'll never betray.

This friendship will never end.
I love you, best friend.

Marrissa Behrens, Grade 11
Belmont High School, WI

Earth and Moon

Earth,
Sphere, creation,
Amazing, rotating, changing,
Globe, planet, spherical, phases,
Orbiting, glowing, showing,
Shadow, crescent,
Moon

R.J. Vantroostenberg, Grade 11
Neil E Reid High School, MI

questions to my uncle

why did you?
smoke?
drink?
why did you have to push it too far?
was it the family?
was it fun for you?
i miss you

i will never be able to get to know you because of
alcohol
cigarettes

you will never be able to see me graduate, married, and my children grow up

you did something horrible not just to yourself but to our family
but
i learned something from you
tell people how you're feeling at that exact moment because you will
never know the next time you will see them

Sophia Pehrson, Grade 11
Deer River High School, MN

Eros' Arrow

Oh, dear friend! Your love is woeful,
And you know it fully well,
That it is not true.
Every time you see her, your heart becomes arrhythmic,
And your eyes spark with joy,
Your face turns into a stupid smile,
Your skin turns pink,
You feel as light as a feather,
And as light as butter,
And you sigh as you see her walk past, feeling utterly euphoric for whatever reason.
But, sir, you are blind to the truth, for you know not what this girl thinks of you;
You can love her all you want, but you will never know what she thinks of her.
Let me tell you, sir, your love is unrequited;
This girl is preposterous and treacherous;
She does not care if someone likes her, and she does not care if someone will give his life,
For as beautiful as she is, she will manipulate you, and will make sure you get hurt.
Stay away, for she is venomous, and will make sure that you suffer;
So do not remain blind to the truth;
Use your senses, and save yourself from Eros' dreadful arrow.

Justin Reamer, Grade 12
West Ottawa High School, MI

Dreams

To close your eyes is to
Wander off and dream.
To see the stars
In all different streams.
To go, to a place and feel open
Where only you can express your emotions.
Being in the real world is hard enough,
Being alone in your dreams is not tough.
It's ok to daydream,
Just don't get lost
The wind will blow but don't get tossed.
Dream aloud don't get frightened
No one can take your dreams,
Hold on tightly.
You can make it all the way,
Just keep your dreams
Life, life, life
Full of dreams.

Isaiah Jones, Grade 11
Visions Jr/Sr High School, WI

Thanks

You're the needle that sewed my heart
When someone else tore it apart.
You taught me how to trust again.
So now I write to you with this pen
The thank I owe you
Because you helped me through
The heartache and the heartbreak.
You held me up when my crutches fell
You brought me out of a living Hell.
When I was alone,
All it took was a call to my phone
To cheer me up in my darkest hours
And now I stop to smell the flowers
Because I am happy now.
And yet, somehow
You still want nothing but to see me smile
More than just once in awhile.

Carli Mueller, Grade 12
Random Lake High School, WI

Death

Death conquers the night
And holds the might.
It shows no light,
But yet is bright.

All are under its freight.
None are safe from its might.
All are slaves of its grasp
None can escape its clasp.
Yet when we die the time is nigh
When we will live forever on high.

James Westphal, Grade 10
Michigan Lutheran Seminary School, MI

Lend a Hand

It seems to me that people
Never like the things they own.
But people out there are starving
And wishing for a home.

Some people weep and mourn
For the ones that just can't come
Back home for the holidays.
Held hostage by the gun.

Some people sit there all alone
Wanting for someone to hear
About their day, about their life,
But no one's ever there.

I pray for all these people
And to hope to plant a seed
Inside the hearts of all I know
To help someone in need.

Kaitlyn Bunde, Grade 10
Michigan Lutheran Seminary School, MI

Slow It Down

We're going fast
It will never last
Until you hit that car
That looked so far

You'll crash and burn
And then you'll learn
That going fast will never last

So slow it down
Drive through town
Nice and slow

So on that cloudy day
That will seem to stay
Could have been better
If they didn't receive that letter

Brandon Benson, Grade 12
Tracy Area Jr/Sr High School, MN

Nature

Nature is beautiful
The smell is soothing
The wind blows and gently hits your face
A warm satisfaction now enters your body
You hear birds far and near
But all around you it's still quest
Peace is with you
Nature is
Simply what we would call
Beautiful

Justin Lunde, Grade 12
Random Lake High School, WI

A Special Time of Year

Thanksgiving:
A time of year
With great food,
And surrounded by people you love.

One of the best times
Of the year,
Filled with gifts from above.

Turkey, potatoes,
Stuffing too;
On to dessert
Now we're through.

There are many ways
For it to digest,
But watching football
Is the best!

Hayden W. Miller, Grade 10
Michigan Lutheran Seminary School, MI

Grades 7-8-9
Top Ten Winners

List of Top Ten Winners for Grades 7-9; listed alphabetically

Leah Berry-Sandelin, Grade 8
Mahoney Middle School, ME

Naomi Davidson, Grade 8
Decorah Middle School, IA

Olivia Estes, Grade 9
University Hill Secondary School, BC

Faith Harron, Grade 7
Horizon Middle School, ND

Lily Lauben, Grade 9
University Preparatory School, CA

Alex LePeter, Grade 7
Oak Knoll Middle School, VA

Sarah Lynch, Grade 7
Holy Innocents School, NJ

Ally Merrill, Grade 9
Hamilton Freshman High School, OH

Shelby Senger, Grade 8
Emmanuel-St Michael Lutheran School, IN

Anna Sixsmith, Grade 7
St Thomas More School, PA

All Top Ten Poems can be read at www.poeticpower.com

Note: The Top Ten poems were finalized through an online voting system. Creative Communication's judges first picked out the top poems. These poems were then posted online. The final step involved thousands of students and teachers who registered as the online judges and voted for the Top Ten poems. We hope you enjoy these selections.

Camping

When camping I've learned, how to light a fire.
Chopped wood and almost hired.
Pitched a tent and froze to death.
Then the day got warm.
And the bees started to swarm.

When camping I've learned, how to jump in the lake.
To sit on the beach and bake.
I could float,
or enjoy the boat.
The joy of camping.

When camping I've learned, to relax.
And explore the rocks,
have long talks.
Walk on the dock,
and hear the birds mock.

When camping I've learned,
Time to have fun,
eating s'mores, and
having good snores.

Thomas Sliger, Grade 7
Sault Area Middle School, MI

Crushed Mistakes

All that I had dreamed for,
just crushed into a million pieces.
All of my hope and faith,
lost with no return.
When will I ever learn from my mistakes?
Who will teach me to never give up?
How could this be?
Every day I wonder if my dream will come true,
but it never does.
So I wait,
I wait for someone to come along.
To teach me,
To help me.
To teach me to learn from my mistakes,
And to help me up on my own two feet.

Jordyn Davis, Grade 8
Perry Middle School, MI

Weekend

I'm waiting for this day to end
Two more days until the weekend
I'm going shopping and I have money to spend
On all of my friends.

Hopefully my money I won't have to lend
I will have to send
A gift to a far away friend
I'm waiting for this day to end.

Quinn Fitzgerald, Grade 7
Riverdale Elementary & Middle School, WI

Stay Strong

I know people like to bring us down.
I know people like to call us names.
We wonder why people like to see us frown.
They just can't accept that we're not all the same.

Stay strong,
This won't be long.
Be brave,
We aren't their slaves.
Just hold on, this will soon be done.
The pain will finally be gone.
We may not be perfect
So don't think you're cool,
Saying we're not worth it,
You know we're beautiful

So love who you are,
Hold on
You're a star!

Martha Benko, Grade 7
Ruth Murdoch Elementary School, MI

The Tree

The chainsaw roared to life.
The tree screeched as it made contact.

The chainsaw growled as it cut deeper.
The tree yelled in agony as the saw picked up speed.

The saw was almost completely through, but suddenly stopped.
The tree was creaking as it swayed from the strong wind.

The saw resumed cutting into the tree.
The tree was now ready to collapse.

Finally the saw cut all the way through.
The tree fell as the man yelled "Timber."

Gabriel Guerra, Grade 7
Nellie B Chisholm Middle School, MI

Life Isn't Perfect

Not everything always happens your way.
Like for me, my birth parents left me
When I was just a few days old
I was put in an orphanage.
And then when I was ten months old
I was adopted by an American family.
Though I am Chinese
I grew up like an American.
When I was only two and an half my adopted mother died
And my adopted father has never married since.
But I don't think he ever will.
Even though you may think this isn't true
But it is and it is my life.

Rachel Colwell, Grade 7
Ruth Murdoch Elementary School, MI

My Loving Father

I miss you. I love you. I will never forget you. Until the day we meet again in heaven,
Will be the best day of my life. The best day of my life.

All my tears have been shed, now it's time to go to bed, and dream of the times,
You were here with us on Earth.

The happy times on your motorcycle you were,
In a rush to get to what's in front and you really started to blush.

I see you in the hospital bed before God has led you through the gates of heaven.
The angels take you up, up far away and up where God is waiting for them to bring his son home.

All the while you watch over us we see you creep, creep around the house, and we know you
want to come back home and be with us to cherish the sad moments and the funny moments
that we still have in our hearts.

The little things went up with you that we gave to you in remembrance of your loving family.
And in each of our hearts will be that broken piece that you will always repair.

You will wipe away all the tears in the sad times, and tell all the funny jokes in the happy times
just to make us laugh and keep us happy.

We will always miss you and never forget you. We will celebrate your birthday like it is a
holiday every year.

I miss you. I love you. I will never forget you. Until the day we meet again in heaven,
will be the best day of my life.

Davina Jemison, Grade 8
Detroit Service Learning Academy, MI

First Day of School

Screaming, bawling, shouting
Pleading to loving ears
The warm soft voice
Ever so comforting
Being pushed forward
Encouraged to take the step
That is a journey

But showing persistent stubbornness
I run back to her
But she's already gone
Scared but with nothing left to lose
I open the door
To a whole new world
Entering…

When she comes back
It is much later but I don't mind
And when she picks me up I am low in spirits
Yet glad
Screaming bawling shouting, again
But for an entirely different reason
And she smiles.

Dilan Dubey, Grade 7
Detroit Country Day Middle School, MI

Eagle

An eagle glides through the sky,
the same eagle that made us cry.
As our loved ones died,
they were swept away with the tide.
But our freedom is almost there.
Our freedom which we fought for,
Our freedom which we longed for,
Our freedom from kings and queens,
because we know what freedom really means.
Our freedom is uncontrolled,
our freedom will never grow old.
As we begin to stop the war,
the bald eagle begins to soar.
It soars high through the clouds
under, over, and above the crowds.
And even if that eagle dies,
the flag for America still flies.

Carl Sadloske, Grade 9
Lincoln Jr/Sr High School, WI

Baseball

Roses are red. Violets are blue.
I love baseball. How about you?
The crack of the bat when you hit the ball.
The feeling of a strikeout beats 'em all.

When I walk up to the plate or to the mound,
All the other kids just drop to the ground.
The curve in the dirt or the heat up high,
Either way you just shouldn't try.
The feeling of the rosin in my hands
Gives me the power like Superman.

You can come from far.
You can come from wide.
If you want to fight, we'll take it outside.
Let's go to the diamond, and then, we'll see.
Do you honestly think you will beat me?

Dylan Olsonawski, Grade 8
Lancaster Secondary School, MN

Homework

Homework I need to check
Gives me a pain in my neck.
I worked hard at school, it's been a long day.
It's very important that I average an A.
Check and recheck, there is a lot at stake
To guarantee I haven't made a silly mistake.
It's time to move on, but there's no time to rest
I'd better hit the books and study for that test.
Hour by hour the night seems to pass,
Before I knew it the sun arose fast.
Getting no sleep and using my brain
Got me an A and was worth all the pain.

Annie Eugenio, Grade 7
Our Lady Star of the Sea School, MI

My Uncle Dave

It feels as if life has no meaning,
My uncle has left, left us all bleeding.

He has gone to heaven, up in the sky,
If only he had let me say goodbye.

I get out of my car, wind whistling in my ear,
I think about my Davy, and how he is not here.

Oh how I miss his scruffy beard,
His voice, his looks, oh how I wish he was here.

But I know he is safe, no more pain,
For I know he has not left in vain.

I say goodbye, tears dripping down my face,
Oh Dave, I love you, you will never be replaced.

Andrew Mckee, Grade 7
Nellie B Chisholm Middle School, MI

School

School can be fun and exciting to attend
When it comes to learning new concepts
Or just playing around with your friends.
School can be boring to some people
But you have to go, it's not an option
Not because your parents told you so
But because it's for your education.
In school you make new friends and do your best
To learn new ideas and pass your tests.
School teaches us how to laugh and cry
You also have to work hard and really try.
School is where ideas come alive
Even though I have to get up at 5.
School helps you learn to communicate
Even though homework keeps me up late.
School is where you get ample knowledge
You learn about life and it prepares you for college.

Daryn Meredith, Grade 8
Gesu Catholic School, MI

Real

I hear the faint echo of my name in the distance.
I don't want to,
But just for the chance that you want the real me
and not the fake me
The one that's just a similar version of you,
I do anyway.
I whip around, my eyes closed and fingers crossed.
Then I saw you...
Turning my switch from fake to real
I began to walk with you,
A smile on my face
And my chin up high.

Hunter Glew, Grade 7
Corunna Middle School, MI

Endless
A day like no other, nothing like we've known, all the fright and confusion in our freedom home.
Fast and furious with a blink of an eye, America as we knew it, unwillingly died.

There were no longer Twin Towers shadowing the land, sense of peace and safety came to an end.
Faith was tested, but how do you study, the ways of the Lord when you're left running.

Running from tears, running from disaster, searching for a happily ever after.
Yet none could be found, blind chances missed, with the sky falling down in a moment like this.

A moment that words could never describe, but with unspoken words, with wide open eyes.
Looking at life as if from below, where the sun doesn't shine and love isn't known.

Pray for a miracle, long for the light, at the end of the tunnel that'll make everything all right.
Right with our souls, right with our hearts, right with the things that couldn't tear us apart.
Proved by the sun that remained shining through, flames of fire, clouds of dust, victors could too.

In the end we all know the reason why, to unveil warriors that have always lied.
Within the midst of the fateful unknown, to rise up, and win back our freedom home.

Michelle Hecimovich, Grade 9
Chequamegon High School, WI

Ready as I'll Ever Be
"Ready as I'll ever be," she says
If only I were too

I seem to get stuck being the third wheel every time
She tells me I just have to get over it, as if I'm the one committing the crime

But I guess she wouldn't understand
She has him, she doesn't see me by hand

And I have no one like him to go to, no one but her
She doesn't understand that I wouldn't leave her for anyone, but she'd leave me, for him, I'm sure

And he'd do anything for her
And I would too, if she'd give me the chance, but that'd never occur

"Ready as I'll ever be," he replies
If only I were too

Tory Clearwater, Grade 7
Freedom Middle School, WI

Katherine
Katherine
Intelligent, loving, fun, athletic
Sister of James and Charlotte
Lover of dance and family
Who feels excited when traveling to new places, happy to see extended family, and sad when a party is over
Who needs love from family, an active life, and adventures with best friends
Who gives love to her whole family, encouragement, and gives the best that she can
Who fears high places, centipedes, and getting bad grades in school
Who would like to see the Seven Wonders of the World
Resident of Royal Oak, Michigan
Gramzow

Katherine Gramzow, Grade 8
Our Shepherd Lutheran School, MI

A Favorite Teacher

A favorite teacher is funny and sweet,
Gives us love and gives us treats.

A favorite teacher is nice and kind,
And always keeps us in mind.

A favorite teacher is always there,
She cares about our welfare.

A favorite teacher never questions,
She always gives suggestions.

A favorite teacher is wise,
She always gives us the prize.

A favorite teacher helps us to prevail,
She will never let us fail.

A favorite teacher is someone we will always treasure,
She is always a pleasure.

A favorite teacher is a friend you will have forever,
We will always think of her.

A favorite teacher is someone you go to,
When you do not know what to do.

We will never let her go,
She is Mrs. Ascencio.
Elizabeth Brousseau, Grade 7
Our Lady Star of the Sea School, MI

The Return

The dark unearthly "thing"
crawled up to the corner of my ceiling
When I gradually peeked out
from under my blanket
It was staring at me its face appeared to be
rotting off but I knew
it was watching me
The goose bumps ran up my spine
then traveled like electricity
throughout my body
it started to crawl slowly heading my way
Breathing deeply I didn't move a single muscle
Fear yet courage stood
up for me in the time it was needed most
"It" was whispering
things I couldn't comprehend
I screamed, What do you want from me?
Then it's gone
Just like two nights before
I slowly relaxed and waited for
The "thing's" return
Karissa Barnes, Grade 9
Allegan High School, MI

Where I'm From

I am from sports, from catching and throwing
I am from the house out of town
I am from playing sports and going to baseball games

I am from the lake, and feeling the cool breeze and water
I am from my parents Jayne and Rodger Wagner
I am from the sports family,
and eating healthy food

From sharing with others, and being nice
I am from a Christian faith based family
I am from Traverse City,
where at home we eat seafood and steak

From the funny stories to the exciting stories
and the far hitting dad as a golfer
I am from Kalkaska, Michigan
That is where I live and have my life.
Sam Wagner, Grade 8
Kalkaska Middle School, MI

It's All About Luck

The other day I went hunting with my dad
The weather wasn't too bad

While it was still dark I heard something come near
It filled me with fear

I grabbed my dad's arm so tight
I didn't know why we came when it was still night

Soon dark came to light
Then something was in sight

Who would have guessed I had this much luck
With only one shot, I got my first buck!
Hannah Hanson, Grade 7
Riverdale Elementary & Middle School, WI

Journey

Traveling through the depths of my soul
The deeper I go, the more confused I get
I try and find the reason for my pain
I wonder why I hurt so much
My body is like a storm and I try to fight it every day
And I wonder when will it stop
The rain and the storms when will they clear
And I think maybe if I find my soul it will stop the tears
But when your soul is as cold as mine
There's nowhere to turn and nowhere to hide
Maybe one day my soul will find its mate
And they'll last together, like that thing they call "fate"
But until that day I will remain searching
And continue on the lost journey through my soul.
Tu'Neija Tornai, Grade 9
McFarland High School, WI

Best Friends

He was a fair little puppy
His eyes were blue
He had barely been with us
He was brand new

I had picked him out
We were instantly friends
For we knew we'd be together
Until our days end

I love my puppy
With his fur so brown
He's just so cute
I can't put him down

If I didn't have him
I'd be lost in my years
I'd always be crying
I would drown in my tears

But since I do
He makes life better
He turns me from a fool
Into a go-getter
Kimberly Montone, Grade 7
Abbott Middle School, MI

Bieber Fever

Fainting girls,
And flashing lights.
Autographs and pictures.
The paparazzi scream.

His smile sparkles in the night.
The girls are going crazy.
The music begins to play.
He suddenly starts to sing.

He is hotter than the sun.
His face is like a dream.
He is loved by many.
How can some disagree?

He gives girls a sickness
That leaves their boyfriends jealous.
This sickness will not go away.
All the girls will suffer from it.

Bieber Fever is impossible to cure.
There is no treatment for it.
Justin Bieber gave this sickness.
No one wants to get rid of it.
Christine Eilers, Grade 7
Nellie B Chisholm Middle School, MI

Away from Home

Flowers bloom,
Balloons fly,
Flies buzz,
Busy people walk around.
But I feel lonely…
I was the one who decided to be away
But I feel gloomy
I knew it was going to be a new life
But I am depressed
I knew this time would come soon
But I cannot adjust myself into it.
My guardians make me up
Yet I am down
Christmas is coming,
Though I feel alone.
It is not the "feeling"
I am alone.
I need your love more, Mom and Dad
I miss you, my beloved family…
Seon Ho Park, Grade 8
Ruth Murdoch Elementary School, MI

Through the Eyes…

Innocence is what he sees
The innocence in the chaos
The rainbow in the mean storm
The good in a nasty villain

A life filled with dreams
Innocence is what he sees
His eyes see beyond the veil
True beauty in an ugly world

The truth he is seeking
Eyes form in every soul
Innocence is what he sees
He has not known, only seen

His eyes see so much, too much
Opinions form, truth dissolves
The one once known is gone
Innocence is what he sees
Paige Aichele, Grade 8
St. Jerome School, MN

Here

You are fragile
You are broken
You are hurt
You are helpless
If I'd care,
I'll be there
So take my hand
'Cause I am here.
Nalie Xiong, Grade 7
Pleasant View School, MI

Hitting 3,000

The crowd,
Roaring in my ear.

The pitcher,
Staring me down.

The count,
Three and two.

I've got no way
Out of this one.

I'm gonna leave here
With a bang.

2,999
Ain't good enough for me.

The pitcher throws
I must swing.

The bat speaks to me,
"Welcome to the 3,000 club."
Lauryn Trudell, Grade 7
Nellie B Chisholm Middle School, MI

Winter

This is the season,
For slowing down to find
A meaning in life

This is the season,
For having snowball fights and
Wiping snow from your face

This is the season,
For sledding down hills, dragging
Yourself up again

This is the season,
For making great big snow forts,
Until the sun sets

This is the season,
For sitting 'round a fire,
Drinking hot chocolate

This is the season,
For making lots of memories,
Taking time for life
Zoey Caballero, Grade 8
Ruth Murdoch Elementary School, MI

Rain Storm

Falling down from the heavens to the earth.
Droplets soaring from the blue sky.
Turned to gray in the bleak sunlight;
Evaporating from the minds of men.

Sprinkles of water dropping rapidly,
Personal demons of an angel's tear
Never returned to the clouds which bore life.
A bolt of lightning takes the night.

In the darkness hear a roll of thunder
Pounding in the very soul.
See it now, rain falling swift
Forming puddles in the streets.

Through a haze of rain and wind,
See the sparks fly in the shadows.
Even in the most deadly rainstorm
There is still hope in light from the sun.

Laura Becker, Grade 9
Wauwatosa East High School, WI

Music

Music is an art that flies through the air
The notes are like free birds that fly with a flair
Flying high and dipping low the notes take flight
They fly and fly until the end of the night

Free as a bird the notes fly
Swirling around me while the time goes by
The language of music is a simple one at that
But it takes many years to master such a unique language like that

My mind follows the music
As I wander into a wonderful dream
The music fills up my mind
While the beautiful language speaks to me

Michelle Huang, Grade 8
Gesu Catholic School, MI

Art

It is a piece of beauty
it can cause peace
it can cause war
it can make one happy
it can make one sad
it can make one angry
it can cause many feelings
it is like poetry or a song
it depends on the feeling or emotion
it affects the sound or look of the song, painting or writing
sad may have more emotion but happy…
it is always better than a sad feeling
even though sad may have a greater feel to it

Cody Place, Grade 8
Perry Middle School, MI

A "Tweenage" Life

Best friends, chores, and algebra.
Candy wrappers, dirty bras.
Pets, and brothers, what's the dif?
Always trying to fit in.

What's for homework? What page did you say?
What did we do in class today?
School's a war zone (that's no joke!)
Info piles on your brain to soak.

Life at home is not much better,
"Whose night is it?"s and "Where's my sweater?"s
Chores and homework (at least an hour)
All this stress can make you sour!

Friendships end every week,
You always swear you'll never speak.
Next thing you know, you're "besties" again,
You've never had a better friend.

In the end, it's all the same
The "tweenage" years are just part of the game!

Anya Miller, Grade 7
Abbott Middle School, MI

Amanda Lynn

She's fun, and she's smart.
She's my leader when I don't know where to start.

She's like the sun when there's a storm
And my best friend since the day she was born.

When her laughter fills the air,
I can't help but stop and stare.
It feels like I'm talking to a bear
Because all she does is whip her hair.

The more we talk, the closer we get,
And I can't help but make this bet…

We will be friends forever that's all there is to say.
I can't imagine it any other way!

Macy Westerberg, Grade 8
Lancaster Secondary School, MN

Shane

In 1889, in the Old Wild West
You only survive if you are the best
You have to carry a gun
Bing, bang, boom, and your life could be done
The days are as hot as a desert
The nights are black
Bob runs and plays
While Shane and Joe work all day

Shelby Klemm, Grade 8
Wauzeka Steuben School, WI

Seeing the Clouds

Now look up. What do you see? Clouds, right?
White, fluffy, huge clouds
When you look at them
You don't just see white, fluffy, clouds
You look at them closely
And create your own image
Right?
You can see whatever you want to
But keep in mind that
Some people see differently
Just like in life
You might see things your way
And some people see it
Another way than you do
Then there are some people that just don't
Take the time to look up
Or see things differently
They just have their way and that's it
I'm thinking they never stop
To look at the clouds

Miles Nielsen, Grade 7
Olson Middle School, WI

Summertime

Running through the pasture,
hearing nothing but laughter.

With the wind blowing through my hair,
Not having one single care.

Watching the clouds as they roll by,
Seeing how fast time flies…in the summertime

Running barefoot through the grass,
Eating ice cream…what a blast!

Running on the cobbled rocks,
Wish I had my trusty Crocs.

Seeing all the flowers bloom,
Looking up at the stars and moon.

Warming up around the campfire,
Summertime is my only desire.

Gabby Schmiedeberg, Grade 8
Lancaster Secondary School, MN

Adventure

It was the summer of '89.
"Boom!" Went the gun and down went Ernie Wright.
Fletcher is filling a few people with fear.
Bob will raise his kids in the same house that he grew up in.
Shane is a bolt of lightning.
Marian is as good of a cook as Rachel Ray.

Samantha Groom, Grade 8
Wauzeka Steuben School, WI

Dig a Little Deeper

Look in a mirror
what do you see
do you see a strange face looking back at you
or do you see a reflection
telling you to dig a little deeper

look in a mirror
what do you feel
do you feel like you're trapped in a box
or do you feel like there's something bursting out of you

look in a mirror
and ask yourself
is this me
or is this what others see me as

look in a mirror
what do you see
do you see a strange face looking back at you
or do you see a reflection
telling you to dig a little deeper!!!

Megan Stafford, Grade 9
Centreville High School, MI

Confusion

As the scorching summer breeze swipes across my hair,
forcing it to weave throughout the others.
I continue to hike up the coast.
Lonely while sand seeps between my bare toes,
the water whistles to waves taller than I.
Besides the natural beach noises,
I begin to hear footsteps of my own feet.
Every step I take,
sand kicks up and hits the back of my floral dress.
Is something chasing me?
I look behind and nothing appears.
I stop, and get lost in my train of thought.
While I stand alone and clueless and confused.
I jump in the water and drown in my dreams,
though when I wake up…
I realize that it was a nightmare.

Devyn Coleson, Grade 8
Perry Middle School, MI

My Grand Canyon Backpack

My backpack is so heavy,
I think my teachers purposely put
a piece of the Grand Canyon in it!
When we aren't looking
they send their agents
to cut the biggest piece to put in my backpack!
It ruins all my stuff like wild fire.
What will I ever do
about the horrible backpack?!

Kara Przybylski, Grade 7
East Rockford Middle School, MI

You

Was everything we had,
Everything that had been said,
Just a big old lie,
A way to make you less shy,
A ticket to the in-crowd,
A chance to be heard out loud,
Did you ever look at me,
Or take time to really look and see,
Who I truly am,
Instead of leaving me for the damned?
Feeling sorry now won't save you from everything said and done,
You take the prize now, you have won,
My heart you will take,
And for sure you will break,
Go find the next victim,
Kill them too,
'Cause you will never think of anyone but
You.

Rochelle Mindrum, Grade 9
Kickapoo High School, WI

Music

Why I love music:
it can express your feelings
  mad, sad, angry, happy,
  excited, funny, and graceful.
It can speak to you,
  everyone loves it.
Favorite singers and songs,
  makes you want to sing along
  and soon enough you get it stuck in your head
Instruments, tempo, and beat,
  makes you want to dance.
The song has an effect on you
  so go on and
  Listen…

Jasmine Cardenas, Grade 7
Pleasant View School, MI

Basketball

Basketball is my favorite sport.
I like to run up and down the court.

If we aren't doing well, the coach might get mad.
That means we play harder and try not to do bad.

If you get five fouls, you are out.
That doesn't mean that you sit and pout.

The ref is the leader of the game.
So do not get into an argument or you should be ashamed.

Even if you have to run,
Basketball can be a lot of fun.

Mason Olson, Grade 8
Lancaster Secondary School, MN

I Wonder…

I wonder how birds soar.
Was there ever something called a dinosaur?
I wonder how God made a tree.
Was it for him, or for me?
I wonder how the monkey got its name.
Did someone get bored and think of something lame?
I wonder how beagles bark.
Did they get annoying on the ark?
I wonder how the kitten can mew.
Did God plan it, or think it new?
I wonder how winter turns to fall
Or how spring can start a winter's thaw.
I wonder how the sun rises in the morning
Does it come up to stop the moon's snoring?
I wonder how people are different colors.
Are they all a form of brothers?
I wonder how women love men.
Or is it that men love women?
I wonder why I'm always wondering…

Traci Langan, Grade 9
Lincoln Jr/Sr High School, WI

Seasons

The leaves fell down on the ground,
The branches shook so hard, over and over again,

Cold winter weather is the worst,
The snow falls on the city like a blanket,

Warm and cold weather is spring,
The flowers pop out and grow,

Summer is the best, no school,
Warm weather, cousins coming to visit,

Summer, fall, winter, and spring
Come together and play a big part in our earth.

Makenzi Clark, Grade 7
Nellie B Chisholm Middle School, MI

Up North

Summer, it screams up north,
it says swimming then hiking to dry up
and going by the fire and roasting up,
that's how my summer passes.

Fall, up north leaves falling, kids raking,
cheers and laughter everywhere.
Fire blazing, lake freezing, but everyone is still smiling.

Winter, bundling up for up north.
Everyone red-nosed and cold cheeks.
The fire is blazing hot.
Ice skating, shoveling, that's how my winter passed.

Casey McKeough, Grade 7
Woodworth Jr High School, WI

Broken

Silent tears, silent pain
Silent fears, I'm going insane.
Torn heartbeats, silent screams
Blood-red tear drops, shattered dreams.
The moments I cherished, are ripped from my heart.
Patches and scars,
From where you tore me apart.
I'm so confused. I feel so alone.
The last thing you said to me,
Was "Answer your freaking phone."
My world was dark. I called your name.
I should have known, you never came.
A picture of us…cuts through my heart.
What you must be thinking, now we are apart.
Don't come back for me.
Don't even try.
Just remember…you made me cry
You pushed me away.
Are you happy now?
Go ahead,
Take a bow.

Jessi Charon, Grade 9
Galesburg-Augusta High School, MI

The Ocean

A vast world of underwater life,
Fish of beautiful colors swimming gracefully,
A lovely world that is void of land,
Shining and glistening like a diamond,
A realm of beauty and serenity,
With dolphins jumping playfully,
Waves created by wind to lull boats
Like a mother rocking her child,
Islands break the view of blue,
The shade of blue as gorgeous as a sapphire,
Plants sway with the current freely,
Orcas jump and play carefreely,
Sharks stalking their prey,
Crashing waves,
Eternal beauty.

Marley Burnham, Grade 7
Woodworth Jr High School, WI

Hockey

His helmet was black as the night.
His strides were strong as a bear.
His blades were cutting in the ice.
He looks at the goalie as their eyes meet.
He shoots the puck as fast and accurate as a snake.
The puck burst through the air as fast as a bullet.
As the puck reaches the net he scores.
The crowd roars with happiness.
He feels like the king of the world.
Their team feels great to win a hard played game.

Bailey Haglund, Grade 8
St Jerome Elementary School, MN

Learning Time

In school I've learned…
How to add read and spell
It's such a great feeling to be doing so well
How to subtract, jump, skip, and climb
How to look at a clock and be on time

How to make friends and share
To be part of a group and have someone care
How to listen, be patient, and never cheat
To do well on your own is such a great treat

How to respect one another
To learn to take turns and not fight with my brother
How to sit in a space for a really long time
How to write poems and make them rhyme

In school I've learned…
How to stand up as a leader
I never want to be known as a cheater

Regan Casey, Grade 7
Sault Area Middle School, MI

Ballerina

Standing in a spiral of light,
Dressed in the flowing dress of an angel,
She saw herself in the face of a hundred shining mirrors,
And she let the music enfold her.
Feeling its magic course through her veins,
She closed her eyes in forfeit.

As she twirled as free as a crashing wave,
Soared as strong as a hawk,
A fire churned in her heart,
A spark flared in her soul.
She took that stage by storm,
And got lost in another world,
Where she found herself at last.

Jiwon Yun, Grade 7
Detroit Country Day Middle School, MI

School

School
Students, teachers, janitors, friends, principal
School
Math, reading, writing, science, social studies
School
Recess, detention, study hall, play, study
School
Band, dance, drama, art, choir
School
Football, basketball, cheerleading, track, soccer
School
Freshman, sophomore, junior, senior, graduation
School

Derrick McKinney, Grade 7
Pleasant View School, MI

Sodapop from "Outsiders"

Sodapop
Movie star-like, kind
Understanding, caring, loving
Mickey Mouse is his horse
Working, dedicating, protecting
Greaser, horses
Gorgeous
Caitlin Darrah, Grade 8
Kalkaska Middle School, MI

Icy Hot

Fire
Red, hot
Melting, burning, smoking
Gases, flames, chill, cubes
Slipping, freezing, breaking
Cold, clear
Ice
Drake Roesler, Grade 7
Nellie B Chisholm Middle School, MI

Two Planets

Sun
Bright, hot
Exploding, burning, erupting
Fire, rays, white, NASA
Changing, moving, spinning
Big, reflective
Moon
Dylan Webber, Grade 7
Nellie B Chisholm Middle School, MI

Burning Ice

Fire
Hot, light
Burning, sparking, destroying
Colors, flames, cube, frostbite
Freezing, sliding, melting
Cold, chilly
Ice
RJ Sellers, Grade 7
Nellie B Chisholm Middle School, MI

Relaxing and Stressing

Vacation,
Quiet, peaceful,
Relaxing, staying, coming,
Pool, sunscreen, papers, pens,
Massaging, helping, teaching,
Painful, long
Work
Veronica Barrientos, Grade 7
Nellie B Chisholm Middle School, MI

Fire

Fire is a wild wolf
    howling with rage
        pulling the world within its grasp.

Fire is a fierce tiger
    roaring with anger
        annihilating everything within its path.

Fire is a ferocious dinosaur
    savage with power
        both strong and merciless as a dozen dragons combined.

Fire is a vicious snake
    swirling with venom
        terminating anything that dares challenge it.

Fire is an enraged lion
    extinguishing in a flash
        foes run away with the first sound of a lion's snarl.

Fire is a furious bear
    sealed with incredible force
        strong enough to roll a 700 pound weight as if it was a beach ball.

Fire is a demolishing herd of energy-packed animals
    weight provides the momentum needed to demolish an entire forest.
Chittesh Thavamani, Grade 7
Boulan Park Middle School, MI

The Hope of Broken Words for Colorless Love

Words,
Left hung, dismantled, broken in the air
The sight is fresh, distinct,
Leaving the unspoken heartache clear as nothing but unfair

Love,
The essence of a smile, the reasoning of a tear
Cherished by nothing more but the significant beauties living
Yet handled so indelicately, by the ones fulfilled with fear

Color,
Faded before her, violent purple, sorrowful blue
Witnessing the sound and feeling of happiness be taken
Unmistakably from her all because of a simple I love you

Broken,
The meaning displayed on the innocents face, vividly scarred upon her heart
Represented by the depressing images, fading memories that would soon enough
Be one of the many reasons as to why she fell apart

Hope,
Emerging weakly, seeking a cure
Embracing scarcely but visibly enough to been seen
For the wanting to once again be pure

Sophia Green, Grade 9
Willow River High School, MN

Grandpa

You were there when I got hurt,
To help me up and say, "It's only dirt,"
You'd chase me around,
Make me laugh until I'd cry.

You always knew how to make me smile,
And would tell me the funniest things to say,
But hey,
You never know what you have until it's gone,

I loved the way you'd hold my hand when I was scared,
And say, "Go ahead I dare ya,"
How I miss the times you'd chase me around,
And throw me around,

You're always in my heart,
And never forgotten,
Grandpa.

Rebecca Tondola, Grade 7
Lincoln Jr/Sr High School, WI

The Ant's Story

I scurry along, I am very rushed.
Must get to my queen, before I am crushed.

I'm leading the way with a leaf on my back.
And then I am blinded, the world has gone black.

I look up and see a terrifying sight,
The laces of sneakers tied up tight.

And then comes the boom, I feel the Earth shake,
I jump out of harm's way and quiver and quake.

The sneakers have caused damage galore,
And sadly I see my ant friends are no more.

Neha Bhatt, Grade 8
Wayzata Central Middle School, MN

Winter Wonderland

I look outside and all I can see,
is lots of snow on the grass and trees.

The cold winter breeze will chill the air.
I walk outside and feel the swaying of my hair.

The snow is sparking as Christmas lights.
On my face I feel Jack Frost's bites.

Watching the snowflakes fall like a tear.
I would not want to be anywhere but here.

This place is not what you call "Bland."
It is Michigan's Winter Wonderland

Holland Welsh, Grade 8
St John Vianney Catholic School, MI

So Confused

In my closet is a bunch of gym shoes
Which pair should I choose?
I have many colors to choose from
I really want to impress my friends
If I don't hurry up I'm going to be late for the fair
I must be there to share a speech
Hurry fast because my mom will screech
I look at the clock as time is ticking
I'm trying to hurry but confused
I'm not sure what shoes to choose
Blue, black and green, plus many more colors
I must hurry or else my day will be a bummer
I finally pick a color and it's blue
I really have to hurry before the clock strikes noon
When I arrive to my destination
I see that everyone is in coordination
To my surprise everyone decided to wear blue
Oh me, oh my, isn't that a surprise to you!

Mone't Brown, Grade 8
Gesu Catholic School, MI

My Birthday

Birthday's are great,
Especially on my date.
My birthday's on the Fourth of July,
When fireworks are as loud as thunder.
When the sky is prettier than a rainbow,
When bodies of water sparkle like diamonds.
My family is as busy as bees,
Shopping for my birthday feast.
During the family feast,
Everyone looks hungrier than a beast.
When we are eating, it is quieter than an empty church.
When we are done eating,
We are as fat as pigs.
When I open my presents,
I am as happy as a lark.
At the end,
My family felt like a rented mule.

Teddy Bleich, Grade 7
Boulan Park Middle School, MI

Thunderstorm

I could see it coming.
Then "Vroom! Vroom!" the thunderstorm roared to life.

It sounded like a race car.
It was like a reckless driver out for destruction.

Then it will calm down
Like a tired little cat.

Then it will be asleep
Like a baby in its bed.

Kaleb Hams, Grade 7
Nellie B Chisholm Middle School, MI

Bump, Set, Spike

In volleyball I've learned…
To run, run, run
But, also just to have fun
How to never let the ball hit the ground
And when you set, there should be no sound

In volleyball I've learned…
To always listen
Because something coach said you'll end up missin'
How to serve
And making sure it doesn't curve

In volleyball I've learned…
That there are no punishments
And how to try to find the fun in it
To always go for the ball
And if you need to, fall

In volleyball I've learned…
To always be friends
And don't stop going for the ball until the game ends

Annie McLean, Grade 7
Sault Area Middle School, MI

To See the World

To see the mountains, in the bright day.
To see the oceans, and the stars above.
To see the rivers, winding their way.
To see the people, finding their true love.

To see the valleys, with the lush green grass.
To see the birds, and the tall sturdy trees.
To see the lakes, with the brown bass.
To see the jungles, and the new green leaves.

To see the brooks, babbling their tune.
To see the sun, with that bright orange light.
To see the fireflies, on a hot summer's June.
To see the snow, on a cold winter's night.

To see Mount Everest, and a golden new age.
With family, adding a new chapter to each page.

Tori Motloch, Grade 7
Malow Jr High School, MI

Differences in Music

Metal music
Loud, sharp
Screaming, head banging, dancing
Disturbed, Dimetree Lynch, John Williams, Opera house
Sitting, waiting, listening,
Long, soft
Classical music

Logan Waruszewski, Grade 7
Nellie B Chisholm Middle School, MI

The Special Call

Unity and oneness as a whole
All striving to achieve the same goal
195 nations all the same as God's creations
Moving together holding hands
Working together and making bands
Our world is divided that's why we fall
Until we hear that special call
United we stand
Or are we just a strand
A strand of hair that can be broken
And torn to pieces
We need not to tolerate but to appreciate
Many religions, acting like separate subdivisions
We need to strive
To keep the children alive, the children of the future
That will someday rise
We don't want to have to look in their eyes
And hear all their hopeless cries
These cries that mean something
United we stand, divided we fall
And that is the special call

Loujain Kouider, Grade 8
Crescent Academy International, MI

Justifying Insanity

I talk to myself
because I am the only sane one

I write nonsense
because I really don't want you to understand

I laugh
because it makes life easier

I try impossible things
because maybe I'll succeed

I live in delusions
because I don't like reality

Sometimes I stop
because I don't have anything to run on anymore

Annika Kohrt, Grade 8
Wayzata Central Middle School, MN

Breathe

I love him,
He's my angel,
But I know from past experience I'll once again meet the devil,
Because I know his type,
And it's not me,
But when I see him,
I still forget how to breathe…

Vita Simmons, Grade 7
Shelby Jr High School, MI

Foolish Love

I can't trust you,
and you wonder
Why
You shattered my heart with no regret.
You still have the nerve to come back and do it again?
You've made me cry and
torn me down with your lies.
Do
you really want it to be like this?
These pieces just don't fit together,
but yet you still found a way to sneak into my heart.
I say I hate you and we're over,
but the truth is
I
can't live without you.
People say it's foolish the way I
Love
you. And I have to ask myself why do I keep coming back?
What is it about
You?

Lauren Steel, Grade 8
Perry Middle School, MI

My Small Little World

My small little world,
In the palm of my hand,
With just one swift movement I'm gone
I forget the world around,
and I enter my small world.
My small little world it's like a blank canvass and empty,
No one now to tell me what to do.
Just me, myself, I
In my little world,
I can be someone else,
I can be a rock star
I can be whoever I want to be
I want to stay in my little world
but something pulls me out
Like cold water being poured on my head
I wake up and get back to the real world.
I look around me and smile,
People wonder why I'm me
and I remember that
My iPod will never leave my side.

Rachel Evans, Grade 9
Lenawee Christian School, MI

Survival

The thorns grab at my feet as I stagger through the woods
The clouds mock me as I struggle to find water
The trees whisper as I pass
The newborn icicles on the branches wisp away my warmth
My only companion is fire
If I can find him.

Josh Wadlow, Grade 7
East Rockford Middle School, MI

Cedar Tree

Piney scent wafting through the air.
Take a running jump and grab onto the lower branches,
Pull yourself up and you're in.
Experience the canopy of needles,
Finding a comfortable branch.
Sitting, listening to the nature around you.
A chickadee lands on a nearby branch,
whistling it's famous tune chicka-dee-dee-dee-dee-dee.
Reaching out to touch it
as it flitters away.
Just as it leaves, a squirrel scatters up the trunk.
It climbs right past to the upper branches,
so you start to climb after.
Needles and cedar berries fall all around.
Climbing higher and higher,
until you can feel the tree sway in the wind.
Stop and take a look all around,
feel the crisp clean breeze blow in your face.
Slowly climbing down, savoring every minute,
as you take a final leap to the ground
thinking about when you can come back.

Adam Wright, Grade 8
Lincoln Jr/Sr High School, WI

Choices, Is Our Future

When kids are young
They have so much time
No worries about anything
They scream all night and day
Parents want their kids to grow up
Behave, start educating themselves
For a better life in the future
But you never want to rush time
Live every moment, and every second
Bad moments will pass
But only the good ones, will last forever
Children are finishing the work you begun
Living the life that they choose
Living the money that they truly earned
Living with the family they deeply love
Live the life you choose and you will get so in return

Katrin Gurvich, Grade 8
Orchard Lake Middle School, MI

School

CLANK!!! As they close the prison bars
We are trapped for seven hours straight
With no contact to the outside world
BEEP!!! The bell echoes off the cement walls
Everyone looks outside drooling
Then SMACK!!!! The teacher slams a textbook
2:29 it's silent…and awkward
BEEP!!! The last bell rings
FREEDOM!!! As everyone sprints outside

Darren Frederick, Grade 7
East Rockford Middle School, MI

Basketball Court

When I step on the court,
I'm not me.
I'm some kind of person,
With a desire to win.
I don't hate the player,
If anything I hate the game,
But my love for the game,
Is so big,
Bigger than my desire to win.
I've been playing since
I was about three,
Ever since then I've been different.
Some people hate,
But I don't care,
I let my haters,
Be my motivators.
I'll be me,
And you be you.
Whether I'm on the court,
Or before the game.
I'm in my zone and can't be stopped.
Chad Zimbauer, Grade 9
Lincoln Jr/Sr High School, WI

The Sun

The sun is bright
just like a yellow light.
The sunrise,
looks like a big prize.
The sun goes down
in every town.
The sun shines
along the coastlines.
The sun is in the sky
it floats up very high.
The sun is hot
on the spot.
The sun is out every hour
it never runs out of power.
The children play outside very long
they sing many different songs.
The sun is very fun
to everyone.
When the sun is done
the moon comes out
with no doubt.
Sara Rochon, Grade 7
Our Lady Star of the Sea School, MI

Butterflies

Butterflies fly,
High in the sky,
Soaring, fluttering,
Passing by.
Jessica McIntosh, Grade 7
Scranton Middle School, MI

God

God is hope,
God is life,
God takes away the painful strife.

God is kind,
God is love,
God's symbol for peace is a dove.

God is joy,
God is light,
God makes our futures very bright.

God is here,
God is present,
God makes everything pleasant.

God is gentle,
God is true,
God brought me here to be with you.
Kayla Gallant, Grade 8
Our Lady Star of the Sea School, MI

Dirty Hippy John

Hippy John is like a fireplace.
He's similar to a log.
He sits in a chair
Like he's covered in smog.

His face looks like a mud pie.
His hands are as black as ink.
I think I'll take him home with me
And lead him to the sink.

John and I will find the soap.
We'll make a lot of bubbles.
We'll probably make a real big mess.
I hope it's worth our troubles.

I now see Hippy John's clean face.
My voice is like a whisper.
Under all those layers of dirt
I realize he's my sister.
James Ramthun, Grade 7
Nellie B Chisholm Middle School, MI

Waiting

As it comes to this time of year,
The leaves begin to change,
The weather gets cold and windy.
Thanksgiving has passed,
And Christmas is yet to come.
The joy of Christmas excites everybody,
Waiting for that last leaf to fall
And the first snowflake to drop.
Kailey Wendland, Grade 9
Round Lake High School, MN

My Dirty Little Room

My dirty little room
has clothes stacked to the ceiling.
I'm telling you the truth
you don't know the pain I'm feeling.

My room is not a normal room
it's not like all the others.
My room is such a dirty room
I share it with my brothers.

There's always food on my dresser
it's starting to mold green.
There's always food in my closet
why can't it be clean?

My dirty little room
looks like tornadoes hit.
Mom please come clean my room
before I throw a fit.
Merritt Hamann, Grade 7
Nellie B Chisholm Middle School, MI

The Frog

The frog had felt smooth
Like a shirt with silk.
The fog had suction cups
Like octopus's arms.

The frog had round eyes
Like a circular ball.
The frog was fragile
Like a wine glass.

The frog was slippery
like soap when wet.
The frog had webbed feet
Like scuba divers.

The frog was green
Like a colored pencil.
The frog had spots
Like a giraffe.
Jered Bass, Grade 7
Nellie B Chisholm Middle School, MI

The Road of Life

Life is like a never-ending road,
You can only see so far in front of you.
You have no idea what lies ahead,
Yet you still keep going.
Preparing yourself as best as you can,
For those unknown factors,
That could just change your life,
Forever.

Luna An, Grade 8
Boulan Park Middle School, MI

Friends

Friends are people you can trust
through good times, sad,
rough times and bad times.
We all need a friend to do something
for us so we can succeed in
education, sports, and other things we love to do.
I love my friends because they
support me even if I mess up on doing something.
They are always there to help me fix what I started and
work harder doing it and it helps having a friend along.
Most believe they don't need a friend
and everyone has someone who loves them.
Everyone has a friend, if it's your mother and your dad
or even your brother or sister.
I have lots of friends, like my family,
and I have friends that are not related to me.
I always talk to them and we are very good friends.
But you always have to keep a good attitude when talking
to a friend and you always love a friend.

Noah Creer, Grade 8
Gesu Catholic School, MI

Thinking About Tomorrow

Yes, I am thinking about tomorrow,
I'm hoping it's good and not full of sorrow.

I want to play with waves rolling ashore,
I want to hear my friends come knocking at my door.

I want to feel the sun shining on my face,
I would like to buy a new dress with lots of lace.

I will hear the bells ringing with joy and delight,
And I'm also hoping ma' and pa' wouldn't begin to fight.

I hope tomorrow goes how I planned it out,
But it probably wouldn't be how it was thought about.

Quinn Pangborn, Grade 7
Our Lady Star of the Sea School, MI

Canvas

You're the one who tricked me a lot.
You're the one with the lies I bought.
You're the one who tore me apart.
You're the one that slaughtered my heart.
You're the one who found it funny to ask.
You're the one who threw me out with the trash.

I'm the one who stuck by your side.
I'm the one who you watched die inside.
I'm the one who let you through the door.
I'm the one who you now ignore.
I'm the one who thought you were right.
I'm the canvas you painted that night.

Jade Driscoll, Grade 9
Kingsford High School, MI

Tears

I know there are tears upon my face.
There is no hiding place,
and I know I will be afraid that you're gone,
but time will soon go on.

I hear Angels calling my name
through the big flame.
By chance, a miracle appears.
They will dry my tears.

Even though you're gone,
Dusk will go to dawn
through every precious moment.
Life means nothing more than you and I.

Having so much to say
watching you walk away
waiting on you like a dove
when I think of our love.

Help me remember that July
when everything was as good as pie.
Back when we were together, not apart,
I just want you to know.
You still have my heart.

Corey Rich, Grade 8
Lancaster Secondary School, MN

Just Here

I am just there,
Not particularly special, not noticeable,
Not beautiful or ugly,
Just there.

I keep my head down, trying to hide my face,
Scared of whispers, scared of rumors,
I am just there.

Like a whisper in the wind I float along,
Prepared for the rumors to start,
But they never do,
I am just there.

I am not in the way, nor am I helpful,
I am just there.

I yearn to break free,
Free of the spell cast on me,
The magic that makes me feel invisible,
This is a battle my Prince Charming can't save me from,
I have to face it on my own.
But how?
So right now I say the same,
I am still just there.

Alexandra Stavros, Grade 8
Scranton Middle School, MI

Where I'm From

I am from the many dust covered books sitting on the shelves; from half melted Hershey's and Cheesy Cheddar Goldfish.
I am from "The house of dead plants," where aromas abound of burnt toast, and hot bold coffee.
I am from the helicopter seeds, slowly falling from the trees in spring, the quiet binding river that never seems to stop flowing.
I am from the Thanksgiving Dinners, Christmas Breakfasts, and humor;
from Hogerheide and Stuck, and Grandpa Butch and Grandma Lou.

I'm from the "Let's do something family," the "Shop till you droppers," unique in our own little ways.
From "Do your best," "Believe in yourself," and "There IS no whining."
I am from the — He sent His only son, that whoever believeth in Him shall never perish but have everlasting life –
I'm from "The Cherry Capital," "The Great Lakes State," where Torch Lake's beautiful colors are my home.
From the peach scented potpourri, the loving grandma, and the silly exploring girl.

I am from my very first jewelry box, containing my whole family in a picture, the 11 years of dance medals, from the walls in my flowing hallway where it seems pictures are never ending, my glittering and gleaming rock collection, my clip-on earrings from 1st Grade, and from the 16 gigabytes of pictures encompassing my life on a hard drive.

Makenna Hogerheide, Grade 8
Kalkaska Middle School, MI

A Night I Can't Seem to Forget

Red lights and wailing sirens, I know them far too well.
That fateful day, they took her away, as I begged them not to go.
They pumped her chest, she was oh so fragile. I pulled him off her, they said
"Take her away, let us do our job." I sat restrained, watching them break my dear lifelong friend.
My friend, my heart, my great-grandmother.

They angered me when they said it, "Take your time, no need to rush."
No need to rush? Who did he think he was talking about?
I made myself believe if I got there fast enough, she'd be waiting.
I asked God why he would take her just now. He said He needed another angel.
I told Him He could have me, He replied that it wasn't my time.
I could understand why God would want her back, only a fool wouldn't.
I know she is here, sitting beside me, watching me write my poem.
I think she would be proud.

Kierra Wright, Grade 8
Gesu Catholic School, MI

Where I'm From

I am from household pets, from Meow Mix and Milk bones.
I am from the green-grass, the smell of flowers and the buzz of bees.
I am from the pine trees, the oak trees, pine cones and pine needles.
I am from Christmas Parties and brown hair, from Trish Kennell, Rich Kennell, and Ellen Kennell.
I am from the chocolate chip cookies and blue eyes.
From don't talk to strangers and never give up.
I am from Christianity, going to church, and believing in Jesus.
I am from Owosso, Michigan where German, French, Irish, Indian, and American are in my blood.
From cheeseburgers and pizza.
From the stories of my dad lobster fishing and getting pulled overboard,
the time when they caught a shark, and the story about my mom breaking her jaw bike riding.
I am from riding in my dad's jeep, 4-wheeling in my cousin's golf cart, horseback riding,
and playing at Lake Michigan in Frankfort.

Brandy Kennell, Grade 8
Kalkaska Middle School, MI

Life on Their Breath

A cool wave rushing
A white cloud drifting
A small whispered wish
A calm peaceful mist
A lust within the mind
A love residing inside
A breeze in the wind
A twinkle in her eye
A kiss on his lips
Life on their breath
A kiss on his lips
A twinkle in her eye
A breeze in the wind
A love residing inside
A lust within the mind
A calm peaceful mist
A small whispered wish
A white cloud drifting
A cool wave rushing

Morgan Johnstone, Grade 8
Roosevelt Middle School of the Arts, WI

Your Heart

Love is like a candle.
It can shine bright like the sun,
Or can be put out in seconds.
Why is love so confusing?

One minute you're happy
The next you are sad
Or furious
Or scared.

Love is strange.
It can break your heart,
Or make your heart
Ten times the size.

Love is wonderful.
Love is full of hugs and kisses.
Love is trusting someone
With your heart.

Marissa LeVasseur, Grade 7
Nellie B Chisholm Middle School, MI

Spring

The season of rebirth and growth,
Plants and animals shed their coats.
Flowers begin their budding,
And birds begin their calling.
Waters break their icy shell,
Waves rippling to and fro!
These are the exquisite signs of spring,
The time when the end is about to begin.

Meaghen Newman, Grade 9
Providence Academy, MN

Christmas

When a kid hears the word, Christmas, they start grinning ear to ear.
Christmas is a kid's favorite holiday.
It is five A.M. and kids are jumping on their parents to wake up.
Parents everywhere are yawning
Every kid is wondering what Santa has left for them
Creak! Rip! are some of the sounds that are heard on Christmas.
"Wow!" "It's just what I wanted!" is what is said on Christmas.
While kids are playing and putting what they got together,
their parents are trying to get some more sleep.
After hours of playing with new toys, it is time for Christmas dinner.
Turkey, ham, mashed potatoes, gravy, green beans, and pie are served.
Presents are given laughs, smiles, acknowledgments, talking,
and children playing all happen on Christmas.
When we think of this holiday, we think about Santa Claus and gifts.
The true meaning of Christmas is Jesus being born.
It is also the time of giving,
Not just receiving, but giving.
This is the true meaning of Christmas.

Mina Spryszak, Grade 7
Gesu Catholic School, MI

Outstanding, Ominous Orange

Orange is the rustling of leaves and round carving pumpkins.
Orange is comforting like a blanket.
Orange is the taste of delicious oranges.
A burning bonfire and a
Beautiful tiger lily smells orange.
Halloween makes me feel orange.
Orange is the sound of booming fireworks and crackling campfire.
Orange is a pumpkin patch and an autumn harvest and a walk in the woods.
Orange is my favorite color out of a Crayola Crayon box.
Drinking hot cocoa on a cool fall afternoon is orange.
Orange is calm and mellow.
Orange is a sunrise in the morning and a sunset at night.

Briana Henley, Grade 8
Menominee Jr High School, MI

Useless Ideas

I stare blankly at the solid piece of paper that was once a broad tree.
With its leaves falling slowly to the ground.
One by one, each day, until it is stiff, and useless. Cold. Empty.
Animals no longer made homes.
Various fruits and plants stopped growing, and eventually, everyone heard the sound.
The light tap of a crisp blade intersecting with the hollow wood of a tree.
Why, when one is useless, must we abolish it?
Why, when one is aging, must we put it away for years to come?
I think of many whys and ifs, but none of them give me an answer.
My thoughts wander in the dark trails of my mind.
I still don't know what to do with this blank, cold piece of paper, that was once a broad tree.
A happy thought. A wonderful idea, that would soon be useless.

Ashley Beise, Grade 7
Mora High School, MN

The Cold

The sun grows blue
The sky grows dark
The grass grows slow
And the flowers
Die.

My heart grows cold
Have I lost control
Like a tiger in the snow
As my parent fight
I grow cold

My tear falls down
As my heart grows cold
You might see the perfect family
But under that is me
Growing cold as frozen snow.

My mind goes numb
As my heart freezes
Lying there
On the pitch black
Cold floor.

Lionel Peralta Jr., Grade 7
Franklin Middle School, MN

Little Girl

I started in your womb
Your little baby girl
To teach and hug
To love and scold
To make a part of your world

And then I changed
No need for help
No need for you at night
No more hugs, no more love
I'm not your little girl

And now I'm here
Not fully grown
But growing up each day
I look at you
And all I see
Is the girl I want to be

So you should know
That though I've changed
And may not have the same needs
Through good and bad, thick and thin
I'm still your little girl.

Emily Stolz, Grade 9
Eden Prairie Sr High School, MN

Home of the Fencers

The strips.
Rough unforgiving pieces of metal
line up in neat rows.
Readying for battle.

The warriors.
Masked faces clad in white
size up their opponents.
Probing for weakness.

The odor.
Pungent smells of effort
permeate every molecule of air.
Hanging heavy over the arena.

The sound.
Harsh clashes of blades
echo loudly in the open space.
Ringing sharp as bells.

The bout.
Intense battle of wills
search for advantage.
Seeking sly touches.

Solomon Polansky, Grade 9
The Blake School, MN

Late

After school in the lobby,
there are five.
They laugh together,
they play together,
but one by one,
they say goodbye
leaving a sickening, hopeless feeling
in their wake.
5, 4, 3, 2…

1

You have been forgotten,
your ride isn't coming.
Outside, the wind tears at your face
as you stare helplessly at the road
for a sign
and the seconds, minutes, hours tick by.
2 o'clock, 3 o'clock, 4 o'clock, 4 thirty,
5

Your ride is late.
You are alone.

Mason Cothran, Grade 8
Hartland Middle School at Ore Creek, MI

The Wolves

The wolves strike again
running through the leaves at
night, as their black and white
fur moves slowly in the wind. The
wolf pack dies slowly as many
days go on, at night each and every
wolf keeps each other warm and
cozy. The train is near as the
wolves chase after it, people wave
from the frosted windows.
All the howls each and every
night, they say hello and they
say goodbye. The wolves would
hunt their food and find lakes or
rivers to drink out of. They try
their hardest to live.

Sasha Chapman, Grade 7
Perry Middle School, MI

Love in Nature

A leaf falls for gravity,
Slowly but surely.
A leaf comes in different shapes,
Depending on the tree.
A leaf changes color,
For the autumn season.
A leaf gets blown away,
By the howling wind.
A leaf lies on the ground and dies,
When they leave their branch.
A leaf loses its color,
As the seasons go 'round.
A leaf gets stepped on,
When people don't watch out.
Nobody cares about leaves,
Until they're pretty in autumn.

Jessi Christopherson, Grade 9
Lincoln Jr/Sr High School, WI

Snowfall

The wind howled
And snowflakes soon followed.

The snowflakes danced all the way down
As they gently fell to the ground

The snow was soon two feet deep.
So the animals soon went to sleep.

Outside was so cold and dark.
It was even freezing the tree bark.

When the sun was in sight
We could see it had been a very cold night.

Karly Thomas, Grade 7
Nellie B Chisholm Middle School, MI

The Many Places We Go
The many places we go,
Here, there
Everywhere we go, or you,
May go to
Antarctica to see all the snow.
No one wants to go to school, but
You may go to
Prague, which is a large interesting city.
London, Paris, Rome, or anywhere!
And there are so many more to name like,
Constantinople or Madrid
Even Washington D.C. There are
So many different places
We can go, but not
Every person will travel to
Greenwich or Chicago, but just remember,
On the way, remember to have fun.
Michaela Postma, Grade 8
Round Lake High School, MN

6 A.M. Don't Come
It's 10:30 p.m.
Dreading the 5:30 a.m. that will be coming
Buzzing goes the clock

It's time to get up
I don't want to go to volleyball
Get there at 5:30 a.m.

Doors don't open wait 'til 6:20 a.m.
Doors finally opened
Wednesdays now I dislike you
Because of you I have to
Run a lot because we lost

I don't like to lose
It makes me feel sad inside
Because we run a lot
Kennice Anderson, Grade 9
Lenawee Christian School, MI

Such Love
I know not what to say
For all words have failed me
The immensity of the Sacrifice
For an undeserving wretch as I
On that dark dismal day
All of heaven was in awe
No mind will ever understand
The amazing love that was
Now whenever I fail
I feel so undeserving
But He still paid my price
Such amazing love!
Jonathan Logan, Grade 8
Ruth Murdoch Elementary School, MI

A Thousand Words
If a picture is worth a thousand words,
Then what about the original?
Do they vanish?
Do they go and hide away?
Or do they "fall off the edge of the world?"
If a picture is worth a thousand words,
Then the original is worth more.
They show what the picture can't.
They are what the picture will never be.
And if they disappeared,
People will care.
Unlike the picture,
The original can change.
They can grow.
And they can dream.
If a picture is worth a thousand words,
Then you can tell them to the original.
Karly Richardson, Grade 8
Dakota Meadows Middle School, MN

Chiller
Standing in the bitter cold
With knowledge that's not yours to hold
Rippling like the midnight sea
Twisting, turning, calling me
Storm clouds brew with a terrible rage
While lightning strikes and rattles the cage
Of the one who waits, seeking the storm
And then through darkness, light is born

Now come with me and close your eyes
The moon still shines 'til morning's rise
Dancing past the skeletal grins
A shadow with a darkness within
There's an eerie melody no one can hear
By the old oak tree there's nothing to fear
So as life slips away lay down your head
As you sing to the ballad of the dead
Skyler Braun, Grade 8
Perry Middle School, MI

Butterball
Butterball is a dog. She eats and eats.
When I take her for a walk
She pulls and yanks.

She barks and tries to pull
Fur out of our rabbit.
See if you can guess what type of dog she is.

She has a little bit of
Everything in her, and
That is why I love Butterball, the fattest dog
I have ever seen.
Alisha Cooper, Grade 7
Round Lake High School, MN

The Wind-Up
Standing straight as a tree
I kick my knee.
I step toward the plate
With the ball feeling like a weight.
I release.
The ball curves
Then swerves
Then reaches the plate.
Strike one.
I see the sign and shake my head,
The next one comes,
A fast ball.
I throw,
It zooms like a harpoon
Right past the batter
And hits the catcher's mitt.
It sounds like a sonic boom,
Strike two.
The last pitch comes,
A slider into his mitt,
Strike three he's out.
Michael Gassen, Grade 7
Our Lady Star of the Sea School, MI

The Mysterious Boy
Who is this boy?
Nobody knows his name.
We know something happened
That now he will never be the same.
This boy is near,
But you will never know that he was here.
There's a story behind this boy
That nobody knows
But this story doesn't bring him joy.
He is very mysterious
He hides in the shadows
He makes us all delirious.
He's very shy but it is told
That he will never die.
He seems very sad
As we can see
But also seems very mad.
One day we will find out
Who he is.
Just never doubt
Who this boy may be.
Isabela Cherry, Grade 8
Round Lake High School, MN

Guitar
Pluck its string
Send sound through the air
Beautiful music
Filled with love or hate.
Riley Williams, Grade 7
Scranton Middle School, MI

From You

Wait…that's dead and gone
a lasting friendship
from both of us
But really, all I want
all you want is unbreakable promises
from me
all you want is forever
from me
all you want is love
from me
oh that's easy to see
from me, what do you need?
All I want is unbreakable promises
from you
all I want is forever
from you
all I want is love
from you…
Danielle Russ, Grade 8
Perry Middle School, MI

Heartache

I came to school not knowing
Tears filled the halls and kept going.
Faces red, and eyes so wet
People's hearts filled with regret.
Wishing they could say goodbye
I didn't realize I would cry…
But after I remember the good times,
I feel the tears well up in my eyes.
Oh Nyree, so kind, so sweet.
In my gut I feel defeat.
I know I didn't know you well,
But still, even I could tell.
A person like you is as good as they get.
So maybe we shouldn't feel regret.
Because, even though you've left.
You're in God's arms — he's saying, it's ok
You're where we'll all end up some day.
In heaven. We'll miss you Nyree.
Hannah Hudgens, Grade 7
East Rockford Middle School, MI

Somewhere

Somewhere on a road up high
A place to be free, a place to fly
Somewhere in the sky to soar
A place of cotton clouds, and more
A place for many beautiful things
Somewhere to discover my wings
Where God makes his creations
Things here need no renovations
Somewhere full of joy and love
A place your life's gate is closed by a dove
Lydia Mendel, Grade 8
Perry Middle School, MI

I'm Not

I'm not wasting away,
I'm simply losing weight.
I'm not dying a little day by day,
I'm just realizing my fate.
My heart isn't weeping,
It has to concentrate on beating.
My skin isn't ripping,
It's just not smooth.
I'm not screaming,
Because I know I'm not allowed.
I'm not dreaming,
Because I've forgotten how.
I'm not purging,
Because I know it's bad.
I'm not telling the truth,
Because I didn't want to make you sad.
Kaitlyn Armstrong, Grade 8
Galesburg-Augusta Middle School, MI

Thanksgiving List

The wonderful smell of
Fried chicken, macaroni and cheese,
And that sweet potato pie.
Hearing the big family
All together again as one.
Tasting the peach cobbler,
7-Up cake
Sweet, tasty pie,
And that gigantic juicy turkey.
Feeling all the wonderful
Ingredients, and
Playing with the mixer.
Seeing all the delicious
Food on the table
From left to right,
Beginning to end.
Asia Dunford, Grade 7
St Clare of Montefalco School, MI

Winter Is Coming

Winter is coming,
it comes every year.
The fragile flakes fall,
and bring everyone cheer.

Winter is coming,
can't you tell from the chill.
From the breeze outside,
you start to feel ill.

Winter is coming,
put up the lights.
Hang up the stockings,
and try to be nice.
Lauren Goralczyk, Grade 7
Abbott Middle School, MI

Northern Pack

They walk through the woods
Quiet and still.
Playing with the ones around them
Biting and jumping with one another.

They walk on, two and four
They are a pack and a family.
Never knowing when it's time to change
But when they do they are in pain.

They want to love
But never can.
They are very lonely
As lonely as a dark room is black.

They walk through the woods
Quiet and still
Howling at the moon
Never knowing what could be.
Jasmine Madole, Grade 7
Nellie B Chisholm Middle School, MI

Wild Horse

Jane is a wild horse.
She lives alone,
On a mystical island.
There, she neighs a soft tone.

Jane loves to gallop.
She races with the wind,
To a place far beyond,
Which makes her determined.

Jane is as a tall as an oak tree.
Her body burns like fire.
When she feels sad,
Her hair turns sapphire.

When the sun goes down,
There are no howls or screams,
Just Jane being peaceful
In her own selfless dreams.
Paige Klein, Grade 7
Nellie B Chisholm Middle School, MI

Lunchroom

The lunch is a party
Too many people to count
It is a break from work and tests
The lunch is a store
Too much stuff to choose from
Then you hear the scream of the bell
And the party's over
Lunchroom
Ty Dalton, Grade 7
East Rockford Middle School, MI

Oranges

I'm so juicy
So round
And so orange.
So how am I still sitting here?
I cure sick people
I provide vitamin C.
So how am I still sitting here?
Can't you see?
I sit in a bowl
On a counter top.
I'm a favorite fruit.
But I wait
And I wait
I just wait to get eaten.

Jerry Verhagen, Grade 7
Lincoln Jr/Sr High School, WI

Books for Me

Books are fun to read,
And many people have agreed.
A book's title can start from A to Z.
You'll have to open it up and see.

The characters can be weak or strong.
Some books are short, and some are long.
Books should be made to perfection,
And they can show much affection.

Every book has a subject,
And it may even have a suspect.
I open up a book and see,
If it's the right one for me.

Lindsay Lesha, Grade 7
Our Lady Star of the Sea School, MI

And Then

Life was great
but something was missing,
so I kept on fishing.
Fishing for that missing piece,
I came up with nothing.
I knew I was missing something.

My friends tried to help,
but it was no use.
I couldn't find the right excuse.
I didn't give up,
though I wanted to.
I kept searching, clue by clue.
And then…there was you.

Brittany Barnhart, Grade 8
Perry Middle School, MI

Sorrow

It follows me around
And can make me sad at times
Its feeling is so real
I could stare it eye to eye
Its weight is on my shoulders
It gets heavier as I go
So I start to trip and tumble
Over my feet and toes
Its powers overwhelming
I can't take another night
So I let it pull me down
And it all fades to white
I wake up just in time
In a pit of evil black
I see a speck of light
And know there is no turning back
I crawl through the crack
Shaken up with fright
But as long as there is no black
My decision's always right

Logan Warfle, Grade 7
Perry Middle School, MI

Blue

The sky is blue,
the water is too,
blue is a feeling,
inside of you,
when you have that feeling,
like a sad little clown,
then you have the blues,
and you're feeling down,
but it is also,
so much more,
it's also the cold,
when you walk outdoors,
like the winter mornings,
they are blue,
and the jeans you just got,
that match your new shoes,
the winter haze,
and the ocean's flow,
but also your shadow,
in the snow.

Brianna Bentley, Grade 7
Perry Middle School, MI

Shooting Star

All of a sudden there was a bright light
Then in a flash it had gone out of sight
As it shot across the sky
I began to wonder why
We can't see these more often
As the dusk light starts to soften

Holly Raby, Grade 8
Our Shepherd Lutheran School, MI

About You

The sky is blue,
just like your eyes in the sunlight.
The sun is golden,
just like your hair in the moonlight.
Blood is for my heart,
that fills up when I see you.
When you smile, I smile.
When you laugh, I giggle.
You're tearing us apart,
pretending like it's all a joke.
I don't care what you think,
all I think about is
one day you'll come up to me
and say 3 words:
I LOVE YOU!

Almerisa Dzananovic, Grade 7
Pleasant View School, MI

You Are with Me

"Grief is part of life."
Last line I heard from you.
A line that must last a lifetime,
forgotten in a few.

Tears will fill my eyes.
But no one will mind.
All too busy trying to be strong.

For years you'll be on my mind.
Never feeling whole.
Images fill my memory of,
that last line you spoke to me.

"Grief is part of life."

Sara Cooper, Grade 7
Boulan Park Middle School, MI

True Friends

True friends you can't live without them
They don't condemn
Whether you're wrong or right
True friends are not uptight
True friends last for life
Fake friends make you sigh
They are nice one day and mean the next
It makes you feel perplexed
True friends laugh even at your lame jokes
They never provoke
True friends are cheerful givers
They aren't yappers
A true friend makes you happy
They try not to make you angry
True friends can't survive without them

Chiyame Elems, Grade 7
Ruth Murdoch Elementary School, MI

My Symbol of Joy

When you get to the line,
And the gun goes off,
You are wondering why you are doing this.

To pass time,
You meet people,
And tell them good luck.

Your fans, cheering and cheering,
Keep you going faster and harder.

Every hill you move your arms faster,
Just as coach told you.

You move faster and pass,
Pass and pass, keep moving up on the line.

You speed even more,
Finally over the finish line,
You think to yourself, wow that wasn't that hard.

With fans, cheers, pride, struggles, and desires you see joy,
You feel good about what you just accomplished,
Just doing it once makes you feel great.

Just follow what you enjoy,
Which for me is cross-country.

Kandi Shramek, Grade 9
Lincoln Jr/Sr High School, WI

Stand in the Rain

She stands in the rain
With her tears running down her face
She wants to give up and fall down
She's had enough of this cruel world

No matter how hard she tries
She can't get the thoughts out of her head
Her fears keep whispering
"You're not good enough"

She stands in the rain
She's at the edge of the road
Wanting to end things there and now
When suddenly she hears a voice in her heart

And it says…
"Don't do this, you're not alone.
I'm always with you.
I love you just the way you are.
You ARE good enough"

Hearing this, she took a deep breath,
Wiped away her tears, and walked away.

Molly Conden, Grade 8
Unionville-Sebewaing High School, MI

Love

The way one looks at another, with a sparkle in their eyes
The way one brings their little cousin up and down the stairs
At least twenty times

The way one stays with their sick little sister
Instead of hanging out with friends
The way one brushes their little kitty's fur
Even though she tends to bite

The way he would do anything for her
Though she wouldn't do the same
The way you chased after me
The way our lips met in the rain

Love
The crazy things it makes us do
Though all is worthwhile
I love you

Brenna Buckwald, Grade 8
Lakeshore Middle School, MI

Falling to the Ground

As the white snowflakes falls to the ground,
The ice skaters on the lake spins around and around.
They drift down in a shiftless way,
I could stare at them for days and days.
I gingerly walked over to the fireplace,
And warmed my hands over the firebrand.
Outside, everything is frozen and still,
All this white is giving me the chills.
The vestiges of grass is long gone,
But I see the footprints of a young fawn.
The heedless placement of the snow,
Has cast everything in a soft white glow.
As the white snowflakes falls to the ground,
Covering everything without a sound.

Hongying Jiang, Grade 7
Boulan Park Middle School, MI

Forest

The leaves gossip among one another
They flutter and fly in the air.

The brook will whirl and twirl
They run fast and vast.

The trees' branches wilt in sorrow
They mourn and hope that the tree will live again.

The rocks inch and shift
The rocks click and clack.

The wild flowers wilt and tilt
They die of thirst.

Liam Connolly, Grade 7
Nellie B Chisholm Middle School, MI

Blossom

Flowers bloom, and trees blossom,
yet I feel life has stopped.
Whispered arguments, and evil glares,
are shared as my tears fall.
I watch from the window as he leaves,
boxes in his hands.
Mother tries to comfort me,
but it is not the same without him here.
Furniture in the back,
we move to the new house.
A new school, new friends and a new start,
but it is no use, I'm still broken.
More boxes,
lead to another house.
Friends I make,
slowly start to heal me.
For the first time in three years,
I'm happy.
Flowers blossom, and trees bloom,
and life has finally begun again.

Samantha Bica, Grade 9
Dakota Ninth Grade Center, MI

Jazzy

I am only twenty-one,
yet the seizures have begun.
It started out as simple colic,
but soon turned chaotic.
I hear them say tumor,
and my owner gets glummer.
It has gotten hard to eat,
and I keep stumbling my feet.
They say they don't know how long,
but I have to stay strong.
Soon is my time to go,
but I will not be sad though.
Again I will see Tony,
and all the other ponies.
I will be in no more pain,
after in the hole I am lain.
Please don't cry for me,
for I will be as healthy as can be.
The angels will sing their song,
and then and only then will I go along.

Halla Kitsmiller, Grade 9
Montgomery-Lonsdale High School, MN

Santa's Sleigh

Santa's sleigh sails silently
So close to the sky
All around the world in one night
Never stopping for too long
To the tips of the world
And all again after another Christmas Eve

Will Darling, Grade 7
East Rockford Middle School, MI

I Am

I am a crazy girl who loves music.
I wonder what it feels like to perform in front of millions.
I hear my favorite songs in my head.
I see the band performing in my head.
I want to be performing with them.
I am a crazy girl who loves music.

I pretend that I am famous.
I feel the excitement.
I touch my pen as I jot down an idea for a story.
I worry about the changes in life.
I cry when reading a sad book.
I am a crazy girl who loves music.

I understand that it's not possible to make everyone happy, but I can try.
I say that if you want something bad enough you can do it.
I dream about going to Oxford University.
I try to do my best in everything.
I hope that one day everyone will be reading a book that I wrote.
I am a crazy girl who loves music.

Isabel Max, Grade 8
St Clare of Montefalco School, MI

Amazing Love

A relationship is a beautiful sunrise in the morn and
A mountain of light setting at night
It's a love so pure and kind that you can't break
Relationships are butterflies emerging from their chrysalis in fall
A relationship is a new experience waiting to happen
It is one amazing love that everyone can relate to
Some are lost but others remain
Like a missing dog may be gone forever or return home again someday
Relationships are rain falling in perfect harmony on a metal roof top
Making its own beauty
A relationship is a beautiful sunrise in the morn and
A mountain of light setting at night

Amanda Strand, Grade 8
Cedar Grove-Belgium Middle School, WI

Remember

I listen to the wind screaming as it did once a long time ago.
I hear the soft notes of my music box.
I feel as a young kid.
Remember.
Remember the house, the yard, the dogs, the love.
I am almost there again.
The pain and the hatred fill my mind.
The hatred engulfs my heart like the flames that consumed my home.
I fall into rage as I remember
    the house is gone
        the dog is dead
            and the cold traces of pain and sadness replace the anger.

Nadia Foster, Grade 7
Pleasant View School, MI

Poetic Symphony

Hands raise,
Then move quickly through the air,
One rising and lowering,
The other tracing invisible patterns in the air,
A hand shoots out,
Palm up, Pointing at me,
It's the moment I've been waiting for,
My hand explores the neck,
Precisely striking points,
My bow, Working completely in synchronization with my hand,
Slamming horse hair sends dust into the air,
The sweet smell of rosin in the airs,
The resulting friction,
Brings forth a beautiful melody,
My arm, Swinging gracefully back and forth,
Slowly,
Different pressure brings forth different tones,
Different sounds,
A quick flick of the wrist,
A soft vibrato,
The heartbeat of the music.

Justin Regina, Grade 9
New Buffalo Sr High School, MI

Fall

Fall is beautiful,
with all the wonderful colors.
Leaves go from green to yellow,
yellow to red,
red to brown.
People with rakes raking away.
Jumping in leaf piles all day.
Smell of delicious dinners for Thanksgiving.
Crackling of leaves stepped on.
Windy wind blowing leaves.
Zippers on coats zipping away the cold.
Screaming of kids playing every minute.
Warm heated houses,
people with blankets warming up.
All I can say if fall is beautiful!

Kelsee Ostrander, Grade 7
Perry Middle School, MI

Garlic Green Gum

Green is the long tall grass, blowing leaves and being happy.
Green is the bursting flavor of green beans.
Fresh cut grass and warm apple pie smell green.
Delicious shamrock shakes make me feel green.
Green is the sound of bursting fireworks and trees whistling.
Green is the green meadow, beautiful woods, and a clover field.
The cheering of a Packer game is green.
St. Patrick's Day is also green.
Green is the exploding flavor of green peppers.
Green is the color of life and the blooming flowers.

Rachel Eickmeyer, Grade 7
Menominee Jr High School, MI

My Passion

Silky, smooth keys gracing my fingers.
Music flying out of the piano, infusing me with joy.
Butterflies gone replaced with confidence.

The faint scent of lemon
From freshly polished wood
Tingles my nose.

My foggy brain straining to remember the notes,
But in the end not needing to,
As the music takes me over.

My emotions, cascading from my fingertips,
Into the piano and tumbling out into the silent air.

I sense eyes on the back of my neck.
The hairs standing up as I shudder,
A chill suddenly filling me.

My tensed muscles soften, realizing they are here to
Hear me play, hear my music, hear my passion.

Ailsa Bentley, Grade 7
Detroit Country Day Middle School, MI

Love and Hate

If people were born to LOVE,
we would be shaped like hearts…but we aren't.
If people were born to HATE,
we would work for the devil…but we don't.
People are people.
We laugh, we cry,
we LOVE, we HATE,
and we make memories!
That is just the way God wants it to be.
If we didn't have those things,
the memories, the laughs, your first kiss, the LOVE, the HATE,
then people wouldn't be people!
Without all of those things, the world would crumble.
Nothing would matter anymore.
The world revolves around LOVE and HATE!

Rylee Thomas, Grade 7
Corunna Middle School, MI

True Love Found in Blue

Cinderella never loved,
Wishing on a star above,
Hoping true love would come,
Waiting for the right gentlemen,
Waiting for a love so true in her dress so very blue,
In the minute she saw his face,
Her beating heart started to race,
She knew she found her true love then and there.
She knew she found someone who cared.

Shania Murphy, Grade 8
Round Lake High School, MN

Bananas

Mysteriously
They stand inside their cozy coat
Oval is their shape
Their yellow jacket
Is one of a few colors
Brown green and yellow
They wiggle around
As you open the peel and
Grab a hold of them
Before you know it
It slips away from your grip
And falls to the floor
Astonished as
You see it rolling in joy
With a yellow blur
When all you can do
Is stand there and think to yourself
That's one funky dude
Chris Drewry, Grade 9
Lenawee Christian School, MI

Paradise

Walking off the plane to see
Where all the birds and trees are free
Everywhere you look is green
Virtually not touched or seen
Somewhere that is so precise
Hawaii is my paradise

Look out at the vast blue sea
I see a surfer wave at me
And while on the sand I lie
I gaze up at the bright blue sky
I slowly sip a coconut
Sad the trip is over but…

I find we're going the next year
Sad to leave but glad to hear
The fantastic news of returning there
That's the story of my somewhere
Charlie Szur, Grade 8
Perry Middle School, MI

Summer Flowers

Flowers, flowers in the summer,
Only last a couple hours.
Flowers flourish and flair,
In the new summer air.
Midsummer, midsummer,
Has a sprinkle of latecomers.
No more flourish and no more flair,
Sadly no more summer air.
No more flowers,
Leave us with Debbie Downers.
Julia Sniezek, Grade 7
Our Lady Star of the Sea School, MI

Cupcakes

Cupcakes are fun
Cupcakes are yummy
Once you eat one
You'll want more in your tummy
You licked the frosting
You ate the breading
Now you realize
Where it's heading
The cupcake is gone,
But that is all right
There is another cupcake
In your sight
Warm and whipped
With chocolate swirl
You look and think
"Oh Mother of Pearl"
It's the last one all alone
Oh Look
An Ice Cream Cone
Taylor Goldapske, Grade 7
Woodworth Jr High School, WI

Choices

The choices we make
in each passing day,
all are important,
in their own unique way.

The choices we make
they're there to remind us,
when we look in the mirror,
how to refine us.

The choices we make
they paint our whole story,
and how they define us,
determine our fate or our glory.

The choices we make
sometimes it's hard to choose,
the wrong one may be easy,
but with the right one, you'll never lose.
Paul Cataldi, Grade 7
Our Lady Star of the Sea School, MI

Basketball

Bailey is my name
Basketball is my game
It won't bring me to fame
But you will remember this name
This is my favorite sport
Because it's on a court
Running up and down
'Til I get the rebound
Bailey Conner, Grade 7
Riverdale Elementary & Middle School, WI

Swaying Off

High, staying wide
Awake.
Failing to repay
The due that life wants you to supply.
    Big,
        Bad,
            Bugging
Noise
Within your ears
Hitting
Upon you like drums
    Slightly,
        Slipping,
            Slowly
Past your mind
Through your fingers
    Deep,
        Doubtful,
            Darkening
Beats
Within your flexible life's story.
Nahal Javan, Grade 8
Marcy Open Elementary School, MN

Seasons

In January, days are short and cold,
Snowflakes fall, snow piles grow tall,
    Snowmen are built
    And hot cocoa is spilt.
        But, by May,
The spring air melts, winter away,
    The leaves grow,
    The grass is mowed,
The children play in the mist of the day,
Then they shout, for school is out,
And the world around us turns green
    The happy kids swim
    And hang on the limbs
    Of the tall, majestic trees,
Until the crisp fall air, comes our way
    And all of summer fades away.
The leaves turn gold, the flowers fold
    As fall gives way
    To the cold short days,
    And the cycle starts again
Mackenzie Simon, Grade 7
Our Lady Star of the Sea School, MI

Shadows

The sun is shining
The shadows are underfoot
But soon things will change
Now shadows are long and thin
And soon they will be all gone
Sean Bacon, Grade 8
Our Shepherd Lutheran School, MI

Shield Your Mind

Let the light
Shine through.
Even
When you are afraid,
Let the love
Settle in you heart.
Even,
If it is not pure,
Shield your mind
From the storm.
For it will crush your soul,
But do not be afraid
Of what is you.
For you are,
The center of the universe.
Your universe,
Our universe.

Abigail Duerkop, Grade 7
Valley View Middle School, MN

Summer Days

The sun is shining in the sky,
watching blue birds passing by.

Splish, splash in the pool,
having fun and staying cool.

Going out for ice cream tonight,
it's summer and it is still light.

Flip flops stomping on the ground,
ah, what a beautiful sound.

We are going to this year's fair,
cotton candy scent is in the air.

I'm really sad today is over,
but tonight I'm going to a sleep over!

Lora Dobbs, Grade 8
Our Lady Star of the Sea School, MI

Trapped

Trapped in a box
that has been pushed off the world
and fallen into space.
No one looking for the girl who can't speak.
Every hour
waking with a terrifying scream.
Opening the box
only to be pushed back down
and thrown off the world again.
Searching for the moment I can get out.
Air is almost gone
and I can't breathe.

Jasmine Helgemo, Grade 7
Pleasant View School, MI

Taz

It's the silly things in life
That when they are gone
They cause you pain

Her fur so black, that
In the sun it was a rainbow

She was a gentle giant
So well-behaved and friendly
She would come and
Sniff your face, but
Never give you a sloppy, wet
Doggie kiss

Sometimes she would wander,
And not be home for hours
Until we would find her
And say "Taz, Taz we found you!"

She was a couch potato
But still a loving pet.
She passed away
7 days from my birthday
But another dog like her again
We will never get.

Jack Bell, Grade 7
Abbott Middle School, MI

Scorching Days

A colorful cup
Of snowflakes
and a small spoon.
A shivering brain-freezing snow-cone
sitting by the pool tempting me.

A big pool,
Kids splashing and
Jumping in clear water.
Waves splashing along the sides.

Swimming
Freestyle when
Water is in my face,
Going faster
Kicking legs,
Harder and harder.

Drying off
with the rigid towel
On the edge of the chair.

A colorful soul
Sitting by the water
In another world.

Nyla Outlaw, Grade 7
Detroit Country Day Middle School, MI

Broken Heart (Dead)

I slowly die inside
From all the times I cried
(I've cried for you)
You look at me
With your beautiful eyes
You look right through me
Like I'm invisible
I've always been to you
Nothing can change that
For some reason I knew
I would always be like this to you
I wish you were missing me
Like I'm missing you
But no matter what I do
I'm always dead to you

Renee Garcia, Grade 8
Unionville-Sebewaing High School, MI

Me, Myself, and I

There I was,
All by myself,
Not a soul was around,
Nor a sound,
Just me and I.
And after I saw it,
Twinkling there,
Reflecting the shadows,
Shining light,
Revealing me,
And swallowing me whole,
After the day,
After time,
It was me,
The light inside of me.

Emily Fisher, Grade 8
Perry Middle School, MI

Family

Family always have your back.
Family will always love you back.
Family will always care for you.
No matter what you say or do.
Family will always show respect for you.
You should respect your family too.
Family is more than just one.
And all their love is never done.
Family may be near or far.
But still with you like a star.
Family may be here or there.
Family sometimes can be anywhere.
Family may not always be near.
But some family members are always here.
That's what makes a family so dear.

Antonio Green, Grade 7
Gesu Catholic School, MI

After

After
she left me
After
you were all I had
After
you were all I needed
After
I found out you were leaving
After
then you left me too
After
I missed you
After
you left me I didn't want you.

Kalin Layman, Grade 8
Perry Middle School, MI

Ice Cream Mountains

Mountains of ice cream,
Piled so high.
I can't resist,
I want it now.
The mountains are so high,
It fills my belly.
I'll wait for tomorrow,
to have some more.
When I piled the ice cream,
I put a cherry on top.
To make it complete,
I pour some chocolate on.

Amanda O'Neill, Grade 7
Lincoln Jr/Sr High School, WI

Abandoned

A sad girl sits in a dark room alone
   with it, the moonlight reflected off
   its black and white keys,
A hand reaches out to her, calling
   to her
She finds a friend who suddenly
   vanishes into thin air
Once more she's alone in a
   dark room
She sits down and starts to play
   her song,
The song of her heart.

Brooke Brandt, Grade 8
Corunna Middle School, MI

Snow

Slippery silver snow falling from the sky
Soft silky snow falling everywhere
Snow is in my sight all around me
No two snowflakes are alike

Sophia Leimgruber, Grade 7
East Rockford Middle School, MI

My Journey Through and Farewell to Gesu

Kindergarten with Mrs. Montbriand was so innocent and sweet
First grade with Mrs. Piotrowski, her singing voice couldn't be beat
Second grade announces Ms. Schick on the first day
Oh how I remember things had to be her way
Third grade was different and an adventure with Ms. Doyle
She adopted little Danny and we all were guilty of his spoil
Fourth grade we started with Ms. Balsam
But halfway through she got married and became Mrs. Beaudry
Fifth grade we were introduced to Mrs. Ball
"Calm your spirit" was her motto and she insisted on the Christlike way
Sixth grade Mrs. Florence was the newbie on the block
We didn't know how to take her but in the end she rocked
Seventh grade presented Ms. Davison and we had to grow up quick
Or receive that dreaded phone call or e-mail about our devilment
Now I sit in eighth grade with Ms. Kuzniar at the top of the heap
Every day we hear that we need not sow what we don't want our futures to reap
In May 2012 this will be a part of my childhood past
Memories of administration, support staff, and team sports will last
Now all that is left for me to say is Farewell to Gesu
I wish only the best for the class of 2012 and to all of you

Daisha D. Brown, Grade 8
Gesu Catholic School, MI

I Am

I'm a courageous dreamer who loves white flowers and Five Guys Burger Fries.
I wonder how vampires look so good when they can't see their reflection.
I hear sorrowful whispers of my determined ancestors in my left ear.
I want to dry their tears and let them free.
I am a courageous dreamer who loves white flowers and Five Guys Burger Fries.

I pretend that my life is a chronic movie.
I feel sometimes my feet are too heavy to lift.
I touch the heavens when I feel my words leave my mouth.
I worry that Nicki Minaj's face will get stuck that way.
I'll cry and smile when my life movie is cut short.
I'm a courageous dreamer who loves white flowers and Five Guys Burger Fries.

I understand why my questions are never answered.
I say everyone's got a talent, it just matters how you use it.
I try to ignore the world and its troubles.
I hope they don't chase me down later.
I'm a courageous dreamer who loves white flowers and Five Guys Burger Fries.

Aureaun Rias-Tribble, Grade 8
St Clare of Montefalco School, MI

Let Go

I hold on too long, I don't know how to let go.
Because before I could even know, every one's already letting me go.
Sometimes it's hard not to show, but no one will ever know.
That I don't know how it feels, how it feels to live a day trying not to die
Sometimes all I do is lie, because behind every sigh it's my temperamental cry.
Will you show me how it feels; will you help me back on to my heels?
Show me the way; show me that you'll stay.
Show me that not everyone has to leave; some are here to stay and please me.

Samantha Keiser, Grade 9
Palmyra-Eagle High School, WI

People Call Me What?

People call me nice
People call me mean,
People call me a nerd
But I don't care...
People say I'm funny
Which I think is okay....
People call me dumb
But I know I am not.
People try to hurt my feelings
But I pay them no mind.
Yes, those are the things people call me.

Charles Timms II, Grade 7
Pleasant View School, MI

Santa Claus

S mart
A wesome
N orth Pole
T rue
A round the world

C ool
L oveable
A t Christmas
U nder appreciated
S uper hero

Hunter Zins, Grade 7
Round Lake High School, MN

Thunderstorm

Boom!
goes the lightning
Pshhhhhh!
goes the rain
as it falls very hard
Ahhh!
go the kids
as the lightning gets louder
Zzzzz!
goes the electricity
as it goes out

Trevor Springfield, Grade 7
East Rockford Middle School, MI

Football

On the line about to snap
adrenaline pumping boys ready to crack
it's third and long
a helpless case
except for those ready to race
final play clock ticking down
the crowd is cheering making sound
the pass is off and spirals away
we win the game with seconds to play!

Andrew Bade, Grade 8
St John Vianney Catholic School, MI

Battle Scars

I sat there in a field
underneath an old birch tree.

Sitting there rocking in the wind
telling stories with its battle scars, some old, some new.

It tells a story, an old wise one, with slash marks.
They were created by Indians for their canoes.

It tells stories of the Civil War,
for its trunk is hollow, just big enough for a person.

It tells stories of wild cats,
running, climbing, and scratching its trunk.

The tree has a recent story, for there is a hole,
It came from a stray bullet from a hunter in the woods.

The tree has many scars, each one has a tale,
Some are new, some are old, some are ones only the tree will ever know.

Liz Christensen, Grade 7
Nellie B Chisholm Middle School, MI

Things I'm Thankful For

The wind whistling through the beautiful trees,
The warm embrace within my family,
The look on my nephew's face when he sees me,
When my grandma's dog and my dog lick me, saying, "they love me,"
The smell of my grandma's cake as it comes out of the oven on a Sunday evening,
The warm loving hugs my mother gives every morning before she leaves,
God telling me He loves me,
The kisses I get from my grandma every time she sees me,
The moonlight that glistens through my window every night,
The sun's rays that glisten through my window at dawn,
The birthdays that I get to share with my family every year,
A roof over my head,
A beautiful Christmas celebrating Jesus' birth,
Every second I'm alive,
These are things that I am thankful for and will cherish for the rest of my life.

Tahitia Smith, Grade 7
St Clare of Montefalco School, MI

Outrageous October Orange!

Orange is a vibrant harvest field.
Orange is a warm and colorful autumn.
Orange is the taste of grandma's fresh-baked pumpkin pie.
Pitch black Halloween nights make me feel orange.
Orange is the sound of crunching fall leaves and the chirping of newborn Oriole birds.
Scary Jack-o-Lanterns are orange.
A roaring bon fire is also orange.
Orange is being with family on Halloween.
Orange is scary and bold.
Orange is me.

Hannah Alguire, Grade 8
Menominee Jr High School, MI

Where I'm From

I am from everyday blue jeans from Levis and Carhart.
I am from the country dirt roads out of town where the sun goes down.
I am from corn, sunflowers, and farm fields, the grass, the trees, to the honey bees.
I am from loving and caring, from grandpas and grandmas and moms and dads.
I am from too busy to know from too busy to care.
From "do your best" and "never give up."
I am from say your prayers and trust in God.
I am from the red white and blue and the great melting pot, spaghetti and blueberry cheese cake.
From loving and cancer surviving Oma, and the hard praying grandma who prayed us through many trials.
I am from rolling hills, barb-wire fences, from the tree lined roads that lose their leaves and fade to snow.

Taylor Cummings, Grade 8
Kalkaska Middle School, MI

Your Call

There's a hole inside my soul and each day it's getting cold
So he says he likes staying friends, but this is not how my story ends
Was it because he doesn't think I'm right for him?
If that's the case, I'll make some changes all because I can.
I can soar above the wind, and set everything right;
I'll show him I think about him, both day and night. I wonder, is it because I'm too nice? 'Cause that's the only reason that comes to mind, when I think about this twice. Remember back in seventh grade, when you asked for advice on your problems with her? I listened and answered in your call. If you won't think about me? That's fine, I'll just show you no affection at all, if you won't answer my call.

Rachel Lederer, Grade 8
Nature Hill Intermediate School, WI

Shane

Shane rode down the road and he stopped.
While being ridden, Shane's horse is a train.
Shane was as smooth as a snake when he got off of his horse.
As Shane went into town and his horse was kicking up dust behind him it was waving him back.
Shane glared at the new guy.
The new guy was even too scared to say hi.
In the other room what I heard from the bar was "BING, BANG, POW."
When Shane was fighting he was slippery, sliding, smiling and smart all the time.

Zach Stluka, Grade 8
Wauzeka Steuben School, WI

Swimming

Swimming is a battle.
You take a look at your opponents as you step up to the block.
You see if the girls are gaining on you as you turn at the other end.
Your heart races as you sprint back to the finish.
As your hand plummets into the wall you look up to the board to see that you have won the race.
You return to your team as they congratulate you on your win.
Swimming is a battle.

Hunter Ignasiak, Grade 7
East Rockford Middle School, MI

Thanksgiving

The turkey is a gift from the gods
The chocolate milk is as rich as Bill Gates
Rolls made from the finest baker in town
Sparkling Grape Juice is as beautiful as can be

Ronnie Ducharme, Grade 7
East Rockford Middle School, MI

Life

Live life to the fullest
Never let you down
Always make sure you are prepared for the worst
But think of the best.

Jasmine Williams, Grade 7
Round Lake High School, MN

Kid World

That special moment
I finally understand
Every world's answer.
The disappearance
of Santa.

Like the magic
of the Christmas lights –
An explosion of colors.
Peace,
Love,
All gone.

I'm lost
In a tunnel of confusion.
Desperate.

My heart is dropping tears,
My mind is growing up,
My eyes are opening
As I discover,
That's just the kids' world.

Asya Mazzardo, Grade 8
West Hills Middle School, MI

I Don't Want To

I don't want to
I don't want to clean
I don't want to play
I don't want to draw
I don't want to shower
I don't want to go walking
I don't want to blow up balloons
I don't want to swim
I don't want to ride a horse
I don't want to stop saying I don't want
but for you I'll do all this and more

Rasha Tiba, Grade 7
Star International Academy, MI

Mom

My mom is extraordinary
She is hardworking and special
To me and other people
My mom feeds me and clothes me
She teaches me right from wrong
My mom is always happy
And in a good mood
She is extravagant and loving
And always does a good job
She means what she says
And she says what she means
I love my mom
And she loves me so much

Jaden Isaac, Grade 7
Gesu Catholic School, MI

What It Takes to Live

Survival is a little boy who's alone and scared,
But keeps hoping for someone to show him what love is

Survival is a beaten horse who has a fear of all people,
And learns to trust again

Survival is a frightened man lost in the wilderness trying to find his way home,
But he doesn't give up

Survival is a dangerous road you take that is covered with ice,
But you make it through anyway

Survival is a wounded soldier who saw his friends die,
And he fights on

Survival is a young girl's horse who dies,
But she keeps on riding

Survival is a friend who saves another person's life

Ashley Navis, Grade 8
Cedar Grove-Belgium Middle School, WI

I Am

I am an intelligent girl who is proud of her African-American heritage.
I wonder what my life could've been like if I was born in slavery times.
I hear the cries of a tribe, torn apart by chains.
I see my future and I know it's bright.
I want to be successful and make my ancestors proud.
I am an intelligent girl who is proud of her African-American heritage.
I pretend I'm Harriet Tubman, and I set my people free.
I feel the pride of many generations surge through me.
I touch my heart and feel my connection to God.
I worry that I will fail and not rise to my potential.
I cry when I think of all the trials my people had to go through to get where we are today.
I am an intelligent girl who is proud of her African-American heritage.
I understand that if I learn from the past that I will go far in the future.
I say "Thank you" to God for all of the blessings He's bestowed upon me.
I dream about a hatred-free world, where one can love thy neighbor.
I try to be a living example of a good Christian and fellow human being.
I hope for a brighter tomorrow.
I am an intelligent girl who is proud of her African-American heritage.

Alana Crawford, Grade 8
St Clare of Montefalco School, MI

Gun Smoke

Shane is a black stallion with his stunning clothes and his quick speed.
Joe is as determined as a lion hunting in the Savanna.
The Starretts live in a valley in Wyoming of 1889.
Swish! The tumbleweed sped by.
There was a group of men outside Grafton's store,
Bob could see them, but Shane could only see one person.
Bob can only have fun,
when he is carrying a gun.
Bing, bang, boom! Guns fired in the saloon.

Kylie Jo Zimmerman, Grade 8
Wauzeka Steuben School, WI

A Different City
New York
Big, loud
Killing, singing, running
Car, gun, football, White Lake
Winning, exciting, amazing
Quiet, small
Montague
Josh Weesies, Grade 7
Nellie B Chisholm Middle School, MI

Full Throttle
Snowmobile
Ear-splitting, full tilt,
Jumping, falling, riding,
Tracks, clutch, throttle, brake,
Racing, shifting, turning,
Muddy, speeding
Dirt bike
Zach Van Nett, Grade 7
Nellie B Chisholm Middle School, MI

Fire and Water
Fire
Wood, smoke
Screaming, yelling, running
Plasma, gasoline, clear, cool
Swimming, squirting, splashing
Cold, fun
Water
Shannon Walus, Grade 7
Scranton Middle School, MI

Fall and Spring
Fall
Chilly, end
Changing, dying, shifting
Leaves falling, flowers blooming
Growing, beginning, living
Renew, fresh
Spring
Emily Castillo, Grade 7
Scranton Middle School, MI

Fun Sports
Basketball
Fun, intense
Running, jumping, dunking
Inside, baskets, outside, goals
Kicking, tripping, scoring
Fast, painful
Soccer
Sydney Stine, Grade 7
Nellie B Chisholm Middle School, MI

When the Geese Come Again
The sun sets and orange rays,
Touch and color the darkest corners
The breeze tells me that soon,
Coldness and frost will settle
I shiver in delight
I hear a faint honk in the distance
Glancing up, I see a graceful formation
Perfectly balanced and symmetrical
A V shaped formation of geese against the faint fading rays of the sun
The orange rays reflect off their feathered wings
Creating a spiral of brightness
A cool breeze beckons and they move forward as one
A rhythm of equality and respect
They honk again and go into the wilderness
When the hills are lush and green
Until the frost melts
And warmth replaces the cold
Until next year when the geese come again
Ellen Zhang, Grade 9
Troy High School, MI

Where I'm From
I'm from hard wooden chairs, from Cherry Cola cans and fantasy books.
I am from the reading home.
I am from the cherry blossom, and the sand that kisses the shore.
I am from singing choir and brown hair, from Gayle and Whiting and LaPierre.
I am from loud and busy, from "Sing more" and "Sit still."
I am from the wooden benches and the stake that held the man
that gave his life for us.
I'm from New Hampshire and knights with blazing armor fighting for
a King, zucchini bread and warm cookies on a cool night
that melt on your tongue.
From the loving grandmother with the famous loving
but with a dash of get to it attitude,
and the grandfather who was taken by sickness in sleep when my mama was just a girl.
I am from the long sandy beach
that holds the shells I love to find, long swims in the pool,
and the flashes of the forest passing by
from the seat of a four wheeler that was a bond, between my father and I.
And I couldn't ask for anything more!
Kaitlyn LaPierre, Grade 8
Kalkaska Middle School, MI

Yearning Yonder Yellow
Yellow is a canary, a burning sun, and being loved.
Yellow is the taste of warm butterscotch.
Fresh-squeezed lemons are yellow and fresh-picked daffodils smell yellow.
Covering up with my cozy blanket makes me feel yellow.
Yellow is the sound of leaves crackling and children's laughter.
Yellow as a corn field, a beach on a hot summer day, a basketball court.
Sitting by a roaring bonfire is yellow.
Shooting stars are also yellow.
Yellow is tremendous joy.
Yellow is what I felt when I hugged my grandma.
Mandy Vretenar, Grade 8
Menominee Jr High School, MI

Engulfed with Empty

awoke by the sadness that seems
to engulf me
sleeping with my dreams
as I wake the dreams seem to just
slip away
into an unknown vast
desert
that's full of everything
ever
dreamed by me
the chances of them ever
coming back is a
far empty chance
one never to be
refilled
or fulfilled
empty

Trista BeDen, Grade 8
Perry Middle School, MI

I Lied

I hate you
You constantly ridicule me

I hate you
You never talk to me

I hate you
You never see me

I hate you
You don't care

But I lied
I love you
And I care

Why don't you?

Cynthia Narine, Grade 8
St Louis Park Jr High School, MN

Bullies

Mean
Back stabbers
Hurtful
Cold-blooded
Liars
Disrespectful
Make your life miserable
Cruel
Hurt feelings
Give you pain
Not trustful
Heartless

Chris Nyquist, Grade 7
Abbott Middle School, MI

Rusty Ol' Car

That Rusty Ol' Car
Never broke down on tar
Always got there no matter the speed
And never broke down.

That Rusty Ol' Car
Never cost me a dime
Never broke a part
And never broke down.

That Rusty Ol' Car
Always got me there safely
Never fought back
And never broke down.

That Rusty Ol' Car
Had to leave her
Never forgot her
And never broke down.

Thomas Cash, Grade 9
Lincoln Jr/Sr High School, WI

Through the Snow

Trudging through the snow,
to the ruins of a giant city.
No one knows,
what to expect.

An untrustworthy stranger
wearing a dazzling green dress,
renews hope.
Soft beds, steaming baths,
vast tables filled with food await.

The roads get rockier,
the snow gets crueler.
Beating mercilessly against your face.

Small flickering lights in the distance,
was all it took.
Happiness filling you from head to toe.
The trip has come to an end.

Efe Osagie, Grade 7
Abbott Middle School, MI

Feelings

Joy is the feeling of happiness
Sadness is the feeling of sorrow
Hope is the feeling of luck
Doubt is the feeling of uncertainty
Pity is the feeling of regret
Sympathy is the feeling of compassion
But above all
Love is the feeling of affection

Katherine Diederich, Grade 7
Boulan Park Middle School, MI

Books

In books I've learned…
Of creatures mean
And gleaming swords with blades so keen.
Of hobbits, rings, and other things
From storytellers' yarn and strings.

Of Ptolemy
And other people greater than me.
Of Mark Twain's life,
And Henry the Eighth's first wife.

About granite rock
Even the creature from the loch
Of UFO's
Deer and does

In books I've learned…
About all things.
Literature has given my mind wings.

Corbin Mcconnell, Grade 7
Sault Area Middle School, MI

Changing of Thoughts

Songs of joy and peace
Landscapes with color like none else
Autumn has arrived

In the morn' I wake
To the scent of changing leaves
And the crisp fall breeze

I step out the door
To feel the dew from the night
Damp between my toes

As I stand alone
A breeze rustles my long hair
Bringing contentment

I think now, of life
Not of the bad or wicked
But of the good times

Abigail Vallie, Grade 9
Lenawee Christian School, MI

The Beautiful Bleeding Pain

Rose
Beautiful, colorful
Blooming, blossoming, sniffing
Gardens, valleys, stem, ground
Bleeding, stabbing, beating
Painful, spiky
Thorn

Mackenzie Bentz, Grade 7
Nellie B Chisholm Middle School, MI

Your Wings of Hope

I fell under. I fell down.
But I got back up,
Because they wouldn't let me lay down,

Not without a fight at least.

I can feel the sadness claw at my spirit.
Bringing me down in utter darkness,
With the silent creeps,
Of its swift feet.

I know they would want me to try,
To be better than this.
To actually show that I made a stand.

I can see them,
The ghosts of their past presence.

Cheering me on,
Begging me to keep walking these long, dreadful miles.
And that there is happiness.

At the end of the cracked lines on this dark road,

I dry the tears, and erase my frown.
I pretend I can hear nothing, not a sound.
And I trudge on.

Searching for a new light, to escape this madness.
Amara Lister, Grade 7
Washington Middle School, WI

Singing

In singing I've learned…
To sing till your death
To wail it out and then take a deep breath
How to sing with emotion
About causing a commotion

In singing I've learned…
To not be afraid
And to stand up on stage
How to let everyone hear the joyous sound
Of me singing nice and proud

In singing I've learned…
That it is okay
To stand out of a crowd some days
How to stand up on stage for people to see
And hope they enjoy my performance with glee

In singing I've learned…
That just one song can make a difference
So listen closely and just enjoy my presence
Michaela Zimmerman, Grade 7
Sault Area Middle School, MI

Art Class

In art class I've learned
How to draw a contour line,
How to draw a flower that looks fine,
How to draw a fire,
And even how to draw a car tire.

How to apply the precise amount of paint,
Before everyone will start to complaint,
How to draw a pumpkin,
Even when it's on a napkin.

How to shade a shading chart,
How to make a work of art,
How to draw a glass jar,
And even how to draw a car.

It doesn't matter if you can't draw a bird's nest,
It just matters that you do your best.
Sharon Ayres, Grade 7
Sault Area Middle School, MI

Christmas

Christmas lights of red and green,
Christmas carols set the scene.

The presents come in different sizes.
The children's faces are full of surprises.

The scent of gingerbread roams the air,
The stockings are hung with such great care.

Christmas trees are all around.
Snowflakes are falling to the ground.

The church is filled with quiet prayer,
Prayers of happiness, not despair.

Christmas is about people coming together,
Family and friends living in the cold weather.
Maddie DesNoyer, Grade 8
Our Lady Star of the Sea School, MI

To Be a Father

To be a father, you must take care of your family.
Being a father doesn't make you manly.

Being a father you are a role model.
You must be strict, but you must also cuddle.

When you're a father, you are the man of the family.
When you leave, you will leave someone in your place.

To be a father, you must take care of your family.
Being a father doesn't make you manly.
Adam Hafner, Grade 7
Our Lady Star of the Sea School, MI

This Boy

There is the boy whose eyes hypnotize me,
Whose voice makes me smile.

There is the boy, who acts too cool to care,
Thinks he's God's Gift, and believes he only deserves the best.

There is this boy, he makes me smile, he makes me laugh.

There is this boy who makes me want to scream,
Pull my hair out in frustration,
He makes me want to yell.

There is this boy who can be selfish,
But he makes me happy.
I shouldn't feel so great around him.

There is this boy,
He doesn't deserve me,
He says it's the other way around.
He doesn't know what he is missing.

There is this boy, who only thinks about himself,
Can be conceited,
Has hypnotizing eyes,
And a voice that makes me smile.

Ally Stavros, Grade 8
Scranton Middle School, MI

King of the Jungle

The tall, tall trees and the waist-thick vines
where leopards sleep and monkeys play.

Where there's no clear path and endless plants
Snakes grow to twenty feet long
and tigers wait for their unfortunate prey.

You'd think that there's only misery,
but if you look hard you can see
tiny cubs, little eggs, baby chimps, and delicate fawns.
They're all part of life, even if
they don't live that long.

There's poisonous fangs,
and leaping lizards,
colorful toucans and
deadly jaws from the rivers' predators.

If you're quiet you can hear
the loud call from the King.
The birds start crying, animals run away,
because if he sees you, the last thing you will see
is his proud mane and deadly jaws
coming down on his prey,
And the lion roars in victory.

Mackenzie Shramek, Grade 9
Lincoln Jr/Sr High School, WI

Arches

Standing high and tall and proud,
Each and every one,
Stretching to its limits,
Under the noon day sun,
Staring upon their massive gapes,
I can clearly see,
A place that gives a view,
Beyond our reality,
As I start the climb to the massive gate above,
I start to dream of what I will see,
From the hole above,
I look on up,
To see the stage,
Where I will stand and see,
The place that will make my dream,
A true reality,
So as I look out through,
The massive eye of stone,
I wonder if I have,
Finally found a home

Maya Turon, Grade 8
Ruth Murdoch Elementary School, MI

Waterfalls

Long and gushing,
All it's doing is rushing.
A pool at the end,
There is no bend.

Mist in the air,
Sometimes they don't dare.
It drops down low,
All it does is flow.

Dive in a splash,
Your life will go before you in a flash.
In order for you to get anywhere you first have to fall,
Most likely everything is just a close call.

The bottom is lined with rocks,
Made up of many stumbling blocks.
You have to work your way around it,
You just can't quit.

Cierra Woof, Grade 9
Lincoln Jr/Sr High School, WI

The Loud and Scary Thunder and Lightning

Thunder
Loud, annoying
Roaring, waiting, poring
Storms, everywhere, electricity, sky
Staring, thinking, screaming
Shiny, blurry
Lightning

Austin Monroe, Grade 7
Nellie B Chisholm Middle School, MI

To the Rescue

Who is your superhero?
Your Guardian Angel?

The one that looks after you
And makes everything ok

The one who is always there
And keeps you safe

The one who gets you through the bad days
And keeps you gleaming through the good ones

The one who helps you in times of need
And keeps your head up

Who is your superhero?
Your Guardian Angel?

Tyler Boyle Hoban, Grade 9
Cannon Falls Sr High School, MN

Halloween Night

Carmel apples ready and dipped,
Pumpkin pancakes just whipped and flipped.
Shaping spooky cookies just like spiders,
Heating up the Halloween cider.
Candy on call,
Soon it will be nightfall.
Jack o lanterns are lit tonight,
So scary and very bright.
Trick or treaters going door to door,
Lining up four by four.
Creepy noises here and there,
A ghostly voice saying, "Enter if you dare!"

Tessa Ulrich, Grade 8
Our Lady Star of the Sea School, MI

The Reality

you're leaving
and soon you'll be gone
you tell me not to cry
and not to worry
but what's the point in saying this
when you don't know the truth

the reality is that now
what happens to you is no longer up to me
and possibly not even you
I want you to prove your points to me
you can do that by coming back from overseas

Emily Martin, Grade 9
Ovid Elsie High School, MI

Love

Everyone falls into it,
someone is meant for everyone.
Love is a strong word,
only say it if you mean it.

I Love You,
The three strongest words you'll ever say.

Whether it's to a friend or more,
It's a word that may be true.
If you love someone,
Tell him, he may think the same.

I Love You,
The three strongest words you'll ever say.

If someone loves you,
You don't have to feel the same.
Love comes from the heart,
Not the brain.

I Love You,
The three strongest words you'll ever say.

Say it only if you mean it,
I Love You...

Kaitlyn Huber, Grade 8
Lincoln Jr/Sr High School, WI

Love Story

She fears she is plain,
Although she's quite vain.
Our friendly little Cole,
Will always be my sweet Cole.

Her cheeks are full of blood-red blush,
For when she sees me she has to rush.
My heart will always be hers,
And I hope hers will be mine.

Her eyes are bluer than the sky,
and in them you can see she's quite shy.
When I see them I think I might faint,
And for her I wish she feels the same.

She's quiet as a mouse,
Even at her house.
We had our first kiss,
I hope it's not our last.

She's pale as the moon,
I hope she'll marry me soon.
When I propose,
I doubt she'll say no.

Kendra Madole, Grade 7
Nellie B Chisholm Middle School, MI

Water and Air

Water
Refreshing, wet
Running, dripping, drinking
Aqua, H_2O, wind, oxygen
Moving, circulating, breathing
Clean, everywhere
Air
Emma Haiser, Grade 7
Scranton Middle School, MI

Be Thankful

Time to appreciate,
Don't be late,
Express your gratitude,
Even for your food,
Be thankful for what you have got,
Whether it is a little or a lot.
Sneha Gorry, Grade 8
Boulan Park Middle School, MI

Erasers

Erasers are like
Mops cleaning up
A pencil mess
They are pink
And very squishy,
Like strawberry Jell-O
Alicia Lamos, Grade 7
East Rockford Middle School, MI

My Locker

My locker hates me
Every time I try to open it,
It messes me up
It hides my math book
And steals my pencils...
My locker hates me
Mary DeBold, Grade 7
East Rockford Middle School, MI

A String

A string, weak and long
All by itself not very strong.
But when you add three, five, or eight
A beautiful tapestry you can make.
See two is better than one
Having more is much more fun.
Jessica Newkirk, Grade 8
Ruth Murdoch Elementary School, MI

Deer

Deer are God's gift
they are peaceful creatures
cute and innocent
Michael Thomas, Grade 7
Perry Middle School, MI

I Won the Spelling Bee

It is not so easy to win the spelling bee.
You get nervous and legs and hands start to shake.
We all sat in a row from smallest to biggest. It is not easy as pie.

But my hands and legs didn't shake. I really wasn't nervous at all.
In fact I was sure I was going to win this. It was easy as pie.

So one by one I start spelling some words.
Few people get out this round. The next few rounds I'm still in.
But now half of the people were gone.

A few more rounds goes by. I'm still in.
There is only five people left, tensions arise the game gets harder.

But not for me. The night before I studied my brains out.
I can still remember the word list. It was kind of crinkled and ruffled.

At last three people left, the people both misspelled palatable
I stepped to the podium already knowing I won,
I carefully spell palatable! There you know it I won.
When I got my award and my prize,
I knew there was a smile and a hug waiting for me at home.
Ryan Victor Joseph, Grade 7
Abbott Middle School, MI

Mr. Stocking

At night I dance around waiting for morning to come
Waiting for one less day till Christmas
Some years the hook they put me on is not the best
My favorite is the reindeer one
Sometimes I get jealous of Mr. Christmas Tree
Always getting presents before me
But that's okay
Because on Christmas Eve Santa comes and fills me with lots of toys
I wait and wait for Christmas morning when little Jimmy and little Susie come down
When Susie pulls me off the hook and looks inside to see what Santa left behind
But then comes the time when my season's over
And down to basement we go
Into the box with Santa and the others
Waiting with one another
To hear the pitter patter of Susie and Jimmy
Coming down the stairs to get us again
Madison M. Nance, Grade 7
East Rockford Middle School, MI

The Beginning of a New Adventure

On a silent, still, sunny day in Wyoming
A boy waits watching the valley around him, it was about midday
The wind blows when a man appears on the road ahead
The boy is playing with a fake gun Bing! Bang! Boom!
The man was coming up the road as fast as a snake striking
He was an alert predator stalking his prey when he came to the house
The family thought he was dangerous but to them he was kind
But there is more to him than meets the eye, this they will find
Alexandra Carter, Grade 8
Wauzeka Steuben School, WI

Sherry's Beauty

Sherry is as pretty as a shining angel,
She's beautiful like the ocean view.
Her love is as strong as a big hard rock,
Her hugs are as powerful as the roaring thunder.

Sherry can be as evil as the devil,
She is perfect like a rose on Valentine's.
Sherry's as old as a picture with dust,
She is built like a hot pocket.

Her sweetness is like soft music to my ears,
She is as cute as a little puppy.
Sherry's heart is as big like a huge panda,
Her eyes are as blue as the sky on a sunny day.

Sherry is as loving as a mother to her newborn,
She is funny like a monkey dancing.
Sherry smells as sweet as strawberries dipped in chocolate,
Her smile is like a gift from God that will not fade.

She is as bright as a twinkling star,
Sherry looks like a pretty princess.
Her hair is as red as an apple,
She walks funny like a dove in clown shoes.

Kelly Jurecki, Grade 7
Nellie B Chisholm Middle School, MI

Words Hurt More Than Sticks and Stones

Looking in the mirror, I wonder
What happened to the time
When I looked there and
I was happy with what I saw?

The word stereotype,
Not only crushes reputations, but the heart.
Because I'm blonde,
I'm stupid.
Because I'm skinny,
I'm anorexic.

Rumors spread like wildfire
Eighth grade girls, the ignition.
Spreading whatever they feel is true.
Breaking the hearts of the victims,
Making us feel lonesome; solitary.
Head down,
Tears rushing down my face,
Leaving the red trail of pain down the side of my cheek.
Wishing I was perfect in the eyes of the "populars."
Nevertheless, I'll never be perfect in their eyes.
I'll never be perfect, but I'll always be myself.

Hanna Wink, Grade 8
West Hills Middle School, MI

A Piece of History

A tiny piece of sterling silver,
Worth nothing to anyone,
Except for me.
A piece of history that holds sentimental value.
That can be passed down for generations.
It was given to my grandmother,
Then my mother,
And now to me,
Then someday to a daughter of my own.
A tiny piece of sterling silver,
That is worn with age.
But holds its young appearance.
Letters of love written on the inside of the band,
Means more than $1,000 to me.
It safely rests upon my tiny finger.
It is like my great-grandmother,
Grandmother, and mother are here with me.
Where ever I go, it will be with me.
A tiny piece of sterling silver,
Worth nothing to anyone,
Except for me.

Ali Stover, Grade 9
Lenawee Christian School, MI

Perseverance

Perseverance can be a big key to success,
It's when you decide whether to go on or not,
It can be any sport, or any game,
Or in school on a test, or a presentation,
It can be standing in front of a plethora of students,
Or the peer pressure you are receiving,
Don't be shy, and don't cry about it,
Because you still have an opportunity to change it,
If you focus, concentrate, and fix in on that what you are doing,
Then you will make it through,
The times you do feel perseverance isn't an option,
If you tolerate perseverance just once,
You may reconsider,
On what it takes to just have,
Perseverance

Noah Huslin, Grade 7
Ruth Murdoch Elementary School, MI

The Amazing Shane

A boy waits watching the valley around him, it was about midday
On a sunny, still, silent day in Wyoming
The wind picks up when a man appears on the road ahead
The boy, Bob, was playing with a fake gun. Bing, Bing, Bang, Boom!
Shane is as fast as lighting doing his work
Bob was staring Shane down like an eagle looking for a fish
Shane was coming up the road as fast as a bobcat

Caitlyn Dable, Grade 8
Wauzeka Steuben School, WI

If It Flies It Dies!

My Dad belongs to a group.
He's told me it's great to be in the loop.
Here's what it is all about.
They send hunting information out.
They say for every season.
There is a reason.
Time for ducks to fly,
And the geese to cry.
When the football game is won between so and so,
Dad and I are off shooting crows.
He says for eating, they're not fit.
It's all right because they're hard to hit.
He's taught me how to gobble, putt, and yelp.
But calling turkeys, I still need his help.
Dad's taken me out west,
Where the hunting is the best.
When the weather is too hot,
We both watch hunting shows…A LOT!
I'm surprised my mom is his wife,
'cause hunting is OUR LIFE!

Aleisha Burns, Grade 9
Lincoln Jr/Sr High School, WI

Better Than Heaven

The only food I need is pizza.
Topped with marinara sauce,
cheese, onions, pepperoni, and sausage.
My senses come alive.
The smell makes my mouth water,
but I can't eat too fast or I'll burn my mouth.
The crunchy crust,
flaky and golden brown.
The melted, golden brown cheese.
I grab a hold of the perfect crust,
and as the pizza arrives at my mouth,
I don't have patience to wait.
The pizza can only sit there silently as I gobble it up.
The sausage and onions make me go back for seconds,
thirds,
fourths,
until I am all filed up.
Once you start eating, you can't stop.
You'll be disappointed when it's gone,
so savor every bit.

Cameron Scholze, Grade 7
Lincoln Jr/Sr High School, WI

Fireworks

Loud and ear-pounding sounds I start to hear
Bright and eye-catching colors begin to appear
The sky used to be dull and bare
But the colorful paintballs invade the air
These loud noises and bright paintballs, children may fear
But just as quickly as they come, they disappear.

Hannah Raby, Grade 8
Our Shepherd Lutheran School, MI

Stupid

Stupid.
Retarded.
Dumb.
Idiotic.

You never know how much those words hurt
Unless they're being used to describe you
At the popular girls' sleep-over
You'll never be invited to.

Who gave them the idea
That it's funny,
Those words.
Or are they weapons?

Why do we
As humans
Have walls
Separating us from each other?
Doesn't that drive us farther apart?
Keep us from becoming better people?

Why must we have feelings
If they hurt us
So badly?

Joanne Wisely, Grade 7
Abbott Middle School, MI

Rushing

Rushing,
Leaves fall as if to say
We're late! We're late!
Painting pictures on the ground of
Yellow, orange, and red
Spinning like ballerinas performing on the theater stage

Rushing,
Snowflakes fall
Covering the paintings left by the leaves,
Just to leave the earth when winter ends.

Rushing,
A stream flows
Free to escape its icy prison,
Leaving no one to wait.

Rushing,
People flood the streets,
Hurrying to fight the crowd
Leaving for the day.

Yet the soil stays,
It does not rush,
To stay forever, and bring us its fruits.

Jessica Stevens, Grade 7
Boulan Park Middle School, MI

For the Survivors

It's hard being a survivor,
When you are the last one,
Still taking a breath,
Fighting to stay on Earth,
For your friends and kin.
It's hard being that only survivor,
When the ones around you,
Seem to be swallowed up,
By the very ground,
Beneath their feet.
It's hard to hold on,
When you feel like it should have been you.
Now you're asking all these questions of why and how,
Why you're still alive,
Why they're gone and you're still here.
You're living in self doubt and self pity,
And pushing away the ones that want to help,
Hurting the ones you love the most.
You were not supposed to leave this world that way,
You were not supposed to leave this world that day...

Kayla Snider, Grade 8
Tomah Middle School, WI

Thanksgiving List

The aroma of familiar smells awakens the children.
Turkey in the oven,
in the early hours of the morning.
Pies, apple, cheery pumpkin, pecan, and sweet potato.
Children awaken to see
the Thanksgiving Day Parade on television.
Mom's in the kitchen rattling the pots and pans.
Turkey and stuffing,
macaroni and cheese,
broccoli casserole.
Dinner's ready!
Mom, Dad, Grandma, sisters and brother, family and friends
all sit down at the table.
Touching one another's hand
in prayer,
giving thanks to God.
Finally
The taste of
a long awaited feast
Provided by our Father above.

Destiny Pitts, Grade 7
St Clare of Montefalco School, MI

Little White Lies

Growing up in small towns,
Will have its ups and its downs.
Rumors are spread,
It seems your life has been ruined,
By a "fair-weather friend" who didn't have a clue.
They tell things about you,
Things you never knew,
But these friends you have, they'll just have to do.
Because growing up in a little square town,
They're all you've got,
Well, that's what you thought.
They all try to be perfect,
Telling lies, spreading rumors,
But you know it's not worth it.
The goal is to be popular,
It's what everyone thinks,
With expensive shoes, and clothes of pink.
Sooner or later you'll realize,
Through your big blue eyes,
What's holding you back, is their little white lies.

Kenzie Finch, Grade 8
Lincoln Jr/Sr High School, WI

I Am

I am an imaginative girl who loves the sea.
I wonder what lies under the sea.
I hear a mermaid's call.
I see her shimmering tail.
I want to swim with her under the sea.
I am an imaginative girl who loves the sea.

I pretend that I am a princess.
I feel the wind in my hair as I ride the Pegasus.
I touch the clouds as I soar through the sky.
I worry that I don't belong.
I cry for the polluted oceans.
I am an imaginative girl who loves the sea.

I understand that the world is in need.
I say that dreams can come true.
I dream of an endless, magical library.
I try to never give up.
I hope that my dreams and wishes will come true.
I am an imaginative girl who loves the sea.

Zoe Jackson, Grade 8
St Clare of Montefalco School, MI

Beautiful, Delicate Butterfly

It's flying towards me with its delicate and colorful wings.
Flapping them gently, following the wind.
Now, it's circling the old willow trees.
So sweet and harmless, so rare and fragile.
Be very nice and kind.
They don't mind.

Megan Costanzo, Grade 7
Scranton Middle School, MI

Shane

"Boom" Shane's gun went,
   the gun sounded like an atom bomb
   and Shane's hand was a machine.
   Like a slippery, slimy snake in slime,
   Fletcher plotted at Grafton's in 1858,
all was still, even the quiet knew not to bother him.

Zachary Asleson, Grade 8
Wauzeka Steuben School, WI

Cavorting Ghosts

Ghosts,
Cavorting the dusty dance floor
The once-gleaming chandelier
Now fallen to the marble floor
Covered in thick dust

Seen only by the ghosts
Cavorting the once-gleaming dance floor
A table, undisturbed, set for many rich
Rotted meat on dust-covered dishes
Not a glass disturbed or broken

Enjoyed only by the ghosts
Cavorting the dull dance floor
The Grand Orchestra
Once the pride of the nation, now gone
Sitting primly in their faded uniforms
Playing a galvanizing symphony, haunting and gentle

Heard only by the Ghosts,
Who cavort on the dance floor.

Ty Smith, Grade 9
Millington High School, MI

Winter Vacation

Fly over the land through the sparkling blue sky,
To the crystal blue sea we go;
Filled with anticipation
About our Caribbean vacation,
We wave goodbye to the frost and the snow.
Fly over the land through the sparkling blue sky,
The promise of warmth grows near!
Oh, how the sun does shine
As I look out along the coastal line,
The day is bright and clear.
Fly over the land through the sparkling blue sky,
We're at the resort at last!
Feel the salty water spray
While in the waves we play,
The days and nights are a blast!
Fly over the land through the sparkling blue sky,
To return to our home once more;
Away from the sun
And nonstop fun
We'll soon be at our front door.

Joel Fershtman, Grade 7
Boulan Park Middle School, MI

Fireworks

Explosions
Vibrant colors flaring up in frenzy
The blasts fill the midnight sky with magnificent color,
but soon it fades to its original shady state
Only the ghosts remain.

Mark Lapinski, Grade 8
Our Shepherd Lutheran School, MI

Trapped

I am lost in this world not knowing
Where to turn, where to run
For everywhere I turn and everywhere I run
I see the pain, I feel the pain
Of the tortured earth

The chemicals, the toxic waste, the wasted life
The peace is gone
The quiet is gone
The love is gone
And it will never return

Plants and animals killed
Habitats destroyed and altered
People pushing through, killing all of it
To create a better world
For themselves

Here I am trapped
Help
Save me from what they have done

Mikayla Galloway, Grade 8
Silver Lake Intermediate School, WI

Hockey…

When you see the lights
Flickering off the ice

You hear the crowd cheer
Your heart jumps in fear

The feel of the cool breeze
You suddenly know that you are going to freeze

Tasting the concession food
All of the sudden changes your mood

Afterward the smell of the sweaty equipment
Makes you want to faint in embarrassment

Gabrielle Guderyan, Grade 7
Ruth Murdoch Elementary School, MI

Will Shane Get Shot?

If Wilson shoots Shane
The Starretts will go through insufferable pain
Bang!
Will a gun go off?

Wilson is a rattlesnake lying in wait.
But Shane is just as heroic as those goofy men with their
Tights inside their underwear!

But will Shane prevail…
Or die?

Megan Walters, Grade 8
Wauzeka Steuben School, WI

Someday

Life has been hard,
Since you went away.
Life has been hard,
I don't know what to say.
Life is so hard,
'Cause I will never forget that day.
That day, you went away.
It was a beautiful November day,
The day you left me here.
I know I will see you, again
Someday...

Hannah Oostdyk-Howard, Grade 7
East Rockford Middle School, MI

Gorgeous Night

I sit and watch the sun go down,
The fireflies all dance around,
The diamond-like stars in the sky,
The moon like a lamp up so high,
It's a gorgeous night.

When we look at the solar system,
it reminds us of all the people.
We miss them.
Oh how it brings a smile to my face
I know that I'm in the right place.

Jordan Flynn, Grade 8
Woodworth Jr High School, WI

Good Old Lake Michigan

The sun dancing off the water.
As if they had rehearsed it.

The sand as hot as lava.
With mixed materials in it.

The water so deep you could
swim for years and not touch bottom.

The hills so old that they
tell their life story.

Ethan Roth, Grade 7
Nellie B Chisholm Middle School, MI

Life Is Like a Song

It's stuck on replay,
never stops,
always playing in your head.
Sometimes you don't know the meaning,
sometimes you do and you love it,
some days it makes you cry,
some days it makes you laugh,
some days it reminds you of him,
then you really can't get it out of your head.

Erin Knight, Grade 9
Sault Area High School, MI

The Tower

As I stood at the top of the tower looking down,
my mind was debating whether to jump or not.
One false step and I was a goner.
My life would be over in a blink of an eye.

All my life's hard work and tough times would be gone,
and the bullying would finally stop.
My parents' screams and tears would end and I would be free!

I believe no one loves me,
so the thought is quite pleasing to me;
being able to wipe my life away.

So I closed my eyes and the unthinkable happened;
just as I was about to face death, the hands of an angel grabbed me and forced me back.
When I landed on the rooftop, no one was there.
God had simply showed me that I was born to do things unimaginable.

I was saved for a reason,
to pursue my dreams.
I was given a second chance,
and now I must make the best of it.

Mikaila Falash, Grade 7
Adams Friendship Middle School, WI

Human Proof

The question is not who are you

It is who is I
If I equals me and me equals I
Then my is less than me and also less than I
But if you is somewhat congruent to I
Then is me congruent to you?
What if me was equal to my but only if my is times 1000 plus 61
Making my equal to I
And also making my congruent to you?
But only with the proportions of my times 1000 plus 61 would you be
    congruent to my
And that is how I equal you and you equal I

Only because I am me.

Elizabeth Weiland, Grade 7
White Pine Middle School, MI

Yahoo, Yo-yo, Yellow

Yellow is the slimy yolk of an egg, a crisp juicy apple and being excited.
Yellow is the taste of warm scrambled eggs.
Macaroni and cheese is yellow.
A warm, soft blanket makes me feel yellow.
Yellow is a sandy beach, the circus and Lambeau Field.
The phenomenal sunset is yellow.
The roaring bus ride is also yellow.
Yellow is unrestrained happiness.
Waiting for the school bus and watching the brilliant sunrise is yellow.

Jenna Bayerl, Grade 7
Menominee Jr High School, MI

Thanksgiving in Missouri

Thanksgiving in Missouri is like staying with monkeys!
The weather is bitter cold,
And malls are packed to the brim with people
But I always know where my family is.

My birthday gets celebrated with presents galore,
Money for shopping and pedicures too.
Always more food than we can chew.
With quad rides in the rain or snow.

Family fun is always happening,
With late nights in the bright lights
Or games that tease the brain.
Even telling jokes, that really are not that funny.

Nothing can beat the smell of hot rolls!
Lamberts' rolls flying through the room,
So you better duck your head!
Nothing is better than Thanksgiving in Missouri!

Hanna Lawrence, Grade 7
Montague Middle School, MI

Why I Like to Dance

I really like to dance
It makes me really happy
It puts a smile on my face every time it happens
Clapping my hands and moving to the beat
Tapping my feet to the rhythm of the beat
It really makes me happy
Singing my song moving all around
takes away all my frowns
Sing with me, move with me
Feel the music all around
Look from inside, Look outside
I can see the trees all around
Dancing with me to the rhythm of the beat
Swaying, flowing back and forth
Can't you see it's really fun?
Dancing to the beat
Why you may ask?
Because it makes me really happy
That's why I like to dance.

Andrea Walker, Grade 7
Pleasant View School, MI

The Beach

The car screeches as we arrive
The sun reflects off the white sand
Making it a million degrees
The waves swallow little kids
I laugh at the seagulls dancing on the water
I love the beach

Ellie Sims, Grade 7
East Rockford Middle School, MI

Bonfire

A spark is struck
It fuels the fire
The leaves are added
The inferno grows

The light show begins
In a burst of color
Of reds and oranges
And lots of yellow

The growing fire
And the dancing flames
Warmed my feet
My hands and face

The air was cooling
As the flames were dying
Its glow was shrinking
The shadows growing

The smoke had floated far away
Giving fresh air a chance to stay
The fire burning strong, had been demolished
Leaving behind a land that was polished

Allison Rolewicz, Grade 7
Nellie B Chisholm Middle School, MI

The Hit

As she got up to bat
All eyes were on her
She waited for the wind up
But nothing would occur

The first pitch was a fast one
She could feel the wind
It was called as a strike
Then the outfielders began to move in

She was ready for the next pitch
She waited for it to come then hit it to the lawn
As she connected
She was sure it would be gone

And so it was
As she rounded the bases
She knew it was
She had never been in one of these cases

As she ran over home plate
Her teammates came out of the dug out
They screamed and huddled
As for she was never out

Megan Peetz, Grade 7
Scranton Middle School, MI

My Best Friend

My best friend is...
Crazy, loving, caring and funny.
She is one of a kind.
I would not ask for anyone else.

She is like family to me.
She dresses weird sometimes.
But it goes with her personality.

She is like my twin.
We like the same things.
I love being around her.
She is very hyper.

We do everything together.
She is always at my house.
We will be friends til the end.
Maddy Leighty, Grade 7
Round Lake High School, MN

Fall

Hear the crunch
The crunch of the leaves
The leaves under your feet
See the colors
The colors of the trees
The trees above your head
Smell the food
The food of Thanksgiving
The food that tastes so good
Taste the fruit
The fruit of the harvest
The fruit that is so sweet
Touch the cold earth
The earth beneath your feet
The earth that is so solid
Here are the senses of fall
I think they are best of all
Eli Geraty, Grade 8
Ruth Murdoch Elementary School, MI

What Is Love

What does love stand for
It can be my parents.
Love can be my friends.
It can be my happiness.
What does love stand for.
Where can this really begin?
Love can mean my heart.
Love can be your smile.
Love's precious from a child.
Love to some is freedom.
To me love is home.
Love is where I belong.
Ellis L. Cox, Grade 7
Gesu Catholic School, MI

Butterflies

Suddenly I get this feeling
My mind draws blank
My hands are slightly shaking
My heart begins to race

I feel like I'm losing control
I'm nervous inside and out
I have an unexplainable feeling
I wish I could figure this out

These butterflies inside of me
Keep fluttering all throughout
I thought they were gone for good
I didn't know they could come out

It must be the way
You get to me like you do
The way you make me feel
The way I love you like I do
Madisen Lamp, Grade 8
Shakopee Area Catholic School, MN

Thunderstorm

The thunder strikes,
a booming sound,
and then there's lights
across the town.

Some people scream,
yet others smile
when the storm comes
once in a while.

But when the storm starts
the wind knocks on your door,
and the breezes carry
a thunderous roar.

The lightning comes
then it fades away
and it's the end
of a rainy day.
Calli McCartan, Grade 8
Stewartville Middle School, MN

Game Winning Shots

Swoosh!
the ball goes through the hoop
BUZZZZ!!!
the final buzzer sounds
It's like a million people screaming
at the same time,
I've won the game!
Joseph Fox, Grade 7
East Rockford Middle School, MI

Dreams

A dream can be simple
It can be sweet
A dream can be gloomy
That makes your heart sink
Dreams are all different
And extremely unique
They can make your heart stop
Or even miss a beat
Dreams can be special
Or mean nothing at all
They can be filled with emotion
Or no tears that fall
Dreams bring smiles
Dreams bring tears
Dreams decide your fate
If you keep them near
Tiffani Dagenais, Grade 7
Boulan Park Middle School, MI

Black

Black says night,
it is the color that means fright,
you get a black eye after a nasty fight.
Black is the ink on this paper,
and the tinted windows on skyscrapers.
It is the color in plain sight,
yet it is in need with a thirst for light.
Black may be death,
but is also life,
as your soul is taken by the reaper's scythe.
Black is cold,
icy water that has froze,
it nips and nips at your nose,
until it is driven by summer winds.
Black makes me feel dark,
until I ignite a little spark.
Spencer Davis, Grade 8
Perry Middle School, MI

I'm Just Unique

Call me a loser,
Call me a geek.
Say what you want,
I'm just unique.

Call me a weirdo,
Call me a freak.
Say what you want,
I'm just unique.

Call me boring,
Call me bleak.
Say what you want,
I'm just unique.
Erica Meyers, Grade 8
Walnut Creek Middle School, MI

Books

Books
Have words
Teach humans
And make them feel knowledgeable
Script
Shavonne Chen, Grade 9
Mayo High School, MN

Christmas

Sleep as it snows
Sipping smooth soup
Baking batches of Christmas cookies
Drinking delightful drinks
Scooping snowy snowballs
Tessa Elizabeth Osborne, Grade 7
East Rockford Middle School, MI

The Bus

The bus is like a monster
Eats up kids in a flash
Takes them to their Death
And never takes them back
Hope I'm not dinner tonight!
Brendan Kennedy, Grade 7
East Rockford Middle School, MI

A Hero of Our Own

Today is the day,
We fight 'til we die.
We'll live like there's no tomorrow.
And we will die knowing,
We saved someone from death.
Karissa Stern, Grade 9
Round Lake High School, MN

Serenity

The ocean is forever,
My eyes follow the sea,
The waves are soldiers,
They continue their journey.
Mikayla Kruse, Grade 7
East Rockford Middle School, MI

Snowflakes

Pointy, thin, little
pieces of nature that fall
down every winter.
Kevin Chen, Grade 7
Abbott Middle School, MI

Fall Leaves

Leaves begin to fall
They blow away in the wind
All various colors
Phillip Kapas, Grade 8
Our Shepherd Lutheran School, MI

Our Power

I'm telepathic.
No wait, you are too.
I'm not joking around here…I've been noticing many things in the past month.
It's strange. Our world is strange.
I believe. That Humans…that's right, us. We are telepathic.
Ever get that déjà vu feeling? And the more you think about it…
You realized you've never had any association about that thought before.
You don't know that person. You don't know their personality.
You've never been in that same situation or arrangement…
You can't predict them. You can't predict anything…
But maybe, just maybe the future.
I believe that humans, maybe just the special ones, maybe not.
But possibly, humans are telepathic.
Think about it.
How psychologically…it actually does make sense.
We may have a power…we may have something that could help us.
In.
The.
Future.
Our Power.

Priya Vijayakumar, Grade 7
Detroit Country Day Middle School, MI

My Family

My family means the world to me
My family is someone that I will always have by my side.
Even though it can get a bit crazy, I still love them.
My family is my life and I don't know what I would do without them.
People say we need our own reality show because we're so crazy.
We may sometimes fight but we still care.
We care enough to show them we care.
Even though we're spread out, we still have reasons to come together.
Together we are strong and nothing can break us.
There are so many things that we could share but couldn't.
It makes me sad that someone I love is hurt or in pain.
My life wouldn't be complete
Every day I wonder if something is going to go wrong.
We piece out like separates but we come back strong.
I am glad God gave me such a wonderful family.
I am even glad for my extended family.
My family is incredible and wonderful.

Czaria Wright, Grade 7
Gesu Catholic School, MI

Hope Is

Found everywhere and in anything.
Hope is blissful and inspiring.
Hope is sanity, encouragement, and laughter.
Hope is Mariah, a cousin, overcoming the physical obstacles that came her way.
Hope is a mother's love that means the world to her daughter.
Hope is goals reached.
Hope is Mrs. Shauver, a great teacher.
Hope is a better tomorrow that I wish to see.
That's what my hope is.

Chontalice Hicks, Grade 7
Pleasant View School, MI

Alma Center

It is a small town
Not many people
Not many houses
Not many stores

Friendly folks
Will help with anything
Always will help each other
Where no one is left behind

Full of farms and fields
Corn and crops
Long as the eye can see
But corn too tall to see over

Also forests
Full of animals
Wild exotic plants
Trees further than you can see

Then my house
A nice house
It is tan in color
By swamps and creeks
This is my small town
Nick Shoemaker, Grade 9
Lincoln Jr/Sr High School, WI

Stay Here Not There

There you go again
Dad left
You keep leaving
Feels like you never come back

You left again
After work
Before work
Feels like you're never home

Where are you this time?
You're gone
Who's going to help?
Where do I go?

Soon you'll never come back
Soon life will be gone
Soon things will be different
Soon I won't see your eyes open

We keep hoping
I hide from my feelings
I cry in the dark
Please I want you here on the ground
Not in the heavens!
Jade O'Neil, Grade 8
Menominee Indian Middle School, WI

The Picture Box

A big old couch and a bag of chips,
Romance movies with lips to lips
Women with cats, and crazy old bats
Pirate people and three-masted ships.

Teenage boys singing pop songs,
Kids staying up too long
Little girls watch their crush,
Other girls watch Big Time Rush
Some people just have to yawn.

Macho guys stay up with all their might,
Just to watch the boxing fight
Baby shows that everyone knows
Will make the kids all right.

Disney, Fuse, and TeenNick,
Some shows just make me sick
Almost every day I'm seen,
Because I am your TV
Now it's time to shut me off.

click

Shiloh Sanders, Grade 7
Lincoln Jr/Sr High School, WI

Life Doesn't Frighten Me at All

Loud noises here and there
Bad nightmares everywhere
Life doesn't frighten me at all
Big ghosts haunting my room
Bad spiders crawling up my broom
Life doesn't frighten me at all

Mean old ugly apes
Coming to my house, eating my grapes
They don't frighten me at all
Big hairy monkeys in the hall
Drawing violent pictures on the wall
That doesn't frighten me at all

When I get scared
I confront my fears
But when they don't answer
My eyes get tears

Life doesn't frighten me at all
Not at all
Not at all
Life doesn't frighten me at all
Pooja Natarajan, Grade 7
Abbott Middle School, MI

Sweet Lola

Lola is a nice and protective dog
She is as nice as a cat
She is as protective as a mother
Lola is my favorite pet

Lola is a noisy and playful dog
She is as noisy as a fire truck
She is as playful as a toddler
Lola is an amazing pet

Lola is a cuddly and fun dog
She is as cuddly as your favorite teddy bear
She is as fun as a summer fair
Lola is a friendly pet

Lola is a fast and strong dog
She is as fast as racing car
She is as strong as a bull
Lola is mine
Seth Sparks, Grade 7
Nellie B Chisholm Middle School, MI

Bump, Set, Spike!

In Volleyball I've Learned…
It's something I like
I can even get a bump, set, or spike
If you try your best
you just might have success

How to work as a team
To do better than you can dream
If you get the serve over the net
You will win I bet

How to slide for the ball
But not to worry, it doesn't hurt at all
Get ready and watch the net
For some of those close sets

In Volleyball I've Learned…
To move your feet
So you don't get beat
Kelsey Pattison, Grade 7
Sault Area Middle School, MI

Joyless to Fortunate

Single
Sad, lonely
Lonesome, crying, waiting
Alone, empty, complete, whole
Celebrating, supporting, loving
Compassionate, happy
Marriage
Madison Smith, Grade 7
Nellie B Chisholm Middle School, MI

My Grandfather's Hat

My grandfather pulled out his favorite hat.
It was ripped up from his vicious cat.
He gave the hat to me with tears in his eyes,
And said that it was a special prize.

I accepted my grandfather's worn out cap.
I looked it over and found a strap.
Attached to the strap was a delightful note.
It was a letter Grandfather wrote.

The letter said, "When ever you are alone,
Think about the lovely hat you own."
I put on the magnificent hat and said,
"I'm honored to wear this on my head."

My grandfather gazed into my big, brown eyes,
And we both let out loud, happy cries.
I gave my grandfather a huge, cheerful smile,
And realized that hat was worthwhile.

Lauren Lesha, Grade 8
Our Lady Star of the Sea School, MI

My Neighbor's Farm

Fun peaceful place.
Full of live living things,
To keep you entertained.
The cows are mooing,
Like screaming kids.
Just watching them roam around in the mud.
Lying in the pasture.
Cows are people walking and running.
Mooing like crazy,
Just to be heard.
The cats secretly walking,
Upon the mice and scaring them away, and teasing them.
Along with the horses,
Full of life, fun to feed, and hard to ride.
Watching a tractor,
Run like a child.
And that's where,
I go to calm myself.
My neighbor's farm.

Storm O'Neill, Grade 9
Lincoln Jr/Sr High School, WI

Tornadoes

Tornado spins round and round. Powerful and scary if they
touch the ground. Dark skies in the afternoon
make me want to hide in my room covers
over my head as I hide in fear
and dread.

Parker Baugh, Grade 7
Forest Hills Central Middle School, MI

The Unseen

What else is it to be alone?
Than a shadow of darkness in my soul
People say they can relate
But they have never felt my pain

It ponders my mind why it had to be anyone, TO BE ME!
I walked into what should've been a safe haven
Completely subliminally
And I was ripped off the tower of confidence

And stripped of my self-esteem, it no longer exists
Little words can go a long way
And it might go unseen, you might not notice just today
But that samurai's sword is piercing my heart

I may have looked fine but that was just the start
It started with such small mockery that seems like nothing
And they think it's cool but that's what got me
Losing everything takes its toll
Now all that's left is a grave stone.
RIP, The Bullied

Aya Beydoun, Grade 8
Woodworth Middle School, MI

Thanksgiving List

The smell of the turkey on Thanksgiving Day,
The taste of all the food,
The sound of the parade going down the street,
The smiles on the faces of my family,
The feel of the warm fire in the fireplace,
The sound of all the laughter,
The smell of pumpkin pie,
The taste of the cool ice cream,
The sound of the music playing,
The smell of the burnt wood in the fire,
The look of festive decorations around the house,
The sound of the football game playing on the television,
The smell of apple pie baking in the oven,
The sound of everyone playing games,
The look of happy faces when dinner is ready.

Brian McNamara, Grade 7
St Clare of Montefalco School, MI

The Storm

The storm cackled and laughed as it rolled in,
The people boarded up their houses,
As the storm BOOOMED, "Your power is no more!"
The storm chuckled as his lightening struck everything in its path,
Sparks flew every which way from where the lightning had struck,
As the storm left, the people cheered,
As he cackled and laughed once more as entering the next town.

Cameron Mckee, Grade 7
East Rockford Middle School, MI

Where I'm From

I am from firm pillows, Jiff peanut butter and crisp yellow lemons.
I am from the dogwoods, white tulips and purple morning glories.
From the hardwood floors and dog fur on the couch.
I am from baking cookies, and hair dye, from Kaye Shmid, Goldie Hotchkiss and Chris Haeker.
I am from clumsiness and arrogance.
From never giving up and looking before you cross.
I am from the Baptists, sons of God, tellers of Christ and the church in the meadow where I worship.
I am from Kalkaska Michigan where the blood of the German, Welsh and Scandinavian
run through my veins, with pizza and cherry pie in my stomach.
From the step-stool my grandfather gave me on witch I stub my toes upon daily.
From the time my great grandfather killed a lynx in Alaska and gave the Kelt to my great grandmother.
I am from the wooden chest that smells of white roses.
In which holds my memories every picture, document and charm reminds me of things I would love to relive.

Samantha Hotchkiss, Grade 8
Kalkaska Middle School, MI

Roaring Rambling Red

Red is a sunset blazing and burning bright, fireworks on the fourth of July. A warm fuzzy blanket is red.
Red is the taste of spicy peppers.
Juicy, big, plump strawberries and sweet-smelling carnations are red.
A deep, blistering cut makes me feel red.
Red is the sound of screaming, wailing sirens and chiming bells.
Red is a bonfire, a hot stove, and the emergency room.
Valentine's Day is red.
Cupid's arrows are also red.
Red is love.
Red is the warmth you feel sitting by the fire on a cold, winter day.

Maggie Smith, Grade 8
Menominee Jr High School, MI

Fighting for Life

I lay there, pain coursing through my body.
I wish I could fight back, wish I could pick up the sword and defend myself. But I can't. I don't know how, don't know why.
So I sit and wait for death to creep up and make the last fatal blow. I wish I had guidance, someone to depend on other than myself. Wish I had pain killers, something that would dull my attacker's swords. Wish I had a star to wish on. Wish I had something that would keep me hoping. Wish I had something that would keep me wishing. But I don't. I don't have hope, don't have guidance. don't have a wishing star, don't have pain killers.
I don't have anything. Don't have anything but pain. After days of pain,
It started to fade. My attackers began to tire. The more they tired, the higher my hopes soared. The more the pain faded, the more I wished. After hopes, wishes, and dreams, it disappeared. No more pain. No more sadness. No more attacks. I had learned how to pick up the sword and fight back. I had learned how to hope, wish, and dream. I learned how to fight for life.

Osa Svensson, Grade 7
Tappan Middle School, MI

Determination

It's nothing that happens on its own.
You have to feel it naturally to drive you to your humble goals.
Instead of saying no to this or that why not go for it, even if it's a huge risk?
As you bet and bet not sure if it's going to happen.
Don't let it discourage you from doing what you've set.
Because, as long as you have the determination what you want will most likely get completed.
Willpower, strength, endurance is what you must have in order not to tank.
Determination no matter how we try can't be put in a definite shape
But, is evolving the more we take that leap of faith.

Ky'la Sims, Grade 9
Edsel Ford High School, MI

Friends Are Family

Friends are family, you may not think so
but they are. Friends may not look
like you but on the inside they do.
Friends are people you let into your
open heart and if they are in your
heart they're your blood, so friends are
your family. You need to love and
cherish that they are part of your family,
and they should not be
ashamed of that.

Madison Christenson, Grade 8
Grand Blanc West Middle School, MI

All About Me

My name is Emily Rose
I enjoy it when it snows
I love to play sports
Even though I'm rather short

I like to read and
I try my hardest to succeed

I enjoy riding bikes
But I do have many dislikes.

Emily Rose Headings, Grade 7
Riverdale Elementary & Middle School, WI

The Night Reflection

The cold night wind will blow
and you will hear wind whistle
In your ear
In the night
It is as dark as it can be
But the moon shines bright
Like the sun and says hello
and the ocean reflects
The light of the moon
And says hello back.

Kaylynn Burke, Grade 7
East Rockford Middle School, MI

Egg

I hate it when
People crack me open
And pour out all my insides
I guess they find me yummy
But it hurts when
They break my tummy
I hate it when they scramble me
And stir me all around
But worst of all I hate it
When they always make me frown

Cesiley Lacourt, Grade 7
East Rockford Middle School, MI

The World as I See It

A dangerous place filled with troubles.
A beautiful place where smiles are born.
A complicated, horrible, wonderful place filled with love and scorn.
An ongoing forest with magical creatures.
A forsaken land with terrible features.
An exciting, adventurous, deadly place where there are rich and poor.
So come all you lovers, haters, and fighters.
Come all you planters, destroyers, and makers.
Come all you from near and far, come see who we really are.
We are people diverse and proud.
We are colorful and we are loud.
We are spiritful and we are shrouds.
We are one big crazy crowd.
Some of us skip and some of us dance.
Some of us sing and some of us prance.
We all come together in a messy soup, all of us do.
All of us who laugh and cry.
All of us who love and lie.
All of us, all of us, and that's who we are
That's our world.
Now let's go see it, so get in the car.

Jacqui McGregor, Grade 7
Dakota Meadows Middle School, MN

Beautiful

You are beautiful when your inside appearance looks better than the outside,
You are beautiful when you help others,
You don't put them down.
You are beautiful when you are smart,
And you try your best,
You are beautiful when you overcome your adversities,
And you keep moving forward,
You are beautiful when you try your best for success,
And help others get to the top with you,
You are beautiful when you are above the influence
And don't follow the wrong crowd,
You are beautiful when you fix your mistakes,
And then you learn from them,
Most of all you are beautiful when you are you,
And you never try to change you.

Arianna Jackson, Grade 7
Gesu Catholic School, MI

Generous, Galloping Green

Green is the swaying grass, a slimy lizard, and a warm, soft blanket.
Green is the taste of crisp dill pickles.
Cool, fresh-tasting mints, and fresh-cut grass are green.
A breezy day in May makes me feel green.
Green is the sound of thundering Packer fans and a chirping grasshopper.
Green is the muddiest woods, a nail biting Packer game, and a clover field.
Immense Christmas trees are green.
The luckiest St. Patrick's Day is also green.
Green is Easter with my family.
Green is the bursting of sprint when winter's snow has melted away.

Taylor Wroblewski, Grade 7
Menominee Jr High School, MI

Christmas Eve

Jingle bells ringing in the distance,
Hoof beats on the roof,
A grunt, and swoosh,
But "This Man" is not at the door,
Down the chimney he had gone,
Not once even covered in soot,
And now Santa Claus walked to the Christmas tree,
Proceeded to put presents for the children under it,
With candy in the stocking for the good children,
And coal for the naughty,
He walks to the table,
That is covered with cookies,
Temptation too great,
He had to munch down to the cake,
"Too delicious," he thinks,
And gives a little wink,
Back up the chimney he goes,
How? Nobody knows,
But off he must go,
And all the over again…
Jingle bells ringing in the distance…

Deborah Kim, Grade 7
Ruth Murdoch Elementary School, MI

Basketball

The best sport is basketball.
There are ten different players on the court at one time.
You could play point or right wing
Or left wing or center or post.
I usually play point
Because I am good at it.
I play wing too.
There is a varsity team
And junior varsity team
And there is a junior high.
There are girls teams too and guy teams.
You have matching uniforms,
A home jersey and an away jersey.
The lower numbers on jerseys are for point and wing.
The higher numbers on jerseys are for post and center.

Travis Behrends, Grade 8
Round Lake High School, MN

Will I Ever Know?

I feel as if my world has no time.
As I see you, time stops and there is no longer any time left.
I wonder if you will ever understand…
    that I like you — I do.
When you're not around
I feel as if time is running out without you there by my side.
Or maybe you do know
    that I feel as if I am falling in love with you.
But are you falling in love with me, too?
Will I ever know?

Raeann Carr, Grade 7
Pleasant View School, MI

Just Me

I am a spirited girl who loves bunnies.
I wonder if there is life on different planets.
I hear the twinkle of the stars.
I see myself having awesome powers.
I want to learn how to break dance.
I am a spirited girl who loves bunnies.

I pretend to save the world.
I feel like I live in Japanese manga's.
I touch the sparkles of a never ending rainbow.
I worry for my friends' and family's well being.
I cry when I think about my grandpa.
I am a spirited girl who loves bunnies.

I understand humans *need* water to survive.
I say practice makes perfect.
I dream of being a ninja.
I try to be the best person I can be.
I hope for a bright future.
I am a spirited girl who loves bunnies.

Ashley Joranstad, Grade 7
Abbott Middle School, MI

Why?

Why do you scream?
Why do you cry day and night?
I just don't see why.
Why do you scream so loud?
And why is your voice so low?
I know you're only six months.
Why do you show?
Why do you speak this language
That I don't know?
Goo-goo-ga-ga
Does that mean you feel alone?
Please don't cry.
Look, I'm here and my arms are wide.
Just crawl in — I know you're wise.
You shall not be surprised.
Your tear will evaporate into the sky, your frown turn upside down.
You will see — together forever we will be.
Beyond all time — watch and see
Knock, knock on the door
Now why do you have to leave?

Nohamys Gatorno-Cisneros, Grade 7
Pleasant View School, MI

Family

F orever and always loved
A lways there — us no matter what
M emories that are unforgettable
I n our minds, hearts, and souls
L oving every moment with each other
Y es, we may have ups and downs, but we are still Family.

Odalyz Ramos, Grade 9
Round Lake High School, MN

In the Upper Peninsula I've Learned

In the Upper Peninsula I've learned
How to rock climb 70 feet
My oh my, that's quite a treat
What goes up must go down, so we learned to rappel
We had a great time and nobody fell

In the Upper Peninsula I've learned
How to catch wind in a sail
And if water comes in to bail
How to get eleven people on a one foot crate
It took a little debate

In the Upper Peninsula I've learned
How to throw a disc golf disc
That isn't such a risk
How to eat in a canoe
We had quite a crew

In the Upper Peninsula I've learned
How to have fun with friends
That isn't something that just passes with the trends

Benjamin Reattoir, Grade 7
Sault Area Middle School, MI

The Pains of Hide and Seek

While days went by and nights passed
Time went by way too fast
Every time an old day died
Nights passed days went by

The wind blew and the rain came
He sat there getting tired of this game
He sat there bored with nothing else to do
The rain came the wind blew.

He sat there waiting for way too long
In the background the bells went dong don dong
Thinking this game of Hide and Seek,
should have ended as he stood on the mat
Waiting there wait too long he sat

Eric Burns, Grade 8
St Jerome Elementary School, MN

Halloween Night

The wind of the fall air slithers through the trees.
The whispers of spirits are carried in by the breeze.
The witches and ghouls are laughing with delight.
As the neighborhood kids run with fright.
The pumpkin lanterns are lit up high.
The zombies are rising from where they lie.
This is the night where the dead arise.
And all that is living will soon die.
It's Halloween night.
Let the frighting begin.

Shantel Jacoby, Grade 8
Unionville-Sebewaing High School, MI

Satisfaction

Consumed by the darkness, never returning to the light
I'm forever lost, my soul wants to be freed
But it's locked inside me, never to know freedom
I walk endlessly, never to reach my destination
Never to know, what is satisfaction
My body is tired, my mind does not care
It is focused on my ultimate goal, to know satisfaction
My mortal form collapses, exhausted from my search
Endlessly looking for the unattainable, what is satisfaction
My body fades, never to return
My soul remains, never to learn
Never did I achieve, my ultimate aim
Never to know, what is satisfaction
But as I look up, I see a light
It is a bright shining white light
As I get closer, I feel a warming sensation
Maybe this could be, what is satisfaction
Finally I touch the light, the darkness inside me flees
I feel greed no more, instead I am content
I know my search has finally ended
Finally I have attained, what is satisfaction

Matthew Lonto, Grade 8
Ruth Murdoch Elementary School, MI

My Girls

We're not an ordinary group of girls,
we are a family.
No one will ever get between us.
We win together,
and lose together.
We don't leave anyone behind.
We support each other.
They're the sisters I never had,
but always wished for.
We count on each other and
stand up for one another.
We've become a family.
We take hits for each other.
No one will break this strong bond we've created.
We play with such…
heart, passion, and love for basketball.

Lindsay Crim, Grade 8
Perry Middle School, MI

Beautiful Spring

The trees dance in the spring breeze
Birds sing like no one is listening
There is a beautiful rainbow after a long shower
The sun shines bright in the sky
The mamma deer plays with her babies
She keeps them safe
"Peck, peck"
Says the woodpecker searching for food
I feel like I have only seen a beautiful day like this in a dream

Lauren Hyink, Grade 7
East Rockford Middle School, MI

Life

In life, I've learned…
That divorce is bad
And it left me very mad
My mom and dad split two years ago
But I'm over that now, let's go

In life, I've learned…
I split my time by two
But this gives me a variety to do
No one can replace my mom or dad
But in my heart it isn't bad

In life, I've learned…
Along the bumpy roads of life
Filled with joy and filled with strife
And with sadness, stress, and no rest
I've learned I can do my very best

In life, I've learned…
That my mother and father still love me the same
And there's no one to blame

Tyler Feltis, Grade 7
Sault Area Middle School, MI

Baby Kammeron

I hear you cry every time I see you,
You're so innocent all you want is your nook,
You liked to be rocked,
With one hand between someone's armpit and body,
The other touching someone's shirt,
Wide-eyed just looking,
Your eyes getting heavy,
Almost asleep then someone else takes you,
As your nook fell out you start to cry,
So your aunt has to give you your nook and rock you,
Then your eyes are getting heavy again,
And then you fall asleep,
Just to wake up and cry again.
Sweet, sweet Kammeron,
So, so innocent.

Holly Lueck, Grade 7
Lincoln Jr/Sr High School, WI

Blue

Blue is the color of the great ocean blue
That makes me happy when I am blue
Blue is the color of the great ocean blue
That keeps me happy from morning till noon
Blue is the color of the great ocean blue
That splashes water on its white sandy shore
And makes me full of joy more and more
Blue is the color of the great ocean blue
That's why I love the color blue

Tsion Getahun, Grade 8
Ruth Murdoch Elementary School, MI

Owl I See, Owl I Do

Owl I see
Owl I do
Wow what an owl
Looking at me so fluffy and plump
Owl I see
Owl I do
Such big brown eyes always watching me
Owl I see
Owl I do
With outstretched wings flying at me,
WOW what a wingspan
Owl I see
Owl I do
As you fly into the night,
It is time to say good bye to the brown beast of the night
Owl I see
Owl I do
Wow what an owl I have seen and now have you

Ellie Capistrant, Grade 7
Parkview Center Elementary School, MN

After

After he left he was gone forever
And I thought he would never come back
After he left I thought I would never love again
After I loved I cared

After I cared I shared my love
After I shared it I loved again
After I loved I never stopped
After that I always loved

After he left I cried
After he knew he came back
After he came back he loved again
After he loved he never stopped

Courtney Barnhart, Grade 7
Perry Middle School, MI

I Am Free*

Though I'm scared I shall not run,
Though I'm cold I burn like the sun.
Though I'm tired I shall not sleep,
Though I'm strong I continue to weep.
Though I'm a fighter I still don't feel right,
I toss and turn and worry all night.
Though I stare at the mountains, giants so high,
I fear I will never be like the peaceful sky.
So for all of the Tibetans, tattered and who mourn,
This is the message to be worn,
For all of those who have kept you in captivity,
They shall know you are Tibetans, peaceful and free…

Justin Christopher-Moody, Grade 7
Abbott Middle School, MI
*Dedicated to the people of Tibet

Look Up

When one fails, one is stomped on.
Broken to pieces, drummed on by forces.
Hit on the head, with truths of life.
Drowned in water, with tears of hatred,
and words that lie.
Crushed in the earth, within the dead
Drilled down and down and down…
Until one looks up,
sees the blue sky,
laughs at the drama,
remembers one is alive
recalls the dictionary,
and that fail is only an adjective,
that needs to be tinkered.
It is only an action,
that needs to be corrected.
It is only the entering pass, the ticket,
the key, the passing fee, to the later success in life.

Chetana Guthikonda, Grade 9
South View Middle School, MN

Regret

Love for you is a flower out of bloom
Struggling to find its way back to you
In your absence, my life is a monsoon
Wind and rain making it hard to pursue

We are a story, our ending unknown
Love is the author, both gentle and cruel
Our love is ashes, burned and left alone
Our passion burned hot, and now is left cool

We are a sea pulled apart by the tide
What now is weak was previously strong
We are storm clouds, pushing the sun aside
What felt so right couldn't have been so wrong

Would you be willing to risk all the pain
Just to be able to love me again?

Emily Ford, Grade 8
Core Knowledge Charter School, WI

Sparx

So furry and cute, but makes my mom sneeze.
Cold ears in the winter and warm in the summer.
I hear her paws hitting the floor and her collar jingling.
Her tail is hitting me and it hurts.
I bend down and pet her on the head.
I kiss her cold nose and scratch her tummy.
My mom bites her and she complains.
Who is this person?
It is my dog, Sparx.
She is playful but getting old,
but I love my dog so much.

Danielle Carter, Grade 7
Pleasant View School, MI

Broken Archer

Threw away all I had
Just to get nothing
Wondering if I should start crying
Or at least say something
Drew back my life
Like an arrow on a string
I forgot to grip the bow first
So it's still missing
Didn't address my target
So now I'm thinking
If I want to have a good life
First I need to start wishing,
Because the best medicine for anything
Is as simple as screaming
Tried to write a script
Of all the songs I didn't sing
Couldn't come up with the words
Cause I'm a bird with a broken wing
I'm going to gather my courage
And screw it to the sticking place
And try to turn this deadly winter into spring

Hawa Salad, Grade 9
Metcalf Jr High School, MN

Discipline of Homework

Homework, homework, bad music I always hear.
Easy or hard, I always am scared.
You get my attention, with your bad infection.
Homework is stuck in my head,
even when I go to bed.
The work that takes up lead
and fights me until the end.
It's work that kills my heart,
with all the sections apart.
Homework, why don't you go?
I finished you a minute too slow.
I wish you would disappear,
because the scar is too severe.
Having homework in my life
is by far the very worst sight.
Homework is obvious evil at work,
but now I must go and finish my homework.

Lynden Badgley, Grade 7
Pleasant View School, MI

Morning Dew

I walk outside all is calm,
The winter's wind cools my palm,
All is quiet.
All is still.
The sun rises above the mill.
The sparkling of the ground blinds me with such beauty.
The moment lasts for but an instant.
I shall enjoy it again tomorrow.

Branden O'Connor, Grade 9
Round Lake High School, MN

Best of Both Worlds

Best of both worlds. Now what do I mean?
This is no fairy tale. Nor a pipe dream.

My mother's Caucasian. Dad — African-American.
Better known as white-n-black
Not trying to confuse you just stating the facts.

Growing up different but all in the same.
My mom loves mashed potatoes. And dad loves pinto beans.

One of my parents loves rap and the other R&B
Sometimes rock and roll and a little country.

I was blessed to have both — some might disagree
If I could change it all I wouldn't change a thing.

Best of both worlds. Now what do I mean.
This is no fairy tale nor a pipe dream.

So if you wonder what's the best of both worlds
Just look at me.

Jordan Eddins, Grade 7
Pleasant View School, MI

Sonnet 25

My love for you only comes once a year
From Santa's workshop and presents galore
To the Jingle Bells and holiday cheer
And wishful wish lists, plus spirits will soar.

Ornaments enhance the beautiful tree,
Anticipation is on Christmas Eve,
All together around the fire are we,
Excitement, cheers, no one will dare to leave.

And who can forget about the reindeer,
Who dared to save Christmas with his red nose,
Or Frosty the Snowman, without one fear
of being silly, cuz that's how it goes.

When the season's done, there will be a tear
or two, but always think about next year.

Isabella Genova, Grade 8
Core Knowledge Charter School, WI

Fire

Fire
Hot   deadly
Burns spreading explodes
"But Martin said it doesn't have to be this way"
Comforting warming   life saving
Beautiful   majestic
Fire

Brandon Brown, Grade 7
St Jerome Elementary School, MN

Again

As I stood there, watching you board the train,
I wondered why you're leaving me here again.
We say good bye,
And because of that, I thought that I would fall and die.
I felt as if my heart would break,
And since it did, here's a piece for you to take.
I would never, ever lie,
So I told you "I can't wait, to tell you 'Hi.'"
I gave you a kiss and dreamed of the day,
That you and I will never say,
"Good bye! I love you."
And, "I love you too."
The day that you would come and stay forever,
So that you and I; will be happy here together.
So you leave me here again,
And as I watch you board the train,
To see you leave me here again,
I dream of the day,
That you and I, will never, ever again have to say,
"I love you."
"I love you too."

Caleb Kim, Grade 8
Ruth Murdoch Elementary School, MI

Cross Between Friendship and Love

You're there when I need you most,
Happy or sad, I know you'll hold me close.
By my side or miles apart,
You'll always be in my heart.
I'll be thinking of you when I feel blue,
Wishing you could help me pull through.
I will shine my love like the golden sun,
And I hope you'll always call me number one.
When I call you mine
I hope you will sign,
Then we can intertwine
And become a lifelong love line.
I know you won't decline,
Because then I would just be a straight line.
I know our love will last
And I guarantee it won't shatter like broken glass.

Kayla Green, Grade 9
Lincoln Jr/Sr High School, WI

A Cataclysmic Color Collision

A cataclysmic color collision caught in black and white
An awe-inspiring epic fairy tale forgotten in time
The perfect final line to a story never written
The inspiring idea of something undefined never to be known…
A good intention found in a tragedy
A small silver sliver in the darkest cloud
One pure heart amongst a thousand greedy souls
One good line in each story as it unfolds

Emily Sandoval, Grade 8
Horning Middle School, WI

Siblings

Siblings are friends!
They hang out with you when friends can't!
They're always there for you!
Siblings are evil!
They tell on you for things you never did!
They try to beat you up but never win!
But all in all siblings are a blessing!

Gertie Venckus, Grade 7
East Rockford Middle School, MI

The Winter

Sled surfing on the snow
Franticly freezing fingers
Candy cane crazy
Holiday hissing hot cocoa
Whistling, wind, wonderful winter
Perfect precious presents
Around an amazing tree

Kameren Butler, Grade 7
East Rockford Middle School, MI

Basketball

Pass the ball
Your teammate screams
Make the shot
Your coach shouts
Swoosh, bounce, YAY!
As you make the winning
Shot

Mariah Taylor, Grade 7
East Rockford Middle School, MI

Homework

Homework is gross
Homework I hate the most.
Especially when you have to add and divide
It's all just a piece of slime.
Sometimes it's all easy,
Sometimes it's all hard,
I really think it's bizarre.

DeShawn Porteé, Grade 7
Pleasant View School, MI

Landforms

Mountain
Rocky, cold
Snowing, freezing, blowing
Rocks, snow, slope, grass
Warming, raining, freezing
Joyful, peaceful
Valley

Logan Halverson, Grade 7
Nellie B Chisholm Middle School, MI

Roscoe, Just My Dog!

He is my other eyes that can see above the heavens
He is my other ears that hear above the winds
He is a part of me that can reach into the souls of laughter and fun

When I am wrong he forgives me
When I am angry he tries to make me smile
When I am happy he is a joy to be around
When I act like a fool he ignores it like it never happened
But when I succeed he brags and smiles

Without him I am different
With him I feel his love and strength
He is very loyal
He has taught me how to be a friend
He now has my trust
And his head on my knee heals me when I am hurt
His presence by my side is protection against my fears of dark and unknown things
He has promised to wait for me wherever in case I need him
I love him I will and always have,
He is just my dog!

Alena Jones, Grade 7
Forest Hills Eastern Middle School, MI

My Hero

He is nameless, faceless, and mysterious
She is cunning and courageous.
A brotherhood, a sisterhood. Shared...
We stand united an American family
He has super powers, traveling by land, air and sea.
She is black, white, Hispanic, Asian, Arab, and Other.
He is Catholic, Jewish, Buddhist, Orthodox and everything in between.
In the same moment we are separate, we are united.
She is bold, fearless like David in the face of Goliath.
He is as giving as Mother Teresa who dedicates herself for the salvation of humanity.
She is as reflective as the Buddha always thinking about peace in times of war.
He fights for me and She continues that fight today.
My hero is a Soldier.

Chris Abdulreda, Grade 8
Detroit Country Day Middle School, MI

Where I'm From

I am from music, from converse, and art.
I am from a lakefront home in South Bordman.
From pink lilies and yellow daisies.
I am from hard workers and hazel eyes.
From Abramczyk's and McCallum's.
I am from hard heads and strong wills.
I am from "children are seen not heard!" and A twinkle in my daddy's eyes!
From popsicles, chicken nuggets with honey, and no bake cookies.
I am from Sunday school and sitting on Santa's lap in the mall.
I am from Fitch's school of dance.
I am from princesses in fairy tales and climbing old pine trees.
I am from Kalkaska Michigan, from a long dirt road winding down little creek.
I am Kirsten and This is were I'm from!

Kirsten McCallum, Grade 8
Kalkaska Middle School, MI

Christmas Day

It was Christmas Eve a beautiful night
The day before Christmas not a snowflake in sight
We wait with hope and excitement too
For a happy Christmas day which was just in a few
Under the tree which was a sight to see
Were our gifts that were waiting with happiness and glee
Near the tree we sat and sang
Our Christmas songs like an angelic gang
The house was happy not a tear in one eye
While our grandma made cookies, and brownies, and pie
The next morning as we all awake
We all ran down to the tree and the sound of slumber breaks
With excitement that follows of course for the gifts
One brave soul remembers with a tear and a sniff
Christmas day is not about receiving
But the joy we get from giving
So remember this holiday season that it's not about us
And consider your reward may God bless

Emmanuel Saint-Phard, Grade 8
Ruth Murdoch Elementary School, MI

Music

It's something I can listen to all day.
It's something that makes me want to prance.
It's something that I can always sing to
and throw up my hands and do a dance.
It's something that I love to listen to
and it describes part of who I am inside.
Without it I don't know what I would do
for it is one of the things that keeps me alive.
Music is so important to me
there are no words to describe.
It gives me hopes and dreams
and it makes me feel good with pride.

Katirah Perkins, Grade 7
Pleasant View School, MI

Gabby: My Friend

A friend like you will never turn me away.
A friend like you will be there for me every day.

Gabby, you mean everything to me.
It could be the smiles I see.

You're such a beautiful friend
So I will be there until the end
As your friend.

As your friend, I do swear to love you.
Because I don't want to lose you.

Allison Engstrom, Grade 8
Lancaster Secondary School, MN

Life

Life is a gift
God gave us this gift
In life we face challenges
Life is short
So we live life to the fullest

They say knowledge is power
But life is the true power
Life we share good and bad memories
Like they always say, life is what you make of it
Your life holds memories that are priceless

Your life is unique
Lives are different in every way
Life is yours to control
Grasp it and take it by the horns
In life we love, cry, laugh, and scream

Life also brings new adventures and excitement
Life can bring mysteries
Life is the true puzzle
Life can be your friend
Or your enemy

Jeremy Miller, Grade 8
Gesu Catholic School, MI

Skiing the Black Diamond

Resting peacefully on a lift
I prepare to dash through
pearly snow,
Riding on my skis
with the bluest sky that I have ever seen right above me.

The lift reaches the summit of the hill,
I begin my descent slowly
then faster and faster 'til the wind is whipping snow in my face.
I zoom down the hill
like an airplane landing on a tarmac.

The speed awakens me,
excites me, and thrills me.
Seconds pass
focusing
Toward the goal —
the bottom.

I spin around at the bottom
spraying snow into the icy air
to look back
at my impressive achievement.

Krishan Amin, Grade 7
Detroit Country Day Middle School, MI

Open Your Door

This is the man who died on the cross
We are fully to blame for the holy soul that was lost
This sad story all began one night
When shepherds looked up and saw a star shining bright

This is the girl who suffered through pain
The journal she kept her only thoughts that remain
She hid in cellars, she thought there was a chance
She was not alone, but still tortured in camps

This is the dream, so many people have had
Where everyone is free and no one is sad
Where humans and humans can stand hand in hand
No matter your religion, your language or land

I've told you of a man, a girl and a dream
Don't say they make no difference, for they are more than they seem
The man gave us faith, the girl gave us courage
The dream gave us hope, so now we are sure
One can make a difference — many can make more
Out the window you see change, so open your door

Megan Hickinbotham, Grade 8
Maplewood Middle School, WI

My Grandmother

My grandmother is the peaceful and leafy palm tree,
Proudly standing on a remote desert island
In the middle of the calm, aquamarine ocean.
Providing comforting shade from the devilish sun
For the abandoned who are washed up on her shores.
She is sturdy and weathered,
And allows to be leaned on.
She is everlasting, surviving throughout the ages,
Enduring catastrophic storms and scorching temperatures.
Selflessly dropping luscious coconuts,
Filled with creamy yet sweet milk,
A delicious gift for the famished.
She becomes a companion to all, an enemy to none,
Turning the lonely mound of sand and dirt
Into a magical paradise.

Janith Jayatilake, Grade 9
Detroit Country Day Upper School, MI

War and Cry of the Sky

The sky was black, the sky was dark
The clouds march in, grasping their flashing weapon
As they march in, they play their loud booming song
The clouds confront the sun as they cover up the brightness
The war is over, the clouds have won
But then they realize that they ruined the day
They all start crying as they leave
Making the day bright once again, where it was destroyed.

Trevor Garlock, Grade 7
East Rockford Middle School, MI

Christmas Tree

Trudging through crunchy, pure, sugary snow
Pondering, surveying, analyzing
Perfect height — check!
Bushy leaves — check!
Big gaping hole
Next aisle
Intention of decorating the perfect tree
Plucking the perfect pine
Strapping the big furry sack on the truck
Flapping in the wind
Cinnamon and pine swirling around my nose
Glistening, twinkling, entrancing garnishes
Dancing around the proud pine
Snowman there!
Teddy bear here!
One by one until finished
A single minuscule click of a switch
Flash!
A present too unique
Light fills my eyes and the room with pure delight
Christmas has started again

Maria Tucker, Grade 7
Detroit Country Day Middle School, MI

In a World Without Make-up

In a world without make-up
The people would be free
To show themselves as who they are
And not as make believe

In a world without make-up
Everyone would be a star
More focused on individuality
Rather than trying to be someone they aren't

So maybe just for a day alone
We could go natural
Not plastered with blush and mascara
But shining from the inside out
In our world without make-up

Josephine Woods, Grade 7
Pleasant View School, MI

Early in the Morning

Early in the morning when the sun comes up
I get up hoping for good luck
No time to stay in bed
You little sleepy head
So I jump out of bed
A good day ahead
Early in the morning when the sun comes up

Emilee Gaiser, Grade 8
Corpus Christi Catholic School, MI

Don't Cry Anymore

I must stop my wailing,
I must avert the tears.
I need to scamper away,
And stand up to my fears.

An instinctive quality, crying was a must.
But now, whimsical tears; I cannot trust.
Now is the time for me to look up,
To my future, my potential is an unfilled cup.

I now fervor my freedom,
I won't take it for granted.
My destiny is shown,
Succor others, let them have it.

Don't be a fowl, I say,
Don't be the runt of life,
Be strong, branch away.
Never lose hope on your fight.

Tony Burton, Grade 8
Clinton Middle School, WI

My Sky

My sky looks down and stares at me.
Now I am not lonely.
It tells me how my day has been.
If happy, it turns sunny.
But if all that I am is angry,
Thunder will shout at me.
Sky is there for the gloomy days,
Where my skies will turn cloudy, and all will be gray.
When I am depressed, the sky turns dark and cold.
And that makes it cruel, to all living souls.
But if there is love,
Then watch the sunset that roams above.
What's your kind of sky?

Nika Orman, Grade 7
Abbott Middle School, MI

Scary

CREEK! the door opens slowly
SMACK! the door slams shut
CLICK! the lights shut off
BARK, BARK! my dog yelps out
I see a figure and jump out of bed like a scared cat
I snatched a flashlight from under my bed
HAHAHAHA! the figure laughs
CLICK! I turn on my flashlight
No one is there
Like a ghost just disappeared
I turn on my light
Nothing here
Except the wind

Kylie Curtiss, Grade 7
East Rockford Middle School, MI

Don't Cry, My Friend

Little tears fall
And cheeks are red
Little hands wipe
You hope life's for the best

Everything changes
And then you have to cry
Try to hide your feelings
But they are still inside

But don't cry, my friend
The worst is all gone
Hold on, my friend
You've done nothing wrong

You may feel like you are losing control
You may feel like you are in a black hole
But you'll realize you shouldn't fear
And I hope you see: that your friends are here

So, don't cry, my friend
The worst is all gone
Hold on, my friend
You've done nothing wrong

Nothing at all

Kavya Chaturvedi, Grade 7
Detroit Country Day Middle School, MI

Baseball

Baseball, baseball, a batting sport,
It is played on a diamond and not on a court.
First base, second base, third base, more,
Once you cross home plate, add 1 to the score.

Pitcher, catcher, outfield too,
Every player has something special to do.
The pitcher pitches the very first ball,
Screaming by faster than them all.

One strike, two strikes, protect the plate,
It's going to be a good battle, we'll just have to wait.
One foul ball, two foul balls, finally a hit!
It didn't go down not even a bit.

Rounding first base, the pressure starts to fright,
Heading to second, with confidence and might.
Over the fence my baseball goes,
Passing third, and onto home.

My teammates await me with hands in the air,
High five's all around, an A plus could not compare.
Looking to the crowd, with smiles abound,
This moment is great, I knew I'd come around.

Joseph Cipriano III, Grade 8
Our Lady Star of the Sea School, MI

Compassion

Compassion is the foster parents who gladly take in a rebellious teen
and give her a temporary home.

Compassion is the adoptive family who takes that precious baby
and gives him a forever home.

Compassion is the courageous soldier who takes the time to sit with a little girl who is lost and scared
Compassion is the gallant man who comes to help a lady when she has her hands full and can't open the door.

Compassion is the selfless nurse who takes the time to really care for her patient
Compassion is a sympathetic listener who helps a friend through every tough time.

Compassion is the reassuring hand that guides you with kind words
Compassion is the comforting arm around your shoulder.

Compassion is the bright, warm sunlight
through the dark, heavy clouds.

Abigail Lavey, Grade 8
Cedar Grove-Belgium Middle School, WI

Where I'm From

I am from pots and pans, from macaroni & cheese.
I am from the squeaky floor of our 35 year old house.
I am from the Tulips and the Fairy Circle.
I am from Donnelly and Hilliker, Grandma Tina and Nana — stubborn and wholehearted,
from shopping to dropping, always ready to laugh or cry.

I am from a world where technology reigns supreme and I am finding a place for me in this big world.
I am from "Do your best and you will succeed," to "Be true to yourself."
I am from the oldest religion, from the cross caring walk, to the crucifixion, to the saving of our sins,
to the home where everyone's welcome.

I am from Up North (God's Country), daughter of vacationing Ernest Hemingway, from the Mackinaw Bridge,
to the Sleeping Bear Dunes, to the beautiful blue waters of Torch Lake, and the colorful outlook of Dead Man's hill.
I am from the "Forever Young" grandma and "Soon to be world traveler," from a great grandma
I never knew I would get my knack of cooking from, and the love of Polish food.
I am from the roomful of just pictures and memories, from my dance medals to my preschool crafts,
to the love of scrapbooking, to the love of my memories.

Emily Hilliker, Grade 8
Kalkaska Middle School, MI

Something Greater

Trees fly by as the engine purrs and the wind weasels its way through my hair.
I look to my side trees fly by like people watching a parade.
As stone becomes vibrant as we approach and tries to calm itself as we pass.
I looked up into the stars hoping they would dance, but as I watched them,
those glowing diamonds surrounded by a dark abyss.
They stood there motionless, as everything zipped by filled with motion, those wonders,
stood there watching us with comfort and ease, like an old man and his favorite chair.
So I think at a certain point in every human's life we realize how small we are
and that there is something out there something greater than life.
So when we find a place that only contains happiness, and is filled to the brim with everything you
once dreamed of, and once we reach this place of perfectness beyond belief we will be able to create
a better future for our fellow brethren or create a masterpiece even greater than life itself.

Garrett Osborn, Grade 8
Perry Middle School, MI

Educational Michigan

In Michigan I've learned…
How to float a boat, milk a goat,
and when to put on a coat,
How to say goodbye and sigh
to all of the people that die.

In Michigan I've learned…
How to walk, how to draw with chalk,
and talk the yooper talk
How to cut down a tree and just be me,
and how to get rid of an unwanted fee.

In Michigan I've learned…
How to play guitar, how to drive a car,
and how to laugh at people when they come out of a bar,
How to ride a bike,
and how to catch a pike.

In Michigan I've learned…
How to be funny, how to raise money,
and how to enjoy honey

Kyle Burton, Grade 7
Sault Area Middle School, MI

The Woods

In the woods I have learned…
How to carry my gun over my shoulder
And be careful not to trip over logs, ruts, and boulders
How to climb up the ladder to my blind
Being careful not to trip up into a bind

In the woods I have learned…
How to dress properly if it might be cold or warm
In case of a very long storm
A hoodie and an orange vest
Will help on my long quest

In the woods I have learned…
How to sit quietly and listen to the sounds
Of all of nature all around
How to listen to the winds blow a cold breeze
As it slowly whistles through the trees

In the woods I have learned…
How to sit and wait for my deer
And when he comes, I silently cheer

Darren Langendorf, Grade 7
Sault Area Middle School, MI

Rocking Chair

It sits there in the attic,
Waiting to be sat on.
So many memories long gone.
Now everyone has grown,
Leaving the rocking chair on his own.
From the children to the old,
The rocking chair is waiting there in the cold.
He has been there, he has seen it all.
Now everything has seemed to fall.
He creaks and squeaks but nobody can hear,
He is sad but does not shed one tear.
He was at one time bright and proud,
His chipped paint was once white as a cloud.
The rotting wood is old and worn,
And the heart of the poor old rocking chair, is now torn.

Tyler Junk, Grade 7
Lincoln Jr/Sr High School, WI

Things I'm Thankful For

Dancing with my father,
And listening to his heart pump.
My baby brother Justin, and his charming smile.
The feel of my mom when she is hugging me.
The warmth that I feel when I come in my house.
When I smell my mom's cooking.
When my dad always smiles when I get in the car.
When my dog wags her tail when I come in.
When my mom cuddles with me.
When I watch football with my dad.
When my mom and dad kiss me on the forehead.
When my teacher congratulates me on an assignment.
When all my classmates come in the door.
When we win a basketball game.
And when everybody is having an awesome time.

Brooke Coleman, Grade 7
St Clare of Montefalco School, MI

Bravery

Bravery is not something earned.
You don't receive it like you would a medal.
No one stands on a podium handing you bravery.

Bravery is already within you.
You have always had it.
Every challenge is bravery playing hide and seek with you.
You just have to look inside yourself to find it.

Joshua Downing, Grade 7
Abbott Middle School, MI

Snowy!

I looked outside and it started snowing.
I walked outside and the wind was blowing.
I knew that it was freezing.
If you had no coat you would probably be wheezing.
It was so cold nobody was outside.
If I ran out there my feet would slide.
I looked outside, the wind was blowing.
Then I saw that it was snowing.

Michael Mayberry, Grade 7
Pleasant View School, MI

His Hands

A little girl, just three or four
her tiny figure by the door
wet tattered shoes upon the floor
her puffy eyes hold two lone tears
her small form shakes from cold and fear
My heart goes out,
I draw her near,
I stroke her face,
I wipe her tear
God speaks to me, his voice is clear —
She's my child, tell her I'm near.
I hold her there
she clings and cries
Emotions rage
tears sting my eyes
I tell her that there's one that loves
that thinks she's special
that gives free hugs
She looked at me with wide, blue eyes —
then turned from me; looked at the sky
I think I know — but wonder why.
Ruth Burn, Grade 7
Ruth Murdoch Elementary School, MI

My Thanksgiving List

My old dog's face,
My puppy's fur,
The sound of cats when they purr,
That new car smell,
A shining star,
The sound of howling from afar,
The taste of turkey,
My best friends' faces,
All safe, warm, and happy places,
My uncle singing
Me a song,
And my cousins singing along,
My TV shows,
My favorite books,
The smell of stew when it cooks,
My family's love,
The chill of water when I swim,
The sound of screaming when I win,
The last is my parents, sister, and cousins,
Even though we kick and shove,
They're the ones that I most love.
Liam Conlan, Grade 7
St Clare of Montefalco School, MI

Winter Wonderland

Winter is my snowboarding highway
Twists and turns
Til you hit that one jump
Winter!
Chase Tweedale, Grade 7
East Rockford Middle School, MI

The Best Room

It was a chill place,
Smell of firecrackers,
We had fun every day,
BB and firecracker wars,
But good times or bad,
We were never sad,
Friends over all the time,
We would play games,
Then go outside,
Our room was the best,
We had a lot of fun,
Like a lion attacking his prey,
Stay up all night,
We played football in the house,
But only when parents were gone,
But the room's not mine anymore,
I got up and moved out,
Hoping another person,
Would have as much fun,
As we had in that room,
I'll miss that place.
Travis Vetrone, Grade 9
Lincoln Jr/Sr High School, WI

Beautiful Daughter

Beautiful daughter,
Why don't you listen?
Beautiful daughter,
Let your brown eyes glisten.
Beautiful daughter,
Get out of this mess.
Beautiful daughter,
I will never love you less.
Beautiful daughter,
Daddy knows what he is talking about.
Beautiful daughter,
Believe him without a doubt.
Beautiful daughter,
I thank God every day for you.
Beautiful daughter,
Remember your daddy loves you too.
Beautiful daughter,
Why don't you listen?
Beautiful daughter,
Let your brown eyes glisten.
I love you…beautiful daughter.
Alessandra Tanner, Grade 9
Montgomery-Lonsdale High School, MN

Life

L ove is in every life.
I n life people love, hate, and forgive.
F un, everyone needs fun in life.
E veryone deserves happiness in life.
Macy Sazama, Grade 7
Round Lake High School, MN

The Dancing Night

In the night the time is right
to sight the high and holy light.

The moon now up, it starts to dance,
the light shines and starts the trance.

And on that night were none to name
for all played in the devil's game.

We drank and laughed through the night.
On that night we named a right:

A vow to make the day go on,
every night, all summer long.

And after then the sun comes round,
And we'll try to keep the sound.

The graceful dance we had that night
and the memories that felt so right.
John Lathrop, Grade 7
Nellie B Chisholm Middle School, MI

I'm Exposed

I can dig like a worm,
But I am quite firm
I can swim like a beaver,
But I don't have swamp fever
I can fish like a flamingo,
But I don't know their lingo
I can see like a bat,
But I'm not a brat
I have a star on my nose,
I guess that's what God chose
Man I love my kind
Because of all the food we find
We even have built-in knives
They come in handy when cutting chives
I don't need a parole
For I live in a hole
I'm all alone there
At least I have hair
I love being star-nosed,
But now I am a mole, exposed
Nathanael Tuckerman, Grade 9
Lenawee Christian School, MI

Summer

The flowers say hello
The sun hugs my back
The wind bites at the back of my neck
The clouds run by,
The leaves wave at me,
And I wave goodbye.
Mallory Parker, Grade 7
East Rockford Middle School, MI

Natter

The voices around
Paint an abstract picture
Varying pitches
Differing sounds
Each voice its own story
Its own idea
But clashing together
Too many to make out any one
They blur
A new image forms
So unsightly
Beautiful
Kaela Schudda, Grade 8
EAGLE School of Madison, WI

Trisha

Trisha
Hilarious, cool, fun, energetic
Relative of Domanic, Alexis, Monea
Lover of Mom, Dad, Family
Who feels happy, sad, mad
Who needs Mommy, Daddy, friends
Who gives love, hugs, kisses
Who fears spiders, bugs, worms
Who would like to see Peace
Hunger, homelessness
Resident of Lansing
Washington
Trisha Washington, Grade 7
Pleasant View School, MI

A Life of Wonder

There's an endless road to wonder,
once you've opened up your mind.
Although we try not to ponder,
it's a part of human kind.
Even our best detectives can't solve,
the mystery of life.
How it tends to always revolve,
around bumps in the road and strife.
True love has no end,
it goes on and on forever.
An angel God will send,
to guide your every endeavor.
Kayla Worachek, Grade 7
Lombardi Middle School, WI

Christmas

Tree as big and bright as the sun
Christmas music as quiet as a mouse
Living room as crowded as a mall
Table stacked with food
Sledding down a hill faster than a jet
Wrapping presents for others
Josh Zmudka, Grade 7
East Rockford Middle School, MI

The End of a Beginning

Lights flicker
Big lights all around; above my head
Like walls of electronic beasts, eating at my sore eyes
Some hang precariously by cables
Jagged blue runs along a few now and then

All is dark besides the spots illuminated in electronic hues
All is silent but white static
And the occasional rumble as another building crumbles at its manmade seams
Thus the ground is littered with debris

It looks as though there is no sky. Only endless black
I believe the stars are cowering behind a film of storm clouds
Or the sun has been taken by ash

I feel no breeze; the air is still
And it is not warm or cold
But I breathe in and taste the dust I had caught floating off the rubble around me

It smells of ash. Of death. The death of a beginning.
The end of a beginning.
Rachel Nagy, Grade 8
West Middle School, MI

Gone

Once there radiating joy and love
Now gone
Arms wide open ready for a warm hug
Now cold and stiff
Ready to softly kiss the pain away
Who will kiss this pain away?
So short so fast
Death is so unforgiving
So cruel and vile
Letting life seep out a little by little until she's just a hollow shell
Getting weaker and weaker until she's just a moving skeleton
Even though you can expect her to die at any second
You plaster on a fake illustration of your once-happy self and stumble on through life
Life moves too quickly just a blur
Once there…now gone
Gone forever
Harini Pasupuleti, Grade 8
Black Hawk Middle School, MN

My Bedroom

My bed told me a story.
The door wished me a good-night.
My window kissed my forehead.
The closet said goodnight and don't let the bed bugs bite.
My bedspread tucked me in.
The lights flickered on and off to a tune so I could fall asleep soundly.
My pajamas kept me as snug as a bug in a rug.
My mother came into my room and said, "I love you!"
Katie Tschida, Grade 8
St. Jerome Elementary School, MN

Out of This World

Aboard the spaceship
Throughout the world
Notwithstanding pressure
Amid the shadows
Beyond the universe
Together with love

Megan Herman, Grade 8
Unionville-Sebewaing Middle School, MI

Painter

Painter
Creative, art
Artistic, open-minded
They make you think about everything.
Artist

Haley Jackson, Grade 8
Perry Middle School, MI

Fall

The wind starts to blow
People begin to wear coats
The leaves fall down to the ground
And leave the trees bare
But the ground filled with color

Colton Joyce, Grade 7
Scranton Middle School, MI

Sun and Moon

glaring so fiercely
enclosed by a light blue
rise and set again
it sits so proudly
stars scattered around it

Madeleine Dahm, Grade 8
Our Shepherd Lutheran School, MI

The Savior of the Sun

Sitting at home
watching the rain pour down
A ray of sunshine
from the corner of my eye
a hope out of darkness

Spencer Carlson, Grade 8
Our Shepherd Lutheran School, MI

The End

From ev'ry ancient city
To populated town, come people
Who foretell the world's end
Only one being knows the answer
God, Lord of all

Sean Sheppard, Grade 8
Our Shepherd Lutheran School, MI

Ariel

Her stall smells of pure Ariel as I come to tack her up.
She nuzzles me as a old friend and waits for me to brush.
She is quickly tacked up as we walk with crossed over feet to the arena.

Her walk is calm but she is ready to go.
As I bump her to a trot she knows who I am.
I pay attention to my hands.
You have to be light but strong.
As I sit for two beats,
She takes off.
At a collected canter she knows her job well,
As we slow to a trot,
The jump comes up.

As she tries to gallop I tell her no and we jump.
One blend of horse and rider but her leg nicks the pole.
She stumbles but holds me with her strong neck to the other side.
As we try the jump again she does it.
She jumps gracefully and I hold on to her thick hair.
Not looking down at the blue jump and brown sand below,
We sail over.
And canter away, looking for the next jump.

Saskia Charles, Grade 8
West Hills Middle School, MI

Thanksgiving List

The sweet smell of pumpkin pie,
My dad making silly jokes,
My family praying to God,
The crisp air across my face,
The warmth of love in the room,
My beautiful sisters laughing, smiling, and singing,
The night sky glistening with stars,
The smell of the Thanksgiving season,
My brown dog barking in joy,
The feel of my grandparents hugs and kisses,
The look of green swishing trees,
The sound of planes flying across the blue sky,
My family gathering around the table to give thanks for what we have,
Praying for people less fortunate,
My friends and family being near me all the time.

Noelle Milton, Grade 7
St Clare of Montefalco School, MI

Gang Green

Green is crisp cool money, slimy leaping lizards and feeling envious.
Green is the taste of Shamrock Shakes.
A warm country breeze and spicy jalapeno peppers smell green.
Salty green olives also make me feel green.
Green is Viking fans and wind whistling in the trees.
Green is a rolling meadow and the Metro Dome and a warm green house.
Tumbling down a hill is green, mowing the lawn is also green.
Green is mint chocolate chip ice cream.
Green is fresh blades of grass on a spring morning.

Dyllan McKenzie, Grade 8
Menominee Jr High School, MI

The Quiet Jungle of Trees

Sunlight falls on the quiet jungle of trees,
The only sound that can be heard is the cold icy breeze.

The sunlight is now high
In the snowy, cloudy sky
As the trees start turning to white.

Then the light grows low
And fades down to a glow,
And that's when it all starts to change.

As you are asleep
Tucked deep in your keep,
As moonlight glows in the jungle of trees,
Two big eyes appear, attached to no head
As raccoons wake up and get out of bed.
Then noise fills the quiet jungle of trees.
The two red eyes fly down with a hoot
To catch a mouse running to a root.

The raccoons run about
As new sunlight comes out
And that's when it all start to change.

Sunlight falls on the quiet jungle of trees.
The only sound that can be heard is the cold icy breeze.

Karissa Mazzara, Grade 7
Our Lady Star of the Sea School, MI

Loneliness and True Love

It's dark, damp, cold,
Where am I,
I'm scared,
Frozen there I stand weeping

Waiting,
Waiting to see what will happen next,
Silence falling in all around me,
It's suffocating me, it won't stop

I can't feel anything,
No happiness, joy, excitement,
Only guilt, sorry, pain

Still frozen in the darkness,
Hearing nothing, but my slow, staggering breath,
Why am I alone?

I suddenly feel warmth,
I turn and see nothing,
But a glimpse of benevolence only you hold,
Then, and only then was the first time,
I felt the passion I seek,
Your true love

Autumn Gare, Grade 9
Montgomery-Lonsdale High School, MN

Daddy's Little Girl

Aren't you proud?
Tattoos and piercings everywhere
Fast cars and motorcycles
Loud music playing till dawn
Aren't you proud?
Your little princess
Turned into the girl you see on TV
Do you still love me Daddy?
Even though I'm a mess
Walking around in tight dresses
Showing everything to strangers without shame
Flouncing around with dyed blond hair
Starving myself to look perfect
Are you still proud?
I know in your eyes
I'm still your little girl
Playing dress-up in huge heels
Fairy wings and pink fluffy tutus
Are you still proud of me?
For what I am now or what girl I was before?
Are you still proud of me Dad?

Claire Nader, Grade 9
West High School, WI

Purpose

Purpose is an idea, a thought, a voice,
There to raise you up or tear you down.
Purpose is a seeing dog,
Trained to walk beside you, leading you in the right direction.
Purpose is a best friend,
There to lean on when things aren't going your way.
Purpose is a young foal,
Romping around a colorful meadow.
Purpose is a thoughtful mother,
Eyeing her mischievous daughter with practiced patience.
Purpose is hope,
The exhilarating zip line after the exhausting climb.
There
Until
The
End.

Maddison Schreurs, Grade 8
Cedar Grove-Belgium Middle School, WI

Life

Life is a mess
When you have to deal with school and home
    it's hard to keep it right.
Life is also not fair.
Someone can mess with you and
    you have to deal with it.
But all you have to do
    is get a notebook
    and write down your feelings.

Tyrone Hooper, Grade 7
Pleasant View School, MI

Lost Treasures and Memories

A hot summer breeze
as we step in the cool lake.
There the treasure lies.
Rusting metal, rotting wood.
What great excitement rushing!

Shocked and amazed,
we step out of the water.
We have to tell someone.
Though our findings are great,
fame never discovers us.

Katie Espin, Grade 8
Our Shepherd Lutheran School, MI

Ice Skating

White and black skates touch the ice,
Sharp blades gliding across the ice,
Beautiful dresses and costumes
Brighten the ice
Spinning and spinning
Jumping and jumping
Being an artist on the ice,
Skating to music of choice,
Winning the gold
For true
Skater heart

Haley Ruesch, Grade 8
Round Lake High School, MN

Up

Up is where the bees are
Up is where the birds go
Up is where the sky starts
Up is where the world glows
Up is where the night is
Up is where the stars shine
Up is where faith is
Up is where my mom went
Up is where life begins
Up is where this story ends

Amber Thomas, Grade 7
Pleasant View School, MI

Skiing

Skiing down the hill,
gives me such a thrill.
I hop onto the chair lift,
up the hill I go.
As I look down,
I see the wonderful glittering snow.
I get to the top,
the lift comes to a stop.
I ski back down the hill,
it gives me such a thrill.

Barbara Davidek, Grade 8
St John Vianney Catholic School, MI

Winter

Winter is when Jack Frost plays
For blows the wind chill, the world cold
Earth she does not like the frost
For she wants her plants to live in a warm world
In summer comes out of her tropical paradise
She goes into the streets, invisible to awaken the plants from
their slumber
With each year, the chill, the cold get closer,
Jack frost gets closer
She is afraid for herself, and her plants
For she might be put in a permanent freeze by Frost and Winter
If this happens the Earth will be ruled by Winter and his son Jack Frost
The world will be changed, the World of Ice
For Earth she needs some place warm to be or this she will die.
The cold is slowly creeping in
Sooner or later Earth will die!
But then a hero could come along
And vanquish the son of winter and defeat his armies of dark.

Matt Twaroski, Grade 8
St Jerome Elementary School, MN

Medicine of Sleep

It is full moon night.
Wolves are barking and barking. Bark! Bark! Bark! Bark!
And owls are hooting and hooting. Hoot — Hoot — Hoot — Hoot —
I am on my bed.
I can't fall to sleep.
I am counting one hundred lambs.
One lamb, two lambs, three lambs, four lambs, five lambs…
I still can't fall to sleep.
Dogs are barking and barking. Bark! Bark! Bark! Bark!
Cats are mewing and mewing. Mew — Mew — Mew — Mew —
I am counting all of my friend's names.
Alex, Eli, Trevor, Max, Caleb, Chris, Johnny, Jonathan…
I still can't fall to sleep.
Baby is crying. Brother — Brother —
He hugged me. I feel so good.
Now I can go to bed.
Goodnight wolves and owls, goodnight dogs and cats, goodnight crickets and mice.
Goodnight my little lovely brother.

Siwon Choi, Grade 7
Ruth Murdoch Elementary School, MI

Lonely Night

I sit all alone over there, pouting and thinking about how it's not fair.
That they get to go and do all the fun things, and I lay on my bed
hoping my phone rings.
I wait and wait for them to get back, and then I remember about the
chores I did slack.
So I do them all and only twenty minutes go by, oh how I wish the
time would just fly.
Then they step in the dark front door, the moment I had waited for.
So that was the consequence that I did reap, now it's all over so I can
go to sleep.

Elexis Chiero, Grade 8
Woodworth Jr High School, WI

Whispers

I can hear them all around,
from leaves rustling and birds chirping,
to seeds buried deep in the ground.
They're in the wind when it blows,
the water when it ripples,
and the grass when it grows.
From waving golden wheat,
and flowers blooming,
to sand under my feet.
They're here,
and they're there
I hear whispers everywhere.

Autumn Ash, Grade 8
Perry Middle School, MI

So?

So you're pretty,
So I'm not,
So you get everything your heart desires,
So I don't,
So you stay,
So I go,
So you don't get your heart broken,
So I always do,
But I will always have,
Something you want,
What is it you ask?
It's so my secret.

Madison House, Grade 7
Perry Middle School, MI

White

We see white in winter
Snow falling
We see the sun shine off the snow
The snow starts to sparkle
We see snow in the trees
We see snow everywhere we go
White is winter
White is the gloss coming off the snow
White is on our roofs
White is on the ground
White is on our houses
White is winter

Adam Galbavi, Grade 7
Perry Middle School, MI

Help Me

Look in my eyes
And
Feel my pain
This is me asking for Help!
Everybody just thinks
I'm a joke.

Jasmine B. Jackson, Grade 9
Visions Jr/Sr High School, WI

This Thing I Found a Love For

Happy, sad, furious, stressed.
These emotions released with what I do the best.
Across the floor moving beautifully.
Feel the music as if you wrote the song.
Leap, turn, kick, stop…I feel unstoppable as I go deeper into the music.
Everyone's watching me intensely,
Every move I make, every mistake.
I've found a love for this thing I do.
Not everyone was born with this gift.
Luckily I was.
To be the best takes time.
Working out, stretching,
All through the blood, sweat, and tears.
Sometimes I feel like giving up
Because of things I don't get.
But good thing I kept going to fulfill my dream
Of even being famous one day.

This is my passion.
I am a dancer.

Jada Page, Grade 7
Pleasant View School, MI

Winter Mess

Winter mess winter mess why are you here?
I thought that the spring was near!
The rain is dropping; the snow is falling, why are you here!
The kids are laughing and also crying because of the mess you have made.
I'm sorry to confess but you are a mess.
Winter mess why are you here.
Unless you leave, the town will weep winter mess why are you here?
Please please please winter mess leave for the town will be happy indeed.
Christmas is near the bells are ringing oh winter please leave.
The merry Christmas will turn into a boring Christmas.
Winter mess we beg leave leave leave it is Christmas Eve
The bells do ring the time is here please leave.
The town will be happy indeed.

Itumeleng Gabasiane, Grade 7
Ruth Murdoch Elementary School, MI

No Need to Fear

I believe in angels, the
ones that God created for me to
become close to. I believe in God, the one who
scarified for me. I believe in friendship the kind that lasts forever.
We talk every night from dusk to dawn, about the ones we see forever
and all day long. Our friendship is like no other, nobody
else but you, you and I, the angels that descended
to us, to guide and protect, to love
and to share. To have joy with and actually care.
You realize in life that everybody is not always there when you need them.
So you just turn right back around and face your fears.
And say, "No need to worry, Jesus is here."

Teshani Hutch II, Grade 8
Gesu Catholic School, MI

Fallen

They guided me towards
the place where I'll fall
binding my wings,
allowing no escape.
I can hear them whispering
but I cannot understand
Looking down, I saw Earth.
One shouted,
the rest cheered
A bell rang in the distance,
and I knew it was time.
Pushed over the edge of the cloud,
the drop seemed endless.
My instincts were to fly and survive,
but I couldn't.
I couldn't even look back.

Sarah Taylor, Grade 7
Perry Middle School, MI

Brothers and Sisters

My sister is weird and annoying.
I am cool and active.
We argue about everything.
But my mom gives her anything
I don't like my sister and
She doesn't like me.

We are totally different.
I like sports and being outside.
She likes reading and writing.
We are nothing alike.

She doesn't like trying new things
And I do.
We're like water and air,
Nothing alike.

Zachary Sheffer, Grade 7
Lincoln Jr/Sr High School, WI

Street Ball

Boom, Boom, Boom, Smash
That's how it goes
Boom, Boom, Boom, Smash
It's the way it is.

He yells and screams,
but gets back up.
Boom, Boom, Smash
Is the way it is.

Boom, Boom, Smash
He gets laid out.
That was the end of
Street ball.

Rudy Janke, Grade 7
Lincoln Jr/Sr High School, WI

The Leaf

My old grandfather
watches from the deck,
the leaves falling from the little oak tree.

One by one the leaves fall,
like the pages from a calendar,
getting ripped off day after day.

The leaves are like Jackson Pollock
making a painting,
on the ground.
Some leaves are colorful,
some leaves are shriveled up.

Grandpa himself is an oak tree.
His face looking older each day,
each time another leaf falls.

As winter grows near,
the faster they fall,
until the last leaf falls,
he stands here and is proud,
of a life well lived.

Clark Chisnell, Grade 7
Abbott Middle School, MI

My Best Buddy

She has blond hair
I have reddish hair.
We both have freckles
But only when the days are hot.
We both have blue eyes,
But mine seem to change as the seasons do.
Hers are dark and bright at the same time.
She's got the brains.
I have the ability.
We love to do art together
and we love to sing.
She's got the words,
but I have the tone.
I have nice handwriting,
And she's got nicer handwriting.

She's 23 and I'm 13.
She might be older,
But she loves me
And I love her.

I don't know what
I would do without her.

Elizabeth Hulett, Grade 7
Lincoln Jr/Sr High School, WI

Sükran Listesi*

The power and will to survive,
The wisdom to lead,
The courage to prevail,
And God to follow HIS word.
    Sight to see the good in life,
Touch to feel my soul,
Hearing to listen to good news,
Taste to enjoy the sweets in my mouth,
And smell to wear cologne.
    Discipline to learn,
Language for communication,
Freedom to follow your dreams,
Passion to occupy me,
And my body to use on Mother Earth.
    Hope to not distress,
Sacrifice to reach a goal,
Logic to make smart choices,
Love to be eternally happy,
And writing so my memories are never lost.
    These are a few pleasures of life,
But I hope you enjoy them.

Ervin Colston, Grade 7
St Clare of Montefalco School, MI
*Turkish for Thanksgiving List

The Outdoors

From the outdoors I've learned…
How to hike up a mountain to the top
To run around a lake until I drop
How to paddle board along the shore
And sit at a campfire and make a s'more

From the outdoors I've learned…
How to make a snowman
And how to say, "Yes I can"
How to downhill ski
and climb a tree

From the outdoors I've learned…
To kayak down a stream
And to get muddy without a scream
How to hunt with my dad
And to fish and be glad

From the outdoors I've learned…
To sit in the sun
And be outside and have fun!

Courtney Arbic, Grade 7
Sault Area Middle School, MI

Time Zone

Time's not slow, nor fast,
Making objects change by force,
And we are its victims.

David Fortune, Grade 8
Perry Middle School, MI

The Story of the Man*

Summer of '89
Someone in dark clothes rode in
He is like a black bat with his black clothes
Said to call him Shane
Seems like he is running from his past
But what?
Works for Starretts

Gets picked on for drinking soda pop
Fletcher's men
Next trip to town got in a fight with Chris
POW! Slam! Whack!
Shane was a strong ox in the fight against Chris

Next fight
Shane and Starrett take on Fletcher's boys
They win
Fletcher leaves
Then no one thinks that Fletcher would bring back a new man
Wilson is the man's name
Marian and Joe stay to play out Fletcher's game

Sophia Sander, Grade 8
Wauzeka-Steuben School, WI
*Based upon "Shane" by Jack Schaefer

The True Meaning of the Holidays

Thanksgiving has passed, Christmas is near
The holidays are full of laughter and cheer
The true meaning, of course, is not presents, ribbons, or bows
Rather to celebrate with friends and foes
We celebrate because we care
About the joy and love He came to share
He came to save everyone
He is our Savior, Lord of Lords, and God's own Son
He gives us life, He gives us health
He paid for us by His own death
And now in the holidays
Let us look at Him and change our ways
Think of others, not ourselves
Speak good words and think good thoughts
And as for Jesus, the babe in a manger, never doubt
That's what the holidays are truly all about

Gillian Kuhn, Grade 7
Ruth Murdoch Elementary School, MI

Without/With

Without this I wouldn't be able to express myself.
Without this my life would be boring.
Without this some things could not be done.
With this you can have fun.
With this you can dance.
With this you can do a lot of things.
Have you guessed what this is yet?
If not, it is music, one of the best things in the world.

Jacob Cherry, Grade 9
Round Lake High School, MN

MSU Spartans

The players took their spots,
After choosing one side of the dot.

B.J. caught the ball,
And brought it to the wall.

We had gold helmets,
Black pants, too.
(There was no green, like the Spartans usually do)
We beat the Wolverines four touchdowns to two.

Before and after a tailgate for all,
My family and I did have quite a ball.

The refs were pretty bad,
Unlike some that we have had
But we still got the win,
And Michigan lost their grin.

Bennett Burke, Grade 7
Our Lady Star of the Sea School, MI

Winter's Death

I shall remember thee on winter's night
The freezing wind swept snowflakes everywhere
So dark and silent, all around no light
Yet still you hear the sound of blowing air

It happened in the evening on a walk
He was alone and filled with lots of strife
This was because his friends would only mock
Too fast the river cracked and took his life

I stared outside at emptiness so much
It felt as though my heart was ripped apart
I miss his warm laughter and gentle touch
At my first sight I loved him from the start

But now you're gone, your lifeless body lies
And I am full of so many goodbyes.

Grace Smith, Grade 7
Parkview Center Elementary School, MN

A New World

There's a whole other world out there,
One for you and me,
It's different there,
And full of peace.
A land where men can get along,
And not worry about war,
It's time for us to go out and explore.
A world of laughter and smiles,
With no fears or regrets.
It's time to change our world,
To make it like the rest.

Sara Heyerdahl, Grade 9
Arrowhead Union High School - South Campus, WI

True Love

It was a hard thing to do
But it came to me and you
To finally see
We were meant to be
With one another
Only you could help me see
You were always meant for me

Sara Hendzel, Grade 8
Perry Middle School, MI

Sidewalk vs Trails

Sidewalk
Hard, rough
Walking, commuting, stepping
People, shoes, tracks, boots
Running, hiking, climbing
Earthy, natural
Trails

Joe Dandron, Grade 7
Nellie B Chisholm Middle School, MI

Outdoor Sporting

Hunting
Exhilarating, dower
Firing, tracking, waiting
Bucks, rifles, minks, traps
Checking, setting, baiting
Loud, simple
Trapping

Keenan Wittebort, Grade 7
Nellie B Chisholm Middle School, MI

Wheels of Steel

Cars
cool, fast
racing, driving, riding
metal, trailers, rubber, tires
dragging, hauling, towing
loud, strong
Trucks

Patrick Pineda, Grade 7
Nellie B Chisholm Middle School, MI

Fire vs Ice

Fire
Hot, Red
Burning, Sizzling, Destroying
Ashes, Flames, Icicles, Frost
Freezing, Melting, Sliding
Cold, Clear
Ice

Sam Siemer, Grade 7
Nellie B Chisholm Middle School, MI

My Favorite Place

In my favorite place,
I feel nice and safe.

Posters of my favorite teams and singers,
Banners of Packer Pride,
And telling about my trip to Florida, hang on the walls.

A card from a deceased family member, has its place next to my bed,
Along with a calendar.
There are also lots of pictures,
Pictures of my friends, family, and favorite athletes.

On the wall, at the foot of my bed, hang my ribbons and medals.
Just above them, is something I couldn't live without, my radio.
Next to my bed, sits the books I am reading and my Bible.

On my dresser, more pictures sit, telling my past.
Along with a lamp, mirror made from newspapers, and a huge seashell.

The last thing in my special place, is my bookshelf,
With not enough room for all my books.
Books sit on top of the ones crammed together,
And they lay on the ground, waiting to be read.

Yes, this is my special place,
My room!

Lauren Anderson, Grade 7
Lincoln Jr/Sr High School, WI

Being Different

Sitting in silence,
In a classroom all by yourself,
No one to talk to you;
No one likes you because you are different.

You are the smart one who knows practically everything,
You are the one, who raises your hand because you know every answer.
Sometimes you even go above and beyond sharing your knowledge,
Yet no one likes you because you are different.

All the teachers adore you;
They would adopt you if they could because you are unique.
You do what is right and respect what others have to say,
Yet no one likes you because you are different.

You do everything with grace
Going all out on what you don't have to do.
You even help your teachers after school because you have the time,
Yet no one likes you because you are different.

No matter what everyone says about liking people who are different,
No one listens to them.
Everyone just acts like they agree with that person,
And you have firsthand experience of this because you are different and no one likes you.

Liliyana Wolberg, Grade 8
West Hills Middle School, MI

I Am

I am the president of the United States.
I am a doctor who cures cancer.
I am a teacher that ends bullying.
I am the engineer who invents flying cars.
I am the greatest NFL player of all time.
I am the scientist that ends hunger.
I am the principal of your grand kids' school.
I am the person who provides shelter for the homeless.
I am the CEO for *Microsoft*.
I am the general that ends all wars.
I am an airplane pilot that flies your family safely.
I am the chief of police that ends crime.
I am a person that makes the world a better place.
I am the person who rebuilds the Twin Towers.
I am the first astronaut that lands on Neptune.
I am the dentist that fixes your teeth.
I am the pharmacist that gives you your prescription.
I am the pastor of your church.
I am the mayor of your city.
I am a 7th grader at Abbot Middle School.
I am the future.

Corey Green, Grade 7
Abbott Middle School, MI

Why

Why do I need to be here
Why do I need to mind
Why do I need to reason
If I don't seem to care
Who are you to tell me what to do
Who are you to tell me who I am
Where were you when things were falling apart
When I was alone
When the time would slow down
When I would speed up
When I would cry out
You never were close
You never came
You never listen or said my name
You never remembered, you never tried
You never loved me, you didn't even try
So I ignored you so I lied
So I told you, you were never on my mind
I was lost and alone, But so were you
You where trying to find your way back to me
Where were you, where were you?

Sharon Quartey, Grade 8
Ruth Murdoch Elementary School, MI

Hope

I hope someday you'll realize…
What true love really means,
Because true love isn't what you gave me.
I hope that girl you left me for…
Gives you what I couldn't,
Because even though I know you deserve better…
She makes you happy, and I didn't.
I hope in the future, you'll learn how to treat people,
Because when I knew you, you lacked class.
I hope no matter what happens…
You'll always be my friend.
Nothing more, just a buddy.
I hope you'll never forget me,
Because I'll never forget you.
I hope one day I'll realize…
You weren't the problem…
But I was.

Cherish Woodworth, Grade 8
Perry Middle School, MI

True Friends

A friend is someone you grow to like
Someone you do everything with
   from talk to travel or to bike.
When you have a true friend
   he/she will support you

But you have to know they will correct you too

Even though this wide obstacle course is really long
You have to slow down and see their talents,
   like making dances or song

When you feel like you can't stand
You can use the hand of a friend
If there hand ain't there…
It's time to start your course again

Paris Henry, Grade 7
Pleasant View School, MI

Beautiful Melody

As your hands swipe across that beautiful wooden piano,
   you play a song so sweet and so soft.
It's like listening to an angel sing a song from the heart.
You never know how true this music
is until you hear it, this is a beautiful melody, if you listen
   closely you may hear the words.
I love you.

Darian Ryan, Grade 8
Perry Middle School, MI

Bored

Bored is what you feel
   when you're doing your homework.
   when you're at school.
   when you're at home all alone, lonely as ever.
   when you're outside and nobody is there,
   right by your side to say hi.
Bored is what I am feeling today,
   right now at this very moment.

Audriana Patino, Grade 7
Pleasant View School, MI

School

School came too soon
I can't wait until June
To lay by the pool
And relax and stay cool.

September quickly turns to
November,
As quick as a flash
Like the 50 yard dash.

February is fading
But summer is waiting.
April and May
Can't wait for the last day.

School is out
Scream and shout.
Nine months pass me by
Each last day I always seem to cry.
Lauren Miller, Grade 7
Our Lady Star of the Sea School, MI

The Locker

I am a locker
Tall and proud,
When you open me
I creak nice 'n loud.

I hold all our junk
Your books, your bag,
A magnetic mirror,
An American flag.

Some people yell,
I am real messy.
I hold your gym clothes.
They are the opposite of dressy.

I am a locker,
Tall and proud
And just for you
I'll creak nice 'n loud.
Lydia LaCost, Grade 7
Lincoln Jr/Sr High School, WI

Summertime

Friends all around, eating s'mores
apple trees, apple cores
great stories and lots of fun
games where we have to run
boat rides and tubing, too
there is way too much to do
dancing, smiling, laughing and
loving life, it's so grand.
Haley Borrow, Grade 8
St John Vianney Catholic School, MI

The Second Coming of Christ

The sun is rising
The new day is drawing near
Christ's second coming

Was a cloudy day
The clouds start to open up
A beam of light shines

I see the heavens
The angels come down singing
Hosanna, praise God!

I see people rising
And I too begin to rise
All the Christians rise

I begin to sing
A song of happiness to
God up in heaven.
Jake Barbieri, Grade 9
Lenawee Christian School, MI

Courage

courage is what makes you
get out of bed in the morning
courage is what make you
go to school
courage is what makes you
get a job
courage is what makes you
face your fears
courage is what
gives you the will to fight
courage is what helps you
speak in crowds
courage is what makes you
get married
courage is what makes
you, you
courage is what makes you
live your life the way you want to live it.
Chris Shue, Grade 7
Perry Middle School, MI

A Monkey's World

the jungle is where a monkey roams
they spend all their day in the trees
games are played throughout the day
bananas divided
they eat for the rest
swing on away
a monkey's
life for
me
Alec Stifter, Grade 8
St Jerome Elementary School, MN

After

After the day, the dark sky falls,
After the day, the sun says goodnight,
After the day, the moon says hello,
After the day, the stars start to show.

Once the day sky falls,
The trees start to rustle,
The crickets start chirping,
And people disappear.

Once the sun says goodnight,
You know the day is done,
Loud noises are silenced,
And the light is gone.

Once the moon says hello,
I watch it slowly rise.
As I stop to admire its glow,
The children get settled into bed.

Once the stars start to show,
The fireflies start to glow.
I've never seen such a beautiful sight,
As I close my eyes and murmur goodnight.
Madison White, Grade 7
Perry Middle School, MI

Disappointed

Time after time,
I try not to cry.
For which I find,
A dirty rumor.

You say that you love me,
How do I know it's true?
A lie that hurts
But you never leave.

I confront you,
I question you.
But all I get is more lies,
From a person that says "I love you."

Time after time,
This has been rough,
I've had enough!

Don't call,
Don't write,
Not even type.
I'm disappointed in you.
Symantha Taylor, Grade 8
Perry Middle School, MI

Heaven in a Blanket

Can heaven really be in a blanket?

Every night, by my side,
Why does it make me feel so loved? so complete? so okay?

She knows everything, she's open and waiting;
She helps me get through my toughest problems.
Like a hug, it wraps around me in comfort;
Soft, and inviting every problem.
She listens; She's there.

The box of Kleenex next to my bed.
Every trouble, at the breaking point;
I let go and tears fall from my face.
Lost and confused; the fabric is wise, and tells me what to do.

Love, sorrow, my life;
My mom —
She is gone, she is in heaven.

Heaven really can be in a blanket.

Katie Berthet, Grade 8
West Hills Middle School, MI

Dream

To desire is to want.
To want is to imagine.
To imagine is to believe.
To have all of these things,
you have to
Dream.

To dream is easy,
but making those dreams reality is hard.
Dreams are complicated things.
Some are hard to understand.
Others easy.
No matter how many you fail,
keep going forth toward your greatest dream.

Jamie DeBruyckere, Grade 7
Lester Prairie Secondary School, MN

Life

Life is a roller coaster
There are ups and downs
The downs can be the scariest moments
Like the events of 9/11
Deaths, fire from the plane crash
The ups are the best moments you can ever have
The best moment would be spending time with people you love
But when you crash you don't know what to do
Like when you are in a car accident
There are huge dents and scars that last until it gets fixed
Again life is a roller coaster

Gabby Rudolph, Grade 8
West Middle School, MI

Dependence

Save me from my unruly decisions
Protect me from my heart
Keep me in your sight so nothing will harm me
I should not fear if you're there to guard me
I cannot stand for an injury
Destruction is my worst enemy
I fear to think those thoughts
Some things that I should halt
Never let me mislead the followers
So please may you guide me
My heart screams, "don't leave me here, I can't take this pain"
Please remain so my heart can sustain
What should stay put together
My puzzle, unraveled by the raft in which you hold
I love to hear your voice because you speak words of gold
My heart is in your hands in which I give to you to hold
Protect me, save me, or at least just keep me claimed
My mind will flow with my heart, unable to be tamed
Please come save me so I can stay the same

Karla Harrison, Grade 8
Gesu Catholic School, MI

Windmill

Slice smoothly through the fabric of the air
Your blades in turning reaching for the sun
Then plunging streamlined towards the earth so bare
Hypnotic circles whirling on the run
The weathered, rough-hewn boards do tell a tale
Of loving hands which nailed each supple board
Of storms whipped into record-breaking gales
Of a gigantic, ancient grain-filled hoard
Now foolish people snap you on the green
As if you existed for them alone
Immortalizing you on silver screens
And copyrighting pictures as their own
Remember those days when kids came from farms
Consoled by gentle turning of your arms?

Caroline Harmening, Grade 7
Valley View Middle School, MN

Sports

Basketball is one of my favorite sports
when the calm, blowing wind passes my shorts
or when I steal the ball and dribble my way
across the court
or when playing football
I catch with full grip and run around
until I score a touchdown
or when on defense I break my way through a group of people
blocking the quarterback
blockers make sure you don't get a sack
there's no one open
and the guards are gone
so the QB is trying to get some yards.

Markeny Belvert, Grade 7
Pleasant View School, MI

Winter

Christmas is the sound of family coming to gather and exchange presents.
Is the smell of cookies and turkey in the oven.
Christmas is the feeling of joy and happiness that everyone is to gather.
Christmas is the taste of turkey and stuffing and cranberry and rolls.
Winter feels like snow rubbing against your face and having snow ball fights with your friends.
Building snow forts and having wars with each other.
Is hanging stockings
decorating the tree and hanging ornaments.
Going to church
I love going sledding
snow is fluffy
snow is cold
snow makes you feel like you like you're an icicle
snow is white
snow is great to play in.
winter is a fun time to play with friends.
Heavy
Light
Gray
slushy
I can't wait until winter comes this year.

Brent Kiefer, Grade 7
St John Neumann School, WI

Wait for Winter

She sits in the window seat. Staring out at the crisp, noisy world. Yellow. Orange. Red.
Children dance gleefully among the colorful piles of leaves. She sighs. Yellow. Orange. Red.
Laughter bubbles perfectly up into the sky like a lost balloon. Frost breathes out in a circle where it brushes the window.
Yellow. Orange. Red.
Adults sashay their hips, raking raking raking. Trails her fingers along the cold glass.
Yellow. Orange. Red.
Rain hovers in the air like a mysterious stranger, waiting to be introduced. A smile.
Yellow. Orange. Red.
Wind blows affectionately, ruffling the leaves who blush deep red 'n gold. A silent, icy giggle.
Yellow. Orange. Red.
Lonely puddles wait patiently for squeaky rubber boots. "Rain…" She whispers.
Yellow. Orange. Red.
Clouds puff their chests proudly but hold it in. She pouts.
Yellow. Orange. Red.
Branches shudder and drop their blankets of fire. Impatient, she trills her fingers against a blue tinted arm.
Yellow. Orange. Red.
All gone…but one. A malicious grin, "Fall." She demands in an excited hiss.
Yellow. Orange. Red.
It shivers. Rustling a few hasty prayers. "Please…" She murmurs at last. Yellow. Orange. Red.
It falls. Winter relieves a baited breath, and with that, flew from the window out into that world. And all is white.

Alexis Arons, Grade 8
Jefferson Middle School, MI

That Thing from Above

That thing form above. That thing from above that makes my heart pound. It makes you wanna drop to the ground. That feeling that people are seeking for but they gotta open that hidden door. The thing that people are begging to keep. That thing that makes their body weak. The thing you can't embrace but warms your face. The thing that can hurt you but you can get through. It makes you cry sometimes but can make you feel good inside. I call that thing love.

Tamara Hunter, Grade 9
Visions Jr/Sr High School, WI

Switch

Let's switch our eyes,
Only for a day
So you will finally see
The way I look at you.
Now, let's switch our feet
For the same day
So you will realize
How safe I feel
Walking in your steps.
Now, give me your arms,
And I'll give you mine
To show you how wonderful it feels
when I put them around you.
Here, try my ears
And listen to the sound of your voice
Like sweet music throughout them.
and at the end of the day,
I'll give you everything back,
and I'll ask you, in a whisper,
"How does it feel to be like me?"

Thalia Cannon, Grade 9
Round Lake High School, MN

Rainfall

Rain is such a peaceful thing,
It always calms my mind.
Whenever I think of pouring rain,
I simply close my eyes.
I think of all the great things
I am grateful for in life.
Even though I'm scared inside,
I always know I'm safe.
So why are some things horrible and cruel?
I open my eyes and whisper to myself,
all the great things I have,
every single raindrop,
calms the common fear,
but I know that nothing will appear.
But then I smile,
for I know that I will manage this,
and I remember all the things,
I have to myself.
So today I'm just going to say,
Be grateful for the rain.

Zoe Myers, Grade 7
Ruth Murdoch Elementary School, MI

Winter

Cold wind whispering in my ear.
Trees' needles singing a song.
The warmth of the open fire.
Snow twinkles by my side.
Roiling hills painted white.
All the things around on a winter night.

Mitchell Crane, Grade 7
East Rockford Middle School, MI

This Is New York

twinkling, sparkling nights
New York
buildings so tall with shiny lights
this is New York

lights glowing on this long winter night
New York
I shiver, but the city hugs me tight

the Rockefeller Christmas Tree
New York
such a beautiful sight for us all to see

carolers in Central Park singing
New York
so beautiful that it sounds like bells of St. Patrick's Cathedral ringing

the place where dreams come true
New York
could this city of over seven million be for me too?

glittering snowflakes fall for awhile
New York
now this is the part where I smile because…
this is New York

Lauren Camacho, Grade 9
Wilmot Union High School, WI

I Am Fall

I am bright orange, yellow, and red. I am whirling to the ground from trees.
I crunch when I'm stepped on. I am fall leaves.
I am cool and peaceful. I swirl with sweet smells.
I am the fall breeze.

I make the children excited, some frightened. I am the screams and giggles.
I give wishing feelings. I am Halloween.
I am soft and crunchy. Children jump in, scattering me.
Rustling away, I am the fall leaf pile.

It seems like forever to bake. Mom's cooking up a storm.
I am the family gathering from near and far. I am yummy Thanksgiving.
I am the breeze getting colder. I am the time for hats and scarves.
I am the cold children.

I am a delicious treat. I warm the children up
I am the mother telling kids to come inside. I am the cookies and hot cocoa being eaten.
I am the children inside more. I am the fireplace crackling with swaying flames.
I am fall ending.

I am the carols. I am the tree with lights and ornaments.
I am the decorations inside and out. I am Christmas coming soon.
I am chilly. I am sad. I am lonely. I am the last leaf and the first snowflake.

Maddie Reid, Grade 7
Woodworth Jr High School, WI

How to Get a Sheep

My eyelids are a vault to my dreams when they close
And I see sheep, jumping like rabbits
I realize that they're all mine
Then I wake up

But then I get a dog
A new house
With the 4-H fairgrounds beckoning a minute away
And a job with puppies

And sheep

When I go to the job
I see a puffy, wooly lamb
And baa-ing rings in my ears
I pinch myself
But it's all real

Now, as I pet my sheep Mocha
I think back to when this was just a dream,
But now I don't have to worry
About waking up.

Abby Glad, Grade 7
Abbott Middle School, MI

Boring School

It's eight o'clock, school is so boring,
If you listen close, you can hear some snoring.
Social studies, math, science, poetry,
All the students do is stare at the trees
Even though it's just the start of September,
Every student tries to remember
The time when school was very fun
But now preschool is over and done.
In the sixth grade, the homework is rough,
And all the teachers are even more tough.
Three o'clock is inching so close,
It is this time of day I hate the most.
At last the happy school bell rings,
And all the students want to sing!
After one long day of torture and pain,
Tomorrow they do it all over again.

Nolan Kirkman, Grade 7
Our Lady Star of the Sea School, MI

If I Had All the Money in the World

If I had all the money in the world I would spend it at every shop
I would go to the candy store and get the best lollipop
I'd travel east to explore the wonders and sights of Asia
Or I'd travel to see all the wild animals throughout Africa
Maybe I would cherry pick the best and most beautiful horse
Maybe I'd buy a jet plane and hire a pilot to keep it on course
As far as I'm concerned that will never ever even come close to be
I probably have so little money that a rock is worth more than me

Alysha Sinner, Grade 7
Wayzata Central Middle School, MN

Hard Work

Without it, we would be nowhere.
No pain or frustration.
No more earning respect.
No more overachievers, no more underachievers.

It defines success.
It separates the winners from the losers.
It is the determination to win and achieve.
It makes up you, and shows what you can do.
It shows the difference of a leader and a follower.
It puts you above others.
It gives you the power to achieve the impossible.

But, who are you?
Are you the person who makes excuses?
Are you the person that dreams, but never does it?
Or are you the one who becomes a leader?
Hard work defines you, and nobody can stop you from doing it.

Grant Coleman, Grade 9
Mayo High School, MN

My Best Friend

I've known her since the beginning.
I'll know her until the end.
I will always love her no matter what
Because she is my best friend.

Just hearing her sweet voice can make my day.
Our friendship is one that nobody can comprehend.
I'll always love her no matter what
Because she is my best friend.

I love her glowing smile, her oh so sweet perfume.
Her sense of humor that will never die out until the very end.
I'll always love her no matter what
Because she's my best friend.

Sydney Sele, Grade 8
Lancaster Secondary School, MN

Friends

The people you count on.
The people that count on you.
The people you hang out with on rainy days.
The people you hang out with on sunny days.

People from school.
People from church.
Even people from your family.

Secrets, stories, smiles and laughs.
Shared for hours or even just a minute.
Making your day full, unexpected and fun.

Friends are just about everyone.

Conner Rose, Grade 7
Abbott Middle School, MI

Poems

Poems can be anything
Poems can be saddening
Poems can be joyous
Poems can be philosophical

Poems can be quiet
Poems can be loud
Poems can tell stories
Poems can describe the world

Poems can be like music
They both tell about life
They both have beats
They both inspire people

Poems can be like paintings
They both create pictures
They both paint moods
They both come from ideas
Ross Grattafiori, Grade 7
Nellie B Chisholm Middle School, MI

The Dusty Pink Sky No More

It was dusk outside
I stood and stared as the sky turned pink
If we keep polluting this world
It will be gone in a blink

Everything we love is going to disappear
We only have a little time
Before the sky is gone
That's why I'm writing this rhyme

The sky and birds will be gone
The stars will cry a tuneless song
Before all of it will be gone
Trust me, it won't belong

We have to help
Before it disappears
Tell yourself, make everyone understand
Take a look at yourself in the mirror
Jamie Bowers, Grade 7
Nellie B Chisholm Middle School, MI

Piano

"Tap tap"
as my fingers tap the keys
A beautiful sound
is coming from the piano
"BUM! BUM!" a loud sound
"bum, bum" a soft sound
is coming from my hands
tapping on keys
Stella Spero, Grade 7
East Rockford Middle School, MI

Miss America

The lights are so bright,
they would blind your eyes.
The sounds of the crowd
beginning to rise.

On the stage walks
fifty beautiful girls,
all of which have
big, fancy curls.

Their dresses so elegant
all reds, whites, and blues,
each of them have
lovely cream colored shoes.

One winner is chosen
above all the rest,
to represent our country,
the country God blessed.
Paige Francis, Grade 8
Our Lady Star of the Sea School, MI

Me

D -man
I ncredible
A mazing
M an
O verplays video games
N ever quits until it's impossible
T asteful
E ntertaining

M ost fun
O n time
N ot a yes man
T able turner
G reat dancer
O verall athletic
M e
E ye grabber
R eady
Y oung
Diamonte Montgomery, Grade 7
Pleasant View School, MI

Torrid, Arctic

FIRE
Sizzling, scorching
Burning, killing, blistering
Wood, fire fighters, water, icicle
Freezing, breezing, soothing
Frosty, frigid
ICE
Johnathon Adkins, Grade 7
Nellie B Chisholm Middle School, MI

The Great Battle

I remember the memory
Of a great battle.
It broke loose between two colonies
Maybe more.
The sun beat down
on the battlefield.
It was terrible
The death and destruction.
I watched from high above.
Safe.
The sounds of war still ring in my ears.
I saw one of them
Climb to the highest point.
It took out two climbing after him
And one from the air.
It is stuck in my memory
Even though it was so small.
But to the ants and grasshoppers
It was chaos.
Brandon Zinn, Grade 7
Lincoln Jr/Sr High School, WI

Grandpa

Pokey but soft
the green grass where Grandpa sits
as I play.

Blue rubber ball I kick
bumps Grandpa as he reads.
Smiling, he throws it back.

Trucks on the highway,
fast and noisy,
driving by…

A piece of gold
from Grandpa's pocket
sweet Werther's in my mouth.

Grandpa tall and strong
scoops me up
piggyback ride!
Raynee Thompson, Grade 8
Lancaster Secondary School, MN

Tired

I was so tired last night
that my eyes shut immediately
I was so tired
that I could sleep for 1 million years
My bed was so soft
that it felt like a pile of fluffy feathers
I laid down and sunk into the mattress
like falling back into a pile of leaves.
Jana Feurestein, Grade 7
East Rockford Middle School, MI

The Moon

Once upon a summer night,
When there was a breeze so slight,
The nesting birds tucked down their heads,
And snuggled in their nice soft beds.
The Moon came out so big and bright,
To wish the world a soft goodnight.
The Moon was full, and bright and round,
It crossed the sky without a sound.
When dawn broke free, all too soon,
Wished the world goodbye, the Moon.

Caitlin Jankiewicz, Grade 7
Ruth Murdoch Elementary School, MI

Shooting

Shane stood in a saloon in May,
Shabby but neat when he
Shot like the wind runs,
Shane's bullet is a silent killer,
His gun was talking to him,
His enemy gets a head start,
BANG, WHUMP, THUMP,
Shane is hurt,
He goes home to recover.

Joel Martin, Grade 8
Wauzeka Steuben School, WI

The Christmas Season

Music is playing cheerfully
throughout the whole town
People are singing,
bells are ringing,
you never see anybody frown.
And on that special day,
we all celebrate as one.
It brings joy when we say,
"It's Christmas everyone!"

Elli Sekelsky, Grade 8
St John Vianney Catholic School, MI

Cat

My cat purrs like
a loud thunderstorm
She is as gray
as a very dark night
She is as quiet
as a mouse
I love my cat

Sarah Clymer, Grade 7
East Rockford Middle School, MI

Desert

A very barren place
the sand whistles in the air
it is very hot

Gavin Sanderson, Grade 7
Perry Middle School, MI

I Am Here

I am here and I always will be
When you need a friend.
You can count on me to take you in.
I could clothe you, feed you.
And do everything you need me to.
I love you and care.
I even bought you a stuffed bear.
As I speak from my heart
I tell you I am here.
Just lean on me when you need a friend.
Always count on me to keep you in.
When you feel a little down and you have a frown.
I could make you turn that frown upside down.
If you really knew I care.
You would know that I will always be there.
If you truly cared.
You should trust me to take you anywhere.
Through hard times and rough you still stayed tough.
So when you're down and you've got a frown and you think I'm near.
Just know I am here.

Jada Warren, Grade 8
Detroit Service Learning Academy, MI

My World!

Doesn't it feel like sometimes
Everything bad is happening all at once?
The problems got me losing my mind; seeking but yet can't seem to find
Some call it a piece of mind
I'm stressing slowly losing strength
And when all else fails motivate with assurance
That's what I tell myself time and time again
And when you reach the end they start over again (and you'll never win)
So then you let your guards down for this this thing called "Love"
Feeling in the end
If you knew what you know now, you knew it then
They call it preparation to better yourself
For the next male or female that you'll end up with
And that's the way love goes
I'm sure you heard it all before
Yea it hurts me to my soul
And leaves me feeling me miserable!

Tyzha Swift, Grade 8
Detroit Service Learning Academy, MI

Why

Why care about anyone else who doesn't care about you?
Why talk to someone who is too busy with other things and doesn't care?
Why hope that you will have a chance when you're already happened?
Why try for something when no ones knows you're trying?
Why speak when you have to watch what you say?
Why try and fix things when you know they're going to get worse?
Why wish for things to be back to normal when it never will?
Why try to be someone you're not just to fit in?
Why ask all these questions when they really can't be answered?

Ja-ae Borth, Grade 9
New Glarus Middle/High School, WI

Where I'm From

I am from the end zone
From shoulder pads
From long grass to wet grass
From why not to where to
From hit hard to hit the hole
From cleat to helmet
From blue and white to black and blue
From the snap to the whistle
From go hard or go home
From extra point to under control
That's where I am from
Kameron Cavanaugh, Grade 8
Kalkaska Middle School, MI

River

Among a forest
Around a steep sloping hill,
There lies a river
In current autumn's chill
Flowing however it will

There it lies still,
A marker, or a sustenance
Where birds sing softly,
It carries fall leaves away
It flows and spouts; a refuge.
Adrienne Sager, Grade 8
Our Shepherd Lutheran School, MI

My Dream

Late at night I close my eyes,
Everything fades away.

Into my dreams time travels by,
Fast asleep I'll stay.

I'll dream of things to come,
Or maybe from the past.

But whatever it is it better be quick,
Because time flies by so fast.
Hannah Mattes, Grade 7
Our Lady Star of the Sea School, MI

Gymnastics

I could hear the tramp
telling me to jump higher
I jumped as high as I could
I felt like a flyer
Then I heard the mat telling me to flip
But I messed up just because
Of one little trip
I got back up to keep trying
Again, I felt like I was flying
Bridget Lass, Grade 7
East Rockford Middle School, MI

Surprise!

Surprises.
Like them or not, they can definitely stop your heart.
My surprise was my dad's new black Mustang!
Cruising in it was fun,
But one problem, a snowstorm, a blistering cold one.
It looked more like a cotton storm to me.

The air felt heavy like I was pushing a train.
It was darker than night, but seemed like morning.
We could only see a few feet ahead of us.
We took a left. Time froze. The car screeched.
A volcano erupted under the hood. We were sent spinning.
The car almost lifted.
It was a helicopter's propellers. A fish out of water.
We hit a tree and stopped.

Silence.
The most dreadful noise I've ever heard.
I look at the tree. It towered over me, standing tall.
I felt like I was in school being taught.
The teacher stared at me.
All that came out of my mouth was, "sorry." I'm sorry for running into you.
The police arrived. I couldn't hear anything. They carried me away.
Brendan Hardey, Grade 7
Abbott Middle School, MI

The Life I Once Had

Memories. They fill our mind, making us laugh and smile.
They allow us to remember the good times, and the loved ones we have.
Moments we wished lasted forever.
And then there are those memories which we wish never existed;
The ones we wish we could erase. Forever.
The ones that form a frown on our face, and sometimes even make us cry.
Memories of tragedies, hard times, mistakes, and accidents…
Loved ones we were at one point close to…Gone…Forever.
I had many memories of all the good times.
When at one point, we were a close family.
But one memory stays in my thoughts; constantly.
Glued to the back of my head.
One memory that I will never forget.
The memory was so clear and graphic to me…
The memory of that day.
The day that changed everything…

Daevis Harris, Grade 8
Detroit Service Learning Academy, MI

Someone to Love

Someone to hold your hand when you feel you're floating away,
Someone to hold you when you're scared,
Or you've done something wrong.
Someone to kiss you and make you feel butterflies in your tummy.
Someone that will say, "I'm not going anywhere and I'll be there till the end."
someone that says, "I love you forever and always."
Haley Sanwick, Grade 9
Round Lake High School, MN

Rain

endless rain falling
drowning the world in sorrow
until the clouds part
sunlight struggles through the dark
hinting at the hope to come
Michael Foley, Grade 7
Perry Middle School, MI

Autumn Leaves

Brightly colored leaves
Covering the autumn ground
Red, yellow, and green
As bright as the summer sun
Will be there until the snow
Paige Hallock, Grade 7
Perry Middle School, MI

Dream-Ridden Night

Laying there waiting
Flipping through the memories
Start softly sinking
Floating along all the dreams
To the castle in the sky
Cheyanne Finger, Grade 8
Perry Middle School, MI

Dove

The heavens cry out
with a roar and trail of tears
waiting for a sign
waiting for something that will
never come but still have hope
Connor Scott, Grade 8
Perry Middle School, MI

Darkness Within

Surrounding within
destroying the happiness
replacing with pain
shutting out all life around
swallowing light with pleasure
Colin Anderson, Grade 8
Perry Middle School, MI

Sunshine

The
sun shines
over the mountain.
The golden sun's bright
light.
Matthew Nimtz, Grade 8
Our Shepherd Lutheran School, MI

The Life of a Tree

I came across an orange leaf,
a lonely orange leaf in a small pile of four.
I picked the fragile leaf up and turned it over in my gentle hand.
I realized the leaf's life had ended.

It started out as a baby, a small bud, full of life.
It grew to be a child, nestled in the arms of a big, brown branch through adolescence,
surrounding itself with other leaves.

Maybe a month later, it reached its peak just in time for autumn.
The big green leaf caught fire like the sky at sunrise and turned to a bright orange.
Too soon winter would come and end its life with cold cruelty.

Soon enough, winter did come and the leaf became cold.
Barely holding on, the leaf was ready to let go.
The leaf was a dancer as it slowly fell and landed softly with some old friends.

The leaf's life had now come to a stop.
However it would not be forgotten.

Someday its tree will give life to a new bud, cycling forever.
Jessica Fair, Grade 7
Abbott Middle School, MI

That's How We Work, My Sister and I

My sister and I are a lot alike: mellow, shy, crazy, and likable.
It seems when she has energy I have none,
When I have energy she has none.
That's how we work my sister and I.
In school she's hyper all the time, but outside she acts like a bump with nobody.
It's strange how we're the same but never at the same time.
That's how we work, my sister and I.
We do have differences for she is clumsy and mean, but I'm smart and nice to everything.
Sometimes when we're bored, she acts like she's 5. She whines and plays for my amusement.
Sometimes I talk funny and she laughs.
I take pity on her since she is weak.
My sister is small with straight brown hair while I'm tall with black curls.
When we fight we do not push or punch we just shout until we ignore each other.
That's how we work my sister and I.
She's a 15-year-old kid and I'm a 12-year-old adult. When I think about our ages I laugh.
We love each other because we're brother and sister.
That's how we work my sister and I.
Rafael Godinez, Grade 7
Lincoln Jr/Sr High School, WI

Roaring, Relentless, Red

Red is a dazzling devil, a bleeding heart, and a beautiful butterfly.
Red is the taste of ripe strawberries, giant raspberries, and juicy cherries.
Red is the sound of screaming sirens, cheerful Christmas carols, and a race car.
Red is the roaring fires of hell, a firehouse, and a hopeful hospital.
Anger makes me feel red.
The violence of war is red.
The cheery Christmas is also red.
Red is fear.
Monique Johnson, Grade 8
Menominee Jr High School, MI

Paint to Age Sixteen

I close my eyes and watch
As me and my memories pass
Each as a car
I'm six now and finger painting
Now ten and sketching to draw
Four paintbrushes to my left
Twenty-eight paint colors to my right
A canvas in front, far too small
To push it away
To paint on the wall
I open my eyes to the road
I'm sixteen and driving
Driving a rusty old truck and back
To an occasion
With paintings of mine
And before me, my sunrise
Of a painting I made
Not to sell
It's mine only
And it's painted on my wall
Kiara Stamford, Grade 7
Pleasant View School, MI

Locker

I have a hungry locker.
It eats my work,
Hides my books,
And crumples my art.
I've tried everything.
Offerings, food,
You name it, I've probably tried it.
It ignores my worthless things
And loves my homework
As if it were a rare delicacy.
Perhaps, perhaps,
My locker is a vortex.
That sucks things in
And spits them out
In places inconvenient to me.
I've tried it all, but nothing will work.
What's that you say?
Organization?
That would never work.
My locker just eats all my folders.
Rine Wakeman, Grade 7
East Rockford Middle School, MI

First Day of School

First day of school,
Waking up too early,
So tired,
Pain and misery,
Watching the clock,
Goodbye summer.
Samantha Endres, Grade 7
Scranton Middle School, MI

Where I'm From

I am from the outdoors,
from playing in the mud puddles.
I am from the play room upstairs.
I am from camping trips and red hair,
from Dawn and Nelson and Plude.
I am from loud laughter and sarcasm,
From it's all about choices and hang up your coat or I'm throwing it outside.
I'm from Kalkaska and Ireland,
Goulash and Potato Salad,
From playing hide and go seek in the dark,
with large Uncle Shawn,
who scared Jessi so bad,
she peed her pants,
and the Giant/Midget combination,
from listening to country music every day.
I am from the pictures in my jewelry box,
my great great great grandmother's dishes,
the yelling of family playing euchre,
summer birthdays at the cabin.
Sara Plude, Grade 8
Kalkaska Middle School, MI

Why He Fights

You stay up late watching TV. He stay up for days looking for terrorists.
You take a warm shower to help you wake up. He doesn't get to shower today.
You have your mother wash your clothes and clean your room.
He wears the same things for days.
You talk trash about your friends when they're not around.
He knows he might not see any of his friends.
Your parents ask you to do something…you don't.
He does exactly what he is told even if it puts his life in danger.
You hang an American flag outside your house.
He fights for the right to represent your country.
You are proud to be living in the land of the free.
He's the proud one who fought for the title
Charlene Tourtillott, Grade 8
Menominee Indian Middle School, WI

Carousel Under the Sea

The water rolls over my porcelain skin, the sun beams bend like lightning.
An army of crabs pass under me, a patch of waves pass over gently.
And everything glows, it's like an underwater meadow.
The horizon smolders above in the reflection, my hands reach out to pet the perfection.
I feel the vibrations of life as it moves, sways, swims, bends, groves.
My breath bobs to the surface like a its in a race, so I dive deeper into the endless blue space.
The colors are my favorite part, each piece of the puzzle is a piece of art.
The rocks are rough but calming, the fish are awkward but charming.
My time with this underwater world is about to end, but it says goodbye like a good friend.
Everyone pops out of their hiding places, they say goodbye with a thousand dances.
All sorts of them start to encircle me...
It's my magical carousel under the sea.
Teresa Sargent, Grade 9
Rockford High School Freshman Center, MI

Migration

A goose sitting on the frozen ground
Spreads its wings and begins a long journey
It soars over the barren snow field,
Leaving the dismal scene behind him.

It sees the vibrant forests,
Verdant and bursting with color,
But it flies on perpetually,
Seeking the safety that awaits.

Over the prairie it soars
Feeling the cool and gentle breeze,
Taking a glimpse of the clear blue sky,
Unfazed, it flies on.

Finally, this goose arrives
To the place his heart so desires,
With the shining sun that gives him warmth
And the gently rolling hills that welcome him.

A goose sitting on the frozen ground,
Spreads its wings and begins a long journey
And a goose landing on the soft grass,
Closes its wings and ends it.

Christopher Chen, Grade 8
Boulan Park Middle School, MI

Do You Understand?

Do you ever hear me?
Do you even care?
This is hard for me to say,
But this just isn't fair.

Did you hear me when I told you?
Or did you just ignore?
I wouldn't be surprised really,
You have done it before.

I try to reach out,
But what do I get?
Little sorrow,
And mostly regret.

You wonder why I don't come around when you please
But if you stepped in my shoes,
You might, for once, see.
I have a life too; it's not only you.

I want to say goodbye,
But can I withstand?
I'm afraid of what will happen,
Do you understand?

Hannah Nicosia, Grade 8
St Jerome Elementary School, MN

Through the Eyes of the Virgin

My eyes are shards of glass
Broken, hidden from the world
Never to see what comes to pass
Never to see a flower uncurled

But her eyes, as big as my hands
Her healing breath warm upon my face
Her eyes can see to all lands
But all I see is empty space

She has no hands, I have no eyes
But together we become one
I see the world, full of lies
The hate, war, as fiery as the sun

Extend your blessing now
Not for me, but for all
Harmony and justice you may allow
For every person, no matter how small

My eyes are shards of glass
But I have seen a world where fighting shall cease
No more blood staining our fresh grass
Where all people can see the love of peace

Allison Rowe, Grade 8
Lumen Christi Catholic School, WI

The First Thanksgiving

In 1620,
that's when it all began.
They traveled across the sea,
to this amazing, newfound land.

They had great hopes
and wonderful dreams.
Made new friends who taught them
to fish from the streams.

There was a great gathering
and an amazing feast,
where the children played games,
and everyone could eat, eat, eat.

The natives and the pilgrims together,
they ate turkey and potatoes and bread of rye.
Pumpkins were harvested to make
the most tasty pie!

So, that's what happened
400 years ago.
Today's Thanksgiving,
To Grandmother's house we go!

Owen Galligan, Grade 7
St Clare of Montefalco School, MI

He

He thinks I'm pretty, he thinks I'm perfect, should I be his girl, is he worth it?
I take a flower, picking petals, he loves me, he loves me not. I ask myself "Does he show me love?", he shows a lot.
He dreams of marriage, I dream the same, is this real, will I take his name?
He makes me happy, he makes me smile. For his love I'll walk the extra mile.
Like Aaliyah, I'm too shy, read my 4 page letter and it will tell you why.
When he opens it, there's my kiss, in the bright red he can't miss.
Together we are one, he wants real love, I have a ton.
As long as he lives, I'm here to give. I'll be there, he's never alone, I'm right next to him to watch the throne.
He is my King and I am his Queen. When I see him I get butterflies, what does this mean?
When I'm with him he is truthful, we have a good vibe, but the others lied.
He is my diary, he knows all my secrets, our trust is so strong I know he'll keep it.
When I cry he wants to feel my pain, wipe my tears with no shame.
He is my shield, protects me from the bad, he is my happiness, cheers me up when I'm sad.
He's on my mind all the time, I try to wait patiently for him to be mine.
But the clock is ticking, my legs are weak, I even see him in my sleep.
With him is where I wanna be, I'm so happy he feels the same about me.

Octavia Coston, Grade 9
Harding Senior High School, MN

Winter

I sit on the sled at the top of the steep hill at Kensington Park,
Ready to slide down.
The snowflakes slowly float downward from the sky,
Like a blanket for the earth.
I glare down the entire challenging hill,
Noticing the fun people are having as they wait at the bottom.
My ears stinging from the crisp chill of the winter air.
I take one deep breath as my brother behind me gives me one strong starting push.
It is always surprising to me how quickly you can pick up speed.
I fly down the hill, only white snowflakes in sight.
Squeals of laughter and cheering surround me as suddenly I lose control and skip off the path into the woods.
I taste a mouthful of cold snow and some heavy on my eyelashes.
But the thrill of this wonderful adventure is irreplaceable.
Friends arrive eager to make sure I am okay and ready to tell exactly what they witnessed.
Pride comes in how much air I gained.
As we begin our trek up the hill, our heart beats excitedly, wondering what thrills lie ahead.

Stephen Kenkel, Grade 8
West Hills Middle School, MI

Thanksgiving

The cool spring winds, the cold autumn chills, the warm summer sun, and chilly winter thrills,
The smell of hot food, the cool, refreshing taste of clean water, my cozy bed, my warm clothes,
The sight of loving friends and family, the feeling of happiness that each day brings,
The sound my mother makes whenever she sings,
For everything, good and bad, especially remembering my loving dad,
Knowing that I am loved and that they all care,
My baby Godson, my energetic little brother, the best sweetest dog in the world,
The beautiful Christmas mornings, the scary Halloween nights,
The glorious Easter Sundays, and the last day of school, which we delight.
All of this is to be thankful for.
I never forget all those who hold me fast, and all those whom I adore.
Knowing that Aunt Bea is looking down on me from a better place,
And the Father loves me with his holy face,
Please bless us all this Thanksgiving, and let us all say our grace.

Matthew Lujan, Grade 7
St Clare of Montefalco School, MI

Bass

In bass lessons I learned…
How to sweep the neck
How to get a show in Quebec
To keep the beat
How to get people on their feet

How to slap the strings
How to play such difficult things
To make the crowed go wild
To make the crowd say "Is that really a child?"

In bass lessons I learned…
How to create a song
How to make a melody sound so strong
To make something easy sound impossible
To make the most difficult possible

In bass lessons I learned…
To try your best
You must try your hardest
Michael East, Grade 7
Sault Area Middle School, MI

Field Hockey

The wind blows gently through my hair
The adrenaline pumps through my veins
There were cotton candy clouds
The crowd cheering, waiting for the pass
As the ball made contact with my stick
I knew the ball would make it across the field
The opponents were creeping up onto the flying ball
The ball reached my teammate's stick
I saw the power and determination in her eyes
As the ball was thrust into the goal
The fans quieted in suspense
GOAL!
The game continued in a new way
The passes hit with more enthusiasm
The drives with more energy
When the game ends
Our team spans the ground
The grass feels gentle under our bodies
It was the first win of the season
We are sure there are more to come
Aneesha Gummadi, Grade 7
Detroit Country Day Middle School, MI

Silence

The silence is deafening
No sound in sight
As I look from face to face
Each one just the same
Scared knowing we would be like this forever
The silence is a black hole waiting to consume us completely
Marlee Busalacchi, Grade 7
East Rockford Middle School, MI

Love

Love is a common word,
But not always used correctly.
People can say they love you,
But do they really mean it?

Do you love everybody?
Or certain people?
Some people don't care for your love.
Spread your love out wisely and
To those who desire it the most.

Don't be sad if people don't
Tell you they love you.
Sometimes you don't want
Everyone to love you.
Love, a common but
Meaningful word.
Use it carefully, that one word
For it is strong when love is heard.
Diamond Buchanan, Grade 7
Chandler Park Academy – Middle School, MI

Transitions

Transitions, in life there will be changes,
There comes a time when everybody's life rearranges.
For instance when you have to say farewell to friends you know,
When everything you have gone through has made you grow.
The life you have grown accustomed to has suddenly changed,
No matter where you turn or look it will always seem estranged.
I wonder how fast change has to take place,
I know in my heart that I'm not in a race.
How can I say goodbye?
To the ones that have made me laugh and cry.
I know that now is time for my last year,
With the friends and teachers that I have come to endear,
This is a transition that must run its course,
How hard it is going to be, and full of remorse.
J'Laina Harvey, Grade 8
Gesu Catholic School, MI

Determination

Determination is the last game of the year
An everlasting competition
Determined to get the starting role
For starting has a bigger rush than a roller coaster
Feels better than opening presents on Christmas day
Getting the ball in your hands feels better than a soft pillow
Determined to make the play of the day when suddenly
You get the last out, basket, touchdown or field goal
The game is concluded
Every player boosted their stats or had them decline
For when the season's fulfilled
Everyone knows their hard work and determination paid off
They are determined to win a championship.
Taylor Holzberger, Grade 8
Cedar Grove-Belgium Middle School, WI

Secret Bird

The sun shines high in the sky, throwing rays of heat down on your skin
A river rushes by, like the blood pulsing through your nervous veins
Balancing on his foot, with his white and black feathered blanket
  is an ibis

You are a tree, tall and majestic, placed in the middle of the grounds,
where you are providing a dark shade that covers the floor with leafy soot

Everywhere, is where you belong but
you must wait to go to the
  other side
for a man whom is wise and curious
is calling out to the world

The sun sets and the moon rises, but the ibis does not stir
The secret is juicy, like the papyrus upon which it is inscripted
Without warning he spreads his wings and jumps into the air
His neck stretched in the stars and his eyes fixed on a hidden point, he soars away heeding the call of
  the
condemned man

The ibis had no way of hearing the call but, knowing the secret lifted him

Audrey Kohl, Grade 7
Abbott Middle School, MI

Falling for Soccer

My sneakers squished and stomped in the
muddy,
bumpy,
messy,
brown mud.
As I twisted and turned rotating my body 180 degrees every move,
I slide past each of the players standing before me trying to knock the soccer ball away from me.
I did a 360 turn of my head and made sure I had a good significant lead running toward the net.
As I saw a player creeping up on me I placed my left foot in front of the ball.
I kicked my left foot back into the dirty brown mud.
I kicked the ball behind me to escape from the desperate opponents doing everything to prevent me from scoring a goal.
After I pushed the ball behind me I faked right and went left. She fell for it(literally) and fell face first in the dirty, spongy mud.
I went back to my concentration, I dribbled easily around the first defender.
The second one looked angrily at me and then at the ball.
I knew this was going to be a battle, a messy one.
I kicked it   over   the short girl's head and ran as fast as I could.
I got there just in time to make a shot on goal.
I brought my foot back and kicked with the side of my foot.
After I kicked the ball, I lost balance and fell face first in the mud.
I got up when I heard screaming.
I had scored a goal!!!

Samantha Tarnopol, Grade 8
West Hills Middle School, MI

Our Love Is Stronger

Our love is stronger than the winds of a cyclone and hotter than the sun beating down on a warm summer day. We used to be as cold as ice, now we are so hot that we are like butter melting on popcorn. We only have each other and if we break, my world will end. Please don't leave me here in this asylum, trapped from ever seeing you again.

Jessica Davis, Grade 8
Cabrini Elementary/Middle School, MI

Mother
Loyal, loving
Patient, caring, helpful
She deserves more than you think
Best friend
Skylar Lynde, Grade 7
Perry Middle School, MI

Grades 4-5-6
Top Ten Winners

List of Top Ten Winners for Grades 4-6; listed alphabetically

AbdurRahman Bhatti, Grade 5
Cambridge Friends School, MA

Katie Dominguez, Grade 4
St Joseph School, PA

Avery Fletcher, Grade 5
Balmoral Hall School, MB

Foxx Hart, Grade 4
F L Olmsted School, MA

Maximiliana Heller, Grade 5
Stanley Clark School, IN

Sarah Kim, Grade 5
Avery Coonley School, IL

Grace Lemersal, Grade 6
Meadowbrook Middle School, CA

Julia Peters, Grade 4
Toll Gate Grammar School, NJ

Lucas Tong, Grade 6
Chinese American International School, CA

Mallory S. Wolfe, Grade 5
North Knox West Intermediate/Elementary School, IN

All Top Ten Poems can be read at www.poeticpower.com

Note: The Top Ten poems were finalized through an online voting system. Creative Communication's judges first picked out the top poems. These poems were then posted online. The final step involved thousands of students and teachers who registered as the online judges and voted for the Top Ten poems. We hope you enjoy these selections.

Halloween

H anging out with all of my friends
A huge sugar rush the next day
L ittle shrieks of terror and horror
L ooking around to see all the cool costumes
O ne whole night of free candy
W aiting at the dentist's to figure out the damages
E veryone is wearing a costume
E ven adults are handing out candy
N ot a single bag empty

Thea Bultman, Grade 5
Zinser School, MI

Rebecca

It means energetic, happy, and joyful
It is the number 19
It is like the sparkling water
It is building a tree house
it is the memory of Joy
Who taught me how to build
When she helped pound the nails
My name is Rebecca
It means to love God

Rebecca Zoetewey, Grade 4
Grand Rapids Christian School - Evergreen Campus, MI

Veterans

V eterans are what make this country proud and free.
E very person has the right to be free.
T he veterans are brave people.
E very person can and should be proud of our country.
R ights are because of our veterans.
A ll of the other countries look terrible next to ours.
N ot another country is like ours.
S ome more people are moving here because we are so free
and the reason we are so free is because of the veterans.

Samuel Schaunaman, Grade 6
Maple Lake Elementary School, MN

Spelling Tests

Oh, how I don't like spelling tests.
They make my life a mess.
Oh, how I wish I could rest,
Instead of studying for those laborious spelling tests.
Oh, how I don't like spelling tests.
They make me frown
Oh, how I wish that spelling tests would just leave town!

Madelynne Elworthy, Grade 5
Mazomanie Elementary School, WI

Whiteboard

White and blank as hence the story is unknown,
For now the tapestry is not shone.
Gone history throughout the year,
Yet not enough to spill one tear.

Kathryn Murphy, Grade 5
Echo Park Elementary School, MN

Leo

Leo the lizard
Small as he was
Was stuck in a blizzard
And had no fuzz

Leo the lizard
Covered in snow
Worn from the blizzard
And nowhere to go

Lana de Graaf, Grade 4
Grand Rapids Christian School - Evergreen Campus, MI

The Minutemen Story

The minutemen were ready to ride.
I know Paul Revere had already spied.
The minutemen used swords to cut,
the logs to build the Valley Forge huts.
The French and British battled on ships,
soon one side lost, and the ship dips.
The soldiers on land built up a wall.
The Colonist won! Yippee for all!

Josh Halbman, Grade 6
Northwoods Community Elementary School, WI

Helpful

It is always nice to be helpful to others?
When I help others it makes me feel good.
It feels good to help someone who needs help.
You can help by cooking, cleaning, or just talking with them.
Did you know some older people don't even get visitors?
They would be very happy to see someone.
It would make them very happy to have someone to talk to.
I think people at nursing homes would enjoy friends.

Sydni Matson, Grade 6
Gilmore Middle School, WI

As I Lay in My Bed

As I lay in my bed,
I think about things going on in my head.
Staring at the ceiling, counting sheep,
Trying so hard to fall asleep.
Thinking and thinking what life's all about,
I'm trying to sleep, without a doubt.
Resting with the pillow cushioning my head,
As I lay in my bed.

Jessica Fisher, Grade 6
Birmingham Covington School, MI

Happy Cat

prancing, purring, sleeping
catching mice, moles, and voles
chasing cats, scaring them up trees
grouchy, grumpy, hot-tempered
angry dog

Zachary Bemben, Grade 5
Grand Rapids Christian School - Evergreen Campus, MI

What I See When I Ride My Horse

Pink is the color of my leather saddle,
Brown is the color of the grazing cattle.

Green is the meadow that I ride by,
Black is the biting fly that I don't want to go by.

Blue is the horse trailer we zoom past,
Tan is Buttercup that loves to go fast.

White is the color of the electric fence,
Yellow is the electricity that makes Buttercup tense.

Purple is the brush I use to reward her,
Grey is the prickly bur I get for sure.

Buttercup and I…full of glee.

Taylor Mattson, Grade 6
Manistique Middle & High School, MI

Forest in the Fall

Red is the color of the apples I chew,
Blue is a bluebird that I knew.

Green is a color of many shades,
Brown is a color that never fades.

Yellow is the color of the bright shining sun,
Blue is the color of the pond of fun.

White is the color of the clouds no doubt,
Orange is the color that I think about.

Purple is the color of the flowers that grow,
Black is the color of shadows, I know.

What do you see?

Tesa Powell, Grade 6
Manistique Middle & High School, MI

Cancer

E melio Garcia is a brave little
M an. At an
E arly age he was diagnosed with cancer.
L ittle did he know that
I t was going to be a tough road.
O ver the next two years, he had many operations and treatments.

G od gave him the strength to endure
A ll of his procedures.
R adiation and chemotherapy were testing his
C ourage.
I n the end he was able to conquer his cancer.
He has been cancer free for over a year now.
A men!

Hannah Frei, Grade 6
St. Gerard School, MI

Shotgun Shooting at Island Lake

Black is the color of the wheel,
Brown is the color of my blue-winged teal.

Red is the color where I hit him on the spot,
Yellow is the color of the shell that I shot.

White is the color of the splash where he hit,
Silver is the color of my dad's knife kit.

Turquoise is the color of his wing,
Orange are his feet that make me sing.

Yellow is the color of his beak,
Pink is my mouth when I shriek.

Duck makes a fine meal!

Zachary Matchinski, Grade 6
Manistique Middle & High School, MI

Fall

As the fresh autumn air whisks by me,
I smell burning bonfires made out of a tree,
The bare trees dance in the moonlight,
While the howling wolves sing in the night,
Hot apple cider swishes down my throat,
As I run my fingers down my new coat,
Jack-o-lanterns sure give you a fright,
While the trick-or-treaters ring your bell at night,
Steaming apple pie taste so yummy,
The scoop of ice cream on my pie fills my tummy,
Salty pumpkin seeds sure are good,
Autumn has the best food!
The cold air stings my face,
While I touch my new hat made of lace,
As the leaves fall to the ground,
I wish autumn was all year round!

Madelyn Hartwig, Grade 4
Floyd Ebeling Elementary School, MI

Going Camping

Red is our car as we head to camp,
White is the camper that keeps us not damp.

Brown is the log that we found in the wood,
Golden is the marshmallow that tastes so good.

Black is the night sky with stars so bright,
Yellow is the flashlight that saves you from fright.

Blue is the shiny crystal clear lake,
Pink is the sweet vanilla cake.

Green is the mighty tall pine tree,
Gray is the flying dove that I see.

Hunter Miller, Grade 6
Manistique Middle & High School, MI

White Is My Favorite Color

White is 4th of July and Christmas.
Making a snowman is fun.
Drinking hot cocoa when you're done.

Marshmallows are sticky
But are good to put in hot cocoa.
It is no joke.

Snow falls on my head.
Stars are white and stars are bright.
Stars twinkle in the night.

Crystal Berning, Grade 4
Platteville Middle School, WI

If I Were…

If I were a popsicle
  I would taste very sweet
  I would be mad if someone bought me
  I would like to be cozy in my freezer
  I'd want to stay in my box
If I were a popsicle
  I would come home with a kid
  I would wish I stayed at the store
  I would love to be in my box again
  I would listen to my friends
  I would want to be back with my friends

Jade Gray, Grade 4
Stocker Elementary School, WI

Football

Football is awesome.
Penalties make it more exciting,
6 points for a touchdown, 3 for a field goal,
Only fun when your team wins,
Fans roaring in the crowd,
Safeties are 2 points, the extra point just 1,
Isn't football very fun?
A lot of exercise,
Running, catching, throwing, and tackling,
More work than everything else,
Football is the best sport.

Sam Pellinen, Grade 6
Gilmore Middle School, WI

Christmas

C aroling with your family
H aving a family meal
R eindeer flying up above
I n the presence of friends and family
S tockings hanging from above
T oys hanging by the fireplace
M aking presents for friends and family
A ll snuggled in bed
S nowflakes falling

Kaylee Melzer, Grade 5
Clovis Grove Elementary School, WI

What Do You Hear in the Fall?

Flocking birds
Leaves
Birds singing one last time
Turkeys bucking
Squirrels collecting nuts
Trick
or
Treaters
I see
Falling leaves
Flowers dying
Deer
Wandering
For
Food
Leaves
Turning
Different colors

Alyssa V. Holston, Grade 5
Riley Upper Elementary School, MI

Inside This Bracelet

Inside this bracelet
Hides
A symbol of friendship
Never ending
Like a line going on forever

A symbol of hard work
Weaving
Colorful string in and out
In and out
Created for someone special

Long thought
And decisions
Of what kind
Or what color to make it
And who to give it to

Megan Richard, Grade 6
T J Walker Middle School, WI

My World of Colors

Blue is the color of the sky,
Red is the color of cardinals flying by.

Green is the color of the grass,
Brown is the color of squirrels that pass.

Purple is the color of my veins,
Gray is the color when it rains.

Orange is the color of the sun setting,
White is the color of a fancy wedding.

Brent Ogden, Grade 6
Gilmore Middle School, WI

Nothing

Roses are red,
Violets are blue,
This poem is boring.
It's time for something…
New.
I've tried it all,
From daisies to lilacs
From green to purple.
There is nothing,
Nothing at all!
There is not a light,
Not a spark,
No inspiration at all!
Wait I got it the perfect poem!
A poem about not knowing
What to write it is perfect!
Just one small problem,
who's going to publish this?

Isabelle Smiley, Grade 6
Franklin Middle School, WI

Poetry

Poems sing
and swing
around in your
mouth.
Poems can be
said or poems
can be read.
Poems can be
sung or
poems can
be hung
in a gallery.
Poems are
inspirational.
Rhyming.
Playing with
words, strong-feeling
and passionate.

Nikki Alvarenga, Grade 4
The Potter's House Christian School, MI

My Awesome Pink Pen

My awesome pink pen
Makes stickmen and buildings
Bright, neon pink
Like a flashback from the eighties
Zoomed through my drawings
Making my stickmen
Dress from Woodstock
And my buildings
Spray painted
Bright, neon pink

Oskar E. Zuchner, Grade 5
Hewitt Texas Elementary School, WI

Holiday

The smell of candles filled the air,
The time is close, I could hardly bear.

The season is filled with laughter and joy,
All the kids wish for their favorite toy.

It's the time for family,
It's the time for love,

It's the time to relax
And have some fun.

Arilee Hays, Grade 6
Gilmore Middle School, WI

The Colt

The colt
that is unstable,
The colt
who loves to run,
The colt
whose name
is Kaboom,
The colt
who will
always be in my soul.
The Colt.

Grace Mitchell, Grade 5
Mazomanie Elementary School, WI

School Days

S ocial studies
C omputers
H omework
O utside
O utstanding teachers
L anguage arts

D aily work
A wesome
Y ard sticks
S cience

Kourtney Tygesen, Grade 5
Zinser School, MI

My Little Turkey

My little turkey waddled away,
I thought he wanted to stay.

My little turkey waddled away,
I found him the next day.

My little turkey can't go away,
For now he's in the oven,
Ready to stay.

Alexis LaLonde, Grade 5
Seneca Elementary School, WI

Finding the Lamp Post

We were playing hide and seek,
my two brothers, my sister and I.
When I found a wardrobe
beautiful to my eye.
My brother Peter I heard
coming towards the door,
So I hid, stepping back
and felt no more floor.
What I felt was cold.
I turned around, it's snow!
So I ventured a little further,
I saw a lamp post with a steady glow.

Abbie Luetmer, Grade 4
Minnewaska Elementary School, MN

Misunderstood

I misunderstood this award
or was it a contest?
I misunderstood how to enter
or how they picked the winner
I misunderstood why I wrote this
or who I wrote this to
or what I wrote this for
or when I get this contest
or was it an award ceremony?
but most importantly,
I misunderstood what a poem was
or was it I didn't listen…

Iqra Ismail, Grade 5
Echo Park Elementary School, MN

One

One thing can change the world.
One person can be a change.
One dollar can buy you food.
One light can light a room.
One doctor can save a life.
One toy can make a kid happy.
One pizza can feed a family.
One car can take you a long way.
One cop can stop a criminal.
One movie can entertain a crowd.
One chip can brake into many crumbs.
It takes *one* point to win a game.

Nick Zopf, Grade 6
St Gerard School, MI

Pink Is…

Pink is the color of a "Mike and Ike"
Pink is the color of my brand new bike
Pink is the color of the ring I wear
Pink is the color of my friend's dyed hair
Pink is the best color of a ball
Pink is my favorite one of all

Gabby Poller, Grade 4
Platteville Middle School, WI

Christmas

C aring
H elping decorate
R est in peace
I nside
S ledding
T asting cookies
M aking cookies
A very good Christmas
S o fun going sledding

Ashley Fields, Grade 4
Dibble Elementary School, MI

My House

This is my house
It is covered in snow
It is very big
Because we started three years ago.

I like my house
It's unfinished but clean
It's a little bit cold
Because it's close to Halloween.

Rebekah Jones, Grade 4
St Paul's Lutheran School, MN

Snowflake

S now that falls
N o purpose
O ver the ground
W ith a gleaming spark
F alling from Heaven above
L ike a ballerina, like
A dancer
K ind and pretty
E verywhere it goes

Makayla Feddersen, Grade 6
Detroit Lakes Middle School, MN

In the Universe...

In the universe there is the Milky Way
In the Milky Way there is our solar system
In our solar system there is Earth
On Earth there is North America
In North America there is the USA
And that's where I'm proud to live!

Christian VanIten, Grade 4
St Joseph Elementary School, WI

Crazy

C uckoo when at a party
R ambunctious children jumping around
A ll wacky and wild
Z any kids full of excitement
Y outhful energy

Evan Zarotney, Grade 6
St Gerard School, MI

Funky Fall Fun

Crackling leaves falling
From the trees
Tiny scarlet red
Big tangerine orange
Maze yellow
Lime green
Leaves
Cider, doughnuts
At apple orchards
Turkey, stuffing, mashed potatoes and carrots
Happy Thanksgiving

Jenan Shareef, Grade 5
Riley Upper Elementary School, MI

Popcorn

If I were popcorn
  I would taste all buttery
  I would be fresh and hot
  I would like to not be cold and stale
  I'd want to make people enjoy the movie by letting them eat me
If I were popcorn
  I would come in a popcorn bucket
  I would wish I was at the movie theater
  I would love to be the best popcorn I could be
  I would listen to the people talk about how good I am
  I would want to be the most popular food in the whole world

Haley Quick, Grade 4
Stocker Elementary School, WI

Music

Music is in the air,
Everything you hear is music.
You can hear music when you walk on the sidewalk.
Of course, you hear it on the radio.
When you walk on the sidewalk you see people everywhere
listening to what?…music.
Music can make people sad, happy, aggressive
it just gives people a new emotion.
When I listen to music we all go and sing.
That's what my family does.
Because where would we be without music?

Erin Tlam, Grade 6
Martin County West Trimont Elementary School, MN

Cry

People hide behind glasses
As they hide behind words
Trusting no one they love
Tears begin to drop
The clock ticks, ticks, ticks…
Next thing people know they're not with us anymore
People hide behind glasses
As they hide behind words
Be a friend to cure the worst

Dakota Hoang, Grade 6
White Pine Middle School, MI

Hold on to Life

Hold on if you want to succeed
Hold on to life as you know it
Even if wickedness tries to pry you away
Hold on to your friends and faithfulness
Even if you shatter in frustration
Hold on to no riches too greedily
Even if you seem to desperately want
Hold on to important memories
Even if you lose their photographs
Hold on to every treasure you possess
Even when luck seems to fall away from you

Dylan Witteveen Lane, Grade 4
Grand Rapids Christian School - Evergreen Campus, MI

Seasons

I see the snow so white and sparkly
And it all melts away in sorrow.
As I see cupid touching hearts.
I see four leaf clovers and I know that spring is here.
I feel eggs, chocolate and flowers
Blooming as summer in Wisconsin is coming.
Fireworks raise off the ground and the crowd cheers.
It gets cooler once night comes
And leaves fall to the ground.
People start to get their jackets on and once
Again play in the snow thinking about next year.

Teagan Bignell, Grade 4
River Heights Elementary School, WI

Cheesecake

If I were a cheesecake
  I would taste like the best cheesecake ever
  I would be set on a plate with whipped cream on top
  I would like to be eaten properly with a fork
  I'd want to not get too old and dry up
If I were a cheesecake
  I would come anytime you wanted a celebration
  I would wish I would taste gushy in your mouth
  I would love to be put in the oven to be baked
  I would listen to the people say, "Delicious"
  I would want to be the most delicious cheesecake made!

Carter Altmann, Grade 4
Stocker Elementary School, WI

Friendship

You may have friends that will last a lifetime,
Or other times when they pretend they are, but they really aren't,
But that will never come close to me and my friend,

We share giggles and thoughts, dreams and wonders, but
A friend we had a part of us,
Moved far far away, and we will never get to see
Our trio will never be the same,
Without that special, funny, spunky girl.

Rose Warosh, Grade 6
Campbellsport Elementary School, WI

I Am…

I am nice and creative.
I wonder if there will ever be peace on the earth.
I see unicorns in my dreams.
I want an iPod touch.
I am nice and creative.
I pretend to be an actor.
I feel happy and sometimes very confused.
I touch cute little puppies.
I worry that I won't ever be able to see my dad.
I cry because I miss my dad.
I am nice and creative.
I understand that if someone does something bad
Or has done something bad they have to pay the price.
I say that Jesus did die on the cross for us.
I dream of being a pediatrician.
I give my best effort in school to get good grades.
I hope one day I'll be able to see my dad again.
I am nice and creative.

Lucia Delgado, Grade 6
Gilmore Middle School, WI

All About Me

Claudia
Loving,
Helpful,
Caring,
Wishes to be a lawyer.
Dreams of helping people who are blind.
Wants to help people who are in trouble with the law.
Who wonders what dogs think about.
Who fears earthquakes.
Who is afraid of roller coasters.
Who likes Halloween.
Who believes in miracles.
Who loves my family.
Who loves going on trips.
Who loves roller skating.
Who loves my pets.
Who plans to go to Harvard Law School.
Gomez

Claudia Gomez, Grade 6
Gilmore Middle School, WI

Leiana

Leiana
It means, funny, creative, smart,
It is the number 55,
It is like the rainbow shine,
It is going to Miami Beach in Florida,
It is the memory of Mamere and Daddywoody,
Who taught me how to golf and bake,
When they tried my patience,
My name is Leiana,
It means I believe in me.

Leiana-Lavette Woodard, Grade 6
Detroit Lakes Middle School, MN

Inside This Wilting Rose

Inside this wilting rose lies a heart full of
Joy for when it was living.
A lifetime full of adventures it had in its life.
But when its petals fell, one memory was
Lost in the flower.

Inside this wilting rose lies a sweet lullaby.
The petals fall day by day but the flower
Still holds on for dear life.
Its beauty appears to be amazing, but when
It begins to become grim the beauty
Appears to be strong.

When it gets plucked a lifetime full
Of joy, happiness, memories, are gone.
But if you listen very close you will hear
A heartbeat beating slowly but gently
A life will appear.

McKenzie Geibel, Grade 6
T J Walker Middle School, WI

Wise Old Mr. Owl

Once, some time ago
I found him sitting in the old oak tree
and asked him
"Who should I be when I grow up?"
His answer irritated me,
"Who?"
Again, "Who should I be?"
"Who?"
Furious, I stormed off.
That was awhile ago,
but now I get it.
It's not who I should be,
It's who I want to be,
Who I am.
Now, if you go to the old oak tree
You will see Wise Old Mr. Owl
with his only answer…
"Who?"

Jordan Stahl, Grade 6
Martin County West Trimont Elementary School, MN

Basketball

B asketball is a fun sport to play.
A three point shot can be difficult.
S lam dunks are awesome.
K eep a good grip on the ball.
E veryone can play basketball.
T eamwork is helpful.
B asketball can be hard if you don't practice.
A good player practices a lot.
L ay-ups are easy.
L ebron James is good at basketball.

Jeremy Guerrazzi, Grade 6
St. Gerard School, MI

Dragon Problems

Stuffed with fire.
Pumped with lava.
I'll tell you about him, he's a liar.

He won't do you a favor.
He's grumpy from all those scales.
It would be like sleeping with a razor.

He's not the best with mail.
Most of it gets burned.
Even if he carries it in a fireproof pail.

His daughter's name is fly.
She's like the Grinch before he loved.
But she'll never touch the sky

Oh my, oh my, he's in the air
His baby's left behind
His daughter can only stare.

Jacob Fischer, Grade 4
Grand Rapids Christian School - Evergreen Campus, MI

I Speak the Language of Wolves

I speak the language of wolves
howling at my pack
grateful for the first kill of the night
I speak the language of wolves
growling at my pups to get to bed

I speak the language of wolves
my pack and I praising the moon
on the top of a hillside before it sets

I speak the language of wolves
now it is 12:00 it's time to sleep
before I go to sleep I steal a drink from a pond

I speak the language of wolves
as I fall asleep all I hear are crickets chirping

I speak the language of wolves
Natalie Hansen, Grade 5
Wagner Elementary School, MN

My Name Is…

My name is Luis
It means nice, polite, funny,
It is 101,
It is like dripping water falling in a lake,
It is Ryan's best friend,
Who taught me laughter and trust,
When he made a funny joke and he kept my secret,
My name is Luis,
It means I know that my friends and family will be there for me.
Luis Mendoza, Grade 6
Campbellsport Elementary School, WI

Happiness

Happiness is being with family.
Happiness is playing sports.
Happiness is giving gifts.
Happiness is making others smile.
Happiness is making new friends.
Happiness is hitting a homerun.
Happiness is laughing at funny jokes.
Happiness is playing games with friends.
Happiness is not leaving anyone out.
Happiness is a sunny day.
Happiness is helping others.
Happiness is doing something you enjoy.
Happiness is going on vacation.
Happiness is learning new things.
Happiness is knowing God is watching over you.
Happiness is knowing that your family is always with you.
Olivia Theis, Grade 6
St Gerard School, MI

Playful Puppies

P laying with their tug toys
U nder the couch and on the chair
P ulling the living daylights out of them
P ouncing and jumping on their best people friends
I n and out of the house
E xtremely cute when they sleep
S nuggling and cuddling in bed with you

A mazing companions to everyone
R un them in the tennis courts throwing the ball
E xhausted you make them after such play

C harming as a prince or princess
U nbelievably adorable
T ilting their heads so cutely
E very little thing makes puppies best friends
Rachel Tetzloff, Grade 6
Home School, MN

Inside My Hands

My hand are my life.
I use them every day, from writing, to eating, to reading.
Inside my hands is the future of my life.
My hands are the United States of America.

Our hands are how we tell people
our emotions that we are feeling inside of us.
Our hands are just like the rest of our body.
Your hands are what we wipe away tears with when we are sad.

Our hands are all different.
From small, to medium, to big.
Our hands are the key to writing.
My hands are the future of my life.
Brittany Nemeth, Grade 6
T J Walker Middle School, WI

Veteran

V ery brave to be in a war
E very day is honored
T hanked for their service
E very veteran's family has a flag hung on their house
R isked their lives for their country
A true hero
N ever forgotten

Jacob Fynboh, Grade 6
Maple Lake Elementary School, MN

Savage

Red is live lava burning through the ground
Red is like criminals breaking the law
Red is as dangerous as murders in giant cities
Red is as upset as a mad person in an asylum
The red is as evil as the underworld
Red is like Lucifer himself

Rachel Westcott, Grade 6
Campbellsport Elementary School, WI

Self Portrayal

My eyes are as blue as the shining sea.
My hair is as short as a leprechaun
My dimples are as unique as a cow's spots
My smile is as bright as an eclipse
My heart holds love that is as bright as the sun.
I live on the ice and eat ice skates.

Kiera Herr, Grade 6
Dr Dyer Intermediate School, WI

I Hate Homework

I hate homework. It's the worst thing in the world.
I never get it done cause I like to dream a lot.
I hate whoever made it up cause it makes me really bored.
I wish it did not like me so it would go to the trash.
But anyway…I'm not in eighth grade so I won't have a lot.
At least I'm in fourth grade so I won't have a lot.

Tina Paavola, Grade 4
River Heights Elementary School, WI

Fishing

I
Like to fish
In the Mississippi River (off shore in a boat)
Right in the afternoon.
Because it's glorious and fantastic to catch colossal fish.

Chase Herman, Grade 4
River Heights Elementary School, WI

What I Think of the Vets

When I think of the vets I think of happiness.
I feel warm and special they make me feel safe.
When I think of the vets I think they are sincere and cautious.
I am proud to be an American.

Lily Mae McCutcheon, Grade 6
Maple Lake Elementary School, MN

A Football Life

Yesterday I
Played full contact football
Started throwing spirals in the fall
Threw my first pass in a game
Had three plays in one game for loss of yards, that's not lame
Also forced two fumbles

Today I
Watch when any team has to play
Love to watch Green Bay all day
See McBain win the game
Play with my friends in a contact game, while trying not to maim
Talk about the awesome game with my friends

Tomorrow I
Will be the best in the game
Will be the QB with the best aim
Will have won the Rose Bowl
Will have won the Super Bowl
Will have won the Heisman trophy in college

Alexander Utecht, Grade 6
McBain Middle School, MI

A Colorful World

Yellow is the color of the sun,
Brown is the color of a bun.

Blue is the color of the sky,
Green is the color of my dad's tie.

Orange is the color when the sun is setting,
White is the color of new volleyball netting.

Pink is the color of a flower
Gray is the color of the Eiffel Tower.

Gold is a color of a ring,
Purple is a color of a shirt in spring.

Red is a color of a rose,
Silver is the color of the top of a house.

Turquoise is a color of paint,
Maroon, such a beautiful color, I might faint.

Haley Epple, Grade 6
Gilmore Middle School, WI

Sky

Soft cuddly blue gleaming eyes, white soft fur,
purring, comforting
What is Sky thinking most of the time?
Blue gleaming eyes
Blue gleaming eyes
Blue gleaming eyes

Dylan Kegley, Grade 5
Hewitt Texas Elementary School, WI

Silence

As I walk out the door
I hear the leaves rustling like they are all wrestling together
If there were no electronics the world would be silent
You could hear the most quietest things
Just think
No cell phones ringing
No playing DS's
Just think

Silence is fragile
It is very valuable like a diamond
It doesn't come that often
When everyone's inside playing on their electronics
I walk outside and hear the branches shake
I hear the crunch of the leaves when my neighbor walk by
Then my dog barks.

Alyx Korth, Grade 5
Clovis Grove Elementary School, WI

Shapes

Shapes are life
Because they have edges and curves
Some are
Round
And some are
Straight
But shapes are like
Life
There are sometimes perfect times
And some bad
But there are thousands
Of shapes
Different sizes and
Curves
Just like life; no one is the
Same

Laura Trettel, Grade 5
Blue Heron Elementary School, MN

Melted Heart

Your fur is as soft as a cloud.
It's as yellow as the sun.
Your chocolate-brown eyes hypnotize me
You have melted my heart.

It may seem ridiculous but you are my best friend.
Your bark travels through the wind.
It looks as though you travel faster than a cheetah—
Once again you have melted my heart.

I love you more than anything in the world.
When you swim with me it is my favorite thing.
You are the best dog a girl could have—
You melt my heart every time I see you.

Samantha Elizabeth Posey, Grade 6
Chisholm Elementary School, MN

At the Lovely Beach

Brown is the color of the warm sand,
Peach is the color of my tanned hand

White is the bottle of my favorite sunscreen,
Blue is when the warm water is clean.

Orange is the sun high in the sky,
Violet is my mother saying "hi."

Pink is the color of my cute hair tie,
Grey is the color of the clouds in the sky.

Teal is when the beautiful sky is clear,
Green is when I know my best friends are near.

Those are the colors I observe at the lovely beach.

Nicole Syers, Grade 6
Manistique Middle & High School, MI

Inside This…Dead Flower

Inside this drooping dead flower, in this lonely
field with strong and healthy flowers.
Lives a tiny amount of life, just lurking to get out and
make this lonely, dead flower strong again

Inside this weak dead flower lives the negative
thoughts in life.
None joyful or happy, just negativity.
The power of this dead flower is unexplainable
It has lived through stomping boots, vehicles
and animals.

Badly wounded this flower fights through sad and hard times.
Sometimes it watches his friends get picked away to freedom.
It still sits here today waiting for its day.
Inside this dead flower I see courage to stand out.

Jaden Stevenson, Grade 6
T J Walker Middle School, WI

Magnificent Sunrise

As I look at the splendor of the leaves
Adorned in tiny sparkling gems of dew,
As I watch the eastern sun glowing pink,
I feel that there is something I must do.

As I feel the tender chill of the wind
And listen to the breeze with my mind,
As I watch primroses burst in bloom,
I feel that there is something I must find.

Farewell, long grass coated with gems of dew;
Farewell, oh wonders I've seen naught before —
For the rays of the bright and dawning sun
Before me seem to be an open door.

Jennifer Wiland, Grade 5
Ann Arbor Christian School, MI

blue is everywhere
blue sky, fresh with clouds
blue water, sparkling with sun
blue eyes, reflect your face
blue tears, sad children
blue birds, soar through the sky
blue on rainbow, God' promise
blue fish, gently swim

Seth Hackbarth, Grade 5
St Paul Evangelical Lutheran School, WI

Snow vs Sun
Minnesota
Warm, cold
Swimming, freezing, skiing
Baseball, loon, movie stars, broadway
Acting, hiking, snorkeling
Fun, hot
California

Chloe Schmit, Grade 6
Detroit Lakes Middle School, MN

Flowing Tears
Flowing through a river of water
are tears of a young boy.
The only one who gave him joy
was a very old, wise koi
which swims in a
flowing river of water
with tears of a young boy.

Alex Struck, Grade 5
Sauk Trail Elementary School, WI

Waterfalls
waterfalls
trinkly, sparkly
falling, splashing, running
Niagara, American, castle, Old-Faithful
spouting, steaming, spewing
steamy, leaping
geyser

Alec Avila, Grade 6
Detroit Lakes Middle School, MN

Football
Football is fun
Football is getting hit
Football is hitting opponents
Football is touchdowns and fumbles
Football is coaching
Football is winning
Football is fun

Gibson Sposaro, Grade 5
Zinser School, MI

Rain/Spring
Rain
wet, muddy
freezing, drinking, relaxing
clouds, thunder, shorts, beach
sleeping, running, burning
pink, sunny
Spring

Joshua Freeman, Grade 4
Stocker Elementary School, WI

Summer/Fall
Summer
sunny, cool
running, jumping, swimming
parties, family, trees, leaves
scaring, trick-or-treating, carving
red, brown
Fall

Zachary Joas, Grade 4
Stocker Elementary School, WI

The First Time I Met You
The first time I met you
I fell in love with your golden fur.
Now you're an old dog and
you can't move the way you did
when you were a puppy.
Even if you're old and gray
I still love you with all my heart.

Sophia Rock, Grade 6
Chisholm Elementary School, MN

Winter to Summer
Winter
white, cold
sledding, sliding, shivering,
Christmas, snowman, birthday, 4th of July
running, riding, swimming
sunny, hot
Summer

Jebea Johnson, Grade 4
Stocker Elementary School, WI

Winter
Winter
cold, snowy
sledding, skiing, snowboarding
snow, hot chocolate, lemonade, grass
swimming, camping, playing
hot, sweaty
Summer

Justin Bohn, Grade 6
Gilmore Middle School, WI

I Fear the Animals
I fear the rattlesnakes for their poison
I fear the skunks for their nasty smell
I fear the raccoon for the rabies they carry
I fear the Asian Carp for their flying talent
I fear the black widow for their red mark
I fear the bears for their big paws
I fear the alligators for their striking ability
I fear the snapping turtle for their bite force
I fear the eagle for their talons
I fear the hawk for their keen eyesight

I fear the animals

Dylan Schutz, Grade 5
Wagner Elementary School, MN

Animals
Always loving,
Loyally sticking close,
Always sweet and cute,
Trying to get outside or
Running on their wheel,
Something's always going on,
In their little minds.
Chewing on their chew toys,
Or your favorite shoe,
Getting into something or
Sleeping all day through.

Alexis Genthe, Grade 5
St Paul Evangelical Lutheran School, WI

Broken 1955 Chevy
Bumpers fell off
Brakes do not work
Tires gone flat
What about that?
Gears rusted up
Axles fell off while driving
Ran out of gas
Windshield broke
Tires fell off — door fell off!
Had a leak
Broken 1955 Chevy

Jeffrey Lokrantz, Grade 4
River Heights Elementary School, WI

Football
F un
O ffsides
O pponent
T ouchdown
B ig plays
A ll four quarters
L ong pass
L ateral

Cameron McCarthy, Grade 5
Zinser School, MI

Heroes of Faith
There are many heroes of faith;
The best place to start is the Bible.
Look up Hebrews Chapter Eleven;
Each person's name listed is rejoicing in heaven.

Take the name Abel, for example,
And see his faith, which was nice and ample.
Abel had given a better sacrifice than Cain,
But his brother in jealousy had him slain.

Another faithful man was named Noah,
Being warned by God built an ark in midst of savannah.
A great flood came and killed everything living,
But Noah and his family were safely floating.

Faithful Abraham God called to a place,
Where his children multiply of a blessed race.
His wife, Sarah, gave birth to a son,
Though she was barely age ninety-one.

Jeanette Wang, Grade 5
Rochester Hills Christian School, MI

No Worries
For tonight don't fright
Bur in the morn when you arise
There will be a dog beside you
No, not just a pet
But your loyal friend
Your friend that leads you and guides you
Even though you may not be able to see
He sees you and in a way you see him
So remember when you arise that dog
No that loyal best friend of yours
Will see the way you want to go
Even though you may not see him
He sees past the eyes of you and me
So when you arise he'll look into your eyes
So no worries
He leads the day
So hand in leash both of you lead each other in an interesting way
So make way
A new guide dog and his best friend are on the way!

Lauren Reid, Grade 6
Franklin Middle School, WI

Life Still Goes On
Life can be like a difficult board game
Or a puzzle with missing pieces
You will never win or lose, and
Life still goes on

Life is important, hard and sensitive
You will only get one chance
So take good care of it and,
Life still goes on

Life is like weather, it changes every day
When the sun comes out to make you smile,
Or the storms rise and they pout and will make you too, but
Life still goes on

And then you come to the point to choose
Does life still go on?
Keep thinking positive and,
Life still goes on

Jenna Chan, Grade 5
Blue Heron Elementary School, MN

You and Me
I try to hide it,
Not to show it,
But the thought of you keeps on goin'
I smile an' I blush,
But still there's a rush,
From the moment we met,
Our destiny was set,
The three words "I Love You" are only just for you,
Take them to heart the way I take you,
You take away my fears but leave just one,
The fear of losing you leaves tears falling behind,
The reason why there's a smile,
Is 'cause you're still here…
The constant want and need leads to an addiction baby,
For me to be your one and only the way you are to me,
I imagine, I believe,
That we are meant to be,
Gaze up at the stars as they translate:
You and Me.

Mumtarin Islam, Grade 6
Beer Middle School, MI

British on Their Way
The British are coming, to stop the protest.
That is making King George the Third mad.
But we were ready for them.
We raised our swords and hid in the woods,
muskets ready to blaze.
They made this war when we tried to protest,
about the taxes the king put on us.
That's what lit the flame.

Michael Bartelt, Grade 5
Northwoods Community Elementary School, WI

Veterans
Veterans are very heroic.
And extremely important people.
Veterans are entirely wonderful.
And terrific as can be.
Veterans are very strong beings.
And really, really brave.
Veterans put their lives at risk of dying but still serve.
They are nicer than anyone else than you will ever know.

Miles Brown, Grade 6
Maple Lake Elementary School, MN

Our Today Is Yesterday's Tomorrow

Yesterday is my past, and that sometimes make me aghast.
I won't have an 8th birthday.
I won't have a Christmas in 2002.
Some days this makes me sad.
Some days this makes me mad.
My past will always be, will stay, will never come again, my past.

I live for today.
I move with motion,
I praise with devotion.
Today, I read a book.
Today, I eat my lunch.
It all happens now in this moment, the present.

Tomorrow never comes.
Once you think you have caught up to it,
It will run farther, to the next day.
Tomorrow holds events, hope, and knowledge.
I might go to college.
I might meet the president.
It is all unknown.
My future, your future, our future, the future.

Lucia Rees, Grade 6
McBain Middle School, MI

Pizza

If I were a pizza
   I would taste of cheese and sauce
   I would be delicious
   I would like to be hot and ready to be eaten
   I'd want to be crunchy
If I were a pizza
   I would come to make your tummy full
   I would wish I would be made perfectly with lots of sausage
   I would love to be covered in sauce, cheese, and pepperoni
   I would listen to the family say, "This is some GOOD pizza."
   I would want to be a healthy pizza.

Carson Bakkala, Grade 4
Stocker Elementary School, WI

When I Grow Up

When I grow up,
I hope I win the lottery,
Or become a rapper,
Possible a famous trumpet player
I may change my mind and want to be a cop,
Maybe a graphic designer,
Or a video game tester (probably not)
I could be a mail deliverer,
A librarian,
A bus driver,
Or an investigator
But when I grow up,
All I want to be is me.

Dave George, Grade 6
Campbellsport Elementary School, WI

What Was, What Is, and What's to Come

Yesterday
Yesterday holds memories and treasure.
Yesterday is something I will remember not regret
Yesterday has some bad memories, but I have forgotten them.
Yesterday has some good memories too, I'll remember those forever.
Yesterday

The present
The present is happening right as we speak.
My present is happy and chic.
The present is now not tomorrow or yesterday.
Live in the present days like they are your last.
The present

Tomorrow
Tomorrow will come sooner than we think.
Tomorrow I hope brings travel for me.
Tomorrow will bring a loving family.
Tomorrow will come, I can't wait!
A happy life awaits.
Tomorrow

Kaya Dahlquist, Grade 6
McBain Middle School, MI

Soccer

Running, passing, kicking, and scoring
Whether it's in the sun
In the leaves or
In the cold
Soccer is always fun
Soccer is a mile because you have to be ready to
Run, run, run.

Soccer teaches us a lot of things like
Teamwork, hard work, and commitment
If you want to play soccer you have to like to
Run, you have to be aggressive, and dedicated.

Whether it's just for fun or in a game
I would always like to play soccer
For me soccer is like breathing because
I would do anything to play soccer
And I know there are a lot of other sports
But for me soccer is
Definitely
The best one.

Elle Hoffman, Grade 5
Blue Heron Elementary School, MN

School

I like math it is fun, reading is fun too.
I go to school because I want to be a smart student.
I want to help other students with their work
I would like to be a gym teacher.

Isaiah Peterson, Grade 4
River Heights Elementary School, WI

Inside This Empty Box

Inside this empty box
Are things never seen
Colors never seen
There are things unthinkable
Unexplainable things

Wonderful things I want to tell that's in this box
But I can't you have to see not with your eyes
But with your heart
To see these unexplainable things
You have to believe you can see them

To see what I see you have to imagine
Inside this empty box there are pictures with drawings
There are words that people throw in that hurt
There are memories left behind
Thoughts and feelings never spoken

There are secrets in this box
Secrets that can change the world

Laural Hermosillo, Grade 6
TJ Walker Middle School, WI

Christmas

A wesome; **B** eautiful tree
C ookies
D uring winter
E lves
F riends and family
G reat **H** oliday
I cicles; **J** ingle bells
K indness; **L** ovely time
M orning surprises
N orth Pole
O pen up **P** resents
Q uick run to your presents
R eindeer; **S** anta
T rain around the Christmas tree
U get lots of presents
V ery glad to see your family
W hen you go downstairs there're presents for you
X -mas is great
Y eah for Christmas
Z ipping through the wrapping paper

Lilliana Harvel, Grade 4
Dibble Elementary School, MI

I Am

I am so cool
I wonder if I am going to be a police officers
I hear birds chirping
I see the sun every morning
I want to catch every ball in football
I am so cool

I pretend that I can fly
I feel goose bumps when somebody says something
I touch the ball every time I play football
I worry that I am going to be bad on my test
I cry when I fall
I am so cool

I understand that you have to listen to the teacher
I say good things to people
I dream that I can fly
I try to keep my room clean
I hope that I can do good at football
I am so cool

Dawson Sugars, Grade 4
Floyd Ebeling Elementary School, MI

I Am

I am smart and a Rosa
I wonder if I will become an artist
I hear dolphins clicking to me
I see my paintings in an art gallery
I want to be a marine biologist
I am smart and a Rosa

I pretend that I'm a teacher
I feel turtles nibbling on my fingers
I touch a microphone
I worry about moving
I cry when I think about my dog, Max
I am smart and a Rosa

I understand why my cousin is in a wheel chair
I say "I love you" to my family
I dream of helping my patients
I try to be a good sport
I hope I can save an animal
I am smart and a Rosa

Cristiana Rosa, Grade 4
Floyd Ebeling Elementary School, MI

Silence

Silence is a beautiful thing that can be broken easily.
It is fragile and a precious thing,
it is a simple treasure like beautiful sparkling jewels.
It's like a breath of fresh air.
It is unowned and free to everyone.
It is peaceful and wonderful.

Ashley Steenis, Grade 5
Clovis Grove Elementary School, WI

Autumn Leaves

Autumn leaves
As the leaves turn red
and they fall from the trees autumn is in the
air the weather turning cold and a distant memory
of a summer that came to an end all the fun that we
had hoping it will come again

Anahi Navarro, Grade 6
St John Kanty School, WI

Shoreline Wonders

Sounds of water glide
Along the shoreline wonders
On the beach I wait

Alexis Russell, Grade 6
Manistique Middle & High School, MI

Whipping

Sledding in white snow.
Cold wind whipping in our faces.
Let's go one more time.

Jaelin Marie Lockwood, Grade 6
Manistique Middle & High School, MI

Winter

The wind is blowing,
Trees lose their leaves in winter,
Winter wonderland.

Connor Murphy, Grade 5
Mazomanie Elementary School, WI

Fawns

Fawns with small white spots
Hiding in the green hemlocks
While predators stalk

Keith Fischer, Grade 6
Manistique Middle & High School, MI

Lonely Moon

Moon in the night sky
Seems lonely and so alone
Is silent as a rock

Isaac Anderson, Grade 6
Manistique Middle & High School, MI

Winter

Branches stretch their twigs
Breezes are as soft as snow
When the grass is white

Vanessa Barton, Grade 6
Manistique Middle & High School, MI

Trees

Leaves falling fast
Skeletal branches reaching
Bare trees creep through the night

Jordan Utterback, Grade 4
Stocker Elementary School, WI

Autumn

Walking through the woods
Rustling of beautiful leaves
Autumn is peaceful

James Oscar, Grade 4
Stocker Elementary School, WI

A Sad Day

I remember the day my dad died.
I remember him leaving the house to go hunting.
I remember watching his green truck drive away in the cold, damp rain.
I remember asking my mom if we could go visit my aunt in Waukesha.
I remember arriving at her house.
I remember my cousin standing at the window pointing at my mom and I.
I remember playing with my cousins Katie and Connor.
I remember my mom answering her cellphone, followed by her crying.
I remember my aunt asking what was wrong.
I remember my mom saying that my dad had a heart attack.
I remember asking if he would be okay.
I remember everyone in a rush.
I remember being in the hospital sitting on my cousin's lap, crying on her shoulder.
I remember my mom saying he was gone.

Samantha Krueger, Grade 6
Campbellsport Elementary School, WI

Life: Inside and Out

Life is something that God brings to the world.
There is light at the beginning and light at the end.
We realize what he brings to us may be temporary,
And when we get attached, it is the hardest thing to let go.
It is next to impossible to know when or where a person is going to pass.
But life is like a tunnel that has many obstacles along the way.
When you enter the tunnel, your life has begun.
In it you will face many decisions and adventures,
And when you have faced enough obstacles and had enough fun,
The tunnel will come to an end.
You never know what life will throw at you, so enjoy the little things.

Megan Gassner, Grade 6
Campbellsport Elementary School, WI

Lava Cake

If I were a lava cake
   I would taste like a good chocolate cake with fudge inside
   I would be made with a good fudge taste
   I would like to be made with French chocolate
   I'd want to be eaten by people who like me.
If I were a lava cake
   I would come from France
   I would wish I would be made with really warm fudge
   I would love to be the best lava cake in the world
   I would listen to the yum sounds the people eating me are making
   I would want to be on display for everyone to yearn for

Tyler Robbins, Grade 4
Stocker Elementary School, WI

Thank You for Serving

I'm proud of my country and I hope you are too.
I'm proud of all the brave people working right now to let our world go round and round.
To stop the wars would be a pretty good thing.
But for now we are going to have to keep fighting as hard as we can.
So thank you vets for all you have done.
But for every good year a new vet will come back.

Jay Rumsey, Grade 6
Maple Lake Elementary School, MN

Thanksgiving

Thanksgiving, Thanksgiving, it's that time of year,
when you eat turkey and
give thanks

Thanksgiving, Thanksgiving, it's that time of year,
when we celebrate
the big turkey dinner
the Pilgrims and
Native Americans
had to celebrate
their friendship

Jonathan Ooms, Grade 5
Grand Rapids Christian School - Evergreen Campus, MI

Sleigh Ride

On a cold Christmas morning
I went for a ride in a sleigh
It was not at all boring
There was no sleeping or snoring
I loved it so much I wanted to stay

I did not want to go home and play
And when I did I thought of soaring.
I wanted to go back the very next day.
If I could go back all my money I would pay.
Next year on a cold Christmas morning.

Lindsey Stinton, Grade 4
Grand Rapids Christian School - Evergreen Campus, MI

Licorice Man

Four
Feet tall,
With a peppermint
Flavor, dots for his
Eyes, a gummy bear servant,
Heart made of jelly, sherbet, and
Ice loves his licorice hates his rice,
Chocolate chip buttons cow tails shoes, tip of
Frosting for his new blues, edible grass for his
Hair, his wardrobe is definitely not a horrid despair

Taylor Marie Wilcox, Grade 6
Campbellsport Elementary School, WI

My Name Is Henry

Henry
It means active, player, friendly
It is the number 43
It is like a soccer game
It is biking 45 miles in one day
It is the memory of my uncles
Who taught me to sacrifice
When they fought for our country
My name is Henry
It means the best sports player

Henry Schenkel III, Grade 4
Grand Rapids Christian School - Evergreen Campus, MI

Inside This Soccer Ball

beneath the old tattered ridges and lowlands
under years and years of redundant kicking
the old vibrant colors replaced by faint sad colors
the worn out bladder has no choice but to go lopsided
yet it's content

inside his neglected ball lies something else
love
a person growing up with this at his feet
immense love instantly get sewed between the two
spending numerous hours together

creating something new
peace
bringing joy to people all around the world
rejoicing the fun times when we were young
slowly rebuilding our world…

Connor Sannito, Grade 6
T J Walker Middle School, WI

Love

Love
Is an ocean of tears.
Breaking,
Binding.
A roller coaster ride of emotions.
Beauty,
Roses,
Midnight dances,
Tender kisses.
Cherishing time together.
Turn forward the hands of time and you'll see:
A white dress floating down the aisle,
While a black tuxedo waits near the altar.
Touching,
Glowing.
Forever ours:
Love.

Emily Ellenbecker, Grade 6
Campbellsport Elementary School, WI

Our Future

As the world is spinning,
we're getting closer
To a specific day,
that's beginning our future
As we're moving and moving,
until we all stop
We're improving our nation,
by taking our spot
From trees, to lakes, and everywhere north,
we're taking our chances with all kinds of work
Now let's keep this day going with things new and fresh,
because this world is changing with all simple steps

Sydney Rowland, Grade 6
Wayzata Central Middle School, MN

Treasure, Emeralds and Diamonds
Treasures and emeralds are
So
Lovely. So are white
Diamonds
They are gems.
The
Treasures, emeralds and
Diamonds
Are
Stunning.
Ethan Kadlec, Grade 4
River Heights Elementary School, WI

Autumn
The crisp fall leaves float around
And touch the ground without a sound
The exciting streets in jeans and boots
Many duets of cellos and flutes
The animals sleep
The chipmunks eat
And get ready for the cold to come in
You feel the known air
And know that it is there
The snow is calling my name
Stephanie Green, Grade 6
Birmingham Covington School, MI

Special Moments
Long walks with my dog
Eating with friends and family
Tiny kisses
Hugs and kisses
O-x-o-x-o-x at the bottom of cards
You and me moments
Getting together with family on holidays
Happy times
Thinking happy
Special moments
Alyiah Schuh, Grade 5
Clovis Grove Elementary School, WI

Exploding Mind
My mind is
Exploding
Like a
Volcano.
So much information
Coming out,
So much going in.
Our mind is
Amazing
Like God!
Harmony Winters, Grade 4
The Potter's House Christian School, MI

McKayla
M arvelous
C reative
K ind
A rtistic
Y oung
L oving
A mbitious

R adical
I ntelligent
C ute
C aring
O utside a lot
McKayla Ricco, Grade 5
Riverdale Elementary & Middle School, WI

Simba
My cat
Extra fuzzy
Orange tabby
Overly plump
Very talkative
Friendly greeting
Plays fetch
Nighttime prowling
Frequent napping
Rumbly purr
Loved him
Miss him
Morgan Barnes, Grade 5
St Paul Evangelical Lutheran School, WI

Hidden by Darkness
When nighttime falls
I am hidden by darkness
I feel like life is done
I walk in my house
I hop in my bed
and I lay there with
thoughts in my head
spinning, twirling, and
dancing until I fall asleep
and before I know it
the darkness is gone
but the cycle will start again
Laney Huhner, Grade 5
Wagner Elementary School, MN

Autumn's Pumpkins
Autumn has orange pumpkins,
Big, fat, heavy pumpkins,
Carved glowing pumpkins,
Small, light, white pumpkins,
And small colorful gourds.
Krista Olson, Grade 4
Sheboygan Falls Elementary School, WI

Winter
I love winter so cool so beautiful
With the white flakes
Like a blanket over everything
The crystals melt on your tongue
And the cool air in your lungs
When animals go to hibernation
While kids come out to play
Snowmen and snowball fights
Then come inside to hot chocolate
Like a winter wonderland on every block
Hang on the fireplace your sock
Go to bed with dreams filled with gumdrops
Wake up to presents and lollypops
With presents everywhere
And decorations hung with care
Such a jolly time
Have a drink with a slice of lime
See the sleigh tracks and the
Plate that was once filled with snacks
That's why I love winter
Meghan Koval, Grade 6
St Gerard School, MI

Jitters
Yesterday was such a day.
I have no need to hide away.
I got a good football game,
Now there is no need for fame,
Because that was yesterday.

Today is a day of waiting.
Today is a day of no sports.
Today is a day of fun.
Today I am hopeful.

Tomorrow the football playoffs await.
Who will win state?
Will it be my high school?
Or some other fools school?
I cannot wait,
I anticipate,
That tomorrow,
My school will rule.
Brett Kamphouse, Grade 6
McBain Middle School, MI

Christmas/Easter
Christmas
cold, snowy
cooking, eating, playing
hot cocoa, presents, eggs, chocolate
hunting, dying, warming
sweet, warmth
Easter
Natalie Kaley, Grade 4
Stocker Elementary School, WI

I Am
I am smart and sporty
I wonder what college I will go to
I see me singing the National Anthem and me getting married
I want to be an artist and a singer
I am smart and sporty

I pretend I am a teacher and a mother
I feel happy and sad sometimes
I touch flowers and my baby brother's hand
I worry about my baby brother and my family
I cry when I get hurt and sometimes tears
I am smart and sporty

I understand my brothers are crazy
I say we should have more MEAPS and soccer season
I try to help out a lot and do my best
I hope all my wishes come true and I get to play soccer inside
I am smart and sporty

I am Kailey Bull

Kailey Bull, Grade 4
Floyd Ebeling Elementary School, MI

Imagination
Imagination waved to me when I was born
Imagination is from the heart and mind
Imagination is more important than any talent or kind
Imagination is a best friend
It's with you until the end

Imagination is so important
Imagination is so amazing
You don't need any talent or specialty
All you need is creativity

Imagination is full of
Colors
Brightness
Happiness
And thoughtfulness

Imagination is a special thing
Never let it go

Natalie Warner, Grade 5
Blue Heron Elementary School, MN

Quietness
Quietness is valuable,
it gives you time to relax and think.
Away from all the noise,
up in a tree or in your bedroom.
It gets you away from relatives,
brothers or sisters that annoy you.
Calm is another word for quietness and peaceful.

Taylor Helm, Grade 5
Clovis Grove Elementary School, WI

A Friend
A friend is like gold as valuable as treasure
A friend is something in which nothing could measure
A friend will always find a place in your heart
A friend will help and make you feel smart
A friend is an angel, a guardian by day and by night
A friend is the one who brings all the light
A friend is there when all is lost
A friend can amount up to no cost
A friend is the one that can make your day
A friend is the one that can shine the way
A friend is the one who gives the love
A friend is like a wonderful dove
A friend is kind, thoughtful, and true
A friend appears like on cue
A friend is with you from school to home
A friend is like a beautiful poem
A friend is with you all the way
A friend is by you every day, a friend to you is always fair
A friend is the one who really does care
A friend is like gold as valuable as treasure
A friend is something in which nothing could measure

Sylvia Sidky, Grade 5
Cedar Ridge Elementary School, MN

I Am
I am in 4th grade
I wonder if I'll find buried treasure
I see Fred giving me $1,000,000 on TV
I want my dad to feel better
I am smart and creative

I pretend I'm on the Cocoa Puffs commercial
I feel the coldness of the igloo
I touch my pencil when I do homework
I worry someone's going to break into my house
I cry when my dad yells at me
I am lovable

I understand my dog isn't going to have babies
I say Halloween's the best
I dream there's only 1 day of school
I try to be the best artist
I hope my 5th grade teacher is nice
I am good at video games

I am Blake Felton

Blake Felton, Grade 4
Floyd Ebeling Elementary School, MI

Mannequins
Do mannequins get tired of standing all day?
Do they wish they could go out and play?
Do they get tired of people changing them?
Do they wish they were real people?

Deanna Maldonado, Grade 6
Gilmore Middle School, WI

I Am

I am energetic and a good gamer.
I wonder how the next day will go.
I hear music playing in my head.
I see math going around in my head.
I want to be the best at whatever I do.
I am energetic and a good gamer.

I pretend to like some things in life.
I feel curious about how things work.
I touch a basketball and all I think about is basketball.
I worry about my grandparents every day.
I cry only when needed.
I am energetic and a good gamer.

I understand some things other people wouldn't understand.
I say I'll get my Master's degree in machines.
I dream of having a big truck someday.
I try to be my best. I hope I will be the best at whatever I do.
I am energetic and a good gamer.

Michael Joseph Wier, Grade 6
Campbellsport Elementary School, WI

Canada

Canada is my favorite place to
take a trip.
When you're driving there and you're having
fun with everyone
it seems like a zip.
When you get there it is easy to make friendships.

My grandma makes great food for
us, breakfast, lunch and dinner.
We always go to sports day
and it would be great
to be the winner.

Now you could be anywhere in
the town of Matlock,
Uncle Brian's cabin, Auntie Laura's cabin or
even the candy store…
Every time I visit it
I love it more and more!

Julianna Rendall, Grade 4
River Heights Elementary School, WI

Purple

Purple is what my wardrobe is, of course
Because I have a purple purse
My purple purse matches my purple shoes
My purple shoes came with my purple skirt
Because I have a purple skirt I have a purple shirt
That is why I have a purple wardrobe
Because I have a purple wardrobe I have a purple room
And everything else purple

Tia Coates, Grade 4
Platteville Middle School, WI

What Are We Fighting For?

Why can't we come to an agreement
about what is right and wrong — aren't we all equal?
Like Martin Luther King Jr. said in 1963
that no matter how you speak
no matter where you come from
no matter your religion we all are equal beings.

Why can't we come together as one?
Why can't we be peaceful to each other?
What's the reason we do things to hurt one another?
Didn't we all agree that we all are equal beings?
What are we fighting for?

Our hearts tell us to avoid hate
Yet we all do the opposite.

Why is it we act like this?
Why can't we all be one nation?
One world? One family?
Why can't we stop the fighting?
Because really what are we fighting for?

Adam Ehline, Grade 6
Saginaw Arts and Sciences Academy, MI

I Am

I am confident and courageous
I wonder how the computer works
I hear the sound of an ocean
I see the waves of an ocean
I want to live forever
I am confident and courageous

I pretend I know everything
I feel angry when someone abuses their pet
I touch the soft feel of a cat's fur
I worry my cat will get sick and die
I cry when I see the movie *Fox and Child*
I am confident and courageous

I understand when someone loses a loved one
I say "Stop it" when someone annoys me
I dream that I will be able to fly
I try to do good in school
I hope my dreams will come true
I am confident and courageous

Shayenne Jaffke, Grade 6
Campbellsport Elementary School, WI

My Favorite Autumn!!

Sitting in a huge golden field,
listening to the wheat swaying in the wind
and watching the geese fly over my head.
Hearing the honk and feeling their wings beat makes me wonder?
Looking at the cows helps me feel like I'm unstoppable!!!

Lily A. Meyer, Grade 4
Sheboygan Falls Elementary School, WI

The Woods

I see a wonderful forest.
The forest has a pretty stream.
I see a deer drinking from the stream.
I hear the birds singing.
I hear frogs croaking.
I hear the leaves rustling.
I smell fresh ground.
I smell dew from this morning.
I smell the animals.
I taste rain water.
I taste fresh picked raspberries.
I taste picked apples.
I feel free.
I feel happy.
I feel alone.
I touch cool water.
I touch the deer's fur.
I touch damp bark.

Allison Creek, Grade 5
Eagle Creek Academy, MI

In the Season of Fall

The wind blowing the leaves,
Making a rustling noise,

The football team practicing,
"SET, HIKE!!"

The girls playing tennis,
Boing, boing

The fall colors,
Red, gold, and bronze

Thanksgiving,
The giant turkey

And school starting

In the season of fall

Kylee Jones, Grade 5
Wagner Elementary School, MN

The Bully

Left on the sidewalk, pushed around,
With the mean you talk, I have found.
Words bring me down most of all,
It's so hard to just stand tall.
Rumors spread across the school,
Why do you need to rule?
The name you called wasn't mine,
Every day you have to shine.
Maybe you'll find in the end,
You could've had a great friend.

Alison Albrecht, Grade 6
Novi Meadows School - 6th Grade, MI

Lion-Lamb

Lion
Majestic, proud
Roaring, snarling, prowling
Mane, muscle…fleece, fluff
Bleating, leaping, grazing
Meek, gentle
Lamb

Uma Prasad, Grade 5
Birmingham Covington School, MI

Lizards

L eaping creature
I ncredible
Z ipping
A wesome
R unning
D aring
S uper cool

Maddie Hensrud, Grade 4
Dibble Elementary School, MI

Fall/Winter

Fall
breezy, chilly
jumping, playing, raking
leaves, Thanksgiving, cold, snow
shoveling, reading, sledding
frosty, icy
Winter

Lee Fulkerson, Grade 4
Stocker Elementary School, WI

The Christmas Tree

The beautiful tree with sparkling
Ornaments streaks of gold and
Pearls of silver.

It has stars of blue and
Snowmen of white
With the beautiful angel on top.

Molly Vanderwood, Grade 4
The Potter's House Christian School, MI

Thanksgiving to Easter

Thanksgiving
light-brown, cool
stuffing, carving, eating
turkey, apples, baskets, colored eggs
looking, feasting, playing
nice, fun
Easter

Jackson Musick, Grade 4
Stocker Elementary School, WI

I Don't Understand…

I don't understand

Why poems rhyme
Why a rhino has a horn
Why a giraffe is tall
Why an elephant has a trunk

But most of all
Why people go to work
Why we have to read
Why we have to learn
Why kids can't drive cars

What I do understand most is
Why the sky is blue
Why we go to school
Why we write

Lo-ammi Moyett, Grade 6
Gilmore Middle School, WI

Inside These Shadows

Inside these shadows darkness
thrives preying off the evil of the free.
In these shadows darkness lives growing
growing never stopping they will never
stop they will never love.

Inside these shadows where light turns
black there is an ache, a need for love
a feeling they have never felt before
they will kill for it but they
will never understand.

Inside these shadows the lonely live
the desperate, the scarred, the scared
they will never live in peace they
will never prosper they will never fly.
When will these shadows learn.

Joey Doucette, Grade 6
T J Walker Middle School, WI

Wonderful Wolf

Wolves live in
Europe, Asia, North America,
Long legs, large feet,
Deer, moose, squirrels and mice,
Gray, brown, red, white, or black
Wolves attack cattle,
Habitats are being destroyed,
People kill wolves,
Spine tingling,
Highly intelligent,
They hunt at night in packs,
Wolves eat meat

Alina L. McLendon, Grade 5
Riley Upper Elementary School, MI

Fall

Fast, whistling winds,
In which colorful leaves catch,
Spinning to the ground.

It gets colder still.
People get out their jackets,
And their warmest socks.

Red apples are ripe.
We pick and eat the good fruit.
It is tasty, crisp.

We carve large pumpkins.
For dark Halloween night,
We put in candles.

Fall is nearly gone.
Soon it will be wintertime
Goodbye, fall! Goodbye!
Amelia Mills, Grade 6
St Gerard School, MI

Monster Trucks

Monster trucks are big,
And weigh 10,000 lbs.
Once you take a look at one
You'll be very excited.

Monster trucks are shiny
They jump big obstacles.
They go to big domes
With a lot of people.

Monster trucks are awesome
They go to different states.
Like Detroit, Texas
Florida, and Vegas too.

Monster trucks are popular
Monster trucks are big.
Monster trucks are shiny
Monster trucks are awesome.
Nicholas Rieser, Grade 5
May V Peck Elementary School, MI

The Ice Within

Ice lives within me.
It flows beneath my skin.
When I pace around the rink
I always have a grin.

The cold air rushes past my face,
A kiss from Mr. Frost.
There is a chap upon my lips.
My eyes are slightly glossed.

Happiness shows on my face.
Practice has finally come!
I make a note to watch my place,
To know where I came from.

The ice lives within me.
It flows beneath my skin.
When I leave the rink each day
I have an enormous grin.
Sarah Kreitman, Grade 6
Detroit Country Day Middle School, MI

Staring at the Sky

I see clouds in the sky.
It is like the sky is not high.
I can't wait for the clouds to change.
The birds chirp.
The leaves rustle.
No one is asking me to hustle.
I smell the leaves.
The flowers too.
Not the smell of old shampoo.
I taste the cool air.
Also the gum in my mouth.
I am not going to pout.
I feel weightless.
I feel calm.
No one can touch my palm.
I can feel the ground.
It isn't very soft.
It is like I am in a loft.
It is fun to stare at the sky.
Nick Manzo, Grade 5
Eagle Creek Academy, MI

Dolphins

What does a dolphin
Know?
Mixture of
Black,
 White,
  And gray
Intelligent and
Playful
Swift swimmers
Needle-like
Teeth
Spindle shaped
bodies
Beak-like
snouts
30
Km an hour
Males are larger than
Females
Michael J. Marlett, Grade 5
Riley Upper Elementary School, MI

Ninja

Still as water
he runs in the night
fights off bad guys
his moves are as calm
and swift as when air
blows in a tree. He
is the ninja. Fast
as the speed of
sound

he is the best
fighter

his suit
is like a shadow
you don't know
his identity. You
can't see him.
He is like air.
Ryan Brooks, Grade 5
The Potter's House Christian School, MI

The Life of a Colonist

Civilian
quiet, rebelling
singing, dancing, fearing
women, girls, men, boys
hardworking, cold
jumping, screaming, yelling
hopeful, scared
Soldier
Anna Coletti, Grade 5
St Paul Evangelical Lutheran School, WI

Football

F un
O uch
O ffsides
T hree point stance
B all
A wesome
L ong throw
L eft tackle
Landon Jones, Grade 5
Zinser School, MI

Veterans

V eterans
E xtreme
T ired
E xciting
R epublican
A wesome
N ice
S avior
Noah Hayes, Grade 6
Maple Lake Elementary School, MN

Thank You

Thanks to the veterans
We all live free
Fighting in World War 1 and World War 2
I have many thanks to you

Brian Heald, Grade 6
Maple Lake Elementary School, MN

Autumn Leaves

Outside, I heard crispy sounds,
leaves were falling, floating around.
People stepping on them
crunchy, colorful leaves abound.

Savanna Ridge, Grade 4
Sheboygan Falls Elementary School, WI

Thank you Soldiers for Our Freedom

Thank you soldiers for our freedom,
Thank you for winning wars,
Thank you for the stars and stripes,
Thank you for our freedom.

Ashley Day, Grade 6
Maple Lake Elementary School, MN

Fall

Chilly, rustling leaves
fires burning, marshmallows roasting
crunchy cool fall nights!

Kalyn Ocampo, Grade 4
Stocker Elementary School, WI

Fall

Playing with the leaves
Geese flying south for winter
Red-orange leaves crunching

Sebastian Rosales, Grade 4
Stocker Elementary School, WI

My Fall

Mourning doves cooing
Birds flying south for winter
My sounds of fall.

Colton Matthews, Grade 4
Stocker Elementary School, WI

Listen Carefully

Slow water hits shore
Listen very carefully
I finally sleep

Renae Schuetter, Grade 6
Manistique Middle & High School, MI

What Is Inside This Blank Piece of Paper?

Inside this blank piece of paper are many things
Stories that have never been told,
Ideas that have never been thought of,
Mysteries that have never been solved
This wise, blank piece of paper wants to tell its tales

Even though no one has ever uncovered or thought of a tale and put it on this paper,
They are alive, hiding
And they are there, waiting waiting
To put those words on this blank piece of paper
Neither fire nor ice can bring them out

They have to be thought of
What will they say?
Will I be able to understand them?
I guess that even though it's blank, there is much more on the inside
For now all I can say is they are waiting, waiting.

Grace Hubbard, Grade 6
T J Walker Middle School, WI

Memories, Adventures, and Possibilities

My past has been filled with many great memories.
Summers spent growing giant-sized pumpkins and prize-winning pigs.
Fishing for salmon with Dad on Lake Michigan,
and fishing for bass with Grandpa and Grandma Z. on Lake Missuakee.
Fun times with my friends playing sports and hanging out.

Today my life is filled with many great adventures.
Competing in travel team basketball league and dodgeball tournaments.
Time spent practicing my trumpet to perfect my musical talent.
Reading my Bible to learn more about God,
and spending time taking care of the family aquarium.

My future is full of many possibilities, only God knows what is in store for me.
I want to have a happy Christian family,
and stay in touch with all the friends I have made.
Reaching my goal of attending Michigan State University,
with hopes of learning how to successfully run my family's farm.

Noah Outman, Grade 6
McBain Middle School, MI

Autumn Days

Leaves are falling
Down
Down
Down
But then…
Bop! A leaf hits you in that noggin of yours.
Also you look down and your shoes and feet are moist from the dew, and the wind is dry.
Then you hear birds chirping and you see them flying south, they must be migrating.
As you look around there are pumpkins and Halloween decorations.
You hear your house door open it's your mother and the rest of your family and she says,
"Come on it's time to go to the cider mill." Then it hits you it's fall!

Abraham Jaafar, Grade 5
Riley Upper Elementary School, MI

Baseball

Baseball is cool
Baseball is fun

You get to bunt,
And you get to run

You get a lot of money
That you don't really need

Baseball players are sweaty
Cool and awesome

They have mitts
That they use to catch with.
Cole Mockbee, Grade 5
May V Peck Elementary School, MI

Snow

The snow begins to fall.
It's fun to play outside.
It's time to make snowballs.

The wind blows the snow in
like tides.

My mom finally calls,
"It's time to come inside!"
Hot chocolate is what awaits for us!

All the kids wait patiently
and everyone gathers aside.
No one makes a fuss!
Celeste Medina, Grade 5
The Potter's House Christian School, MI

Basketball

As I glided through the air
I felt like a bird soaring through the air.
The ball hit the back board with a thud,
And fell gracefully through net.
Cantering my horse gives me a steady beat,
Up, down, up, down. It is the coolest feeling.
Riding feels like you are a part of the horse.
Wind whistling against your face,
With the sun beating down on you.
My future plan is to be a photographer.
To be able to give cherished memories,
And photos as keep sakes.
Capturing moments that need no words.
Like shooting a hoop. Or riding in the wind.
Taylor Schonert, Grade 6
McBain Middle School, MI

Dance

An experience I
will never forget.
It is the feeling of being
free, free at last.
Watching it or doing it
you will feel good inside.
The gracefulness of dancing
is something you will
feel throughout your life.
It is this feeling, a feeling
that you will have forever.
Audrey Biemeret, Grade 5
Mazomanie Elementary School, WI

Together

Together we can
Together we can stop war.
Together we can make peace.
Together we can make a difference.
Together we can build hope.
Together we can save a life.
Together we can save the world.
Together we can stop crime.
Together we can stop global warming.
Together we can stand up for what's right.
Together we can
Karlee Peacock, Grade 6
St Gerard School, MI

Awesome Fall

Leaves crunch as you
Step outside
Red
Yellow
Green
Leaves, fall
Down
Down
Down
Branches breaking plants dying
The best things about fall.
Annalise J. Connelly, Grade 5
Riley Upper Elementary School, MI

Nature

Nature is colorful and beautiful,
Nature is peaceful.
Nature is wild,
Nature is full of surprises.

Nature is full of beautiful sounds,
Nature is full of life.
Nature is soothing,
Nature is all you can imagine.
Bryce Arredondo, Grade 6
Corpus Christi Catholic School, MI

Subs

Subs are good
Some are big, some are small

Some have lettuce, some have tomatoes
Some have pickles, some have peppers

Some have turkey, some have ham

Some have Swiss, some have American
Some have mustard, some have mayo

Any way you make it
I'll eat it
Yum yum!!
Felicia Borchardt, Grade 5
Hewitt Texas Elementary School, WI

My Scout Troop

M y scout troop is a lot of fun
Y ou know. I

S ay that because we go
C amping all
O f the time. It's nice to sleep
U nder
T he stars.

T hat is what I love about it. Although we
R un all
O ver the place there is time for
O urselves to
P lay card games, which is very fun!
Jonathan Brandell, Grade 6
St Gerard School, MI

Veterans

Veterans fight,
All through the night
When we sleep,
Without the fright

Americans,
Don't understand
While they fight,
With command

So many make a stand,
Maybe it'll be you
Remember, if you go,
You'll fight for the red, white, and blue!
Maggie Miller, Grade 6
Maple Lake Elementary School, MN

All About Me

Smart,
Kind,
Nice,

Wishes to be a teacher.
Dreams of love.
Wants to teach young people.
Who fears spiders.
Who is afraid of basements.
Who likes boys.
Who believes in God.

Who loves to read.
Who loves mom's cooking.
Who loves family and friends.
Who loves everyone I meet and am close to.

Who plans to be a good friend to everyone.
Who plans to be a faithful wife and person.
Who plans to live a wonderful long life.

Whose final place after life is heaven.
Alexis Radliff, Grade 6
Gilmore Middle School, WI

Thank You Vets

Thank you vets.
For all you have done.
There have been some hard times.
And people have fallen.
Don't feel sad.
Still stick up.
We will win this war.
One day or another.
Blake Ogilvie, Grade 6
Maple Lake Elementary School, MN

Michael

M uscodian
I ntelligent
C ool
H itter
A thletic
E nergetic
L efty

S mart
C aring
H appy
A wesome
E ven
F un
E ntertainer
R unner
Michael Schaefer, Grade 5
Riverdale Elementary & Middle School, WI

You

Look up,
Look down,
Look all around.
Up high,
Down low,
But just for you to know,
You'll never find someone
Quite like you.
Sarah Kotajarvi, Grade 6
Abbott Middle School, MI

My Friend

I have a friend hidden away,
He loves me so.
He has stayed with me always,
and when I need Him, He is there.
We have fun together all the time,
I read His word every day,
and that is why I love Him too.
Kaila Abrahams, Grade 5
Home School, WI

Summer/Snow

Summer
Dark purple, sunlight
Walking, relaxing, fishing
Fireworks, parties, snowmen, snowflakes
Sculpting, migrating, freezing
White, cold
Snow!
Sydney Block, Grade 4
Stocker Elementary School, WI

Winter/Fall

Winter
snowy, cold
shoveling, playing, shivering
Christmas, hot cocoa, leaves, Thanksgiving
tasting, gobbling, raking
yellow, windy
Fall
Alex Henry, Grade 4
Stocker Elementary School, WI

About Me

S mart
T ruthful
E xciting
P arty Animal
H elpful
E ager
N ot nauseous!
Stephen Juracka, Grade 4
Dibble Elementary School, MI

Libby

Libby is so golden brown,
Not too dark, but not too light.
She rolls on the ground,
But still is very bright.

She always makes me smile,
Even when I'm blue.
Just her howl,
Will change my mood.

Oh Libby, my beautiful dog,
You are perfect.
Taylor Charon, Grade 5
Zinser School, MI

Love

Love tastes like a velvet mint.
It smells like roses.
It feels like a roller coaster ride.
It sounds like a waterfall.
It looks like a sunset.
Love is a virtue.
God is love.
There is romantic love.
There is family love.
There is universal love.
There is unconditional love.
That is love.
Michael Bennett, Grade 6
St Gerard School, MI

Hope

Hope will never let you down.
Hope can be wisdom.
Hope can be a thought.
Hope can be a plan.
Hope can be a name.
Hope can be shared.
Hope can be given.
Hope can be happiness.
Hope can make you smile.
Hope is always there.
Hope will never leave you.
Hope will go with you anywhere.
Grace Bellgowan, Grade 6
St Gerard School, MI

Friends

We will be friends
Till the end
Through snow and the blow of cold wind.
We will be friends
Through heat to sleet.
We will be friends!
Jared Mickelson, Grade 5
Mazomanie Elementary School, WI

Veterans

The veterans are strong
They fought all night long
Veterans are courageous
They have been for ages

The veterans fight at any price
They have great sacrifice
Veterans are incredible
They are always dependable
Katelynn Kramer, Grade 6
Maple Lake Elementary School, MN

Soldiers

Thank you soldiers,
For all that you do,
For fighting for our freedom,
And yours too.

Thank you soldiers,
We're proud of you,
You should come home,
Because we all love you.
Jason Webb, Grade 6
Maple Lake Elementary School, MN

Thank You

T eam work
H ang on tight
A dmire your strength
N ever out of my heart
K ind to everyone

Y ou will never be forgotten
O bservant to everyone
U ltra strong
Sienna Ortiz, Grade 6
Maple Lake Elementary School, MN

Walking in Autumn

Trees with naked arms
reaching for the blue skies
walking in the crunching leaves,
hearing birds…
tweet, tweet, tweet.
Fatima Magsaysay, Grade 6
St John Kanty School, WI

Aaron Rodgers

Aaron
Better than Favre
Super Bowl MVP
Sharp quarterback for the big Pack
Rodgers
Trevor Ramthun, Grade 6
Campbellsport Elementary School, WI

I Fear the Owl

I fear the owl out at night
I fear the owl he gives me a big fright
I fear the owl he stands so still
I fear the owl he watches me all night
I fear the owl he goes "hoo-hoo"
I fear the owl he finds a place to sit
And sits there until the moon sets
Quinten Engelson, Grade 5
Wagner Elementary School, MN

The Color of Blue

Blue is the color
of the sky above me
of the flowing river
of the water in the lake
on a boy's favorite shirt
of blue jeans
of a blue couch or chair
Carter Kexel, Grade 5
St Paul Evangelical Lutheran School, WI

The Special Flowers

The flowers are gleaming in the night,
And shining oh so bright.
A sad song fades away,
While the skies turn gray.
As the flowers die,
So do I.
Samantha Sheldon, Grade 6
Gilmore Middle School, WI

Sports

Sports are fun.
You can jump, hit, fall, and run.
Swing, swim, and throw.
You can get tired,
But the best part is
Sports are fun.
Nicholas Wesolowski, Grade 5
Mazomanie Elementary School, WI

Easter

Easter is super fun
Celebrate Jesus died for us
You finally really won
The devil can never claim us!
Teagan Kokesch, Grade 4
St Paul's Lutheran School, MN

Flowers

Flowers bloom and reach for the sky.
My, oh my, they do grow high.
Do you like flowers? I really do.
The petals' colors are red, white, and blue.
Emma King, Grade 5
Mazomanie Elementary School, WI

In the Far North

Arctic
extreme cold
few communities
snowy, windy, quiet
Tundra
Jacob Ulrich, Grade 5
St. Paul Lutheran School, WI

Smelly Beast

Animal
Cute, rough
Squealing, splashing, snorting
Great playmate for mud
Pig
Benjamin Bournelis, Grade 6
Campbellsport Elementary School, WI

All About Katy Perry

Famous musician,
Awesome voice,
Stylish fashion
Rocks the stage,
Katy Perry
Katrina Blaisdell, Grade 5
St Paul Evangelical Lutheran School, WI

Thank You Veterans

Time has been done,
Wars have been won,
Lives have been lost,
Thank you veterans,
For the blood you have shed.
Andy Mavencamp, Grade 6
Maple Lake Elementary School, MN

Winter

Winter's icy breath
Chills the woods and the hillsides
Trees look like crystals
Jack frost nipping at your nose
White is almost everywhere!
Sydney Bruce, Grade 6
Abbott Middle School, MI

Me

Gabe K
Playing soccer
Likes nachos and tacos
Watches a lot of videos
My life
Gabe Koebbe, Grade 4
Dibble Elementary School, MI

Give

Give to people who have nothing at all,
Give hope to people who have none,
Give comfort to people who need it,
Give back to your community,
Give a smile to someone who needs it,
Give ideas to create something big,
Give money to find a cure,
Give inspiration to a child,
Give a cheer to encourage someone on,
Give time and listen to someone,
Reach out and find what you can give.

Katy Shannon, Grade 6
St. Gerard School, MI

Americans

A mazing
M iracle
E xperts
R eady
I nspire
C aring
A wesome
N ation
S pecial

Mean a lot to me

Anna Becker, Grade 6
Maple Lake Elementary School, MN

Best Friend

B rittney
E ver so nice
S pend lots of time together
T ries to make me laugh

F riend
R uns around with me
I s so cool
E ver so funny
N ever gets angry
D oes not leave me

Carly Strauss, Grade 5
St Paul Evangelical Lutheran School, WI

Kevin Hart

Kevin Hart is funny
He has so much energy.
On stage he talks about people a lot.
He went to jail once.
He is a very short guy.
He has two children
that get on his nerves
a little too much
but he loves them.

DéVante Barry, Grade 5
May V Peck Elementary School, MI

Simple Pleasures

Silent night
  Imagination
    My family
      Pets
Listening to noises
  Eagles soaring through the sky
    playing with friends
Laughing
  Entering the park
    After a good day
      Simple silence
        Under a tree
Reading a book
  Entering a new place
    Snowy nights

Hannah Porto, Grade 5
Clovis Grove Elementary School, WI

Forever

You mean the world to me
Nothing will ever come between us
No matter what anybody says or does
You will always be in my heart
Forever and ever.

Your spot will never be replaced
You hold the key to my heart and
You have since we met
I will love you forever

No matter how much we fight
  Things will be okay, like I said
    I will love you forever
      No matter what.

Ashlee Surface, Grade 6
Chisholm Elementary School, MN

Lucus

L ikable
U nbelievably smart
C an behave
U nafraid of challenges
S ometimes silly

S ometimes friendly
C ourageous
H elpful
N ice
E nergetic
I ncredible
D oes like football
E xercises
R eads a lot

Lucus Schneider, Grade 5
Riverdale Elementary & Middle School, WI

A Ride on My Bike

It's the wind through my hair
As my bike catches air
It's the feel of a jump
When I ride over a bump
It's the drip of my sweat
As I ride like a jet
It's the pump of the wheel
As my bike's made of steel
As I use my legs
I pedal my pegs
As I ride my bike
I'm glad it is not a trike
As I go around a bend
My ride starts to end
As I ride so fast
I never come in last

Grant Weed, Grade 5
Blue Heron Elementary School, MN

My Colors

Blue is the color of a sunny day.
Red is the color of Santa's sleigh.

Gray is the color of clouds about to rain.
Silver is the color of a shiny train.

White is the color of a fancy wedding.
Brown is the color of the dog I'm petting.

Black is the color of darkness.
Pink is the color of harmless.

Green is the color of money.
Gold is the color of honey.

What are colors to you?

Mitchell Krien, Grade 6
Gilmore Middle School, WI

Spartan Sports

S partan…soccer
  P aintball
    A rchery
      R ugby
        T ennis
      A rm wrestling
    N et ball

S partan…shuffleboard
  P ing pong
    O ff road skating
      R owing
        T rack and field
      S wimming

Matt Statly, Grade 6
St Gerard School, MI

Grandpa's Going

I remember when Grandpa got cancer
I remember, "Is it bad?"
I remember Mom saying yes
And then it got better
I remember when he got it back
I remember it was worse
I remember taking him to therapy with Mom
Even when he was stopping therapy
I remember Mom telling me he was going to die
I remember we all went down to see him
Then I started to cry and Mom told me it would be okay
I remember he only had 2 weeks to live
I remember going to see him in the home
I remember the final 24 hours
I remember the death of Grandpa
And the funeral, the hardest part of all

Dalton Fleischman, Grade 6
Campbellsport Elementary School, WI

In My Backyard

Red is the color of my shirt,
Brown is the color of the ground's dirt.

Blue is the color of the day sky,
White is the color of the birds that fly.

Yellow is the color of the sand over there,
Pink is the color of flowers in your hair.

Black is the color of my dog running around,
Silver is the color of the cars going to town.

Orange is the color of the bright firelight,
Dark blue is the color of the cold summer night.

Now, what are the colors in your backyard?

Lexi Johnson, Grade 6
Manistique Middle & High School, MI

Fall

The seasons are changing,
The colors of leaves are fading,
The sound of leaves crunching under my feet,
Fall is such a wonderful treat!

Juicy warm meat of the turkey running down my throat,
Apple juice to wash it down,
Good old Thanksgiving dinner will never give you a frown!

Apple picking, strawberry picking, harvesting too,
Fall has so many things for you to do!

Jumping in leaf piles,
I hope this season stays a while!

McKenna Gingery, Grade 4
Floyd Ebeling Elementary School, MI

The American Revolution

That crazy king!
On every finger was a ring!
Cruel and mean, royal and mad!
Thought up with all the power he had,
some large taxes, that brought us to our maxes.
This became known as the Boston Massacre
which was a great disaster!
Five of our men died that day.
So then we thought of a plan to get our way!
We dressed as mighty Mohawks, and with our tomahawks,
we boarded a ship of Boston tea that night
and we gave the sailors such a fright!
The captain we didn't see, but there were his mates.
Then we started dumpin' those British tea crates.
There was no solution.
This became known as the American Revolution.

Bridget Rich, Grade 5
Northwoods Community Elementary School, WI

Harvest

Harvest is in the fall time,
So busy farmers are in the field.
Grain carts and semis are everywhere,
Beans and sweet-smelling corn is getting picked.
Combines start on fire, so does the corn.
Flat tires and a bean head are getting fixed.
Morning to nightfall is when they work
Dryers and legs are running.
Bins are getting full.
Harvest is so much fun,
Let's go for a ride
Our farm is really busy at this time.
Meals are in the field.
This is my favorite time of the year.
This is harvest time.

Katie Ebeling, Grade 5
Martin County West Trimont Elementary School, MN

Dreams

When I lay in bed
Dreams fill my head
Of the book I just read
The fish that didn't get fed
And the test that I dread

The snow on the ground
Cars driving around
The penny that I found
The frozen ant mound
And a dreadful sound

But when I wake
I give a shake
And say "what a great poem this will make."

Courtney Kuipers, Grade 5
Grand Rapids Christian School - Evergreen Campus, MI

My Trampoline

Jump, jump up and down
On my trampoline, hear
It shriek and squeak
When you jump,
pretty neat.

Trampolines are really
Fun, hope you get to
Jump on one.

Sometimes you jump so high
You almost touch the sky.
It's like you fly.
I like to jump with friends
On Friday, do you know why?
Because it's fun and fantastic.

Sammy Lund, Grade 5
Blue Heron Elementary School, MN

15 Letters of Me

A nnoying
B ubbly
I mpatient
G abby
A ctive
I mpulsive
L eadership

S assy
C onfident
H ard headed
A ide
L oyal
L ovable
E dgy
R isky

Abigail Schaller, Grade 5
Riverdale Elementary & Middle School, WI

Music

Music is love,
Music is life,
Music makes people and family unite.

Music inspires me to do better,
Music is the earth, the air, and weather.

Do you hear the music play,
As it brightens and lightens up your day?

Music can dance and sing
Music is what makes me say…

DANCE WITH ME!

Rayven Craft, Grade 6
Gilmore Middle School, WI

Slithery Snakes

What does a snake
know?
Rows of scales,
Mice and rats,
Vibrations in the
ground,
Hissing sound,
Slender and swift,
Hawk and owl,
On the prowl,
Desert sands,
Wrap around prey like
rubber bands.

Stephen M. McDonald, Grade 5
Riley Upper Elementary School, MI

Heroes

My heroes are the firemen.
They come by in a big red van.
Then out comes a man carrying a hose,
Strong enough to blow off your nose.
If it weren't for the firemen,
Lots of people would be dead.
I think firemen are heroes;
They don't have laser power
Or the power to fly,
But every time they go by,
They are going to help people not die.
I think firemen are heroes because
They save lives.

Jordan Toma, Grade 5
Rochester Hills Christian School, MI

Who Am I

Who am I?
I teach many
about God.
Who am I?
I am God's only son.
Who am I?
I never lied
in my whole life
Who am I?
I died on the cross
for our sins.
Who am I?
I am Jesus Christ!

Stephan Bracey, Grade 5
The Potter's House Christian School, MI

Pizza

Pizza has pepper —
onions and cheese or peppers
ham and pineapple

Bradley Dutcher, Grade 4
Dibble Elementary School, MI

Weightless

Swish, swish
I swim deeper
It gets dark; my ears would pop,
if I had any.
I am no longer seeing darkness
an invisible force is pulling me,
yet I stay calm.

I see light,
I am soaring, higher and higher,
evaporating;
I am in a cloud now
I feel the cloud get heavier;
each drop of my brethren making it shake.
Finally, I am weightless,
falling, like I was meant to,
a weightless raindrop.

Isabel Canales, Grade 6
Saginaw Arts and Sciences Academy, MI

My Dog

He chews on everything,
Like a bobcat on prey
But I love him anyway
He sits down, and he also lays,
Plus rolls over when he wants a treat

I pet him all day over and over
Then I comb his hair,
And brush his teeth

We play Frisbee,
And throw ball,
In the front yard,
While the neighbors stroll by,
On their daily jogs
I walk him
But sometimes he walks me

Jack Kirchner, Grade 5
Blue Heron Elementary School, MN

Colors

Yellow — The color of a daisy in the day,
Blue — The color of a fresh water bay.
Orange — The color of a big flamed fire,
Black — The color of a nice round tire.
Red — The color of a big barn,
Pink — The color of pigs on the farm.
Purple — The color of a plum,
Brown — The color of a chocolate yum.
Gray — The color of a rainy sky,
Tan — The color of breading on a pie.
Colors really mean a lot for me,
They open my day as you can see

Alec Spang, Grade 6
Gilmore Middle School, WI

Fire and Water

Fire
Hot, rapid
Wild, burning, blazing
Water is fire's weakness
Cool, relaxing, refreshing
Everything lives because of it
Water
Nathan Buxton, Grade 6
Gilmore Middle School, WI

Grandpa

Loving,
Gardener, teacher
Cook, friend, partner
Heart attack
Sad, hospital, surgery
Funeral, pain, loneliness
Death
Kristin Garibay, Grade 6
Gilmore Middle School, WI

Halloween/Thanksgiving

Halloween
windy, cool
trick-or-treating, scaring, sleeping
pumpkins, candy, football, pie
gobbling, tasting, cooking
cool, sunny
Thanksgiving
Ria Patel, Grade 4
Stocker Elementary School, WI

America

A rmy
M arine
E xciting
R espect
I love America
C orps
A ir force
Catie Fobbe, Grade 6
Maple Lake Elementary School, MN

Miss You Forever

I miss you for now I will miss you forever
You will always be remembered
You fill me with joy you fill me with love
Even though you're not here with me
Forever and always we still are together.
You are still fighting for our country
For now and forever.
Abby Fredrick, Grade 6
Maple Lake Elementary School, MN

School

School
Learning, teaching
Listening, talking, answering
Math, Social St., Science, English
Conversations, working together
Solving problems
School
Onyx Magno, Grade 6
IQ Academies/eAchieve, WI

Veterans

Veterans are brave
Everyone will honor you
Right there with us
Always in are memories
Trustworthy
Everlasting in our hearts
Never ending
Rylee Shaw, Grade 6
Maple Lake Elementary School, MN

Freedom

F aithful
R oses
E verything
E ndless Freedom
D efinite
O utstanding
M emorial
Emily Rasset, Grade 6
Maple Lake Elementary School, MN

Veteran

V eterans served for our country.
E ntirely helpful to us.
T he American flag.
E ndless freedom.
R eally important to our country.
A mazingly brave when they fought.
N eeded their help for war.
Lance Jude, Grade 6
Maple Lake Elementary School, MN

Deer

Stunning, magnificent, graceful,
Swiftly moving,
Pausing to graze,
Observing me cautiously,
Rapidly running away!
In awe of God's creatures,
Formidable buck!
Richard Pricop, Grade 6
Detroit Country Day Middle School, MI

Autumn Sunset

I stroke you across my smooth canvas,
Leaving color behind.
Color so pure and rich
With no drips.
Colors and colors mixing together
Every second more intense.

Blues with purples,
Yellows with greens,
And pinks with reds.
No noises.
The sound around is completely dead.
I stroke you across my smooth canvas.
Celia Allen, Grade 6
White Pine Middle School, MI

Me

My hair
In despair
Looks like a black bear.
My eyes
Are like spies
Soaring the skies.
My ears
All they hear
Are things I despise.
My heart
Holds rage
As you turn the page
With a picture of bizarre me inside.
Blake Johnson, Grade 5
The Potter's House Christian School, MI

Sergio Garcia

S acrifices
E ffective
R eckless
G lorious
I nteresting
O utstanding

G lamourous
A mazing
R eliable
C ontagious
I rresistible
A stonishing
Sergio Garcia, Grade 6
Gilmore Middle School, WI

Ocean

Waves hitting the sand
Sparkling light of the ocean
Crashing in the night
Faith Griffith, Grade 4
Stocker Elementary School, WI

Freedom

Thank you soldiers, for all the things you do and thank you veterans too
Thank you for giving your country freedom too because freedom gives us the rights to do whatever we want to do
We really appreciate what you do thank you
Our whole country feels so lucky on Veteran's Day and always
So thank you, thank you, thank you, very much

Hanna Stewig, Grade 6
Maple Lake Elementary School, MN

Leaf Dance

As I step outside, the crisp fall air wraps its arms around me. Step by step I get closer to the towering trees, until finally they devour me! The beautiful fall leaves cling to the delicate branches, but the crisp air loosens their grip. The sun streams through the mustard colored leaves, making them appear golden. The red and orange leaves make a fiery path for the golden leaves to dance through. Though I don't want it to be true, I know their sweet ballet will end soon.

Halle Blauwkamp, Grade 5
Bauer Elementary School, MI

The Parting

We are patriots of the British, so they tax everyone! We go on a boycott, and weave our own clothes and make our own tea. We have done a ton. We also took stamp men and tarred and feathered them all. We took up arms for our new nation and answered the call. This led to the Boston Massacre, where it all started. The colonists and the British are now parted.

Liz Boehm, Grade 6
Northwoods Community Elementary School, WI

The Family Tree

The tree is your gift;
part of your family
growing in your backyard
by the care of your hands.

You are the Master Gardener
Creating the tree of love for your family to treasure

You are the waterer — nourishing its roots,
so that it can...
shelter your home,
produce fruit for your family,
house the nests of birds,
and warm you from the fires of its branches.

You are the care giver — protecting its life,
so that it can...
welcome children to climb in it,
stretch its long, strong branches to
safely support tree houses,
and provide hours of swinging from the tire swing.

A family treasure.
A gift of love.
The family tree.

Olivia Steinmetz, Grade 6
Saint Francis of Assisi School, MN

Autumn

Red, orange, yellow, and brown
Splattered upon trees as their leaves propel down
Twirling, circling, fluttering in the breeze
Landing perfectly on the Earth with ease

As I look upon the ground and stare
I wonder, is there anything that could compare
To this beautiful sight with perfect crisp air

The leaves flew up and circled me
I was the center of a twister, a treat to see
Some are yellow, some are red
Some are even brown and dead

Each leaf is unique in its own way
But when mixed together they all lay
As a painting in your mind that will always stay
A gorgeous mural spread across the ground
Rustling and moving with a melodious sound

Another name for autumn is the season of fall
But you may say any name you wish to call
Some people take fall for granted
But I gaze upon this season completely enchanted

Maya Rajan, Grade 6
Detroit Country Day Middle School, MI

What's in My Computer Tower?

Inside our computer tower
are dark, clicky things
Screws, bolts, wires, and fans
that sometimes swirl into a dark, black hole
and make a low humming noise,

like little whispers in the dark
or the wind through the trees.
What will they say?
Hello?
Goodbye?

Nobody knows.
They're dark, clicky things
that hold secrets
That will never be heard
Unless they're discovered within.
Kayla Pruden, Grade 6
T J Walker Middle School, WI

Trophy

Inside this trophy is a song
A song that won me a trophy
Inside the song is a message
A message about a girl
Who won everything

My trophy may not be big
It may not be grand
But it means a lot
And it can stand bright,
Brighter than a polished Eiffel Tower

Now it stands alone
In a cold, dark place
My name carved on it
In the dusty room
Stands a trophy
Mikayla Eliyha, Grade 6
T J Walker Middle School, WI

The One and Only Me!

K ind
E nergetic
N ice
Z esty
I nnocent
E ntertaining

O utstanding
L eader
S mart
O riginal
N eat
McKenzie Olson, Grade 5
Riverdale Elementary & Middle School, WI

Inside a TV

Inside a TV
There are items waiting
Weather reports to be heard
Video games to be played
Football games to be watched

There is electricity buzzing
As it moves through wires
And transmitter
Picture and sound signals
Magically appear

Stories
Sports
Events
Waiting to come to life
When you hit the button
Jack Richard, Grade 6
T J Walker Middle School, WI

Christmas

Christmas is here!
It's finally here!
Presents are waiting
down stairs.

I have lots
and lots of presents

Presents that are big and tall
and some that are small

I like giving
presents to others
and seeing their faces.

That's why I'm saying
Christmas is here!
Jatara Nash, Grade 4
The Potter's House Christian School, MI

Loneliness

She feels unloved and alone,
Everyone makes fun of her,
She has no one at home,
her voice is never heard,
She wakes up every day,
Wondering if her life is worth it.
She could no longer stay,
She would finally admit,
She could not take it anymore,
On that day she ended her life,
And every day I cry
For that poor girl that died.
Sierra Varebrook, Grade 6
Gilmore Middle School, WI

The Magic of Music

Music is strong,
Music is a song that we all sing along.

Music is a way of life,
Music is what tells us what's right.

Music is a story,
Music shows us all the glory.

Music will never be the same,
Music can never be tamed.

Music is what makes us love,
Music is from the ground to above.

This is the magic of music…
Maddie Crenshaw, Grade 6
Gilmore Middle School, WI

Hope

Hope is family.
Hope is friends.
Hope is singing.
Hope is our talents.
Hope is listening to others.
Hope is being respectful.
Hope is being nice.
Hope is being positive.
Hope is believing you can do anything.
Hope is courage.
Hope is trusting others.
Hope is giving money to the poor.
Hope is happiness.
Hope is about our faith.
Hope is GOD who gave us 'us' so we could
have HOPE.
Christina Williams, Grade 6
St Gerard School, MI

Mudding

Bright
Blue
Sky
Sun shining down
On
Me
Mud
Flying through
The
Air
Excitement
Screaming engines
Roar of the motor,
Roar of the motor
Hunter S. Quinn, Grade 5
Hewitt Texas Elementary School, WI

I Wish

I wish I had a sister
I wish to be a writer

I wish to have lots of snow cones
I wish to have a big January birthstone

I wish I had a dog
I wish I had a frog

I wish to have lots of gum
I wish I could eat every cookie crumb

I wish to go on a cruise
I wish I could wear red high-heeled shoes

I wish…
Well I wish for a lot of things
But what I have is enough.
Klarese Applebee, Grade 4
River Heights Elementary School, WI

If I Were

If I were a tornado,
I wouldn't even touch down
to the earth.

If I were a storm
I would only rain
with no thunder and lightning.

If I were a blizzard
I wouldn't blow hard at all
I would only snow.

If I were you
I would have fun
while it lasts and
try to be as smart as your
teacher.
Mine is Mr. Gutbrod!
Devon Jones, Grade 5
Blue Heron Elementary School, MN

Gymnastics

G o ahead, have some fun!
Y ou can do anything if you believe!
M e? Of course I believe!
N o one can put me down
A whole class in on floor.
S ome kids are on bars.
T ime to go home!
I had a
C aptivating
S ession today!
Samantha Hazeldine, Grade 6
Detroit Lakes Middle School, MN

Fun with Leaves

I climb a tree then shake the leaves.
When the leaves start to fall
I tumble and hop in them all.

I bury myself in a hurry.
I will not worry!
I hear a giggle and a hoot,
I jump out of my hiding place
and yell "BOO!"

My friends ran this way and that.
Over each other and each other's hat!
So that was that.
I knew it would come soon
now I'm stuck in my room!
Abi Charbonneau, Grade 4
Sheboygan Falls Elementary School, WI

The Luminous Light

Bright
Bleached
Light

Wonderful
Joy
Amazing

Calm
Quiet
Still

Peaceful
Peaceful
Peaceful
Cassie E. Lambrecht, Grade 5
Hewitt Texas Elementary School, WI

Friends

Friends are fun.
Friends are helpful.
Friends are loving.
Friends say hi.
Friends are encouraging.
Friends have things in common.
Friends aren't mean.
Friends give hugs.
Friends always share.
Friends are nice.
Friends are smart.
Friends are responsible.
Friends stand up for each other.
Friends go places.
Friends entertain you.
Jacob Fischette, Grade 6
St Gerard School, MI

Veterans

V ictory
E ach other
T rained
E arns respect
R eady
A merica
N avy
S trong
Joe Elsenpeter, Grade 6
Maple Lake Elementary School, MN

Veterans

V eterans
E ncourage
T ough
E fficient
R espect
A dmire
N ice
S trength
Brooke Sawatzke, Grade 6
Maple Lake Elementary School, MN

Veterans

V ietnam War
E nemy
T ough
E quality
R escue Mission
A mbitious
N avy Cross
S acrifice
Kaitlyn Murphy, Grade 6
Maple Lake Elementary School, MN

Veterans

V ery strong
E xciting
T rusting
E nthusiastic
R emember them
A chievers
N ever gave up
S o brave
Sam Zappa, Grade 6
Maple Lake Elementary School, MN

Flower

F ull of great smells
L ovely colors
O riginal
W onderful shapes
E verywhere
R idiculously beautiful
Samantha Osenga, Grade 5
Zinser School, MI

Math
Math
Addition, subtraction
Is basic facts
Times, divide harder facts
Put it all together we get math
Fractions, decimals, place value can be facts
A lot of things we do in life has to do with math
Math!

Allyssa Sanderson, Grade 6
Galesburg-Augusta Middle School, MI

October
Leaves fall, rip, crumple and start to get old.
The weather makes people shiver and start to get cold.
Snow reflects sunlight and it looks gold.
Snow piles itself big white bold.
The grass bends down in green and white folds.
The wind changes as the weather turns cold.
The leaves fall, rip, crumple and start to get old.

Alina Bowser, Grade 4
Grand Rapids Christian School - Evergreen Campus, MI

Nikki
Nikki is as sweet as an angel.
She might be tiny.
She might be feisty.
She is the best. You can't beat that can you?
When she talks her voice is as soft as a cloud.
What a sweet angel.
What a sweet girl.

Jasmine Hernandez, Grade 5
The Potter's House Christian School, MI

Thankful
I am thankful for God giving me the life that I live,
and I am thankful for my friends.
I am thankful for my family that I live with today,
and when I leave I am going to cry.
Because I am going to remember my childhood,
and I am going to miss everything.
I do not want to grow up.

Imani Rodriguez, Grade 5
Clovis Grove Elementary School, WI

Simple Pleasures
As I drifted into sleep
It felt like I was floating on a cloud
Thinking only one thing could make this better
My dog Snickers, but…
Once I open my eyes there he is
Laying there peacefully sleeping
Laying there at my feet

Jack Skaletski, Grade 5
Clovis Grove Elementary School, WI

Timothy of the Cay
Timothy
Strong, helpful, old, foreign
Lover of Phillip
Who feels outrageously happy
Who needs food
Who gives everything
Who fears the jumbi
Would like to see a plane
Resident of The Devil's Mouth
Wise old man

Liam Guikema-Bode, Grade 4
Grand Rapids Christian School - Evergreen Campus, MI

The Saddest Day
It was the saddest thought
A girl could think,
As a tear rolled down my cheek.
I went in the basement trying to hide
The aches and pains
I felt inside.
I couldn't stand the news from my mother…

She told me I was getting
a little brother!

Starr Altizer, Grade 4
River Heights Elementary School, WI

Volleyball
V olleyball is extremely fun!
O nly in late summer and early fall
L ikes to play tricks on your mind
L ove the floor because you need to dive
E ntering a game you'd better be ready
Y ou need to have the right equipment
B all is extra hard so you need to be strong
A lways need to practice
L ove the game or don't play
L uckily you don't get hurt often

Hannah Bliesmer, Grade 5
Martin County West Trimont Elementary School, MN

Escape
I want to escape from the dark places in my mind
Find a place where I can see the light
Free to be myself
Free to accept who I am
I want to escape
To find my identity
Escape to realize what I can do
I want to escape from the people who don't believe in me
And find people just like me
I just want to escape

Sydney Smith, Grade 6
Saginaw Arts and Science Academy, MI

Fireworks

I speak the language of fireworks
Fireworks on the fourth of July
I hear people saying "oo ahh"
I hear the fireworks going "boom"
I see them fade away in the night sky
All I dream about are fireworks
I am a firework in the night sky
Because...
I speak the language of fireworks

Madison Shoultz, Grade 5
Wagner Elementary School, MN

Squirrels

S ame old
Q uiet trees
U tter
I ncredible learning
R ights to
R eason for
E njoyment and
L earning animals are
S quirrels parroting trees

Taylor Mosher, Grade 6
Detroit Lakes Middle School, MN

Veterans

V ietnam
E ndless freedom
T he flag
E ducated
R ed, white, and blue
A braham Lincoln
N ever give up
S oldiers

Kora Fuller, Grade 6
Maple Lake Elementary School, MN

Swimming

S ummer
W ater
I love to swim
M elt the ice after winter
M ichigan's Lakes
I rresistible
N ature
G oing to the beach

Hali Blik, Grade 5
Zinser School, MI

Sports

Athletic, awesome
Tiring, thirsting, sweating
Improves shooting the ball
Basketball

Gretta Kumrow, Grade 6
Campbellsport Elementary School, WI

Our Country

Our flag is red, white, and blue
with stars for each
and every beautiful state in our country
our country is free
our country is brave in every way
we fight for our people
and our people fight for us
thank you America
for the red white and blue
we now know because of you

Katelyn Fuller, Grade 6
Maple Lake Elementary School, MN

Gymnastics

G ood feeling
Y our turn on vault
M ore responsibility
N o stopping
A ll the way
S trong body
T rust
I n your team
C oaches are there for you
S tay in the sport

Kira Avila, Grade 6
Detroit Lakes Middle School, MN

Love

Love is the reason
we live our awesome lives
the way of writing it is a heart. A
very dark red heart. So dark like
the color of human blood. With
out love the world wouldn't
get bigger. Love is the
reason all this
world is
here!

Mayar Zamzam, Grade 6
Birmingham Covington School, MI

Simple Pleasures

Reading under a tree.
Playing with kittens.
Planting flowers.
Family time.
Walking the dogs.
Spending time with friends.
Playing with my cousin.
Holding my cousin.
Laughing.
Writing.

Naomy Tangness, Grade 5
Clovis Grove Elementary School, WI

Cherries

Cherries are red,
Cherries are good,
Cherries are good on ice cream,
Cherries are at the store,
Cherries are in a jar,
Cherries are good plain,
Cherries are in my mouth.

Danielle Oliver, Grade 5
May V Peck Elementary School, MI

Fall to Summer

Fall
crunchy, cool
jumping, raking, playing
candy, leaves, trees, flowers
riding, camping, hiking
light, sunny
Summer

Hay Tharler Thee, Grade 4
Stocker Elementary School, WI

Halloween to Thanksgiving

Halloween
cold, foggy
trick-or-treating, carving, walking
candy, pumpkins, stuffing, turkey
eating, feasting, harvesting
windy, crisp
Thanksgiving

Ashley Falduto, Grade 4
Stocker Elementary School, WI

Feet

Feet make a steady beat and
help you walk, stomp,
jump. Feet have toes that stick
out, and are very smelly,
hairy, dirty, shiny, and clean.
Every living thing has
feet except ocean animals.

Iven Daood, Grade 5
May V Peck Elementary School, MI

October to November

October
spooky, scary
carving, trick-or-treating, eating
Halloween, candy, turkey, Thanksgiving
eating, socializing, playing
cool, fun
November

Curtiss Tolefree, Grade 4
Stocker Elementary School, WI

The Snow Fall

One snowy day
the snow was falling.
The sparkles of the snow
made me want to go outside.
It was so beautiful in the sunlight
it almost made me cry.

Jerry Singleton, Grade 5
May V Peck Elementary School, MI

Marvel Man

Super hero
Big hammer
Lives in Asgod
Fights frost giants
Marvel avenger
Thor

Lucas Schneider, Grade 5
St Paul Evangelical Lutheran School, WI

Autumn Leaves

The leaves are all falling down,
Not one of them makes a sound.
Yellow, orange, red, and brown,
All falling down, down, down.
A pretty sight to see,
Very nice for you and me.

Erin Sime, Grade 5
Seneca Elementary School, WI

Autumn

Look at the leaves falling down,
They can be red, yellow, green, or brown
Rake them up in a pile,
You can play in them for a while.
Jump in the pile and have some fun,
Until finally you can't see the setting sun.

Jared Payne, Grade 5
Seneca Elementary School, WI

Drawing

I
Love to draw and paint
At home
In the middle of the day
Because I'm the only judge of my art
Not you

Joslynn Groff, Grade 4
River Heights Elementary School, WI

Rain

Rain, rain
Falling like crystals
Making icy mirrors in puddles
On the Arctic.

David Holtrop, Grade 4
The Potter's House Christian School, MI

Slinky

I remember getting in the car.
I remember my dog running toward the car.
And me telling my dad to stop.
I remember hearing a yelp.
I remember getting out of the car and running toward him.
I remember when my sister and I had a funeral for him in the backyard.
I remember crying my eyes out in my room directly after.
I remember waking up the next morning confused about where he went.
I remember that he has passed on.
I remember.

Bryce Vogt, Grade 6
Campbellsport Elementary School, WI

Basketball

B asketball is a great sport to play and watch.
A thleticism is a big part of basketball. Athletes with a lot of
S kill usually make it to college basketball, some even to the NBA.
K icking is a foul in basketball.
E lite NBA teams like the Dallas Mavericks usually have the best players.
T eams in the NBA may not have a season this year because of a lockout.
B asketball tournaments are very fun to play in. Basketball is a boy
A nd girl sport. The professional girls' league is called the WNBA.
L arge amounts of people play basketball every year.
L ocal Catholic schools play in the Catholic Youth League.

Ryan Pence, Grade 6
St Gerard School, MI

One Day I Will…

One day I will graduate from high school.
One day I will got to college at UWM, Boise St., or University of Texas.
One day I will get drafted.
One day I will play in the NFL.
One day I will be a millionaire.
One day I will win a Super Bowl.
One day I will sign thousands of autographs.
One day I will be on the cover of a video game.
One day I will retire.
One day I will get inducted into the NFL Hall of Fame.

Payton Johnstone, Grade 6
Gilmore Middle School, WI

Simple Pleasures

Cooking with my mom.
Going to the park with my nephew.
Singing to my cat and my cat listening to me.
Playing with my nephew, hide-and-seek, and him saying "Turn the light on."
Listening to Mr. Staehler with his amazing stories!
Going dress shopping with my brother's fiancé.
Hanging out with my sister and going to Tom's Drive-In with her.
Going down to my dad's workshop and helping him make wonderful things.
Watching scary movies with my sister.
Eating at the supper table with my family.

Anna Hansmann, Grade 5
Clovis Grove Elementary School, WI

Butterfly High

If I were a butterfly,
I'd fly above the sea.

I'd walk across
the bright green grass,
then sniff
the flowers clean.

Next I'd fly up very high,
and make the clouds sound loud.

Then I'd spread
my wings so wide,
and try to touch
a cloud.

I'd fly down to where I belong,
to a place that I call home.

In the meadows
so very warm,
is the place
I've always known.
Isabel Ledin, Grade 5
Blue Heron Elementary School, MN

Music

I hear music everywhere and every day
then I sing and I sing and I sing away
I sing as much as birds in a bath
splishing and splashing
as I stroll down the path

Then I see squirrels gathering nuts
I hear the squirrels talking as
they go into their huts

Music is a wonderful thing
Music makes me
sing sing sing

Then I hear the snake hissing
and oh how I keep wishing
I could be a singer singing
music in every which way

I hear music everywhere and every day
then I sing and I sing and I sing away
I sing near and I sing far
I sing all over even in the car
Kendall Kramar, Grade 5
Blue Heron Elementary School, MN

One

One wish on a star goes a long way.
One day things could change.
One God is all there is.
One dream is all you need.
One chance and you could make it.
One song is something everyone needs.
One word can show that you care
One picture is worth a thousand words.
One memory can make you happy.
One friend always helps.
One smile can make a day.
One laugh could lead to laughter.
One reaction causes another.
One step forward is better than a step back.
One person can make a difference.
Mattie Mason, Grade 6
St Gerard School, MI

The Football Game

The quarterback threw the football,
it soared through the air like a
shooting star.

The runner caught the football
AND
got the winning touchdown!

Cheerleaders waved their pom-poms
and they danced in the air
like fireworks on the 4th of July.

The crowd's screams
whirled in the air
like the wind on a beautiful fall day.
Mackenzie G. Lohse, Grade 5
Blue Heron Elementary School, MN

Mining for Gold and Silver

G et digging
O ld man
L ose some weight
D ig dig dig

A ppalachians here we come
N othing will stop us
D on't stop working

S leeps little
I f you don't work hard
L ittle faster
V ick struck gold
E mpty your bucket, it's too full
R est it, starts all over tomorrow
Peter Zambo, Grade 5
St Paul Evangelical Lutheran School, WI

Night

Crisp clear moon,
Suspended in the sky,
Stars sprinkled high,
Above me.
Frost sparkles on the grass,
And on my window,
This is the night.

Crickets chirp in the grass,
Owls hoot in their trees.
The leaves rustle,
And blow in the breeze.
This is the night.
Sydney Green, Grade 5
Mazomanie Elementary School, WI

Amanda Ruchti

A mazing, awesome, athletic
M agnificent
A pple-eater
N ot as cool as the rest of my family
D arling
A lways fun to be with

R eally cool
U seful
C ute
H ilarious
T alented
I mportant person
Amanda Ruchti, Grade 4
River Heights Elementary School, WI

Christmas Tree

Green is the color of my Christmas tree,
Rainbow lights shine so beautifully.

Black is the color of the sky so grim,
Red bulbs hang from every limb.

Purple packages lay under the tree,
A blue tag says one's for me.

Silver tinsel glitters in the light,
Yellow garland wraps the tree up tight.

And, a golden star shines through the night.
Ava Curran, Grade 6
Manistique Middle & High School, MI

Frogs

Cool rushing river
Frogs jumping onto soggy logs
Landing gently on logs
Kiara Cooper, Grade 4
Stocker Elementary School, WI

My Mom Is My Hero

Roses are red,
Violets are blue;
My mom is my hero.
Roses are red,
Violets are blue;
My mom helps me
With my homework.
Roses are red,
Violets are blue;
My mom cooks dinner for our family.
Roses are red,
Violets are blue;
My mom tells me
What not to do.
Roses are red,
Violets are blue;
My mom buys me clothes.
Roses are red,
Violets are blue;
I love my mom
And she loves me, too.
Carolyn Zink, Grade 5
Rochester Hills Christian School, MI

Me, Myself and I

Me, Myself and I
No one knows why
I sit in corner
readjusting my personal borders
sitting by myself,
slouching.

Everyone says that
I'm as creepy as a snake,
Just because I'm nice I like it this way.
So I sit alone

It's quiet.

So, if you see me by myself
leaning
in my corner,
moving my borders
don't ask me why.
Just Me, Myself and I
Tyrique Moten-Porterfield, Grade 6
Saginaw Arts and Sciences Academy, MI

Rocks

R ough
O val
C olorful
K eep
S everal
Kailyn Cunningham, Grade 5
Zinser School, MI

Three Boy's Adventure

The three boys,
Wandering in the woods,
All through the night,
Across Florida,
Looking for a home,

The three boys,
Searching the rain forest,
In the afternoon now,
Through the everglades,
Still without a home.
Jacob Wilson, Grade 6
Gilmore Middle School, WI

Angels and Demons

Angels are nice
and friendly ones.
Angels have powers
never seen before.
They're God's assistants.
They're in heaven.
Demons are evil and vicious.
They're he ones with pitch forks.
They're also nasty. They're also creepy.
They both have powers
never seen before.
Tony Bernardi, Grade 5
May V Peck Elementary School, MI

Be a Reader of Dogs

In my dogs' eyes I am their master
When I say "go eat" they listen

In my dogs' eyes I am there for them
If they get hurt by another animal

In my dogs' eyes I am their doctor
In my dogs' eyes I am their best friend
In my dogs' eyes I will always love them

In my dogs' eyes
Emma Doty, Grade 5
Wagner Elementary School, MN

Autumn

Autumn
The change of the season
air turning cold, leaves changing
color and a past summer.
Full of joy that comes
To the end with
Autumn on its way
It will be a good
Change.
Alexis Navarro, Grade 6
St John Kanty School, WI

Trees

Climbing trees is fantastic.
Climbing trees is fun.
Apple trees are the best
To pick the apples down.

Some trees are comfy.
Some trees are not.
Comfy or not it's still fun.

Flower trees smell good.
Apple trees give food.
Normal trees are normal.
I climb them all.

I'm like a monkey.
I love to climb.

I like to sit in a spot
And look down at the world.

When I climb trees I feel
Alive!
Abby Swim, Grade 5
Blue Heron Elementary School, MN

Birds' Song

Birds are musical
Floating through
The air
Sounding like a song

Their flapping
In the wind
Is like the beating
Of their music

Birds' chirping
Is melodious
In perfect
Harmony and sound

Birds go back
To their tree
Sleeping until
Dawn when they will
Wake up singing
Their beautiful song
Ellie Jensen, Grade 5
Blue Heron Elementary School, MN

Bud

B rave uncle
U nder fire
D id the best he could
Hunter Manka, Grade 6
Maple Lake Elementary School, MN

Anger

Anger is red like blood and also like fire
It swims through my mind
It makes me feel weird like
Stepping in peanut butter with your bare feet.
It makes me want to…SCREAM!!!

Lydia Ankrum, Grade 5
The Potter's House Christian School, MI

The Night Comes Alive

Close your eyes
Turn off the lights
Dream of happy things
But as you are dreaming
The night comes alive

The monsters under your mattress
The creatures in your closet
The werewolves watching
The night comes alive

The vampires venturing
The Loch Ness monster looking
The witches wandering
The night comes alive

The mummies marching
The ghosts glowing
The skeletons sneaking
The night comes alive

They wake in the dark
Watching the streets and the town
But when the sun peeks over the horizon
The night disappears

Chelsea Rowe, Grade 6
Lumen Christi Catholic School, WI

The Pink Mystery

I have a mystery
for you to figure out.
It's almost like a round about.
Who is the Pink Mystery?
It has feathers, but it's not Heather.
Who is the Pink Mystery?
It stands on one leg,
almost like a peg.
Who is the Pink Mystery?
Just one clue to show who
the Pink Mystery is.
It has a beak, so it's
not weak.
Who is the Pink Mystery?
You guessed it!
It's a flamingo!

Cassie Parrell, Grade 5
Mazomanie Elementary School, WI

All About Me

Anika

Caring,
Tall,
Talkative

Wishes to go to Miami, FL.
Dreams to get more As.
Wants to get more bracelets.
Who wonders if he likes me.
Who fears getting rejected by her crush.
Who is afraid of getting no sleep.
Who likes boys who are nice.
Who believes in love.

Who loves her family
Who loves herself
Who loves boys
Who loves hugs

Who plans to be successful
Who plans to be careful
Who plans to not be so clumsy

Kissh

Anika Kissh, Grade 6
Gilmore Middle School, WI

When I Met You!

When I met you,
I was like woah,
We could be best friends forever.

It turned out to be that way!
I trust you with anything.
We met in the 3rd grade.

We're as close as peanut butter and jelly.
We'll be best friends until the end.
I love you!

You're a good friend to me,
I'm a good friend to you.
We also have the greatest memories.

I knew you were the missing piece,
For my puzzle!
You were the prefect fit!

You made me the way I am now,
I'm glad we met!
When I met you.

Katelyn Larson, Grade 6
Chisholm Elementary School, MN

Fantastic Fall

Crunching leaves,
Leaves fell
Down,
Down,
Down,
Down,
To the ground,
Waving trees,
Frosty breeze,
"Trick or treat,"
Enough to eat,
Pumpkin pie,
Red hair dye,
Air huffing,
Lots of stuffing
Valerie M. Tant, Grade 5
Riley Upper Elementary School, MI

Bright Light

I melt the winter snow,
I help spring flowers grow.

I am very bright,
For I am a light.

I stay in the sky,
I am very high.

I'm always out in May,
When the children play all day.

When it's time to go to sleep,
You must say goodnight,
To my bright light.
Stephanie Johnson, Grade 6
Gilmore Middle School, WI

Kimberly

K ind
I nteresting
M e
B rown eyes
E xcited
R especting
L ikable
Y oung

W as 11 but now 12
A wesome
L ikes pie
S weet
K nows 6*6=36
I s a Bear fan
Kimberly Walski, Grade 5
Riverdale Elementary & Middle School, WI

Winter

The snow is falling.
Everyone is bawling

Because they got frost bite.
Someone started a snowball fight.

How I love candy canes!
Hold on tight to sled reins.

Oh no! We're going on a jump!
Ouch! I hit a bump.

Got to go —
Going to shovel snow.

Heave-Ho!
Justice Szotkowski, Grade 4
River Heights Elementary School, WI

Every Day in the Fort

A fort shakes like me.
A fort is like a shield from wind and storms.
I am cold like a freezer in the morning.

I love it in the fort.
It is so fun.
You can see my house from the fort.
You can see my fort from the house.
My fort is small.
I could barely get into it.

You should build a fort.
Forts rock.
You can do anything with them.
Forts are yours.
Do whatever you want with them.
Zachery Leonard, Grade 5
Blue Heron Elementary School, MN

Magnificent Fall

I smell tasty turkey
I feel the warmth of a fire
I taste Thanksgiving feast
I see a full moon
I hear a crackling fire
I smell a lovely pie
I feel a smooth rake
I taste colorful candy
I see rainbow leaves
I smell cider
I feel rough candy
I hear screaming fans
I smell a feast
I smell lots of candles
Jonathon Berzins, Grade 4
Floyd Ebeling Elementary School, MI

Fantastic Fall

Chilly cold
Leafs rustling
Birds migrating
In big flocks
Trees dying
The smell of delightful maple syrup
Big fat jack-o-lanterns
People in frightening costumes
Apple cider
Doughnuts
Smoking hot chocolate
Bonfires
People celebrating
Turkey ham
Mashed potatoes
People having feasts
Going places
Do not think of the dreaded winter
For who knows what could happen?
Jeswin David, Grade 5
Riley Upper Elementary School, MI

The Color Blue

Blue,
the color of the beautiful ocean
where the colorful fish swim by.
Blue, the color of a marker,
you could make wonderful
pictures with the
color blue.
Blue, the color
of a brand
new car,
the perfect color
for a summertime car.
There's a lot of
colors close to
blue, but the
color blue
is a very special
color, just like a
person like you.
Spencer Korth, Grade 5
St Paul Evangelical Lutheran School, WI

Veterans

V ery brave
E quality
T hank you
E nemy
R epublic
A merica
N ational Guard
S acrifice
Erica Preusser, Grade 6
Maple Lake Elementary School, MN

Halloween to Thanksgiving
Halloween
cloudy, spooky
shivering, eating, trick-or-treating
candy, pumpkins, cornucopias, turkey
shivering, tasting, feasting
crisp, bare
Thanksgiving
Ian Metzger, Grade 4
Stocker Elementary School, WI

Fall to Winter
Fall
crunchy, windy
harvesting, playing, jogging
Halloween, candy, cold, family
eating, slipping, snowing
white, foggy
Winter
Angel Bucher, Grade 4
Stocker Elementary School, WI

Winter/Fall
Winter
cold, white
snowing, playing, sledding
Christmas, icicles, Thanksgiving, turkey
raking, sleeping, shouting
cool, crunchy
Fall
Brittney Garlic, Grade 4
Stocker Elementary School, WI

Holidays
Halloween
Spooky, Ghoulish,
Munching, Crunching, Walking
Candy, Crazy, Presents, Christmas tree,
Tearing, Opening, Screaming with joy,
Joyful, Exciting
Christmas
Katie Lancaster, Grade 4
Floyd Ebeling Elementary School, MI

Dogs and Cats
Dogs
Cute, Soft
Runs, Rolls, Sleeps
Fluffy, Smooth, Lazy, Small
Playful, Loves yarn, Funny
Kind, Mean
Cats
Selena Nasr, Grade 4
Floyd Ebeling Elementary School, MI

Beautiful
America is beautiful
It has hot and cold skies for fall.
Wind and snow for winter.
Flowers in the spring,
And sun in the summer!
America is special…
It is one of a kind
like you and me!
Kaylynn Maddix, Grade 4
St Joseph Elementary School, WI

In the End
In the end,
It will be warm again.
In the end,
It will be all grass.
In the end,
There is no snow.
In the end,
I can go in my pool again!
Heather Winn, Grade 5
May V Peck Elementary School, MI

The Wandering Dog
There was a dog.
It lived in a log
In the wandering fog.
It couldn't find its way out,
Until it heard a great shout.
It followed the voice in rejoice.
It was happy, and very nappy.
It was fast, and was at home at last.
Abimbola Oyeneyin, Grade 4
Academy of Westland, MI

Christmas
Christmas is great
You get new things
You're happy and glad
You make cookies.
Santa eats them
It snows a lot
Let me see,
I want to put up my tree.
Jalen Perryman, Grade 5
May V Peck Elementary School, MI

What Is Silence?
S ounds are not there
I nteresting sounds are quiet
L etters not spoken
E choes are gone
N othing heard
T alking is not outside
Allegra McBride, Grade 5
Clovis Grove Elementary School, WI

Beautiful Autumn
Hot chocolate and marshmallows
Cider and doughnuts
Candy and
Jack-o-lanterns

Leaves CRUNCH, Crunch, crunching
People and their multicolored
Leaves
Squirrels getting ready to
hibernate

Those delicious pumpkin
seeds
The lovely feast
The cold wind blowing on
Me
Me jumping in multicolored
leaves

Gorgeous mums
Pumpkins and pumpkin seeds
Trees losing their chilly leaves
Hailey N. Maples, Grade 5
Riley Upper Elementary School, MI

Sydney
Sydney
S ticks with me
Y es, my sister
D eer hunting is something we both like
N amed me Hannah to rhyme with banana
E ven nicknamed me Beeners
Y es, I love my sister
Sydney
Hannah Schmidt, Grade 5
St Paul Evangelical Lutheran School, WI

Jayden
J olly
A wesome
Y oung
D etermined
E xciting
N ice

M ale
A rtistic
R eally cool
A lways funny
B oy
E xcellent at sports
L ikes sports
L ikes having fun
I ntelligent
Jayden Marabelli, Grade 5
Riverdale Elementary & Middle School, WI

I Am

I am chipper and energetic
I wonder about what I will be in ten years
I hear God saying, "Stop, is that right?"
I see my great-grandma holding me in her arms
I want a cure for cancer
I am chipper and energetic

I pretend to be a veterinarian
I feel happy when I feel the little hand of a newborn baby
I touch my dog's nice soft fur
I worry about having nobody
I cry when people hurt animals
I am chipper and energetic

I understand my life
I say I'm fine when I'm not
I dream of saying it's going to be okay
I try to cheer people up
I hope I get the chance to raise a family
I am chipper and energetic

Delainie Casey, Grade 6
Campbellsport Elementary School, WI

Happiness

Happiness is joy.
Happiness is love.
Happiness is excitement.
Happiness is a smile.
Happiness is a laugh.
Happiness is petting my dog, Cocoa.
Happiness is playing with my hamster, Blackjack.
Happiness is fishing with my dad.
Happiness is shooting with my grandpa.
Happiness is biking with my grandpa.
Happiness is camping with my cousins.
Happiness is playing cards with my family.
Happiness is skiing with my family.
Happiness is going trick-or-treating.
Happiness is playing football.
Happiness is track.
Happiness is basketball.
Happiness is snow.
Happiness is family.
Happiness is friends.

Matthew Abdullah, Grade 6
St Gerard School, MI

School

School is a place to see my friends,
school is a place where the fun never ends!
School is a time to learn something new,
school is a time for me and you!
School has many qualities, just for you and me,
but the best part is the teacher's qualities!

Jenna Stein, Grade 5
Bauer Elementary School, MI

Spaghetti

If I were spaghetti
    I would taste so good that they'd want to play with me
    I would be a good spaghetti dish
    I would like to be smelling good like I took a shower
    I'd want to be paired with garlic bread
If I were spaghetti
    I would come out of the pot smelling good
    I would wish I would be scrumptious
    I would love to be with my noodle friends
    I would listen to the water boil
    I would want to be poured over meatballs and marinara sauce

Alexis Karls, Grade 4
Stocker Elementary School, WI

Scary Salad

Scary salad dodges my fork
like a fly dodges a fly swatter.
The tomatoes, carrots, and cucumbers flip
and dash from my fork like an acrobat.
The tomatoes, carrots and cucumbers poke fun
because I am not done.
But then I puncture my fork deep in the tomato
like a musketeer stabbing an evil man.
Then, the vegetables all file up in line
because they know that it is over.
Then I gobble them all up.

Toby Reinsma, Grade 5
The Potter's House Christian School, MI

Soccer

I pass the ball to my friend.
He accidentally passes it to the wrong person.
He tries to stop the ball,
But the "Maths" score!
My team, the "Red" play our hardest.
We score four points.
When half time comes,
I pass the ball to C.J.
He kicks it and we score.
The next game the "Maths" win it!
A TIE!!!

Odasi Irankunda, Grade 4
The Potter's House Christian School, MI

I Live in the City of Rain

I live in the city of rain
It rains all day every day.
It gets in our house, in our beds, in our cars.
It floods the streets at night.
I bet people could even swim in it. It is so deep.
You barely see people outside playing or out on a walk.
At school we have to stay inside all day long.
I wish it did not rain all day every day.
    I live in the city of rain

Keegan Linsmeier, Grade 5
Wagner Elementary School, MN

The Last Working Light on a Christmas Tree

When I plugged in the Christmas tree lights
they were not working except
one
one very mighty one
that shined with all its might

one that wasn't afraid
afraid to stand out
one that shined as beautifully as a new
Christmas tree
as this bulb shone it kept going

this little bulb
shone like its last day
to be alive
just like a person who is not afraid
to stand out

Bailee Nessinger, Grade 6
T J Walker Middle School, WI

Five Little Turkeys

Five little turkeys on a gate,
One got off for his date.
So there were four little turkeys.

Four little turkeys swimming in the lake,
One ran off because he had to bake.
So there were three little turkeys.

Three little turkeys waddlin' in the sun,
One waddled off to have some fun.
So there were two little turkeys.

Two little turkeys walking through the woods,
One waddled off to go get some goods.
So there was one little turkey.

One little turkey — BOOM!

Emma Payne, Grade 5
Seneca Elementary School, WI

Me and You Forever

There's one spot in my heart for you.
And I hope that there is a spot for me.
If we are together I hope it is forever and ever.
If we are together I hope it is happily ever after.

It was love at first sight. The way you looked at me and
the way I looked at you. It's how we are together.
It makes me think we are together forever.

Now you asked me to go out and I said yes.
So I believe we will be together forever and ever. When
I said yes our lives changed. So now it is a happily every after.

Katlyn Wolfram, Grade 6
Chisholm Elementary School, MN

Inside the Heart

Inside all hearts are gloomy blobs.
But, the heart won't stop pumping.
Through the toughest of times
your heart will fight, fight to
beat to beat and let you live.

Underneath all the gloom your heart
chooses, chooses what to believe
in. Your heart keeps working, even
when you sleep. When your heart
stops, you stop.

When a business loses its best
advisor, the business usually fails
Unless they get help.
Just like you, hearts contain love so
everyone has love, no matter how deep, it's there.

Kekoa Bicoy, Grade 6
T J Walker Middle School, WI

One Red Leaf and the Rest Are Green

One day I went outside to play
Then I went by a tree and tried to climb it
I couldn't and I slipped, but landed on my feet
Then I went to go on my play set to swing
I swung on the swing and noticed something

I noticed something peculiar
There was a tree with one red leaf and the other were green
So I stopped swinging and stared at it
Then I kept staring an the wind blew
Some of the green leaves fell

The wind blew even harder
Then the red leaf started to fall to the ground
I caught it and it blew out of my hand
I started to chase it but it went down the street
Then all the leaves of the tree fell to the ground

Jacob Edwards, Grade 6
T J Walker Middle School, WI

My Garden

I have a garden big and bright
In my garden, I grow greens the shades of an army uniform
flowers the colors of toucan's beaks
and peas the shape of golf balls
My dog sneaks up to the lilies
and sniffs them, only to get an orange pollen nose
Each day I weed, water, and pick veggies
only to have a sore back and to be bitten by mosquitoes
At night, I sit down and relax
My neighbors and I spend hours admiring my garden
When the bumblebees, butterflies, and hummingbirds come
they enjoy my amazing garden.

Kaija Johnson, Grade 5
Poplar Bridge Elementary School, MN

Robbed from Perfection

When I watched Sunday's Packer game
It really was such a big shame
They didn't seem to care
They looked like such fools out there
The fact they lost to the Chiefs was lame

Jacob Kressin, Grade 6
Dr Dyer Intermediate School, WI

Horses

Horses
muscular, white
cantering, galloping
running grace fully over the hill
long tail

Leah M. Stittleburg, Grade 6
Buck Creek Mennonite School, WI

Roses

R eally pretty
b **O** uquet
expen **S** ive
E legant
valentine **S**

Nickolas Russo, Grade 6
Corpus Christi Catholic School, MI

Winter

Winter is very fun
I will throw a snow ball
We will make a snowman so tall
But in winter there's almost no sun.

Brynja Mielke, Grade 4
St Paul's Lutheran School, MN

Saying Thanks

Thank you for your freedom
And for your soldiers we really need 'em
Thanks for all you did for me
A free country we will stay and be.

Kaleigh Beehler, Grade 6
Maple Lake Elementary School, MN

Papa

P atriotic
A ir force
P rotective
A lly

Jaeger Johnson, Grade 6
Maple Lake Elementary School, MN

Woods

Walking through the woods
Crunching colored leaves under feet
Leafless trees are empty

Cody Cox, Grade 4
Stocker Elementary School, WI

I Am

I am dazzling and glamorous
I wonder how my life is going to be ten years from now
I hear my grandma and grandpa in heaven telling me when I cry they have my back,
and everything will be fine
I see the sadness and fear
I want all fashionable clothing in the universe
I am dazzling and glamorous

I pretend like I am perfect
I feel like I have the world at my feet when someone gives me a compliment
I touch the silk of the baby blanket
I worry about my family splitting apart
I cry when imagining having no one by my side pointing to tell me what's next
I am dazzling and glamorous

I understand the difficulty of life
I say, "Whatever comes to your mind, do it."
I dream about living in a huge house in New York City
I try to be the best I can be and never let anyone make me feel like a disappointment
I hope I never have to see one of my family members go
I am dazzling and glamorous

Leigh Pollpeter, Grade 6
Campbellsport Elementary School, WI

Among These…Piano Keys

Among these piano keys lies a song
a song waiting to bloom…
a song that makes the world a better place
or a broken heart happy again
they stay there for days, months, year…times disappearing

Waiting…patiently…quietly…
for someone…that someone comes, a little girl with hair like golden sun drops
as if she were sent here…for a secret mission
she sits…plays
what's been waiting inside these piano keys for so long
emerges from deep inside its soul

She sits there for what seems like forever, playing its song
the worlds seems to have frozen, as if happiness is there
Forever, and ever…child memories are regained
and for once, the world seems in peace
I don't know what this song has done…
But it has changed SoMeThInG…

Alexandra Isaksen, Grade 6
T'J Walker Middle School, WI

Minutemen

It started with men with guns.
We, the Minutemen — will not do what you — the King — wants us to do.
We will fight, even if it takes our lives we say.
We will not run.
We will win we say.
We — the Minutemen — will be ready because Revere rides to warn us all.

Joshua Doro, Grade 6
Northwoods Community Elementary School, WI

The Park
Feet moving to the park
Leaves falling
The crunchiness hurts the ears
Cars coming by
Hearing wind coming near
Screaming kids while the sun's shining bright
Mulch scattering all around
10 minutes later our feet moving back

Suzanne Jurkowski, Grade 6
St John Kanty School, WI

A Trip to Paradise
I loved our family trip to Mexico,
We were at a perfect place.
A beach, palm trees, and seashells,
It was my idea of paradise.
Swimming with dolphins, watching sea turtles hatch,
And many more adventures that we had,
And memories that we made that will last forever.
All on a trip to paradise.

Mariah Warnecke, Grade 6
Campbellsport Elementary School, WI

Roasting Marshmallows While Camping
I like camping in the summer and roasting marshmallows.
I block out the sound of people.
I look at the fire and think.
I get a stick, and roast a marshmallow.
The fire smiles at me.
As I look out in the forest I see the tree wink at me.

That's why I love roasting marshmallows while camping.

Katie Moseng, Grade 5
Blue Heron Elementary School, MN

The Lake
T he place I love to camp, swim, and grill.
H as all my friends and family, like Katie, Carter, and Hunter.
E veryone loves to go there.

L ike everyone, I think the water is wonderful.
A ll of my friends gather up on the paddle boat.
K atie, my friend, always comes on with us.
E veryone loves to go out to the island.

Ashley Lyon, Grade 6
Martin County West Trimont Elementary School, MN

Hiding Behind a Leaf
I am an ant hiding behind a leaf
Hiding from the children's magnifying glass
Hiding from that hot little dot.
I am an ant hiding behind a leaf
Hiding from the birds when it is snack time
For I am not on the menu.

Jonathan Kellen, Grade 5
Wagner Elementary School, MN

White Water Rafting
White water rafting down the Poudre.
It was scary at first.
The water only 42°F
Going over grade 4 waves
The huge waves were called
Mad Dog and Kamikaze Corner.
The river was in Colorado.
Once we got in,
I was scared.
But once I hit that first wave,
I wasn't scared any more.
Once I went the first 2 miles,
I thought it
was a
thrill.

Derrek Russenberger, Grade 5
Martin County West Trimont Elementary School, MN

Giving Praise
Give praise for songs that people sing.
Give praise for love throughout the world.
Give praise for heaven above the Earth.
Give praise for the oceans, lakes, and rivers.
Give praise for our families, friends, and neighbors.
Give praise for food that God gave us.
Give praise for the sun, which lightens our day.
Give praise for shelter, which gives us protection.
Give praise for rain, which waters our plants.
Give praise for all humans, we are all made in the image of God.
Give praise for Mary, the mother of Jesus.
Give praise for our leaders, so they lead us with justice.
Give praise for trees and plants, they provide us oxygen.
Give praise for the Holy Spirit, which helps us through our day.
Give praise for all good things, God gave us all of them.

Tara Fedewa, Grade 6
St Gerard School, MI

The Key to John Deere
The key to John Deere,
Is not love or passion.
It doesn't need to
Touch, smell, hear, taste, or see.
You need to trust it.
You need to have confidence in it.
You need to believe that it will work.
Get the GPS…you will see how straight your rounds will be.
Nuts and bolts are no problem…
Great service for your questions
Big or small…doesn't matter.
New tires, treads and all
Duals look cool.
Go through mud with tracks.
That's not all you will see if you believe in me.

Carson Kahler, Grade 5
Martin County West Trimont Elementary School, MN

Fight for Freedom

It started with the Boston Massacre.
King George III started over taxing,
but we colonists refused to pay.
Gathered up some patriots,
to help fight for freedom.
We won some, we lost some.
Victory in Yorktown!
All done fighting battles,
we have earned our freedom!

G. Connor Cooper, Grade 5
Northwoods Community Elementary School, WI

Green Is Great

Green is the color of springtime
Green is the color of a just ripened lime
Green is my favorite color
And I will never pick any other

Green is the color of the classroom globe
Green is the color of the grass that has just been mowed
Green is the color of some peppermints
Green is the color I will never forget

Morgan Mumm, Grade 4
Platteville Middle School, WI

Blue

I like the color blue
It reminds me of blueberry pie
And sometimes it reminds me of blue moon ice cream
And blue is my favorite color tie

The sky is blue and cool
And most of the time birds fly
High in the air
In the blue cool sky

Haili Hottenstein, Grade 4
Platteville Middle School, WI

Dylan

I LOVE YOU SO MUCH
For being my brother,
You were there for me when I flipped my ATV,
You play games with me such as dinosaur bowling,
Even if we get in trouble slamming the door,
We're best buds; on November 29, 2011,
I forget to tell you that I LOVE YOU SO MUCH.

Derek Bublitz, Grade 6
Campbellsport Elementary School, WI

Leaves All Over

They love to cover like a blanket on the ground,
It seems like they are all around.
Some are yellow, some are brown,
Some look like they are flying all around.

Rachael Roberts, Grade 5
Seneca Elementary School, WI

Change

Change can be awful,
But it's good too.
If change hadn't come,
I wouldn't know you.

Change takes good people away,
But it brings new people in.
None of them take the place of a loved one,
But that doesn't mean they aren't a friend.

Life would be boring without change,
Which is why I say, "Come on in, friend!
Change, you may not be my favorite thing,
But you're what makes life interesting in the end."

Natalie Nichols, Grade 5
Cedar Ridge Elementary School, MN

My Little Sister

My little sister's name is Bria,
She is very cute, and a lot of fun!
Bria loves to play outside,
She is very smart for the age of one!
Bria knows a couple words,
She can say my name!
Bria calls me "Lys,"
"Ring Round the Rosy" is her favorite game!
Whether it's reading a book,
Playing Patty Cake!
Jumping on the trampoline,
We have fun together,
I love her!

Alyssa Williamson, Grade 5
Martin County West Trimont Elementary School, MN

Orange Is…

Orange is the color of the leaves I see
Orange is the pie that my mom made for me
Orange is the orange juice that I think is yummy
Orange is the color I see

Halloween has orange in it
Orange is the color of the hat that my grandma knit
Can't you see it?
Orange is the best and you know it

Brianna Poller, Grade 4
Platteville Middle School, WI

Tranquil

Ocean waves lapping the shore
Steaming cup of chai in the winter
Relaxing by the fire
Reading the best book ever
And me
Enjoying these peaceful, serene times of the year

Paige Taylor, Grade 6
Dr Dyer Intermediate School, WI

Senses

Sight is a gift of light waiting to be unwrapped
Sights are balls of mystery to be told
Sights are a ribbon of great power

Sounds are never ending vibrations
Sounds are heavenly birds singing and breathing
Sounds are the rustle of a small old tree

Smells are paths waiting to be walked on
Smells are a force no one can break
Smells are a message from the angel of peace

Taste is a touch of God
Taste is a present from Heaven
Taste is the spirit of life

Emotions are solid hearts never broken
Emotions are a strip never cut
Emotions are glory

Touch is a kiss from the universe
Touch is a chain with no ending
Touch is the Earth

Megan Myring, Grade 5
Eagle Creek Academy, MI

Friends

True friends are for life
Until the end
They're more than special
They're your bestest friends.

They're the ones you can go to
When you're in despair
The ones that'll help you
Even when you got gum in your hair!
My best friends are true

They're the ones who'll laugh
And go laughing with you all through the night
The ones who'll help you
Help you with all their might

To have a good friend
You have to be one
So be nice to one another
So you can be friends forever
And that's how to be the best friend you can be

As far as I can see.

Carlos Rizo Rivas and Logan Lynn, Grade 6
Heron Lake Okabena Elementary School, MN

No Fair

No fair! she gets all the toys
She makes all the noise
She slams the doors,
While I clean the floors
She can't sing a tune
She never cleans her room
I do all the work,
While she sits there with a smirk
As you have seen,
She is so mean, It's not fair!

Miya Johnson, Grade 4
Grand Rapids Christian School - Evergreen Campus, MI

Baseball

Baseball is awesome.
A baseball field is shaped like a diamond.
You use bats to hit the ball.
You use gloves to catch the ball.
To get a homerun you have to hit the ball over the fence.
To protect your head you use a helmet.
TO be a better batter you should go to the "cage" which means
where you go hit a ball inside a building.
You have to run the bases.
Homerun season, here we come.

Christopher Sikora, Grade 5
May V Peck Elementary School, MI

Fall Sunset

Leaves of red, brown and yellow.
Cold breezes and the moving leaves.
When I walk I hear the crunches and crackles
of the leaves I walk on.
The sun is going down on this fall evening.
The colors of pink, yellow, orange and blue
waiting for the sun to come down and the night sky to come up.

Silence, silence, silence
Kaitlyn M. Koehler, Grade 5
Hewitt Texas Elementary School, WI

No Taxation Without Representation

The Boston Massacre started it.
No one knew who fired first.
Men dumped crates of tea in the ocean.
For the unfair tax, we tar and feather them.
Paul Revere warned us all that the "Redcoats are coming"
The loyalists wanted us to stay loyal to the king.
"No taxation without representation," we say!
That's why we didn't pay taxes.
Then we went to war!

Emilee Pontell, Grade 6
Northwoods Community Elementary School, WI

Beyond Beautiful

The beautiful flowers are blooming;
along the oceans that are soothing.
The mountains climb so high;
to touch the cerulean sky.
The rivers flow;
where the weeping willows grow.

Luke Foley, Grade 4
St Joseph Elementary School, WI

America

America is great!
The plants and flowers are beautiful.
All of the lakes and streams are cooling.
The sun is bright and warming.
Everything God made is terrific!
I love America and its citizens.

Olivia VandenPlas, Grade 4
St Joseph Elementary School, WI

Hannah

H ot day in the summer
A s I get water on me
N ot a good thing
N ot! It was fun and awesome
A s I go in the pool it is cool
H ot hot day goes by.

Hannah Fleming, Grade 4
Dibble Elementary School, MI

Leaves

L ittle kids
E njoy
A ll the leaves
V ariety of colors
E ase through the woods
S ilently sighing

Katrina Okeson, Grade 6
Detroit Lakes Middle School, MN

Paris

P eople all around
A city of love
R unning all around the Eiffel Tower
I n a wonderful place
S omewhere great!

Emily Borucki, Grade 5
Zinser School, MI

My Turkey

For Thanksgiving we should have turkey,
The day was all cold and murky.
We heard something quick,
That stepped on a stick.
Now, we've got a big, fat turkey!

Emily Garfoot, Grade 6
Seneca Middle School, WI

Amazing Autumn

Leaves hanging on their last limbs just
Waiting to fall Down
Down
Down
Changing from a grass green to a maze, crimson, tangerine
Kids swarming the street going door to door saying "Trick or treat!"
Munching on candy, pumpkin pie, and delightful doughnuts while chugging down
some delicious cider
Breezy winds and
Raindrops crying from the sky
Gooey pumpkin guts,
Creepy faces and thick brown stems
Fall,
Fall,
Fall,
What an astonishing season!

Mason Miller, Grade 5
Riley Upper Elementary School, MI

Autumn's in the Air

SWISH, a leaf hits you right on your head.
You look up, all the trees are bare and
the wind is stinging your face.
The steam of the hot cocoa warms you right up.
You snuggle in your toasty warm blankets and watch as the leaves go
Down
Down
Down
to the ground.
The wind is wrestling the trees and making piles of old crunchy leaves.
You see geese as they migrate south for the winter
as well as squirrels getting lots of acorns for hibernation
Fall
Fall
Fall
you will be missed.

Nina M. Wojtowicz, Grade 5
Riley Upper Elementary School, MI

Fire

I like fire because you can roast marshmallows
If you look in the fire you can see all the different colors
Blue, red, orange.
I like fire because you can have a camp fire at a camp.
I like fire because you can roast sausages.
I like fire because it lights up the night.
I like fire because they are what light up fireworks.
I like fire because in the stove it makes your food.
I like fire because when you light the fire and it's burning paper
the sparks in the sky so it looks like fireflies.
I like fire because you get to warm up with your family on a really cold night.
I like fire because it's cool to start it.
I like fire because it scares away mosquitoes.
I like fire because it is what lights up candles.

Alexis Finley, Grade 5
May V Peck Elementary School, MI

Monarch

The size of a pinhead on a milkweed leaf
The egg hatches, the larva exits.
It starts to eat
He takes fast chomps, for days he eats
Getting tighter and tighter.
Something is happening
He sheds his skin and eats some more.
To him it's good
But to others it's poisonous.
His food protects him.
As he eats he grows bigger and fatter.
Now he's shedding another time
But he's hanging this time, he looks like a "J."
What's happening?
A hard chrysalis is forming around him
He hangs there, now a pupa,
For a long time
Until he comes out
An adult butterfly
Warming his wings until he can fly.

Emma Novak, Grade 5
Amery Intermediate School, WI

I Am

I am flexible and athletic
I wonder what I will be when I grow up
I hear my dog snoring when he sleeps with me
I see myself winning the lottery
I want to travel the world
I am flexible and athletic

I pretend to be a groomer
I feel joyful all day
I touch the cold air in the morning
I worry about strangers
I cry when I hurt myself or if I feel blue
I am flexible and athletic

I understand how to be a good friend
I say good night to my mom and dad every night
I dream of being a veterinarian
I try to be my best in every thing I do
I hope to be successful in my life
I am flexible and athletic

Jordan Widener, Grade 4
Floyd Ebeling Elementary School, MI

What and Whom I Am

My hair gets as white as a jackrabbit in January.
My skin is rough like an alligator's back.
My hands are soft like a new bed.
My feet are small like a baby mouse.
My heart holds too much energy that is released like the sun's heat.
I live in a radio station and eat the music being played.

Dexter Horn, Grade 6
Dr Dyer Intermediate School, WI

I Am

I am silly and smart
I wonder if I will invent something amazing
I hear waves crashing on the shore
I see me counting my millions of dollars
I want a new puppy
I am silly and smart

I pretend I just won the lottery
I feel happy when school is over
I touch my dog when I pet him
I worry when I'm alone in the dark
I cry when I get a shot
I am silly and smart

I understand you have to work for what you want
I say you can do anything you want if you try and don't give up
I dream of my future
I try to be nice to people
I hope I get into U of M
I am silly and smart

Gianni Rosa, Grade 4
Floyd Ebeling Elementary School, MI

I Am

I am friendly and athletic
I wonder about what position I will be put on in the army
I hear the wind whistling in my ear
I see ghosts roaming the hall of a haunted house
I want to be the best I can be
I am friendly and athletic

I pretend to be in the army by using fake obstacle courses
I feel happy as a dog with a treat
I touch my dog's fur
I worry about my family
I cry when I am hurt or sad
I am friendly and athletic

I understand how I am going to get in the army
I say I am going to win the war
I dream to get into the army
I try to get past big obstacles while training
I hope I will get into the army
I am friendly and athletic

Dillon Bielicki, Grade 4
Floyd Ebeling Elementary School, MI

Yum, Yum, Yum

Yesterday...
The trees turned into chocolate bars, and the grass turned into fries,
the flowers turned to candy canes, and the snow started to cry.
My head became a jawbreaker, my shoes turned into jelly, I ate my
veggies during dinner...
They went straight down to my belly!!!

Nicole VerBeek, Grade 4
The Potter's House Christian School, MI

If I Were...

If I were an apple
    I would taste sweeter than candy
    I would be shinier than a shiny new red car
    I would like to be eaten by an athlete
    I'd want to stay fresh
If I were an apple
    I would come from a tree
    I would wish I could walk on two legs
    I would love to be eaten by a kid on a summer day
    I would listen to leaves rustling in the trees
    I would want to be a super apple

Connor Lees, Grade 4
Stocker Elementary School, WI

If I Were an Ice Cream Cone

If I were an ice cream cone
    I would taste very good and soft
    I would be made with chocolate inside me
    I would like to be drizzled with sprinkles
    I'd want to stay in the freezer forever so I can live
If I were an ice cream cone
    I would come from Woodman's
    I would wish I could be cold instead of warm
    I would love to be with my ice cream family
    I would listen to myself and my instincts
    I would want to be remembered by the kid who ate me

Abby Flores, Grade 4
Stocker Elementary School, WI

Donut

If I were a donut
    I would taste like chocolate sprinkled goodness
    I would be nice with vanilla filling
    I would like to be smothered with whipping cream
    I'd want to be warmed in the oven
If I were a donut
    I would come with some nuts
    I would wish I could cool off in a window
    I would love to be right next to the cinnamon roll
    I would listen to be by the musical speakers
    I would want to be eaten by a nice little boy

Evan Engel, Grade 4
Stocker Elementary School, WI

Art Can...

Art can be anything you want it to be
Art can be simple
Art can be an imaginary window to the universe
Art can make you see the true beauty in everything
Art can make you feel like you're floating, flying into the clouds
Art can make you lose track of the real world
Art can help you visit loved ones
Art can also help you on your way to understanding
Art is beautiful, wonderful, the one thing anyone can be happy with.

Sabrina Layton, Grade 6
Sashabaw Middle School, MI

Jalapeño Pepper

If I were a jalapeño pepper
    I would taste hot, spicy, and a hint of sweet
    I would be small and green with little seeds
    I would like to be big and red with a lot of seeds
    I'd want to be stuffed with jambalaya
If I were a jalapeño pepper
    I would come to your mouth and burn it
    I would wish I could be prepared nicely
    I would love to be riding on shrimp stew
    I would listen to you scream when I burn your tongue
    I would want to be remembered as the hottest jalapeño ever!

Isabel Rodriguez, Grade 4
Stocker Elementary School, WI

Strawberry

If I were a strawberry
    I would taste sweeter than candy
    I would be small and perfect
    I would like to be a super strawberry
    I'd want to grow larger than the other strawberries
If I were a strawberry
    I would come in a package with all my strawberry friends
    I would wish I would get eaten every day
    I would love to be sweet and juicy
    I would listen to the people picking me off my plant
    I would want to be the best snack you've ever had!

Jordan Musick, Grade 4
Stocker Elementary School, WI

If I Were a Pizza

If I were a pizza
    I would taste very good
    I would be the best pizza ever
    I would like to be bought by someone that loves me
    I'd want to be picked up by gentle hands
If I were a pizza
    I would come to be a very nice pizza
    I would wish I was carried by someone nice
    I would love to be eaten by a slow mouth
    I would listen to the children talking
    I would want to be with a happy family

Nahyla Wright, Grade 4
Stocker Elementary School, WI

Spring Once More

Snow is melting, no soul woeful of Winter's death
Flowers blooming, the scorching sun floats sky high
Melting the bitter ice that freezes thy heart
Whilst the trees be resurrected?

Passion and feelings of warmth bloom with the flowers
When the sun descends, whilst thou rise once more?
The sorrowing clouds draw ever closer, rain falls
Marking vile King Winter's rebirth soon to come.

Sam Roach, Grade 5
Roosevelt Elementary School, MN

My Dog Luther

My dog Luther was a Saint Bernard.
He was the biggest dog ever!
We played tag, fetch, and he loved to swim.
He would jump on our backs,
He would even take pictures with us.
Luther would roll in the snow and eat the snow.
He would even tackle us in the snow.
Luther would sleep outside or inside.
Luther was so cute and small when he was a puppy.
He got bigger by the time I was born.
By 2008 he had died in our barn.
We miss you Luther!
Have peace in heaven.

Dawson Weber, Grade 5
Martin County West Trimont Elementary School, MN

Duluth in the Summer

A nice swim in Lake Superior.
Time to look for beach glass.
I hear seagulls screech.
I like to feel different rocks, some smooth, some not.
Let's have a bonfire, let's make some s'mores,
it's the best to be there.
The lake is cold like snow icy chills going up my spine.
I wonder if the fish are as cold as me.
Fish are swimming away, I just jumped in the cool water.
It's a hot summer day in Duluth.
Next summer I will come back, but just imagine cool waters.
Put sunscreen on and you will be safe from the sun.

Cora Brewster, Grade 5
Blue Heron Elementary School, MN

I Speak the Language of Birds

I am a crow soaring at the break of dawn
trying to find a bite to eat
I speak the language of birds
I am a hawk flying for days to find a water hole
I speak the language of birds
I am a robin my belly as red as a cherry
I speak the language of birds
I am a pelican swimming in the lake and
dipping my head in the water
I speak the language of birds
I am a loon the state bird of Minnesota
I speak the language of birds

Jadyn Deitchman, Grade 5
Wagner Elementary School, MN

Disguised as Trumpets

Disguised as trumpets, getting headaches all day.
When my friends try to talk to me I say "WHAT!"
Disguised as trumpets, all woozy from bing bong smash crash.
When I'm at concerts it's the worst but when it's all over
I go back in my case to take a nice nap.

Simon Mueller, Grade 5
Wagner Elementary School, MN

Home

Memories made here
Throughout the ages
Some say it's boring in one place but,
You will be homesick
How I shall hate to make my own and leave my family so alone
Eventually I shall call it my own
Maybe…
Maybe…
It is a long time to maturity
But, life is short
Home
Memories made here
Throughout the ages
Memories…
Memories…how I shall hate to make my own
And leave my family alone
Home

Ryan Schneeberg, Grade 6
Campbellsport Elementary School, WI

Dance

Dance is silly, funny, and difficult.
It can be filled with laughter or sadness.
One moment it is quiet, the next it is loud.
Sometimes, I wish it was every day.
Other times I'm glad it's just once a week.
Some steps are difficult…
Others are easy.
Occasionally we dance with black lights…
When we do it's amazing we don't run into each other.
We dance to all kinds of music …
Fast, slow, medium and sometimes…
TOO FAST!
We practice slow and then faster.
After I'm done I'm tired,
Why?
Because I'm there for two hours!

Jackie Frerichs, Grade 6
Martin County West Trimont Elementary School, MN

On the Court

Orange is the color of a basketball,
Black is the color of a scoreboard on the wall.

Purple is the color of my bruise,
Red is the color of the other team's face when they lose.

Green is the color of the door,
White is the color of the net when we score!

Brown is the color of the bleachers where I hear cheering,
Peach is the color of the people screaming!

What colors do you see on the court?

Erica LaBar, Grade 6
Manistique Middle & High School, MI

Halloween
Huge round pumpkins
Carving scary faces
Jack 'o lanterns lit.
Valerie Kaley, Grade 4
Stocker Elementary School, WI

Birds
Pretty birds chirp soft
in the summer, spring, and winter.
Do you hear birds chirp?
Chloé DuBois, Grade 4
Dibble Elementary School, MI

Nature
Streaming rivers fall
The flowing logs are coming
Water is drifting
Morgan Morrow, Grade 6
Dr Dyer Intermediate School, WI

Fall
Itchy, crunchy leaves
Weather is rainy and foggy
Many colors of leaves
Casey Cox, Grade 4
Stocker Elementary School, WI

Goodbye My Dear Summer
As grass dies away
Autumn leaves fall to the ground
Waiting for snowfall
Serenity Hawkins, Grade 6
Manistique Middle & High School, MI

Summer
It is almost here
Flowers blooming everywhere
Summer is coming
Angela Hepfer, Grade 6
Manistique Middle & High School, MI

Kangaroos
Kangaroos have joeys
Kangaroos are animals
Kangaroos are soft
Rhea Chhoker, Grade 4
Floyd Ebeling Elementary School, MI

Fall
Red, orange, yellow
Leaves blowing off the trees
Squirrels storing nuts
Kristal Nava, Grade 4
Stocker Elementary School, WI

Zoey
I remember when we found you 4 months ago,
I remember when we took you from the dark street,
I remember when you got home you went nuts on the couch,
And for sure you loved the other dog that you chased,
I remember you lying on my lap sleeping watching tv,
I remember when you went up the street then waited an hour till you came back,
I remember when you went into the house and lied there,
Even though you knew you were in trouble you laid on my lap,
I remember when we had fun but no longer more.
Zachary Carey, Grade 6
Campbellsport Elementary School, WI

I Remember
I remember my uncle.
I remember him moving into his new house.
I remember him buying a new pickup and coming to show my brother and me.
I remember him buying a new Harley and coming to show us.
I remember going fishing and catching one after another.
I remember him building monkey bars for us to play on.
I remember taking pictures of him on his new Harley which is now mine.
I remember going to his funeral, I cried all the way through.
Colton Gerlach, Grade 6
Campbellsport Elementary School, WI

Christmas Wonderland
Candy canes are striped, Christmas trees are green
When you look outside you should not be seeing green, but white.
When Santa checks his list you know what list you should be on, the nice list
Candy canes are striped, Christmas trees are green
Those presents under the tree mean only one thing, Christmas is here.
Candy canes are striped, Christmas trees are green
The star on a tree as bright as the sun.
Skylar Daray, Grade 6
Knapp Forest Elementary School, MI

Children Are Angels Sent from Above
Children are angels sent from above.
They are light as a feather, beautiful as a dove.
We should all share with them our love.
Some are round others don't make a sound.
Some are tall, some are small, but you see you never leave them behind,
and that is why you are forever mine.
Children are angels sent from above.
Meghan Reid, Grade 6
Franklin Middle School, WI

Tragedies
I am tragedies, the coldness and bitterness of the world
I broke your heart a million times and I will do it again
I make you taste the real world
I am death, sickness, the things that break your heart
I am tragedies, the cold memories that roam inside you until you burst out crying,
Do not forget me for I will haunt you forever
I am, tragedies.
Arianna Davis, Grade 5
Echo Park Elementary School, MN

Ice Hockey
As I arrive at the rink
On a cold winter day
With all my tools I need to play

I tie on my skates
I put on my gloves
I grab my sticks and
Put on my helmet

I get on the ice and
Dump all my pucks
My skates go shhh
When I go to stop
I shoot on the net
And score a goal
I wish I could play
All day long
Garett Hoch, Grade 5
Blue Heron Elementary School, MN

Sunlight Afternoon
The beautiful sun
Setting behind
Some trees,

The late afternoon
Sky with the trees
Showing the beauty

The roar of the ATV,
And peace in my mind

I want to go on the ATV every day
And see the sunlit afternoon

Beautiful sun
Beautiful sun
Beautiful sun
Blake C. Pozorski, Grade 5
Hewitt Texas Elementary School, WI

Shelby Styer
S uper cool girl
H yper but ok
E specially smart
L ow on a bunch of sugar
B rings it on
Y ah, I'm the best you can imagine

S tylish and magnificent
T rouble, but not to bad
Y up, I'm cool!
E veryone loves me
R ight I'm awesome!
Shelby Styer, Grade 4
River Heights Elementary School, WI

Cheerios
How much have these Cheerios
traveled to get to
my bowl, thousands
of miles it traveled to the store
just so I can buy it.

These Cheerios have traveled all
of this way to
make me happy,
wake me up
in the morning,
and give me strength
and energy. These Cheerios
you think is so small,
but big in the travels it took.
Logan Holbrook, Grade 6
T J Walker Middle School, WI

What Does a Dog Know?
What does a dog
Know?
Each paw has a soft pad and a claw
Twenty teeth on upper jaw
Twenty-two teeth on lower jaw
Barks and growls
Perfect, playful family
Pet
Wild relatives hunt for food
Carnivores
Eat meat
Different size and color
Helps blind
People
More than 400 breeds.
Kaitlyn Heffington, Grade 5
Riley Upper Elementary School, MI

Rain
The rain
is like a
MONSTER
that gnaws
on flowers,
and jiggles
like jelly,
and shuffles
across umbrellas.
When it
dries out,
a rainbow
rolls out
into a
dancing cloud
Rebekah Sisco, Grade 4
The Potter's House School, MI

Cold Fun Fall
Apple cider,
Bears snoring,
Chocolate chip
cookies,
Dirty football boys,
Football games going on,
Halloween will spook
you out,
Wear jackets to keep
you warm,
Kicking leaves,
Eating mashed potatoes
On Thanksgiving,
The terrific smell of
Pumpkin pie,
The most rojo red,
The most wonderful things of *Fall*
Robert M. Cavin, Grade 5
Riley Upper Elementary School, MI

A Gift Inside
Every gift has a story
it could be good or bad
not any gift
but that once in a lifetime
never again time of surprise

This isn't a gift under a tree
or hidden around the house
this isn't to play with
nor to sell
but to give

Everyone has a gift
if you dig deep enough
you can find
a gift
for all to see
James Dickson, Grade 6
TJ Walker Middle School, WI

Brandon Baer
B rave
R elaxed
A ctive
N oble
D elightful
O utgoing
N ice

B right
A wesome
E nthusiastic
R owdy
Brandon Baer, Grade 6
Gilmore Middle School, WI

Dogs
Dogs
Loving, kind
Barking, panting, protecting
Dogs are super awesome
K9
Ethen Goebel, Grade 4
River Heights Elementary School, WI

Ornaments
A flash of light
Bursting with holiday cheer
Sparking with jewels
With glitter all over
Reminders of Christmas
Dylan Morrow, Grade 6
Dr Dyer Intermediate School, WI

Dogs
Dogs
Sweet, cute, small,
Chewing, eating, playing,
I love my dog
Oscar
Annie Price, Grade 4
River Heights Elementary School, WI

Nervous
My heart pumping super fast
The gun just about ready to shoot
Me and all the other racers take off
I am dirt biking for the championship
And me up in first place
Cody Badger, Grade 6
Dr Dyer Intermediate School, WI

Wish
I wish I were
A photographer
Working over here and there
Taking pictures everywhere
Stunningly
Emaleth Johnson, Grade 6
Gilmore Middle School, WI

Bad Boy
There was a boy who was bad
and his mom was very mad
he got sent to his room
with a very loud BOOM!
and he was very sad
Zander Gjurashaj, Grade 6
Birmingham Covington School, MI

A Fun-Filled Day!
The river was flowing so gently, with the water rushing over the rocks.
Autumn leaves falling through mid air so quickly.
The wind blowing whisperly with the trees swaying softly.
Salmon jumping for some new fresh fall air, and
Families taking walks in the cold October breeze
Kids throwing rocks from the bridge to the water.
Families taking pictures for their new frames to fill!
Alivia Wisnefske, Grade 6
Campbellsport Elementary School, WI

At the Beach
At the beach I play in the water.
I see people playing with water guns and some snorkeling.
I see seagulls flying like airplanes who are searching for food.
When I snorkel I look for fish and the fish look for me.
The minnows swim away from me but I chase them until I lose sight of them.
Then I go in the sand and play water guns with my brother.
I always win and sometimes I hide in the water and wait to jump out and scare him.
Austin Imsland, Grade 5
Blue Heron Elementary School, MN

Me
My hair feels like straw and is as brown as coffee and as curly as an onion ring.
My eyes are as black as my black binder.
My nose smells wonderful things and my mouth tastes delicious things.
My heart holds love like a love song.
I live in my body and I eat the music notes when I dance.
Kyla Dukes, Grade 5
The Potter's House Christian School, MI

Test
This test is getting me stressed,
and having stress during a test, will get you in a mess.
And if you get into a mess, during a test, an F will surely be your guest.
Brayden Bowers, Grade 4
East K-7 School, MI

Heroes
Cops are nice;
They are as cool as ice.
Cops are fun;
They have a really cool gun.
When the cop speaks,
Everyone will pay heed.
When the cop is around,
Nobody will speed.
When cops visit my school,
They all look really cool.
Cops are neat;
Their cars are so sweet.
Cops will protect your city.
When you see a criminal get caught,
Do not feel any pity;
It is their own fault.
Shawn Suttie, Grade 5
Rochester Hills Christian School, MI

Broken
On the sand you lie during the cold night
Shattered, torn and washed away
Like a broken piece of glass
So worn and weary
Shattered
Destroyed

As a person you have worked so hard
In return you were given so little
Now you are left behind
Like you do not matter
Even though you do
So now you lie all alone
You have endured it all
But now you are
Broken
Tess Monahan, Grade 6
Corpus Christi Catholic School, MI

Dancing

The lights go down,
People look to me,
My heart starts to race,
I can't breathe,

I hear the beat,
And start to move in an unusual way,
I feel as if someone let me free,
To dance in the spotlight,

Though I feel as if I am in the dark,
Moving like an angel,
I'm trying not to trip,
I think about how I hate to dance so gracefully,

So I lock up my body,
And start to do some hip hop,
I do some flips,
And some complicated foot work,
Then I stand still,
And hear the audience roar,
I take a bow and leap off the state,
With a smile on my face.

Alley John, Grade 6
Campbellsport Elementary School, WI

Heroes

The heroes I know are brave and courageous.
David is one;
A tiny boy like he killed great, strong Goliath.

Esther the Queen fasted for days to save her people.
The king agreed. Haman was hanged.
Mordecai was next to the king.

Paul, the preacher, traveled here and there
Preaching the word of God. He was put in prison,
Marked and beaten, yet he kept right on going.

Joseph, the favorite, was sold as a slave to Egypt,
Locked in prison for years yet he never complained.
God let Pharaoh raise Joseph as second in command.

Moses the leader, obedient to God,
Led the Israelites out of Egypt, heading for Canaan.
Though he never made it, God blessed him greatly.

Noah, the man who obediently built an ark as God had told him.
Two by two, the animals came into the bin in Noah's ark.
Here the flood came. Noah was safe since he was obedient to God.

Kathleen Fan, Grade 5
Rochester Hills Christian School, MI

Inside This Broken TV

Inside this broken TV
Was once a loving family
Who sat down and watched this TV
They watched all sorts of shows and movies
But now it's just sitting in a junk yard with no owner

Now comes a guy
He was just here to put junk on me
Now comes another guy
He's picking me up and taking me home
He's fixing me

I'm now at a store for sale
Here comes a family
They got a bigger TV than me
Here comes a small family
He's picking me up and paying for me

He's now taking me home
He's hooking me up
They're turning me on
They're watching movies
They like me

Michael McGinnis, Grade 6
T J Walker Middle School, WI

Ashley

Loving,
Awesome,
Laughable,

Wishes to meet new people.
Dreams of a bigger house.
Wants to laugh every day.
Who wonders what will be happening ten years from now.
Who fears scary things.
Who is afraid of really small spaces.
Who likes people with brown eyes.
Who believes that something bad can be good.

Who loves playing my violin.
Who loves listening to music.
Who loves running track.
Who loves her friends.

Who plans to be a teacher.
Who plans to never leave Wisconsin.
Who plans to see a Bruno Mars concert.

Who is never going to change.

Ashley Nelsen, Grade 6
Gilmore Middle School, WI

Christmas

Christmas time is almost here, with lots of fun and lots of cheer.
There are decorations in every yard. My aunt making fruitcake that is really hard.
It's a wonderful time to play in the snow. But don't forget that it's very cold.
It's a great time to spend time with family. Or very close friends that make you happy.
When Santa puts presents inside your house, he has to be quiet like a little mouse.
Good kids get presents on Christmas day. Bad kids get coal or dirt they say.
Santa Claus lives at the North Pole. He has elves with very nice souls.
He also has nine reindeer that fly on Christmas Eve. You can track them on the internet or on your TV.
His reindeer are Dasher, Dancer, Prancer, Vixen, Comet, Cupid, Donner, Blitzen, and Rudolph.
Rudolph is very special because he has a red nose. But that's not all because it also glows.
The reindeer ride on Santa's sleigh, and these are the reasons why Christmas is my favorite holiday.

Sarah Spagnuolo, Grade 6
St Gerard School, MI

Inside This…Telescope

Inside this telescope are sights and things people have never seen before.
Inside this telescope there are things that can change what we see in the world
Like beauty, devastation, and sadness

But it is your design to see what you want to see.
Inside it there is mystery, questions, and love because it will show you anything and everything.
It may look small, round funny looking, and not special
But it will not be special if you do not take care of it and nurture it.
The telescope will show you great things but you can only find them if you take a look.

Nathan LeRoy, Grade 6
T J Walker Middle School, WI

My Sister

I love my sister a lot.
We fight, sometimes we laugh, and sometimes we never even talk.
Sometimes I think that she never has any time for me anymore.
She's either texting someone that she just saw a second ago, or just plain ignoring me.
I know that whenever we're in a fight, she still loves me.
Sometimes she can be so mean, she can give me 24 hours of pain.
Sometimes when she's mean to me, I always tell her that I won't talk to her but I always give in.
One thing I know about my sister is that she still loves me in her heart.

Kaitlyn Ebert, Grade 6
Campbellsport Elementary School, WI

Energized

Yourself…running on a treadmill, listening to music, letting you last just one second longer.
At a famous concert…listening to the booming music, urging you to dance.
Waiting for Christmas to come, staring at all the presents under the tree, and taking out the advent calendar, having to remember how much longer you must wait.
First day of school…curious about who your teachers and classmates are.
And me…
Remembering all the emotions around myself.

Ana Tinder, Grade 6
Dr Dyer Intermediate School, WI

Thank You

All of the proud, strong, veterans, I would love to say, "Thank you a ton!" For those who killed Osama bin Laden, thank you, because now we have no bombs dropping on our beautiful country, thank you to who are serving our country and did serve! Thank you for having my family safe and sound, and have freedom to do whatever we want to do.

Amber Zeidler, Grade 6
Maple Lake Elementary School, MN

America Is Beautiful

Beautiful because
she has long, green, grassy plains,
home to many creatures.
Tall, icy, cold mountains, very awesome.
Hills and cliffs
I could not count;
green, lush, perfect valleys.
So cool to live in:
beautiful, quiet lakes,
calm ponds,
rushing rivers.
Little quiet towns;
loud big cities;
huge, silent countrysides;
surrounded by gigantic, outstanding oceans,
the Pacific and Atlantic.
A free land,
A great place to live.

Anna Audrey Senjem, Grade 4
St Joseph Elementary School, WI

I Am

I am loud, outgoing
I wonder if I look as good as I think
I hear crowds screaming my name
I see stars all around
I want to sing
I am friendly, passionate
I pretend I'm on stage
I feel strong when I walk into a big crowd
I touch a microphone
I worry about how much I talk
I cry when I'm happy or at a funeral
I am goofy, silly
I understand I need to take things seriously
I say stand up for yourself
I dream I will live my life to the fullest
I try to do my best
I hope that everyone will see me for who I am
I am nice, outstanding

Ja'Quarrious Person, Grade 6
Gilmore Middle School, WI

Family

Family is there to back you up.
Family is there to take care of you.
Family is like your best friend.
Family lets you play pretend.
Family loves you dearly.
Family will be with you always.
Family loves you no matter what.
Family keeps you safe.
Family will be by your side even through tough times.
Family will always forgive you because they love you.

Zoey Alvarado, Grade 6
St. Gerard School, MI

Who I Am

I am comfortable and confident
I wonder if dogs think like us
I hear violins in my head
I see a better day in the Village
I am comfortable and confident

I pretend to be popular
I feel honest like Abe Lincoln
I touch the blue or gray clouds
I cry when I think about moving
I am comfortable and confident

I understand people and their feelings
I say that you should try, try again and to not reflect on the past
I dream of staying here in Campbellsport forever
I try to be caring to others
I hope to be smarter
I am comfortable and confident

Ryker Jeffery, Grade 6
Campbellsport Elementary School, WI

Bullying

I have gotten notes,
I have had pictures drawn of me.
This happened to me by a group of my friends.
Yes, I have been bullied,
And I HATED IT!

My friend is getting bullied.
She HATES IT TOO.
She is getting bullied by her old friend.
She has an ugly picture drawn of her.
She is getting notes.
Just like I did.

People are getting bullied.
We need to stop them,
And soon.
So the same thing doesn't happen,
That happened to my friend and me.

Dakota Jade Hamman, Grade 6
McBain Middle School, MI

My Name Is

My name is John,
It means creative, funny, fast,
It is the number 81,
It is like snowy snow,
It is racing in the cold thick forest,
It is the memory of Emily,
Who taught me to have a fun time when you're bored,
When she jumped off the hill into the water,
My name is John,
It means revenge is not as sweet as it seems

John Lechner, Grade 6
Campbellsport Elementary School, WI

School

Students like rare gemstones,
each different in their own way.
Teachers nice as an ice cream,
on a hot summer day.
Books like candy,
can't get enough.
Write in your journal like a madman,
when your days get rough.
Your brain moves at ferocious speed,
like an eagle, soaring in the sky.
And information gets packed in me,
like a computer about ready to fry.
But all that matters is that it's fun,
like a game, underneath the sun.
School.

Caleb Miller, Grade 6
Eagle Heights Spanish Immersion School, MN

The Music That Flows Through My Ears

Smooth music flows through my ears
Keys moving in all ways
Fragments of songs weave in my mind
A flower drops on the piano
I hold it in my hand
It pricks my finger
The flower drops
I press my fingers on the keys
High, low, up, down
The music of the piano
drives me to sing
The keys press in my fingers
and fade away
Oh, the sweet music
Oh, let it play

Jennifer Haely, Grade 6
Abbott Middle School, MI

Poetry

Poetry
Spelled P-O-E-T-R-Y
Read by you and I
Poetry is like a song
That you can sing all day long
Rhyming words, adventure galore
And so much more to adore
Silverstein, Dr. Seuss
Poetry can even be about a goose
The words are like vines
And the roses are what happens to people's lives
On day you will see
How it came to be
In poetry

Gabriella Dias, Grade 5
Divine Child Elementary School, MI

I Fear the Ghosts

I fear the ghosts when they hide from me.
I fear the ghosts when they pull me out of bed.
I fear the ghosts when they climb under my blankets.
I fear the ghosts when they take my pillow from me.
I fear the ghosts when they hide in my shower.
I fear the ghosts when they scream at me.

Chelsey Bram, Grade 5
Wagner Elementary School, MN

Life

I feel as if something is watching me.
Something is following me.
I don't think it's a ghost.
It might be a demon.
I see shadows when no one is there.
If I move to a different house it follows me there too!

Alexis Yaeger, Grade 6
Campbellsport Elementary School, WI

Lime Green

Lime green is grass poking through the snow
Lime green is nail polish glistening in the light
Lime green is the lettuce waiting in the aisle
Lime green is balloons floating in the air
Lime green is everywhere

Hannah Tucek, Grade 5
St Paul Evangelical Lutheran School, WI

Thank You Soldiers for the Stars and Stripes!

Thank you soldiers for all you have done.
Making our country number one.
Even though a lot of people have died fighting for freedom.
They have sacrificed their lives to save ours.
So thank you soldiers for the stars and stripes.

Alexus Ann Marie Jackson, Grade 6
Maple Lake Elementary School, MN

Music

Music is something that relaxes me
Music is something that you can sing along with
Music is something that you can dance to.
So when you're sad, mad, or glad
Play your favorite song and sing along.

Jenna Zielinski, Grade 5
May V Peck Elementary School, MI

The Game

Bump, set, spike
The noise of the crowd in my ear
The ref stands on the side, nodding me to give the ball a ride
I step and smack, jump towards the net, ready to defend
Bump, set, spike, the rally has finally begun.

Karly Madey, Grade 6
Dr Dyer Intermediate School, WI

loudness

barking in midnight
thunder booming
loud cars driving
lightning strikes
and me
hating it all
Skylar Olson, Grade 6
Dr Dyer Intermediate School, WI

Winter

W inter is cold
I gloo
N ice white snow
T ea and hot cocoa
E ggnog
R unning through snow
Chris Maurer, Grade 4
Dibble Elementary School, MI

Austin

A wesome
U are cool
S o not an idiot
T oo good at sports
I ntelligent
N ice
Luke Wenzel, Grade 4
Dibble Elementary School, MI

Summer

S unny days
U nderwater fun
M eeting with friends
M elting ice cream
E xcitement
R unning and playing
Caleb Faulkner, Grade 5
Zinser School, MI

Soccer

S pectacular
O ut of bounds
C ompetitive
C ooperative
E nergetic
R unning
Sam Siciliano, Grade 5
Zinser School, MI

Ferocious

The tiger has had a bad day
The leopard is in a bad mood
I found that out the hard way
And now my name is cat food.
Peter Smith, Grade 4
St Paul's Lutheran School, MN

Beach

I see the ocean
I see the sand
I see seagulls
I hear the waves
I hear the gentle wind blowing in my face
I hear the seagulls
I smell sea water
I taste ice cream
I taste delicious fruit
I feel happy
I feel joyful
I feel relaxed
I touch the soft bed of sand
I touch the warm beach blanket
Morgan Hubert, Grade 5
Eagle Creek Academy, MI

Music

I can feel it everywhere
Pulsing through my heart
Like the wind in the willows
Rushing through my hair
Like flowers with delicate blooms
Tiny roots clinging to the solid ground
Like the birds that sing at my window
Fluttering, curious, ready to play
Like the maple leaves that fall around me
Whistling a tune to which I dance
The sweet melodies of life
Each has their own special song
Feel the music
Melissa Beyrand, Grade 6
Detroit Country Day Middle School, MI

Soldier

S acrifice
O verturned glass
L iberty
D ied with honor
I nsurmountable
E ndless freedom
R estlessness
Shauni Johnson, Grade 6
Maple Lake Elementary School, MN

Baseball

Helmet
Shin guard
Bat
Ball
Screaming people
Having fun
Winning
Celebrating
Austin Meyer, Grade 5
St Paul Evangelical Lutheran School, WI

I Am

I am 9 years old and funny
I wonder if the world will end
I hear my sister yelling
I see Jesus on the cross
I want to get Modern Warfare 3
I am 9 years old and funny

I pretend I am Daniel Craig
I feel my hands touching a piano
I touch a football
I worry if I get a cavity
I cry when I get hurt
I am 9 years old and funny

I understand why toys cost money
I say to praise when I'm at church
I dream I'm taking a bath in money
I try to do my best in math
I hope I make it to the NBA
I am 9 years old and funny

I am Anthony Shkreli
Anthony Shkreli, Grade 4
Floyd Ebeling Elementary School, MI

Autumn Apples

In autumn, apples are maroon.
We are going to the apple orchard soon.

There are plenty of types of apples to buy
for my grandma to make apple pie.

I love when Grandma bakes me a treat.
They are always very good to eat.
Grace Louko, Grade 4
Sheboygan Falls Elementary School, WI

How Many Ways to Say I Love You

I love you!
You're a nice person!
I love you
Do you need help?
I love you
I need a hug.
I love you
Mom and Dad
I love you
Hey, sister
I love you
Nature
I love you
God
I love you
Oh, I love you
Abigail Gerdes, Grade 5
St Paul Evangelical Lutheran School, WI

Soldier

S o grateful
O ur heroes
L oving and caring
D etermined
I nspiring
E very one trusts
R eady to fight for America
Greg Mattson, Grade 6
Maple Lake Elementary School, MN

Rain Forest and Desert

Rain forest
Watery, natural
Raining, singing, growing
Animals, trees, Africa, camels
Flowing, heating, drying
Sand, cactus
Desert
Cherish Johnson, Grade 6
Detroit Lakes Middle School, MN

Quinn

Quinn
Q uinn means the world to me
U would be blessed to know him
I nteresting to watch play football
N ew things about the world he tells me
N icest brother in the world
Quinn
Caleb Bilitz, Grade 5
St Paul Evangelical Lutheran School, WI

Mom and Dad

Mom
Nice, busy
Working, cleaning, cooking
Woman, Mrs., Mr., man
Sleeping, driving, dreaming
Lovable, quiet
Dad
Casey Ponyicsanyi, Grade 5
St Paul Evangelical Lutheran School, WI

My Pets

Dogs
Loyal, strong
Fetching, running
Bones, collars, yarn, mice
Meowing, purring
Playful, smart,
Cats
Jacob Reichmann, Grade 4
River Heights Elementary School, WI

Yellow Is…

Yellow is the color of the cake that I eat
Easter is the holiday that is neat
Yellow is the color of my bike
Yellow is the color of my trike

Yellow is the color of the bees
Yellow is the color of the cheese
Yellow is the color of the showers
Yellow is the color of the flowers.
Ayden Ubersox, Grade 4
Platteville Middle School, WI

Halloween

H orror
A rmor
L icorice candy
L eaping goblins
O range pumpkin heads
W ary streets
E erie signs
E xtra scary
N eat treats
Katie Bergsma, Grade 5
Zinser School, MI

Christmas

C heerful faces on children
H ollering from the parents
R unning around joyfully
I t is a wonderful holiday
S inging songs of joy to all
T o say "Merry Christmas" to relatives
M any presents to give and receive
A loving reason to share and care
S o, how do you celebrate Christmas
Diana Turcotte, Grade 5
St Paul Evangelical Lutheran School, WI

Fall

The leaves in fall
Make air smell fresh.
Fall makes nature look beautiful.
The leaves I step on
Are crunchy
It makes me want to laugh.
Kevin Rodriguez, Grade 6
St John Kanty School, WI

Rosie

Rosie is a **R** ough dog.
Rosie is **O** ut of control.
Rosie is **S** weet.
Rosie **I** s a princess.
Rosie is **E** legant.
Megan Irwin, Grade 5
Zinser School, MI

Dogs

Playful dogs jump up
While drooling all over me
Making me laugh hard!
Abbigail Smith, Grade 6
Detroit Lakes Middle School, MN

Fall

Leaves are falling
Winter is coming soon
Fall is great.
Ivan Gomez, Grade 4
Stocker Elementary School, WI

Autumn

Eating candy corn
Geese flying south for winter
Leaves falling off trees
Steven Rickman, Grade 4
Stocker Elementary School, WI

Index

Author Autograph Page

Author Autograph Page

Author Autograph Page

Author Autograph Page

Author Autograph Page

Author Autograph Page

Author Autograph Page

Author Autograph Page

Author Autograph Page

Author Autograph Page